Oil Shale, Tar Sands, and Related Materials

Oil Shale, Tar Sands, and Related Materials

H. C. Stauffer, EDITOR

Gulf Research & Development Company

Based on a symposium

sponsored by the

Division of Fuel Chemistry

at the Second Chemical Congress

of the North American Continent,

Las Vegas, Nevada

August 25–29, 1980.

A C S   S Y M P O S I U M   S E R I E S **163**

AMERICAN CHEMICAL SOCIETY

WASHINGTON, D. C.   1981

Library of Congress CIP Data

Oil shale, tar sands, and related materials.
(ACS symposium series, ISSN 0097–6156; 163)
Includes bibliographies and index.

1. Oil shales—Congresses. 2. Oil sands—Congresses.
I. Stauffer, H. C., 1922–   . II. American Chemical Society. Division of Fuel Chemistry. III. Chemical
Congress of the North American Continent (2nd:
1980; Las Vegas, Nev.) IV. Series.

TN858.A1038   665'.4   81–10948
ISBN 0–8412–0640–6 AACR2 ACSMC8 163 1–395
                                                  1981

ACS Symposium Series

M. Joan Comstock, *Series Editor*

FOREWORD

The ACS Symposium Series was founded in 1974 to provide
a medium for publishing symposia quickly in book form. The
format of the Series parallels that of the continuing Advances
in Chemistry Series except that in order to save time the
papers are not typeset but are reproduced as they are submitted by the authors in camera-ready form. Papers are reviewed under the supervision of the Editors with the assistance
of the Series Advisory Board and are selected to maintain the
integrity of the symposia; however, verbatim reproductions of
previously published papers are not accepted. Both reviews
and reports of research are acceptable since symposia may
embrace both types of presentation.

CONTENTS

PREFACE

Domestic oil shale and tar sand deposits constitute a tremendous resource. The proven, recoverable oil shale reserves alone far exceed those remaining for petroleum. In light of this fact, it is not surprising that there are many people having trouble comprehending our vulnerable energy position.

Attempts to develop a commercial oil shale industry historically have been on-again, off-again efforts. In almost yearly cyclical fashion, one has heard or read at least one paper enthusiastically suggesting the general theme, "An Oil Shale Industry—Just Around The Corner." Until now, however, the corner has never been turned and the development pace of this sorely needed resource has been low key at best. All of our domestic heavy oil production and tar sands development endeavors have been in much the same category.

The ability to turn the corner always has been stalled by unfavorable economics. Some combination of factors arises which continually delays the development of these alternative energy resources because of their noncompetitive position compared with the price of foreign oil. In reality, this has obscured the real issue—the fragile nature of our domestic energy structure which is so dependent on the ready availability of imported crude.

Hope springs eternal, however, and recent developments have indicated that the corner may indeed have been turned at last. Although the DOE oil shale research, development, and demonstration program has been trying to foster a technically and environmentally sound industry capable of meeting the President's goal of 400,000 bbl/d by 1990, the recent sign ing of Senate Bill S.932 should provide a significant and needed impetus. This bill, The Energy Security Act, provides for a United States Synthetic Fuels Corporation which has the mission of encouraging the production of 500,000 bbl/d from alternative sources by 1987 and 2,000,000 bbl/d by 1992. Even more recently, several major developers have announced definitive plans for tract development. On-site activity has commenced to achieve a production goal of 50,000 bbl/d before 1990.

These are most worthy goals, but past procrastination will make them difficult to attain. It should not be surprising that in situ retorting is still in its early development stage; that a single, commercial surface retort module has yet to be constructed and successfully demonstrated; or that a full slate of products refined from syncrude has still to be proven acceptably interchangeable with those derived from petroleum.

With respect to recent events the timing of this symposium was only coincidental. Its content, however, is not. The participants have recognized the diverse problems, and many of them are addressed in this volume. The novel concepts of oil shale fracturing and retorting as well as tar sands recovery processes need to be evaluated. Much needed input has been provided on rubbling and retorting kinetics and mechanisms, which still are poorly understood. Our tendency to look for simple solutions to complex problems is apparent in the discussion of "simple" hydrogenation of shale oil to products of questionable and perplexing stability characteristics. In view of our long-term domestic energy deficit, the stimulating discussion of the potential for a very large-scale oil shale operation merits serious consideration.

Nature's petroleum supply is constrained now by what remains in the ground; development of our oil shale and tar sands resources appear only to be constrained by our own actions.

The credit for the content of this symposium belongs to the participants and their sponsors. I sincerely appreciate their contributions and wish to acknowledge P. C. Scott and C. W. Matthews for their help in its organization.

H. C. STAUFFER
Gulf Research & Development Company
P.O. Drawer 2038
Pittsburgh, PA 15230

April 10, 1981

The Department of Energy's Oil Shale R, D, & D Program: An Overview

ARTHUR M. HARTSTEIN and BRIAN M. HARNEY

Office of Oil Shale, Department of Energy, Washington, D.C. 20545

The largest untapped fossil fuel resource in the United States is the oil bearing shales in the western part of the country and the black shales in the east. The oil shale resource concentrated in three western states is estimated to be equivalent to more than two trillion barrels of crude oil. An additional two trillion barrels of oil exists in the lean deposits of the Eastern U.S.

Since the earliest commercial interest more than 100 years ago, the history of oil shale has been one of ups-and-downs. In almost cyclical fashion, the shale industry has appeared to be on the verge of expanding rapidly, economics have appeared potentially viable, and the problems have seemed minimal. But then, a combination of factors, such as jumps in construction costs or the discovery of new conventional oil resources, have led to delays and in some cases, decisions to drop shale oil development.

Recent events, however, have reversed this trend. The ever-rising price of imported petroleum, the continuing volatile situation in the middle east and the passage by the Congress of a variety of significant financial incentive programs for synthetic fuels has stimulated a new interest in moving previously dormant oil shale projects ahead.

The Department of Energy (DOE) has established a research, development, and demonstration (R,D&D) program for encouraging the development of the country's oil shale resource to help in the mitigation of the present and future energy demands. The aim of the Oil Shale R,D&D Program is to stimulate the commercial production of shale oil by eliminating technical and environmental barriers. This paper provides an overview of the DOE Oil Shale R,D&D Program, addressing its essential elements. It should be noted that budget constraints do not permit all portions of the program plan to be supported as yet. Moreover, in many cases, the program areas are addressed jointly with industry. Oil shale program funding for the plan is $31.3 million in Fiscal Year 1981.

Program Goal and Objectives

The Department of Energy's R,D&D oil shale goal is to permit the entire oil shale resource, both east and west, to contribute to domestic energy proportionate to the resource and with a recognition of the unique environmental character of the oil shale areas. In concert with this goal, the objectives of the R,D&D program are:

o   To overcome technological barriers to oil shale commercialization

o   To foster development of innovative processes for all shales that reduce environmental impact

o   To obtain accurate environmental data and demonstrate or develop adequate environmental control systems

The analysis of commercialization incentives and mitigation of institutional barriers is the responsibility of the Assistant Secretary for Resource Applications. R,D&D activities are the responsibility of the Assistant Secretary for Fossil Energy, although the lead for environmental planning rests with the Assistant Secretary for Environment. The R,D&D program, however, integrates the activities under the Assistant Secretary for Fossil Energy and the Assistant Secretary for Environment.

Program Strategy

In essence, the DOE program goal is to develop the technology necessary for the production of oil shale on a commercial basis and in an environmentally acceptable manner. The DOE strategy to accomplish this end is comprised of two major activity elements:

o   Research and Development

o   Development and Demonstration Support

Through the existence of these parallel activities, the DOE Oil Shale R,D&D Program focuses near term research and development (R&D) on supporting industrial development while maintaining an adequate level of more advanced R&D attuned to future needs. The technology developments that will result by achieving the program's objectives will be made available to the oil shale industrial community. Industrial participation in DOE sponsored demonstrations is encouraged as means of maintaining the technological alignment of the R,D&D Program with the needs of industry. These demonstration activities involve the DOE Program

in the industrial decision process and facilitate oil shale
industry growth. Information and experience gained through the
construction and operation of any facilities resulting from
these industry supportive activities will be used defining future
R&D requirements which may be satisfied directly by the private
sector through the program. The program is designed in concert
with and in support of increasing industry activity.

The Program's R&D activity elements are structured to
parallel and complement activities that industrial developers
would need to perform when establishing a commercial oil
shale operation. The initial activities of a developer
include tasks to characterize the resource under consideration and site planning for resource development. Following
this, the developer needs to consider the potential physical
environment and socioeconomic impacts before committing to a
proposed project. Oil shale resource development and extraction entail site preparation, mining (except for true in situ
technologies), and rubbling the in situ retort in preparation
for in place combustion or transporting the mined oil shale to
a surface retort. Retorting would then be undertaken, after
which the shale oil would be upgraded and refined. At each
point in this sequence, the oil shale program will develop
enhanced technology to establish a potential developer's
effectiveness.

Key Technical and Environmental Needs in R,D&D

Technical. The Oil Shale R,D&D Program is directed toward
developing a greater understanding of the oil shale resource and
perfecting an effective means for the recovery of shale oil.
Program activities are directed toward the solution of key technical and environmental needs representing significant barriers
to commercial oil shale development. Based on a review of technology required for oil shale development, the following Key
Technical Needs have been identified as those that should
receive the highest priority in the R,D&D Program:

o Efficient Oil Shale Rock Breakage and Retort Bed Preparation Techniques,

o Development of Retort Diagnostics and Instrumentation,

o Development of Retort Control Procedures,

o Systems Engineering Methods for Total Oil Shale Process
   Development,

o Efficient and Effective Oil Shale Mining Systems,

o   Advanced Shaft Sinking Technology,

o   Chemical Kinetics of the Total Pyrolysis Process,

o   Understanding Retorting Mechanisms and Developing a
    Prediction

o   Development of Alternative Retorting Procedures.

Rock Breakage and Retort Bed Preparation. Efficient
recovery of oil from shale depends critically upon having a
bed of oil shale rubble that is relatively uniform, both in
particle size and void fraction. Mining and rubbling methods
must be developed to assure optimal uniformity. Otherwise
sweep efficiency will be poor, and significant amounts of oil
shale rubble will not be retorted.
    It is expected that the R,D&D effort will result in the
development of technology for breaking oil shale for mining
and preparing rubble beds such that efficient and productive
shale extraction and modified in situ retorting can be accomplished. Retorts will be designed and constructed which meet
the processing requirements for particle size distribution,
uniform permeability, uniform void distribution, and bounding
of the fractured region.

Retort Diagnosis and Instrumentation. The development of
control instrumentation and methods for in situ retorting is
important for determining retort performance and yield efficiency. The effort of the RD&D program will result in the
design of thermal sensors, gas sampling devices, pressure
probes, remote sensing devices, strain and displacement
gauges, and health and safety monitoring equipment. This
equipment will be designed and then tested and modified
through use in several field tests.

Retort Control Procedures. The development of retort control and operating procedures is crucial to the success of both
in situ and modified in situ retorting of oil shale. The R,D&D
effort will establish a set of baseline operating plans from
data collected from laboratory experiments, field tests and the
outputs of predictive models. From the data collected, an
evaluation will be made on the effects of intermittent air
flows, liquid water additions, and other control parameters.
The result of this effort will be a retort operating plan
that maximizes retorting rate and yield while controlling
temperature and burn front symmetry.

Systems Engineering. A systematic procedure for resource

identification and characterization and for determination of
appropriate recovery processes is needed to assure efficient
and effective use of all domestic oil shale resources. The
need related objectives of the R,D&D program are: (1) to
develop and utilize methods for the planning of oil shale
development by matching oil shale resources with appropriate
recovery processes; (2) to develop planning tools (e.g., equipment selection criteria, production models, economic models)
which will aid in the design and analysis of efficient shale
oil production facilities; and (3) to determine the overall
economics for the recovery of energy products from oil shale
by the alternative processes.

Oil Shale Mining Systems. Equipment and methods now used
for coal and hard rock mining are well developed but are not
always applicable to the demands of oil shale mining. Research
and development is needed to meet the particular requirements
of the oil shale industry. The objective of the R,D&D program
is to develop technology and equipment for high volume, cost
effective, underground and surface mining methods for extracting
oil shale for subsequent surface and modified in situ processing.

Shaft Sinking Technology. The development of shafe sinking
systems is crucial for the large scale commercial utilization
of oil shale. The R,D&D effort will carefully examine the
current state of the art in shaft/slope development. A compre-
hensive research and development plan will be established that
attacks all the major deficiencies in the current state of the
art for accessing oil shale resources. Access development system
concepts will be defined after a series of tasks which examine
cutting and drilling methods, water/ground control, and large
scale drilling. The expected result of this effort will be the
development of techniques for efficient, safe, and environmentally acceptable shaft sinking.

Chemical Kinetics. Several models have been developed
which simulate the physical properties of oil shale retorting
(e.g., shale composition, retorting rates, particle sizes,
porosity distribution, etc.). For the models to accurately
simulate retorting, they should include the details of the
major chemical reactions in the system. The R,D&D program will
develop the basic data on chemical kinetics needed to model the
complex reactions taking place in retorting. Among these
reactions are mineral decomposition, especially that of
carbonates, which are large consumers of energy; reactions
char with steam and carbonate to produce valuable CO and
hydrogen; degradation (loss) reactions of oil; gas phase
reactions producing hydrogen and CO_2; gaseous sulfur evolu-

tion; etc. More work is needed on gas phase reactions,
especially on water gas and water gas shift reactions, oil
cracking stoichiometry of hydrocarbon combustion, and sulfur reactions in shale.

Retorting Mechanisms. Retorting is only crudely understood in lab and field retorts. Important operational problems include control of burn front, startup and sweep
efficiency, effect of particle size distribution, inlet gas
composition, especially steam and air mixtures, bed irregu-
larities, flow rate, permeability changes during retorting,
and temperature control. Program research will address key
questions in the area of retorting mechanisms. A knowledge
of the mechanisms taking place during retorting is required
to interpret results of experiments in pilot and field retorts
to develop predictive models, and finally to suggest process
modifications in order to optimize retort performance,
especially oil yields, and production rates. The development
of retorting models will also be pursued as a means of understanding and predicting retort behavior.

Alternative Retorting Procedures. Oil shale retorting is
approaching commercially viable levels of development. However, the technology is not sufficiently advanced to assure
that optimally efficient and cost effective retorting methods
are employed. The R,D&D program will examine alternative retorting processes with the objective of improving extraction efficiency and economics. Studies will include: (1) the use of
oxygen (instead of air) plus steam to obtain high BTU outlet gas
and reduce exit gas handling and cleanup; (2) the substitution
of water mist for steam to improve heat balance; (3) determining
retorting conditions to produce various optimum product mixes,
e.g., maximum naphtha, minimum residuals, etc.; and (4) determining retorting conditions to produce minimum environmental
effects (e.g., lowest sulfur in outlet gas, least soluble spent
shale, etc.); (5) use of fluid beds to increase throughput,
improve yield and lead to more favorable economics.

Environmental R&D Needs. The environmental research in
the R,D&D Program represents a significant portion of the DOE's
Environmental Development Plan. The overall objective of the
Program's Environmental Activity is to develop solutions to
environmental problems associated with the process technologies
involved in oil shale production. To achieve this objective, a
series of Key Environmental Needs have also been established:

    o Development of Environmentally Acceptable Retort
       Abandonment Strategy,

o   Guidelines to Ensure Health and Safety of Workers
    and General Public,

o   Development of Solid Waste Management Systems,

o   Development of Water Treatment Systems,

o   Development of an Emission Control Strategy,

o   Mitigation of Ecological Impacts,

o   Mitigation of Social and Economic Impacts,

o   Development of Compliance Plans, and

o   Development of Subsidence Control Procedures.

Development of Environmentally Acceptable Retort
Abandonment Strategy. The spent shale remaining in underground
retorts after product recovery contains salts and carbonaceous
residues that can be leached by groundwater and thereby con-
taminate aquifers. In addition, some caving in from the weight
of the overburden may occur resulting in subsidence at the surface.
    The research related to this need will determine (1) the
potential for groundwater intrusion, what materials are likely
to be dissolved in groundwater, the permeability of the geologic
media to the soluble components, the toxic properties of these
components, and the persistence of any toxic leaching and subsidence. The more general problem of subsidence in underground
mines, the safety and ecological aspects, are dealt with in a
separate area.

    Guidelines to Ensure Health and Safety of Workers and
General Public. Operations of an oil shale industry will introduce a new set of industrial working conditions and possible
public health risks as a result of plant operations or product
distribution. The research directed toward this need will
examine the potential health and safety risks to workers and
the general public. All aspects of the fuel cycle will be
examined from the mine and retort to the refinery and end use of
the shale oil products. Protective measures, whether they be
through controls, process modifications, or isolation of high
risk areas, will be evaluated and effective measures will be
applied.

    Development of Solid Waste Management Systems. Surface
processes produce extremely high volumes of solid waste in

the form of spent shale. This research will evaluate methods
of compacting and stablizing spent shale and other solid wastes
such as sludges and spent catalysts. The research will lead to
the evaluation of alternatives for stablizing and achieving
self-sustaining ecosystems on the solid waste piles with minimum
potential for water and wind erosion of toxic materials.

Development of Water Treatment Systems. In situ processes
produce approximately one barrel of retort water contaminated
with carbonaceous residues for each barrel of shale oil recovered. Surface processes also produce retort water but in lower
quantities. Although current plans do not call for discharge
of wastewater, it much be cleaned for reuse in the process and
other uses, such as dust control and solid waste management.
An objective of this research is to identify components in the
wastewater that present either a health or environmental hazard
with respect to the intended use of the water and to develop
systems to remove these components. Another objective is to
determine the consumptive water requirements of different oil
shale processes.

Development of an Emissions Control Strategy. There are
two major components to the emissions control need. One is
directed toward determination of the emission control requirements based on the projected emission rates and composition of
the emission streams. In the case of criteria or regulated
pollutants, systems must be engineered to maintain ambient air
quality within the region. In addition, modification of available technology and development of new systems may be required
if risk analysis indicates that unique substances in the emission
stream required removal.

The other component is directed toward estimation of the
capacity of the region to accept industrial development--the
regional carrying capacity--based on the meteorological characteristics of the region. More specific needs are (1) more
accurate atmospheric models to predict the transport and dispersion of atmospheric pollutants, (2) determining rates at which
pollutants are removed from the atmosphere, and (3) quantitative
information on the effects of air pollutants on critical atmospheric processes related to undesirable effects, e.g., precipitation quality, decreased visibility, and local climate modification.

The research tasks that compose this segment of the plan
lead to the development of workable emission controls and
estimates of effects of industrialization on regional air
quality.

Mitigation of Ecological Impacts. Oil shale operations
will cause much disruption of the surface environment through
normal construction and operation activities--large amounts of
solid waste stockpiles on the surface, water treatment operations, steam generation, mining, material handling, etc. The
objectives of the ecological research, in addition to that
which is an integral part of other activities such as the solid
waste management system, will be to (1) evaluate overall effects
of the operation on the ecological communities (plants, wild-
life, fish) and (2) develop ecological test procedures that will
be used by other parts of the program to evaluate systems performance with respect to ecological criteria. This work will
be geared to the environmental impact approach described above.

Mitigation of Social and Community Economic Impacts. The
social and community economic aspects of technological developments are among the most difficult to deal with. To a large
extent, this is due to the fact that solutions involve institutional arrangements and legislative initiatives beyond the scope
of most R&D operations. The problems do not lead themselves
to controlled experiments that can be carried out in the field
or laboratory. Installation of mitigating measures such as
front-end financial support to communities for planning and
development will be dealt with in DOE's industrialization plant.
This part of the R,D&D plan will focus on the social and economic
issues for which solutions are not known and which therefore
require additional research.

Methods for Controlling or Preventing Subsidence. Underground mines are always susceptible to subsidence, which presents a concern for safety and environmental disturbance,
including aquifer disruption and changes in the surface land
form. Some of the retort abandonment control measures will
also act to prevent subsidence. The R&D conducted to satisfy
this need will focus on general underground mining whether related to underground processes or surface retorting processes.
It will be closely tied to the mining tasks and include
analyses of safety, hydrological disruption, and changes in
surface features. The research will focus primarily on pre-
vention or planned, controlled subsidence.

Development of Compliance Plans. The R,D&D tasks, for
environmental as well as the other three activities included in
the Management Plan are carried out in conjunction with, or as
part of, major field projects. These projects, which involves
engineering and construction activities, must comply with
Federal, state, and local standards, and in particular, with
provisions of the National Environmental Policy Act (NEPA).

DOE prepares Environmental Assessments, and Environmental Impact Statements when appropriate, for those major field projects. Air, water, and other environmental monitoring, as required to demonstrate compliance with NEPA and applicable permits, is conducted as part of this need; that data is made available to other tasks for various analyses and decisions.

Process Specific R,D&D

In addition, to satisfying key needs which presently impede oil shale commercialization the Oil Shale R,D&D Program will simultaneously address the following processes.

Surface Processing. The DOE is pursuing a surface module demonstration program as described in P.L. 95-238. This program will result in both design and business proposals for the construction of a surface retort module. A decision to proceed with construction of designed modules on a cost shared basis is being held in abeyance pending industrial actions and the availability of other financial incentive programs such as those to be provided by the newly formed Synthetic Fuels Corporation. Other research and development supporting surface retorting is mainly focused on mining and environmental effects with long term R&D directed to improving surface retorting processes.

In Situ Processing. The current near term emphasis of the Program's research activities is on developing and expanding in situ retorting process technology, with particular emphasis on modified in situ methods. This programmatic direction is based on the fact that in situ oil shale technology has not advanced to the point where it has been proven to be technically or economically feasible. Engineering analyses indicate that in situ processes have the potential to be more cost effective and less disruptive to the environment than surface retorting. Therefore, the program is focused on developing the necessary technical and environmental information from which an economic and environmentally acceptable in situ technology can be engineered.

In addition to this technology base program, the DOE is also sponsoring several major in situ oil shale field demonstration tests. The field demonstration test program and the technology based R&D programs are integrally related, in that field demonstration sites are often used as sites for R,D&D program efforts and information gained from the field tests is used to guide the overall R,D&D program. Each of these projects has been evaluated to determine the program technology requirements that can be met by ongoing industry contract and the other tech-

nology requirements that can be achieved through modification
of the ongoing effort. In addition to providing valuable technology base information, it is anticipated that one or more of
these projects could provide technical evidence of process feasibility. Use of existing projects to accomplish planned tasks
will be maximized to reduce total program costs.

Novel Processing Techniques. In addition to the development of more advanced aboveground and in situ methods, research
is being conducted into new and novel technologies for extraction
and processing of oil shale products. Although not currently
competitive for near term commercial development, these efforts
are indicators of likely second generation advances in oil shale
technology.

The novel technologies being developed are in two general
categories.

o Radio Frequency Heating

o Hydrogen Retorting

Program Operating Plans

The Oil Shale R,D&D Program is defined in a draft document
which include two main sections: a Management and Strategic Plan
which describes the R,D&D program management structure and the
long term strategic aspects of the Department of Energy's program
for achieving its technology objectives, and an Implementation
Plan which details oil shale R,D&D activities over the next
several years to the subactivity task level. In contrast to the
Implementation Plan, the Management and Strategic Plan describes
the Program's objectives as they will be attained by satisfying
a series of technological needs, each of which may require the
successful performance of one or more sets of tasks sometime in
the future. Described are oil shale R,D&D activities for a
multiyear period in terms of needs, with emphasis placed upon
solving key technical and environmental needs inhibiting oil
shale commercialization and developing an activity baseline for
each of several candidate technologies to establish program
direction, resource requirements, and expected accomplishment.
Both plans serve as a basis for developing and justifying future
budget requests over their respective periods.

Strategic Plan. The policy, management, organization, and
long term aspects of the Oil Shale R,D&D Program, as directed
toward satisfying its goal and objectives, are described in the
Management and Strategic Plan. The discussion is in three parts
addressing planned program efforts concerned with:

o Key Technical Need R,D&D

o Key Environmental Need R,D&D

o Process Specific R,D&D

These efforts are defined at the fundamental needs level,
each R,D&D objective (a key need being one such objective) requiring the fulfillment of one or more of these fundamental
needs before it is obtained. This is in contrast to the manner
in which the Implementation Plan is defined, wherein needs are
specified in terms of the detailed tasks required to satisfy
them. Strategic plans are outlined in a plane higher than that
used in the Implementation Plan. Another distinction between
the two is in their planning time horizon. Strategic plans are
defined over a long term period, generally about ten years,
whereas the Implementation Plan concentrates on the near term
period not exceeding five years. To show continuity between the
two plans, the time span addressed in the Implementation Plan is
also defined with the strategic plans and need identifiers uni-
quely assigned in the Implementation Plan are referenced in
the Strategic plans.

Implementation Plan. Short term plans are defined in the
Implementation Plan in terms of the activities and tasks to be
performed. Outlined within the Plan are the research tasks that
will be performed during the next five year period to enhance
and encourage commercial oil shale development. The R,D&D tasks
are described with respect to major activity areas (resource
characterization, environment, development and extraction, and
processing and instrumentation). Component subactivities within
each of these activities provides a framework for organizing
tasks around specified technology areas. For each program task
the performance periods are specified in conjunction with task
deliverables and participating organizations. The Plan, conceived as a working document which is annually updated, thus
serves as a basis for implementing the R,D&D Program by the
various research and industry participants.

RECEIVED March 19, 1981.

Computer Simulation of Explosive Fracture of Oil Shale

THOMAS F. ADAMS

G-6, Mail Stop 665, Los Alamos National Scientific Laboratory,
P.O. Box 1663, Los Alamos, NM 87545

A necessary first step in the recovery of oil from oil shale is the reduction of the rock to rubble. In mining operations, the oil shale is blasted loose and hauled to the surface for further crushing or direct processing. In *in situ* methods, the oil shale must be rubbled in place, with little or no direct access to the resource bed. The efficiency and economic viability of shale oil recovery, therefore, depend directly on blasting technology. The optimization of existing blasting methods and, especially for *in situ* applications, the development of new methods beyond the current state of the art will be needed to use our oil shale resources effectively.

Advances in blasting technology could perhaps be made by trial and error, but experiments on the required scale are costly. An alternative approach would be to develop analytical and computational methods to simulate blasting in rock, and to use the computer to aid in the design of new methods and the planning and analysis of critical experiments. The computer would not in itself specify blast patterns or delays, but would allow the basic phenomenology of blasting to be studied. Computer codes would become tools to study the effect of changing design parameters such as the depth of burial or explosive type on the results of blasting. New ideas could be explored at modest cost before going to the field for large-scale tests.

Computer Simulation

Computer simulation of explosive fracture of rock can be carried out with finite difference stress wave propagation codes, such as the YAQUI code (1). YAQUI integrates in time the coupled partial differential equations for the conservation of mass, momentum, and energy. For a compressible fluid, these equations are

$$\frac{\partial \rho}{\partial t} + \vec{\nabla} \cdot (\rho \vec{u}) = 0 \quad , \tag{1}$$

0097–6156/81/0163–0013$05.00/0

$$\frac{\partial \vec{u}}{\partial t} + (\vec{u} \cdot \vec{\nabla})\vec{u} + \frac{1}{\rho} \vec{\nabla} p = 0 \quad , \tag{2}$$

and

$$\frac{\partial}{\partial t} (I + \frac{1}{2} u^2) + (\vec{u} \cdot \vec{\nabla}) (I + \frac{1}{2} u^2) + \frac{1}{\rho} \vec{\nabla} \cdot (p\vec{u}) = 0 \quad . \tag{3}$$

Here, $\vec{u}$ is the velocity, ρ is the mass density, p is the pressure, and I is the specific internal energy. Viscous terms, not shown here, also enter the equations.

Rock is a material with strength. Therefore, in the solid dynamics version of YAQUI, the pressure terms in the momentum and energy equations are replaced with analogous terms involving the stress tensor. YAQUI is a two-dimensional code, so it can treat problems in plane strain or cylindrical symmetry. This is sufficient for many blasting applications, such as a cylindrical charge in a borehole drilled in perpendicular to the rock face. YAQUI is an "ALE" (Arbitrary Lagrangian-Eulerian) code (2), although for these applications the Lagrangian option is generally used.

Numerical methods to solve fluid flow and stress wave propagation problems have been developed over the years at Los Alamos. Given these methods and large modern computers, the difficulty in solving these equations lies in specifying the initial and boundary conditions and in the model used to describe the material response. In practice, this means simulating numerically the detonation of the high explosive and the subsequent behavior of the reaction products, and developing a constitutive relation. In fluid problems, the analog of the constitutive relation is the equation of state, which gives the pressure as a function of the density and internal energy. The specification of the equation of state closes the set of equations (1-3) and makes a numerical solution possible. The constitutive relation for rock serves the same role, except that it involves the stress and strain tensors. It must be written in incremental form, since the current state of a solid depends on its loading history. The description of rock fracture and fragmentation is an integral part of the constitutive relation.

Explosive Behavior. The behavior of the explosive must be accurately described, since the explosive is the source of energy in blasting. Numerical methods for modeling explosives and the properties of many common explosives have been discussed in a book by Mader (3). An ideal detonation is one in which the chemical energy of the explosive is released nearly instantaneously at the detonation front. Many military explosives are ideal in this sense, while commercial explosives, such as ANFO, are non-ideal. In non-ideal explosives, the chemical energy is released over some distance behind the detonation front. The behavior of such explosives, including the detonation velocity,

Chapman-Jouguet (C-J) pressure, and the detonability, can depend strongly on the charge diameter, confinement, and method of initiation. It is, therefore, important that commercial explosives be tested under circumstances as close as possible to those where they will be used in the field.

The behavior of ANFO in 0.1- and 0.2-m-diameter cylinders has been studied in field tests (4, 5). Most of the data were obtained in high-speed photography of detonations of explosive-filled plastic or clay pipes immersed in water. The detonation velocity can be determined quite accurately and in the water tank tests, the propagation of the shock in the water and the motion of the interface between the water and the pipe can be followed. An equation of state for the explosive reaction products is then calculated with a chemistry code. The equation of state is used in a two-dimensional stress wave code to simulate the water tank test. The equation of state is modified in further chemistry calculations by varying the degree of combustion at the detonation front until the simulation closely reproduces the actual test. The data obtained for ANFO are summarized in Table I. Several commercial explosives besides ANFO have also been characterized in this way.

Table I
Behavior of ANFO in Various Diameters (4)

Diameter	Detonation Velocity	C-J Pressure
0.1 m	3500 m/s	2.4 GPa
0.2	4100	3.6
infinite (ideal)	5400	7.3

Constitutive Relations

Geologic materials like oil shale are commonly treated as elastic/plastic solids. Fracture under intense loading is then modeled as an extension of plasticity or is treated with a separate fracture model. In applications like rock blasting, the latter approach is preferable, since fracture of rock is qualitatively different from plastic flow. Even so, continuum damage models have been used to model blasting for engineering applications. Some calculations with such a model will be presented below.

Fracture Model. A powerful fracture model based on Statistical Crack Mechanics (SCM) is being developed at Los Alamos (6). In this model, the rock is treated as an elastic material containing a distribution of penny-shaped flaws and cracks of various sizes and orientations. Plasticity near crack tips is taken into account through its effect on the fracture toughness.

The SCM model makes use of two results from fracture mechanics: the condition for stability against crack growth for an arbitrary state of stress, and the reduction in the effective elastic moduli of a body containing a penny-shaped crack. The first result is a generalized Griffith criterion, which can be used to say which cracks in the statistical distribution will grow given the applied stresses. The second result allows the weakening of the rock as it is fractured to be modeled.

The use of the generalized Griffith criterion not only allows cracks to extend under tensile loading, but also allows cracks to extend in shear, even under moderate normal compression. This means that closed shear cracks can extend under intense loading (as near an explosive charge), causing the material to be much weaker under subsequent tensile loading. The reduction in the elastic moduli is also important in that it leads to the correct directional response as the rock is fractured. Thus, phenomena such as spall are modeled in a realistic fashion.

The SCM theory is being implemented and tested in stress wave codes at this time. Early results are encouraging, and this approach holds great promise for the future.

Damage Model. It is possible to extend the usual elastic/plastic theory for solids to include fracture phenomenologically in terms of a "damage parameter." This has been done by various investigators (7, 8), including Johnson (5) with his Continuum Damage Model (CDM). In the CDM, the damage parameter varies from zero to one as the rock goes from fully intact to heavily broken. The constitutive relation in the CDM is a standard elastic/plastic model, except that the failure surface is a function of the damage parameter. The damage parameter can be interpreted as a measure of the loss of shear strength at zero confining pressure. The level of damage in a computational cell increases during plastic flow.

The CDM has two additional features that allow it to represent fracture in rocks. First, there is a brittle/ductile transition pressure. Above this pressure, the rock behaves as an elastic/plastic ductile solid, the failure surface is independent of the level of damage, and the damage is not allowed to increase, even if the failure surface is exceeded. Second, the CDM allows for non-vanishing plastic volume strain to approximate the dilatancy observed in certain laboratory experiments on oil shale.

The CDM has the disadvantage of being built around plasticity, which is inherently different from fracture. In addition, as a scalar model (fracture described by a single damage parameter), it cannot represent the tensor response of rock as accurately as the SCM model. Nevertheless, it does have appropriate phenomenological features and, properly calibrated, should allow useful engineering calculations.

Material Constants. Elastic wave velocities have been obtained for oil shale by ultrasonic methods for various modes of propagation. Elastic constants can be inferred from these data if the oil shale is assumed to be a transversely isotropic solid (9). This is a reasonable approximation considering the bedded nature of the rock. Many of the properties of oil shale depend on the grade (kerogen content), which in turn is correlated with the density (10). The high pressure behavior of oil shale under shock loading has been studied in gas-gun impact experiments (11).

Data on the strength of oil shale are more difficult to obtain, especially data for the intermediate strain rates ($10-10^3$/s) relevant to blasting. Extensive quasi-static triaxial testing data are available for oil shale of two grades at a range of confining pressures (12). These data were averaged over sample orientation to give mean yield strengths. It has been shown that yield strength varies significantly depending on the orientation with respect to the bedding planes (13), at least in quasi-static tests.

The triaxial testing data and other data (e.g., from three-point bending tests) can also be interpreted in terms of the fracture toughness of oil shale. Rather than referring to a plastic yield strength, the fracture toughness serves as an input constant for the SCM fracture model. Other input data needed for the SCM model include the mean crack (or flaw) size and density as a function of orientation throughout the sample. These data could be obtained directly by examination of samples or indirectly in simple laboratory tests.

Regardless of the material model being used, data at intermediate strain rates under controlled laboratory conditions are needed. Such data should be obtainable soon with the new large diameter gas gun and Split-Hopkinson Bar facilities being established at Los Alamos.

Comparison between Calculations and Field Experiments

Any complex code, such as YAQUI, must be calibrated and verified by comparing calculations with the results of realistic field experiments. A series of explosive field tests using ANFO in oil shale has been conducted in the Colony Mine near Rifle, Colorado. These experiments were performed under DOE auspices with the cooperation of Atlantic Richfield, TOSCO, and the Colony Development Corporation. They were conducted for comparison with code calculations and to obtain empirical information about blasting in oil shale.

Field Experiments. Fifteen intermediate-size experiments were conducted with amounts of ANFO ranging from 5 kg to over 100 kg. Three of the experiments were heavily equipped with stress and velocity gauges in separate instrumentation boreholes and diagnostic cables inside the explosive boreholes (to give real-time data on the detonation). The other experiments had varying levels of instrumentation. Extensive pre- and post-shot geologic mapping were conducted at each experiment site. Pre- and post-shot core samples were taken in the vicinity of some of the experiments. Where rubbling extended to the surface, crater profiles were measured and data concerning the rubble were taken.

A complete analysis and correlation of the data is in progress and will be published elsewhere. The analysis is being done partly in the framework of scaling relations, where various experiments are compared after removing first order effects due to different charge size or depth of burial. This aids in quantifying effects, such as the influence of site-specific geology (e.g., joint and fault structures), on crater size and shape.

In the remainder of this report, we compare three YAQUI calculations with the results of the corresponding field experiments. The calculations and experiments to be discussed all involved single cylindrical charges of 0.15-m-diameter ANFO emplaced in boreholes drilled straight into the mine floor. The charge lengths and depths of burial are given in Table II. The detonator was placed at the bottom of the charge in each case.

Table II
Data for Three Oil Shale Blasting Experiments

| | | Depth of Burial | |
Designation	Charge Length	Charge Bottom	Charge Top
79-7	0.99 m	4.57 m	3.58 m
79-8	0.99	3.30	2.31
79-10	1.73	3.30	1.57

These three experiments form an interesting subset of the larger series. Experiment 79-7 was buried deeply enough that it was fully contained, with no crater formation or even surface flaw activation. Post-shot drilling did reveal a rubbled region around the charge. In experiment 79-8, the same size charge was used, buried 1.3 m closer to the surface. An extensive shallow crater was formed, starting about midway from the top of the charge to the mine floor and extending outward. The crater was asymmetric as a result of the influence of the local joint structure. Finally, experiment 79-10 had the same charge bottom depth as 79-8, but had more explosive. This experiment produced a roughly conical crater starting near the center of the charge. This crater was affected very little by the joint structure.

YAQUI Calculations. The YAQUI code described above was used to simulate experiments 79-7, 79-8, and 79-10. A continuum damage model similar to the one developed by Johnson (5), using Johnson's damage constants, was used with a rate-independent elastic/plastic routine. It is instructive to follow the sequence of events that occurred in experiment 79-8. Figures 1-4 show the location of the shock wave and the extent of the "damage" 0.2, 0.6, 1.0, and 2.0 ms, respectively, after the firing of the detonator. At 0.2 ms (Figure 1), the detonation front has moved more than halfway up the charge. The upward-moving shock can be seen along with the region of intense damage around the bottom of the charge. By 0.6 ms (Figure 2), the detonation is over and the shock wave is propagating through the oil shale toward the free surface. Extensive rubbling has occurred in the vicinity of the charge.

The shock wave is approaching the free surface at 1.0 ms (Figure 3). Some additional damage has now occurred in a region bounded roughly by an inverted 45° cone extending upward from near the top of the charge. This is the region where the maximum shear loading occurred during the first passage of the shock wave. The 45° angle is related to the ratio of the sound speed in oil shale to the detonation velocity in ANFO. Had the SCM model been used instead of the damage model, closed shear cracks would have grown in this region as the shear wave passed.

A tensile relief wave propagates downward after the shock reaches the free surface. This causes a layer of spall damage to occur near the surface above the charge. By 2.0 ms (Figure 4), the spall layer has formed and the full extent of the computed damage can be seen. The calculation was carried out long enough to follow all the dynamic phases of the blast, but not long enough to follow the throwout of debris or the formation of the actual crater. The combination of heavy damage near the charge, the shear-damaged region, and the spall layer presumably represent the crater that will be formed. The calculation does not, in fact, show complete rubbling in the region above the charge. This is consistent with the fact that in the field only a shallow crater, heavily influenced by the local geology, was formed.

Figure 5 shows the extent of damage calculated at 2.0 ms for experiment 79-7. The regions of damage around the charge and shear damage above the charge are visible, as in the calculation for experiment 79-8. However, neither damaged region reaches the surface, and the tensile relief wave was too weak to produce a spall layer. Thus, the calculation is in good agreement with the observation in the field that there was no surface damage, although there was an extensive rubbled region around the charge.

Figure 6 shows the calculated damage distribution at 2.0 ms for experiment 79-10. The relatively shallow depth of burial for this charge results in intense damage. The three regions of damage seen in earlier calculations now merge to form a crater much like the one that was observed. The intensity of rock breakage shown in the calculation makes it easy to understand why the joint structure had little influence on the crater in the field.

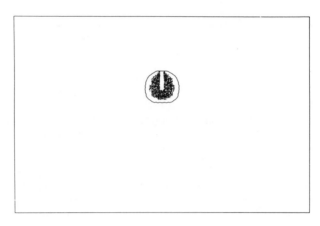

Figure 1.   Damage distribution and mean stress contour plot at 0.2 ms in computer simulation of Experiment 79–8.   The mean stress contour level is 10 MPa compressive.   The distribution and density of the dots show the extent of the damage.   The blank region inside the damaged area is the explosive, which lies on an axis of cylindrical symmetry.   The dimensions of the plot frame are 14 m × 9 m.   The top boundary is the mine floor.   At this time, the detonation front is traveling upward through the explosive. A shock wave is propagating upward and away from the charge, and damage is occurring near the portion of the charge that has been detonated.

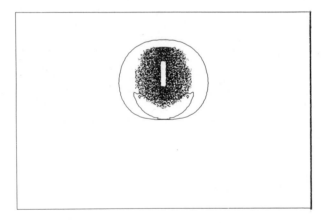

Figure 2.   Damage distribution and mean stress contour plot at 0.6 ms in computer simulation of Experiment 79–8.   The contour level and plot dimensions are the same as in Figure 1.   At this time, the detonation is complete.   A shock wave is propagating upward toward the free surface.   Extensive damage has occurred around the charge.

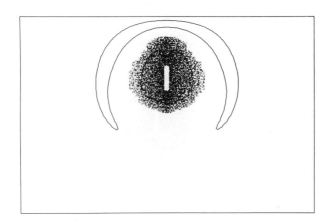

Figure 3.   Damage distribution and mean stress contour plot at 1.0 ms in computer simulation of Experiment 79–8.   The contour level and plot dimensions are the same as in Figure 1.   At this time, the shock wave is approaching the free surface. Damage has occurred above the charge in addition to the damage around the charge.

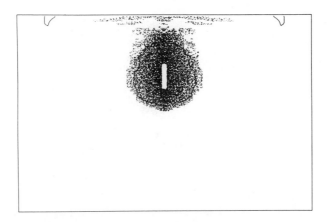

Figure 4.   Damage distribution and mean stress contour plot at 2.0 ms in computer simulation of Experiment 79–8. The contour level and plot dimensions are the same as in Figure 1. At this time, a layer of spall damage can be seen near the free surface. It developed as the tensile relief wave propagated downward following the interaction of the explosively generated shock with the free surface. This figure shows the final computed damage distribution.

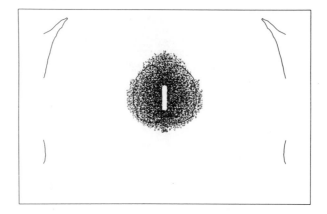

Figure 5. Damage distribution and mean stress contour plot at 2.0 ms in computer simulation of Experiment 79–7. The contour level and plot dimensions are the same as in Figure 1. Note that the charge is buried more deeply here. This figure shows the final computed damage distribution. No spall damage has occurred near the surface because of the increased depth of burial.

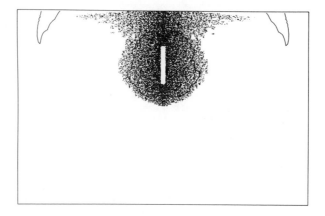

Figure 6. Damage distribution and mean stress contour plot at 2.0 ms in computer simulation of Experiment 79–10. The contour level and plot dimensions are the same as in Figure 1. Note that the bottom of the charge is at the same depth as in Experiment 79–8 (Figures 1–4), but the charge is larger and extends closer to the free surface. The shallower effective depth of burial has resulted in the formation of a crater-shaped damage region, much as was observed in the corresponding field experiment.

Conclusion

The steps in assembling the computational tools needed to simulate the explosive fracture of oil shale have been described. The resulting code, with its input data, was then used to simulate three explosive field experiments. The results of the calculations are in good agreement with what actually occurred in the field. Further detailed comparisons are in progress for these experiments and the others that have been conducted. As this is done, improvements will be made in the input data and in the code physics.

The development of computer codes as tools to predict rock breakage makes a variety of interesting studies possible. The properties of the explosive can be changed to see how the extent of rubbling is affected. Studies of spacing and delays for decked charges are also possible. Finally, the codes can be applied in situations, such as confined-volume blasting, at the frontiers of blasting technology. These areas are vital to the effective utilization of our oil shale resources, especially with *in situ* techniques. Computer simulation will play a central role in the development of new technology for energy and mineral resource recovery.

Acknowledgment

This work was performed under the auspices of the U. S. Department of Energy.

Literature Cited

1. Amsden, A. A.; Hirt, C. W. "YAQUI: An Arbitrary Lagrangian-Eulerian Computer Program for Fluid Flow at All Speeds," Los Alamos Scientific Laboratory report LA-5100, March 1973.
2. Hirt, C. W.; Amsden, A. A.,; Cook, J. L. "An Arbitrary Lagrangian-Eulerian Computing Method for All Flow Speeds," J. Comput. Phys. 1974, 14, 227.
3. Mader, C. L. "Numerical Modeling of Detonations"; University of California Press: Berkeley, 1979.
4. Craig, B. G.; Johnson, J. N.; Mader, C. L.; Lederman, G. F. "Characterization of Two Commercial Explosives," Los Alamos Scientific Laboratory report LA-7140, May 1978.
5. Johnson, J. N. "Calculation of Explosive Rock Breakage: Oil Shale," in "Proceedings of the 20th U. S. Symposium on Rock Mechanics," U. S. National Committee for Rock Mechanics, June 1979, pp. 109-118.
6. Dienes, J. K.; Margolin, L. G. "A Computational Approach to Rock Fragmentation," presented at the 21st U. S. Symposium on Rock Mechanics, Rolla, Missouri, May 1980.

7. Butkovich, T. R. "Correlations between Measurements and
    Calculations of High-Explosive-Induced Fracture in a Coal
    Outcrop," Int. J. Rock Mech. Min. Sci. and Geomech. Abstr.
    1976, 13, 45.
8. Kipp, M. E.; Grady, D. E. "Numerical Studies of Rock
    Fragmentation," Sandia Laboratories report SAND-79-1582,
    presented at the 2nd International Conference on Numerical
    Methods in Fracture Mechanics, Swansea, July 1980.
9. Olinger, B. "Oil Shales under Dynamic Stress," in
    "Explosively Produced Fracture of Oil Shale, April 1977-
    March 1978," Los Alamos Scientific Laboratory report
    LA-7357-PR, November 1978, pp. 2-10.
10. Smith, J. W. "Specific Gravity-Oil Yield Relationships of
    Two Colorado Oil Shale Cores," Ind. Eng. Chem. 1956, 48,
    441.
11. Carter, W. J. "Hugoniot of Green River Oil Shale," in
    "Explosively Produced Fracture of Oil Shale, March
    1976-March 1977," Los Alamos Scientific Laboratory report
    LA-6817-PR, September 1977, pp. 2-6.
12. Johnson, J. N.; Simonson, E. R. "Analytical Failure
    Surfaces for Oil Shale of Varying Kerogen Content," in
    Timmerhaus, K. D.; Barber, M. S., Eds., "High Pressure
    Science and Technology, Sixth AIRAPT Conference," Vol. 2;
    Plenum: New York, 1979, pp. 444-454.
13. McLamore, R.; Gray, J. "The Mechanical Behavior of
    Anistropic Sedimentary Rocks," J. Eng. Ind. 1967, 89, 62.

RECEIVED January 19, 1981.

Fracturing of Oil Shale by Treatment with Liquid Sulfur Dioxide

D. F. BUROW and R. K. SHARMA

Department of Chemistry, University of Toledo, Toledo, OH 43606

Development of oil shale deposits as sources of fuels, lubricants, and chemical feedstocks is being considered as an alternative to present reliance on conventional petroleum reserves. Procedures, advantages, and disadvantages for mining/ surface processing and for in situ retorting have been widely discussed (1, 2, 3). In the former approach, crushing of the shale is essential for efficient oil recovery. As a result of tests with a variety of mechanical crushers (4), it is apparent that the effectiveness of mechanical crushing is limited by the characteristics of the shale. A slab-forming tendency allows large pieces to pass through many conventional crushers. The resilience and slippery nature of the shale limits the effectiveness of mechanical impact. Furthermore, shale abrasiveness and a tendency for the shale to adhere to crusher surfaces causes maintenance problems with crushers. In situ retorting is enhanced by fracturing with explosive charges or expansion of existing fractures with fluids such as water. Fracturing by explosive charges is frequently limited to the vicinity of the charge since the explosive shock is dissipated by shale resilience. Efficient fracturing by aqueous fluids is limited by a tendency for capillary adhesion of water in the fissures and by available water supplies in arid regions where oil shale deposits often occur.

Employment of chemical comminution techniques for surface processing of oil shales could circumvent many of the limitations to mechanical crushing as well as reduce or eliminate capital and maintenance costs of crushers. For in situ processing, such techniques could provide an alternative to explosive or hydro-static fracturing. Our recent success in comminuting and desul-furizing coal by treatment with liquid sulfur dioxide (5, 6), suggested that similar treatments might be successfully applied to oil shale processing.

Liquid SO_2 is a remarkably subtle and selective solvent with moderate Lewis acid properties, a substantial resistance to oxidation and reduction when pure, and a propensity to support a

0097–6156/81/0163–0025$05.00/0

variety of ionic, free radical, and molecular reactions (7).
Physical properties of liquid SO_2 which can be exploited advanta-
geously include: a $-10°$ bp, moderate vapor pressure at room
temperature, high density, low viscosity, and low surface tension.
Since SO_2 has a boiling point of $-10°C$, it is easily liquified
and/or removed after reaction; it can be easily manipulated
without the need for exotic construction materials. Furthermore,
it is an inexpensive material which is readily available in large
quantities from smelting and fossil fuel combustion; if not
utilized, it must be disposed of in some stabilized form at considerable expense. Thus, the direct use of sulfur dioxide could
provide an alternative means of cost recovery for pollution
abatement technology.

Here we wish to report the results of preliminary experiments in which oil shales are treated with liquid sulfur dioxide
to effect fracturing; observations made during these experiments
suggest that liquid SO_2 may also be of utility in other phases
of oil shale processing. We are, presently, unaware of any
previous reports of such experiments.

Experimental

Sulfur dioxide was dried and manipulated as described elsewhere (7). A 1-liter stainless steel autoclave (Parr Model 4641)
was utilized for processing at pressures in excess of ca. 3 atm.
In experiments utilizing larger shale pieces (6-8 cm), clamped
shale samples, or supercritical conditions, samples were placed
directly in the autoclave. For sub-critical experiments using
small shale pieces, samples were sealed in fritted glass tubes
with liquid SO_2 (ca. 2:1 or less SO_2/shale by weight) to
facilitate recovery of extracts. Sulfur dioxide was distilled
on to the shale at $-78°C$; the system was then sealed and brought
up to processing temperature. Temperatures of 25, 70, and $170°C$
were used; supercritical conditions for SO_2 were achieved at
the latter temperature.

Processing time was ca. 2 hours for elevated temperature
experiments; for room temperature experiments, the time ranged
from 2 to 24 hours. No mechanical agitation was employed. Upon
cooling, the SO_2, shale, and extract were recovered. The shales
were inspected immediately upon recovery and at several intervals
thereafter. Sulfur analyses and infrared spectra of the shales
were performed on original, processed, and processed/heated
samples to determine residual SO_2 content. Infrared spectra of
the extracts were also obtained. All infrared spectra were
recorded on a Perkin Elmer Model 621 spectrophotometer; solid
samples were examined as KBr pellets and shale extracts were
examined as thin films (neat) between NaCl plates.

Shale samples were also treated with gaseous SO_2, liquid
CO_2, liquid NH_3, water, and several organic liquids at $25°C$ for
2 days. Procedures equivalent to those used with liquid SO_2 were

employed for treatment with gaseous SO_2, liquid CO_2, and liquid
NH_3. Treatment with other liquids consisted of immersion of
shale samples in the liquid contained in covered beakers.

Samples of Antrim, Green River, and Moroccan oil shales were
obtained from the Laramie Energy Technology Center. The composition of typical samples of these three shales is illustrated in
Table I.

Results and Discussion

Upon exposure of the shales to liquid SO_2, highly colored
solutions develop due to formation of donor-acceptor complexes
between extracted oil constituents and the SO_2. Green River
shale produces red-brown solutions, Moroccan shale forms orange
solutions, and Antrim shale forms yellow solutions; in each case,
these colors are more intense when higher processing temperatures
are used.

Fracturing of Shales. Liquid SO_2 causes extensive
fracturing in each of the three shales examined in this preliminary study; Figure 1 illustrates representative examples of this
fracturing. This fracturing occurs both along and across
laminations. With the larger lumps, laminations are frequently
expanded to 1-2 cm; fractures across laminations are less
pronounced but distinctly visible. Green River shale exhibits
numerous small cracks whereas the other two shales exhibit a
fewer number of larger cracks. With processing temperatures
below 25°C, the degree of fracturing is greatest in Moroccan
and least in Antrim shale; with higher processing temperatures,
differences in degree of fracturing are not so apparent.
Samples of each of the shales, rigidly clamped both across and
along laminations also exhibited extensive fracturing. Immediately upon recovery from the reactor, the samples are so
brittle as to be easily broken with the fingers; after standing
for a time, the samples become slightly less brittle but all
fracturing is maintained. Although no quantitative tests of
mechanical properties have been made, it appears that little of
the resilience and slipperyness of the original shales is retained. Surfaces of the processed samples have a soft lusterous
appearance.

Shale samples were subjected to treatment with other fluids
at 25°C to provide comparative data on their ability to fracture
these shales. From among these fluids only gaseous SO_2, liquid
NH_3, and methylene chloride were effective fracturing agents
under these conditions. The results are summarized in Table II.
Under the same conditions of temperature and pressure, gaseous
SO_2 is less effective than the liquid in producing fractures.
Both liquid NH_3 and methylene chloride produce roughly the same
degree of fracturing as liquid SO_2. Liquid NH_3, however, appears
to produce the greatest fracturing with Antrim shale and the

Table I. Typical Composition of Oil Shales[a] Examined

Green River (Colorado)[b]

Organic Matter:	14% (mostly aliphatic)[d,e]
Oil Yield:	∿25 gal/ton
Dolomite and Calcite:	43%
Feldspar and Plagioclase:	16%
Illite, Montmorillinite, Muscovite:	13%
Quartz:	9%

Antrim (Michigan)[c]

Organic Matter:	9% (1:1 aliphatic/aromatic)[d,e]
Oil Yield:	∿10 gal/ton
Illite:	45%
Quartz:	30%
Pyrite:	5%
Carbonates:	5%

Moroccan[d]

Organic Matter:	11% (3:1 aliphatic/aromatic)[d,e]
Oil Yield:	∿18 gal/ton

a. Samples provided by F. Miknis, LETC
b. Ref. 8.
c. Ref. 9.
d. Ref. 10.
e. Aliphatic/aromatic ratio established from solid state ^{13}C nmr spectra, Ref. 10.

Figure 1. Representative examples of the fracturing of oil shales by liquid SO_2; (left) treated samples; (right) untreated samples; (a) Antrim shale treated at 170°C for 2 h; (b) Green River shale treated at 70°C for 2 h; (c) Moroccan shale treated at 70°C for 2 h.

Table II. Fracturing of Oil Shales by Various Fluids[a]

Fluid	Shales[b]		
	Antrim	Green River	Moroccan
SO_2			
Gas (~3 atm)	-	MF,E	-
Liquid (-78°C)	N	MF,E	HF,E
Liquid (25°C)	MF,E	HF,E	HF,E
Liquid (70°C)	HF,E	HF,E	HF,E
Supercritical (170°C)	HF,E	HF,E	HF,E
CO_2 (Liquid, ~60 atm)	N	N	N
NH_3 (Liquid, ~10 atm)	HF,E	HF,E	HF,E
H_2O	-	N	-
CH_3CN	-	N	-
DMSO	-	N	-
DMF	-	N	-
HMPA	-	N	-
C_6H_6	-	N	-
H_2CCl_2	-	HF,E	-

a. Except for liquid SO_2, tests were run at 25°C for 2 days.

b. N: no apparent fracturing, MF: moderate fracturing, HF: extensive fracturing, E: extract observed.

least with Moroccan shale; this trend is just the opposite of
that observed with liquid SO_2. Our results with liquid CO_2 are
in apparent conflict with results reported by Miller, et al. (11)
for treatment of Devonian shales with CO_2 fluids. From among
the fluids tested, liquid SO_2 has several advantages as a
fracturing agent for oil shales: it is low in cost, it is
available in quantity, it is not derived from either petroleum
or natural gas, and it is readily manipulated due to its moderate
vapor pressure.

The sulfur content of the shales is increased somewhat by
processing in liquid SO_2; residual sulfur increases significantly
with the temperature of the treatment, however. For example,
at room temperature, residual sulfur increases by 1-2% but at
170°C, it increases by 5-10%. Comparison of infrared spectra of
untreated and treated shale samples (Figures 2-4, A and B)
indicates that this increased sulfur content is due to formation
of sulfur-oxygen containing residues, probably sulfites and/or
sulfates, in the shales. It might appear that the increase in
sulfur content of any shale fractured by liquid SO_2 would be
deleterious to oil produced in a subsequent retorting step.
However, since this retained SO_2 appears to be in the inorganic
part of the shale as adsorbed SO_2, sulfites, or sulfates, little
contamination of the retorted oil should occur: adsorbed SO_2
can be removed in a mild preheating step and the sulfite/sulfate
species are sufficiently stable to remain intact during any
retorting step. Sulfur elemental and infrared analyses of
treated shale samples, performed before and after mild heating,
demonstrated that adsorbed SO_2 can be removed easily.

Preliminary SEM/EDXA results for Green River Shale indicate
that these sulfur-oxygen residues are apparently associated with
selected inorganic constituents of the shale. EDXA of untreated
Green River shale samples indicated a Si/Ca ratio of ca. 1.5;
this ratio corresponds closely to that expected from the bulk
composition of the shale (Table I). The sulfur which is present
in untreated samples was observed to be correlated with Ca
rather than Fe locations, suggesting that little pyritic sulfur
was present in these particular samples. Treated samples of
Green River shale exhibit erosion and pitting of the surface in
Ca rich areas but no apparent changes in Si rich areas. The
pits have diameters in the 2-10 μm range. In treated samples,
the Si/Ca ratio was often found to be significantly higher than
in untreated samples; this observation suggests that liquid SO_2
causes a surface depletion of Ca ions. The increased sulfur
content of treated samples is readily apparent in the EDXA
results; this increased S content is associated with Ca rich but
not Si or Fe rich regions in the shale. These SEM/EDXA data
suggest that liquid SO_2 attacks the calcite and/or dolomite
constituents of Green River shale and, perhaps, thereby causing
the observed fracturing. Similar data on the other shales were
not obtained during this exploratory work.

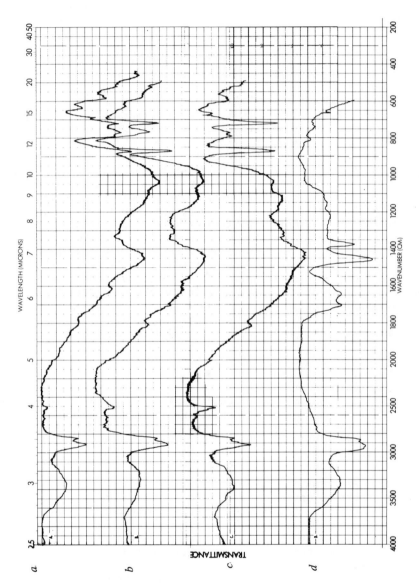

Figure 2.   IR spectra of Green River oil shale: (a) untreated sample; (b) sample treated with liquid SO₂ at 70°C for 2 h; (c) sample treated with SO₂ fluid at 170°C for 2 h; (d) extract isolated from treatment in b.

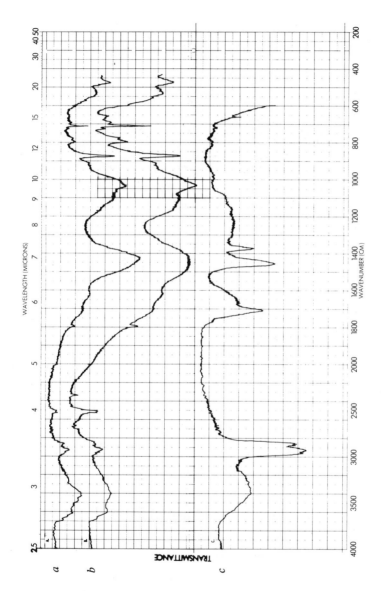

Figure 3.   IR spectra of Morrocan oil shale: (a) untreated sample; (b) sample treated with liquid SO₂ at 70°C for 2 h; (c) extract isolated from treatment in b.

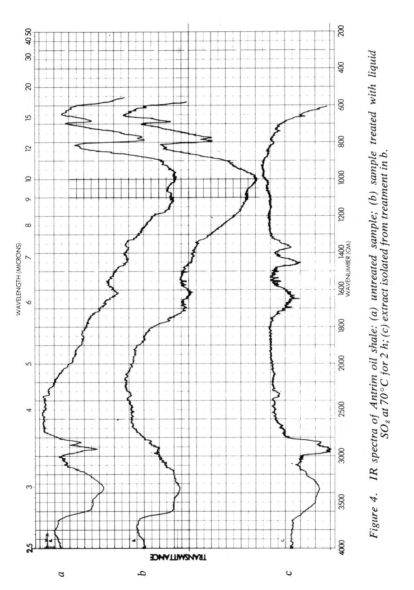

Figure 4. IR spectra of Antrim oil shale: (a) untreated sample; (b) sample treated with liquid SO₂ at 70°C for 2 h; (c) extract isolated from treatment in b.

Fracturing of Model Minerals. Further insight into the processes responsible for liquid SO_2 fracturing of these shales is
provided by the behavior of several minerals when subjected to
liquid SO_2. Authenic samples of calcite (crystals), dolomite
(hard lumps), gypsum (hard lumps), and illite (hard lumps) were
treated with liquid SO_2 at 25°C for 2-5 hours; after removal of
the SO_2, the treated minerals were heated for 2 hours at 100°C;
infrared spectra and sulfur analyses were then obtained. Calcite
crystals developed numerous fine cracks and a fine powder flaked
off. Although the powder contained no sulfur (elemental
analysis) or S-O moieties (IR spectra), the cracked crystals were
shown to contain 0.18% sulfur in the form of sulfur-oxygen
structures. Although these data are consisted with a 0.7% conversion via

$$CaCO_3(s) + SO_2(\ell) \xrightarrow{\quad 25°C \quad} CaSO_3(s) + CO_2(g)$$

other processes cannot be excluded at this stage. Dolomite, on
the other hand, did not appear to be effected by liquid SO_2 under
the conditions employed: treated dolomite exhibited no fracturing, no sulfur content, and no mass change. Gypsum chunks were
fractured by liquid SO_2. Infrared and sulfur analyses indicate
that liquid SO_2 interacts with gypsum in two ways: first,
simple extraction of water of crystallation and, second, reaction
with a portion of the remaining water of crystallation to form
H^+ and HSO_3^-. Large cracks develop and a powder flakes off when
illite lumps are treated with liquid SO_2; sulfur analyses indicate approximate compositions to be $[KAl_4SiAlO_{20}(OH)_4]\cdot(SO_2)_{0.3}$
(lumps) and $[KAl_4SiAlO_{20}(OH)_4]\cdot(SO_2)_{0.4}$ (powder). Infrared
spectral changes suggest partial reaction of the OH groups to
form SO_3H groups.

Fracturing Mechanisms. These observations with model
minerals suggest that several mechanisms be considered for the
observed fracturing of oil shales by liquid SO_2. Partial conversion of carbonates to sulfites could disrupt microcrystalline
lattices in carbonate rich shales. Partial reaction of the OH
groups in alluminosilicates could cause similar changes in
siliceous shales. Extraction of or reaction with water of
crystallization in shale components could be operating in both
types of shale. Purely physical processes, perhaps involving
penetration of pores and microscopic vacancies with subsequent
adsorption to modify surfaces or displace surface water, need to
be considered as well. Finally, our observations that the
vitrinites are extensively fractured when coals are treated with
liquid SO_2 (5, 6) suggests that swelling and/or extraction of
organic constituents of the shale may also play a role. At this
stage, it is believed that the fracturing of a particular type
of oil shale by liquid SO_2 is probably due to a combination of
several of these modes.
    Initial comparison of the fracturing results obtained via

liquid SO_2 treatment with those obtained via liquid NH_3 treatment might suggest that the differences could be attributed simply to differences in the acid/base characteristics of the liquids and the shales. Further consideration of the possible mechanisms involved in liquid SO_2 fracturing, however, would suggest such an explanation to be overly simplistic. Establishment of fracturing mechanisms for these fluids must await the results of future experiments.

Extracted Material. Extracts, comprising 2-4% of the original shale mass, were isolated by filteration and subsequent evaporation of the liquid SO_2 solutions which were in contact with these shales. Although no attempt was made to extract these shales exhaustively, it is apparent that appreciably more material can be extracted by liquid SO_2 under rather mild conditions. The bulk (90% or more) of the extract is organic although some water is removed and small amounts of colorless or light brown crystalline material are found in the cracks and fissures of treated shales. Infrared spectra (Figures 2-4) of the extract reveals aliphatic CH and carbonyl groups in the Green River shale extract; the Moroccan shale extract has a similar content. These extracts represent bitumen portions of the shale. Kerogen fractions, presumably, remain in the shale; infrared spectra (Figures 2 and 3, Traces B) indicate considerable organic content remaining in the treated shales. The extract from the Antrim shale is somewhat different from that of the other two shales in that both aliphatic and aromatic C-H but little carbonyl is present (Figure 4C). The aromatic content of this extract is not unexpected since the organic constituents of Antrim shale are highly aromatic (Table I). Although more definitive data is necessary to substantiate the proposition, it would appear (Figure 4, A and B) that a significant portion of the organic matter is removed from Antrim shale by treatment with liquid SO_2.

Extracts of organic material were also obtained with other fluids as indicated in Table II. Although no detailed analyses of these extracts were obtained, it would appear that these extracts are of the bitumen fraction as expected.

Summary

Preliminary experiments have demonstrated that liquid SO_2 is effective in fracturing and embrittling both carbonaeceous and siliceous oil shales. Liquid SO_2 has advantages over other fluid fracturing agents, viz., low cost, availability in quantity, and non-petroluem or natural gas origin. Several possible mechanisms for shale fracturing have been suggested for future exploration. Organic components can be removed from the shale under mild conditions. On the basis of these results, further efforts in the use of liquid SO_2 for oil shale processing are justified. The general applicability or limitations of these procedures need to be established; a knowledge of the mechanisms of shale fracturing would aid in this development. Enhancement of organic constituent recovery needs to be explored. Adaptation of these procedures to practical and economical processes in both surface processing and in situ recovery could result. Several of these areas will be discussed in future reports.

Acknowledgements

The support of this research by the U. S. Department of Energy under Contract No. ET-78-G-01-3316 is gratefully acknowledged. Provision of oil shale samples and documentation by Dr. F. P. Miknis (LETC), mineral samples by Dr. W. A. Kneller, preliminary SEM/EDXA results by Dr. S. N. K. Chaudhari, and aid in obtaining the mineral/SO_2 results by Mr. R. Carter are also gratefully acknowledged.

Literature Cited

1. Perrini, E. M. "Oil from Shale and Tar Sands," Chemical Tech. Rev. No. 51, Noyes Data Corp.: Park Ridge, N. J., 1975.
2. Yen, T. F. "Shale Oil, Tar Sands, and Related Fuel Sources," Adv. Chem. Series, No. 151, American Chemical Society: Washington, D. C., 1976.
3. Yen, T. F.; Chilingarian, G. V., Dev. Pet. Sci., Vol. 5, Elsevier: Amsterdam, 1976.
4. Matzick, A.; Dannenberg, R. O.; Guthrie, B. "Experiments in Crushing Green River Oil Shale," Bureau of Mines Report No. 5563, 1958.
5. Burow, D. F.; Glavincevski, B. M. "Preprints", Div. of Fuel Chemistry, American Chemical Society, Vol. 25, No. 2, 1980, p. 153.
6. Burow, D. F.; Sharma, R. K. "Liquid Sulfur Dioxide Treatment of Coal," Conf. Chem. Phys. of Coal Utilization, Morgantown, W. Virginia, 1980, Paper T-4.
7. Burow, D. F., In "Chemistry of Non-Aqueous Solvents"; Lagowski, J. J., Ed.; Academic: New York, 1970, Vol. III, Chapter 2.
8. Yen, T. F.; Chilingarian, G. V. Ref. 3, Chapter 1.
9. Musser, W. N., Dow Chemical Co. Report FE-310, 1976.
10. Miknis, F. P., private communication.
11. Miller, J. F.; Boyer, J. P.; Kent, S. J.; Snyder, M. J. Morgantown Energy Technol. Center, Spec. Publ. (METC/SP-79/6) 1976, 473; Chem. Abstr. 1980, 93, 49920j.

RECEIVED January 19, 1981.

Chemistry of Shale Oil Cracking

A. K. BURNHAM

Lawrence Livermore National Laboratory, University of California,
Livermore, CA 94550

Oil shale contains organic material consisting mostly kerogen (a solid polymer) and a small amount of bitumen (a soluble, high-molecular-weight material) (1). Most currently proposed methods for recovering the energy from oil shale involve the pyrolysis of kerogen (and bitumen) to shale oil at temperatures of about 400 to 550°C. Depending on the processing conditions, part of this oil may be degraded into less desirable products: coke and gas (2-11). Previous work here at Lawrence Livermore National Laboratory (LLNL) developed a quantitative kinetic scheme for the degradation of liquid oil to mostly solid products (coking) at temperatures below 450°C (9,12). We now describe a kinetic scheme for the degradation of vapor-phase oil into mostly gaseous products (cracking) at temperatures above 500°C.

Shale oil cracking can be significant in an indirect-heat retort in which the oil shale is pyrolyzed by contact with hot solids or hot oxygen-free gas. To minimize the shale residence time in surface processes, the retorting temperature is frequently maintained above 500°C. The residence time of the shale oil vapor in the reactor may be long enough that a significant amount of thermal cracking may occur, especially in a hot-solids retort to which no sweep gas is added.

Significant shale oil cracking can also take place in an in-situ retort in which thermal cracking may occur both inside large shale blocks and in the gas stream. If the thermal gradient within a block is large, oil produced near the center of the block can crack (mostly to form gas) as it travels to the hotter block surface. More important, the oil emerging from the block enters a gas stream that may be 200°C hotter than the block surface (13). Because this gas stream may also contain oxygen, high-temperature oil-yield loss in the gas stream may take place by both combustion and associated cracking.

In this work, we report kinetics for the thermal cracking of shale oil over shale. The data are most appropriate for thermal cracking inside large blocks during in-situ processing and in the TOSCO-II and Lurgi processes, where relatively low temperatures

0097–6156/81/0163–0039$05.50/0

(500 to 600°C), relatively long residence times (several
seconds), and nearly autogenous conditions prevail. We
previously gave a more detailed report of our kinetic
measurements (14). We also demonstrate the effect of thermal
cracking on shale oil composition and present results of C, H,
and N analysis, capillary-column gas chromatography (GC), and
GC/MS. We compare the compositions of shale oil samples produced
under laboratory conditions with those of samples produced in
large-scale experiments. A more detailed investigation of oil
properties including IR and ^{13}C NMR spectra (15) and a
resulting diagnostic method based on oil composition (16) have
been reported earlier.

Experimental

Figure 1 shows the apparatus used in the cracking
experiments. This assay apparatus is a modification of the LLNL
modified Fischer assay apparatus described previously (17). It
is used for a complete mass- and carbon-balanced assay under
various heating schedules. For the cracking experiments, a
second furnace and reactor were added. Both reactors were made
of Type 304 stainless steel. A 165-µm stainless steel frit
(6.3 mm high by 32 mm in diam) allowed gases but not shale to
pass through the bottom of the reactors.
Raw shale samples were taken from a 92-litre/Mg (22-gal/ton)
master batch (17) of Mahogany Zone oil shale mined from the
Department of Energy facility at Anvil Points, Colorado. The raw
shale had been ground to pass a 20-mesh screen (< 841 µm) and
then spin-riffled to obtain 95-g aliquots. The shale contained
9.9% organic carbon (12.2% kerogen), 22.2% acid-evolved CO_2
(48.3% calcite and dolomite), and the remainder mostly quartz and
silicates. All percentages are calculated on a weight basis.
Organic carbon is determined by the difference between total
carbon and carbon from acid-evolved CO_2.
Raw shale contained in the top furnace and reactor was
retorted at a linear heating rate. Gases and vapors evolved
during retorting passed through the second reactor at 504 to
610°C where the oil was thermally cracked. Temperatures were
measured at the center of the bottom reactor by a
stainless-steel-sheathed thermocouple (Type K). Temperature
variation across the reactor was less than 3°C. To simulate
conditions inside a shale block, the bottom reactor contained
pieces of shale. We used burnt shale (mostly silicates and MgO)
in most of the experiments because it is thermally stable above
500°C. In two experiments, we used retorted shale (2.7% organic
carbon, 24.4% acid-evolved CO_2) and no shale, respectively.
The rate of gas evolution was monitored by a pressure
transducer in the collection bottle. The rate of gas evolution
peaked sharply during the kerogen pyrolysis at about 460°C. To
minimize differences in residence times caused by the

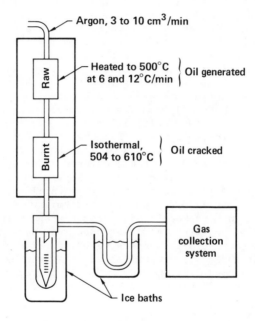

Figure 1.   Experimental apparatus used in the gas-phase cracking of shale oil over shale

time-dependent gas evolution rate, we purged the reactor with a
slow sweep of argon (3 to 10 cm^3/min). (The argon constituted
10 to 20% of the collected gases.) The average residence time
was varied by changing both the heating rate and the volume of
the second reactor.

Products were collected and weighed to determine a mass
balance. Except for two experiments, in which the volume of
gases exceeded the capacity of the gas collection system and the
last portion was vented, the mass balance ranged from 95 to 98%
(14). We measured C, H, N, and acid-evolved CO_2 content for
all retorted shales and for some burnt shales from the cracking
experiments. Oils were analyzed for C, H, and N. Gases were
analyzed by gas chromatography (thermal conductivity detector for
H_2, CO, CO_2, N_2, and CH_4; flame ionization detector for
hydrocarbons) and by mass spectrometry. The analyses permitted
an organic carbon balance to be calculated for the four
experiments in which the shale in the bottom reactor was
analyzed; values from 100 to 105% were obtained (14).

Further measurements were made on the oil samples. In
addition to the samples prepared on the above apparatus, other
oil samples were obtained from the LLNL 6-ton retort, the Laramie
Energy Technology Center (LETC) 150-ton retort, the 1972 TOSCO-II
semi-works operation, Occidental Oil Shale's modified in-situ
experiment No. 6, and LETC's Rock Springs No. 9 true in-situ
experiment. Spectroscopic techniques used were capillary-column
GC/MS, IR, and ^{13}C NMR spectroscopy. These studies have been
reported in detail previously (15). Only capillary-column gas
chromatography results are reported in detail here.

A Hewlett-Packard Model 5880 chromatograph with a
flame-ionization detector (FID) was used following a previously
described procedure (16). Samples were made by dissolving about
0.5 ml of neat shale oil in 2 ml of CS_2. A Quadrex
fused-silica column (0.23 mm i.d. by 50 m) coated with SP2100
(methyl silicone oil) was used. The temperature was programmed
from 60°C to 275°C at the rate of 4°C/min and held at 275°C for
30 min.

Results

Kinetic Measurements. The results of the shale oil cracking
experiments are summarized in Table I. Oil yields are reported
as a percentage of the LLNL assay result on both a condensed-oil
basis and a C_{5+} basis. To conduct the kinetic analysis, an
effective residence time had to be determined. It was assumed
for simplicity that the gas-and-oil evolution profile could be
approximated by a square pulse. The average residence time was
calculated by multiplying the void volume of the bottom reactor
by the time interval over which three-fourths of the products
were evolved and then dividing by the total volume of gases and
vapors at the cracking temperatures (14). The void volume was

Table I: Conditions for preparation of laboratory oil samples.

Experiment number	Temperature of bottom reactor (°C)	Residence time (s)	Shale in bottom reactor	Oil yield (wt% of assay)	
				Condensed	C_5^+
111	508	7.0	Burnt	95	96
113	610	3.8	Burnt	55	59
115	505	10.4	Spent	90	91
119	558	4.9	Burnt	81	83
121	504	9.3	Burnt	91	92
123	585	2.5	Burnt	77	82
125	585	2.7	Empty	87	89
127	610	2.0	Burnt	68	74

determined by subtracting the volume of the burnt or retorted
shale from the volume of the empty reactor. (The former value
was calculated by dividing the weight of shale by its density,
which was determined by mercury porosimetry).

This method of determining the residence time was checked
for Experiment 115 by using a more complicated method. A
time-dependent gas and oil-vapor evolution rate was estimated
from oil-and-gas evolution rate measurements (12,18). Residence
times calculated from this rate ranged from 80 s at 350°C to
about 6 s at 450°C. A weighted average of this residence-time
distribution gave an average residence time of 11 s, which was in
surprisingly good agreement with the value of 10.4 s determined
by the simple method. However, the more complicated method is
also approximate because the calculation of the residence time
does not allow the extent of cracking during the experiment (and
hence instantaneous product volume) to depend on the
instantaneous residence time. For this reason, we have used the
simpler method to estimate residence time. This introduces a
systematic uncertainty into the kinetic parameters.

In our previous report (14), we determined a global rate
constant at each temperature on the basis of the yield of
condensed oil. The resulting four rate constants were then
fitted to an Arrhenius expression. In the present report, we use
a slightly different technique. The typical first-order rate
expression,

$$- \frac{dy}{dt} = k_f y = yAe^{-B/T} \, , \qquad\qquad (1)$$

can be rearranged to give

$$\ln \left(-\frac{\ln y}{t} \right) = \ln k_f = \ln A - B/T , \qquad (2)$$

where y is the yield of shale oil and A and B are Arrhenius parameters. In effect, a first-order rate constant is determined from each experiment, and a rate expression can be determined from a typical Arrhenius plot. The resulting plot is shown in Figure 2 for the yield of C_5+ oil. This gives a rate expression of

$$k_f \ (s^{-1}) = 4.8 \times 10^8 \ \exp \ (-19340/T) \qquad (3)$$

This rate constant has a slightly higher activation energy and is 1.2 times less at 550°C than the rate constant reported previously ([14]) for the yield of condensed oil. Given the systematic uncertainty in the residence time, the differences are not significant.

Two additional cautions should be mentioned concerning the use of Equation (3). Experiment 125 (no shale in the bottom reactor) was used in neither kinetic analysis because the conversion was substantially lower than expected on the basis of the other experiments. This discrepancy may have resulted from either a catalytic effect of the shale or a heat-transfer limitation. In addition, Dickson and Yesavage ([19]) found that there is a 60 to 70% conversion limit for shale oil cracking. This results from the presence and additional formation of aromatics, which are resistant to cracking. This implies that our expression will fail at high conversions.

Table II gives the product distribution for thermal cracking of shale oil. We defined oil as the sum of condensed oil and C_5-C_9 hydrocarbons in the gas. The amount of each gaseous product was determined from the slope of the curve plotting gas production versus cracking loss (conversion) ([14]). The amount of coke produced was determined by difference, but it agreed well with the measured value for the few experiments in which carbon was analyzed in the shale from the bottom reactor. The alkene/alkane ratios in the gas depended more strongly on the cracking temperature than on the extent of conversion. This topic is discussed in greater detail in another paper published in these proceedings ([20]).

Oil Properties of Laboratory Samples. The properties of the liquid also change during the conversion of a hydrocarbon liquid to gas and solid. Specifically, the H/C ratio decreases and the concentration of aromatic molecules increases greatly. Elemental and spectroscopic analyses confirmed these trends for the shale oils produced in our experiments.

The H/C ratio and percentage nitrogen are plotted in Figure 3 as a function of conversion to gas and coke. It is

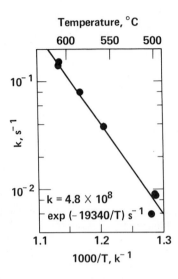

Figure 2. Arrhenius plot of shale oil cracking data from which the rate expression in Equation 3 was determined

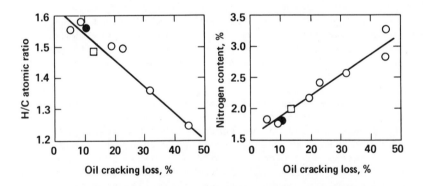

Figure 3. The effect of oil cracking on the H/C atomic ratio and nitrogen content of the shale oil. The data points indicate cracking over burnt shale (○), retorted shale (●), and in an empty reactor (□). The H/C ratio is probably a function of both cracking temperature and loss. Aromatic nitrogen compounds are concentrated selectively by cracking.

Table II. Products from shale oil cracking.[a]

Compound	Volume (cm^3/g at STP)	Weight (g/g)
H_2	184	0.02
CO	22	0.03
CH_4	151	0.11
C_2	155	0.20
C_3	85	0.16
C_4	68	0.17
Coke	--	0.31

[a] $C_5+ \equiv$ oil.

evident that the H/C ratio decreases as cracking increases. Of
further interest is the increase in nitrogen content as cracking
increases. This increase occurs because the nitrogen in shale
oil is contained in aromatic molecules (7), which are resistant
to cracking (i.e., thermodynamically more stable). As the
alkanes and alkenes are partially converted to gases, the
nitrogen compounds become selectively concentrated. Therefore, a
50% cracking conversion results in a doubling of the nitrogen
content.

The trends reported here for cracking are the direct
opposite of those observed by Stout et al. (8) for oil coking
(Figure 4). Oil coking is caused by liquid-phase polymerization
and condensation reactions. It is most important at low
temperatures and slow heating rates--conditions under which
residence times in the liquid phase are greatest. Nitrogen
content in the oil is reduced and the H/C ratio is increased by
oil coking because the aromatic nitrogen compounds are apparently
the most susceptible to coking reactions. Lower temperatures
also favor alkane rather than alkene formation in the oil, as
demonstrated elsewhere for ethane and ethene (20).

In Figures 5a and 5b, we compare the FID chromatogram of oil
produced under Fischer assay conditions with oil that has
undergone extensive thermal cracking at 610°C. Specific aromatic
compounds formed in shale oil by thermal cracking were identified
by IR and capillary column GC/MS (15); alkyl-substituted
aromatics are especially prevalent. Because of their usefulness
as indicators in combustion retorts (16), we show three
1-alkene/n-alkane ratios and the naphthalene/(C_{11} + C_{12})
ratio, respectively, as a function of oil-yield loss by cracking
(Figures 6 and 7). (In this case, C_{11} is the sum of n-undecane
and 1-undecene and C_{12} is the sum of n-dodecane and
1-dodecene.) Alkene/alkane ratios are shown for C_8, C_{12}, and
C_{18} because these regions of the chromatograms appeared to be

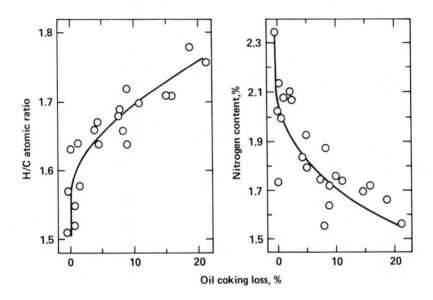

Figure 4.   The effect of oil coking on the H/C atomic ratio and nitrogen content of the shale oil. Coking reduces the alkene and aromatic nitrogen content of the oil.

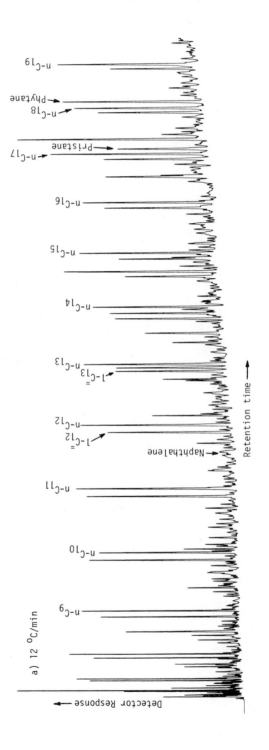

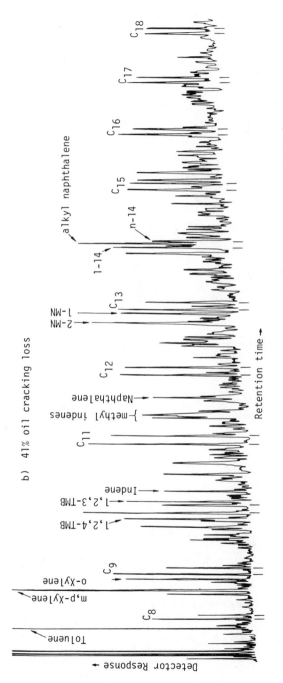

Figure 5. A comparison of the FID chromatograms of (a) shale oil produced under Fischer assay conditions and (b) shale oil that has undergone extensive thermal cracking (41% conversion to gas and coke). The proportion of aromatic hydrocarbons in the cracked oil has increased dramatically.

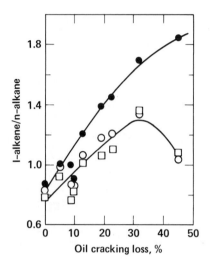

Figure 6. Effect of the extent of cracking (condensed-oil basis) on three 1-alkene/ n-alkane ratios. The ratios were determined by capillary column chromatography with an FID detector. C_8 (●); C_{12} (○); C_{18} (□).

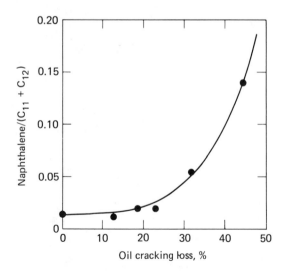

Figure 7. Effect of the extent of cracking (condensed-oil basis) on a naphthalene/ ($C_{11} + C_{12}$), where C_{11} and C_{12} are the sums of the respective n-alkanes and 1-alkenes. Comparing these results with those in Figure 6 shows that cracking to 30% conversion produces primarily alkenes and that further cracking produces primarily aromatic compounds.

particularly free of interfering compounds. For C_8, the 1-alkene/n-alkane ratio increases with conversion. For longer chains, the ratio becomes constant or even decreases at the highest conversion. For comparison, the ethene/ethane ratio seemed to correlate better with cracking temperature than with the extent of conversion (cracking loss).

We also made two qualitative observations on oil quality. First, the viscosity of the oil appeared to decrease with cracking. A small amount of cracking to reduce viscosity (vis-breaking) is a common industrial process (21). Second, the oils with 19% or more cracking loss did not solidify on cooling to -15°C. This might be expected since the pour point is dominated by long-chain alkane components (wax), which are the most susceptible to cracking reactions (21).

Pilot and Field Retort Oil Samples. The data we have presented to this point are for oil cracking at relatively low temperatures (500 to 610°C) and long residence times (2 to 11 seconds) under an essentially autogenous atmosphere. These conditions exist in at least two aspects of oil shale retorting: 1) a hot-solids retort such as TOSCO-II or Lurgi, and 2) the interior of large blocks in an in-situ retort. In the TOSCO-II process, ceramic balls heated to 600°C are mixed with raw shale to heat it to about 500°C (22). Local hot spots or long residence times can cause shale oil cracking. For large blocks in an in-situ retort, the temperature of the interior typically lags that of the surface by 200°C. Oil generated in the interior can be cracked as it migrates to the hot block surface. However, we demonstrate below that high-temperature cracking in the gas stream is more important in combustion retorts.

We first consider the oil from the 1972 operation of the TOSCO-II semi-works. Figure 8 shows the FID chromatogram of this oil. In comparison to Fischer assay oil, significantly higher concentrations of aromatics are evident. We determined 1-alkene/n-alkane and naphthalene/(C_{11} + C_{12}) ratios from the FID chromatogram. We obtained C_8, C_{12}, and C_{18} ratios of 1.36, 1.22, 1.05, and a naphthalene/(C_{11} + C_{12}) ratio of 0.047. These ratios also indicate a yield of from 75 to 85% on a condensed-oil basis and 80 to 85% on a C_5+ basis. In contrast, TOSCO reports a 93% yield for its 1972 run (22).

A probable source of this discrepancy is the difference in pyrolysis temperature. There is nothing in the mechanism described in our introduction that requires absence of oil coking in a Fischer assay (12°C/min). In fact, it has been demonstrated that yields greater than 100% of Fischer assay (i.e., less coking than in Fischer assay) might be obtained under very fast heating rates and higher pyrolysis temperatures (10, 23). However, our experiments were conducted so that the maximum possible yield (no cracking) would be 100% of Fischer assay. This is not necessarily true in the TOSCO-II process. Therefore, further

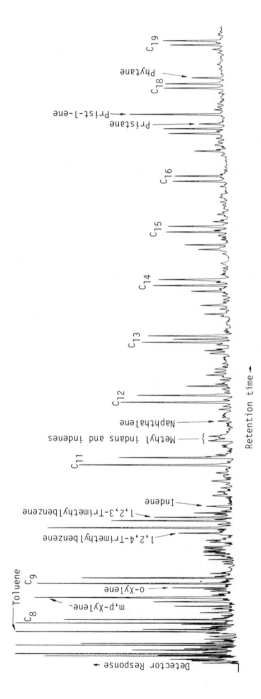

Figure 8.   FID chromatogram of TOSCO-II oil from the 1972 semiworks operation.   The 1-alkene/ n-alkane ratios and aromatic hydrocarbon content are high compared with those of the Fischer assay oil (see Figure 5a).

experiments are required to develop a quantitative method to
determine oil yield from oil composition for hot-solids retorts.

We next compare the compositions of our cracked shale oils
with those from combustion retorts. We show in Figure 9 the FID
chromatogram of shale oil from Rock Springs No. 9, one of LETC's
true in-situ experiments. Several differences are evident
between the chromatogram of this sample and those shown in
Figure 5. Oils produced by combustion retorting usually have
much lower C_6-C_9 content than those produced in retorting
experiments with no sweep gas. A corresponding increase is
observed in the C_6-C_9 content of the offgas from combustion
retorts compared to the gas collected from the laboratory
experiments. It should be noted that some of the light ends of
the laboratory-produced samples evaporated during handling.

The low 1-alkene/n-alkane ratios indicate that more than 20%
of the oil generated was converted to coke because of the low
retorting temperature. The high concentration of naphthalenes
indicates that high-temperature thermal cracking occurred to part
of the generated oil. However, this thermal cracking occurred in
such a way that essentially no 1-alkenes were formed. As
discussed below, this is characteristic of oil burning in a
combustion retort.

The capillary GC/MS was quite helpful in establishing the
difference between oil cracking in our laboratory experiments and
that associated with oil burning in a combustion retort (15).
Naphthalene/2-methylnaphthalene ratios were determined from the
relative 128- and 142-m/e peak heights in specific-ion-current
chromatograms from the GC/MS when the concentrations were too low
to be measured accurately from the FID chromatogram. To convert
the ion ratios to weight ratios, we compared the ion ratios to
area ratios from the FID chromatogram of Samples 113, Oxy No. 6,
and Rock Springs No. 9. In Table III we list the
naphthalene/2-methylnaphthalene weight ratios determined for
these and other samples. We also list some previous results
obtained by Dinneen (24).

One trend that stands out from Dinneen's data and from
Experiments 113 and 127 is that the naphthalene/2-methyl-
naphthalene ratio depends strongly on the temperature at which
oil cracking occurs and only weakly on the amount of cracking.
This apparently occurs because the activation energy for
dealkylation of aromatics is higher than for aromatic formation.
Even at very high conversions, this ratio in oils cracked near or
below 600°C is not dramatically different than that in assay
oil--even though the amount of naphthalene has increased tenfold.

The naphthalene/2-methylnaphthalene ratio in oils from
combustion retorts in which a significant amount of oil burning
has occurred is substantially higher than the ratio in assay
oil. This indicates that most cracking in in-situ retorts occurs
at high temperatures associated with combustion. Preferential
oxidation of alkyl aromatics may also contribute. At these high

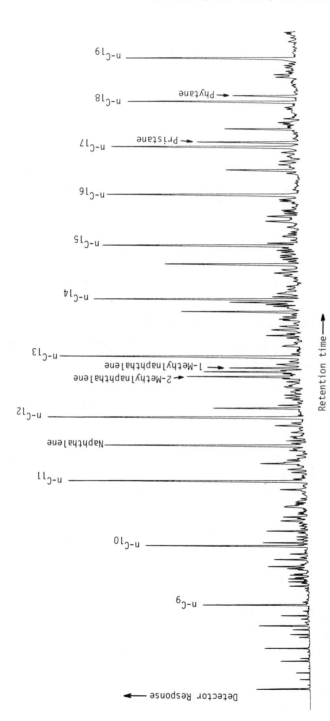

Figure 9. Chromatogram of shale oil from Rock Springs No. 9, a true in situ experiment. The alkene/alkane ratios are very low (coking) and the naphthalene content are very high (combustion and associated cracking). The naphthalene/methylnaphthalene ratios are high compared with the cracked shale oil in Figure 5b.

Table III. Effect of pyrolysis conditions on the
naphthalene/2-methylnaphthalene ratio.

Sample	Heat Source	Yield (% of Fisher assay)	Ratio
Assay (~470°C)	Inert	100	0.4
Exp 127 (610°C)	Inert	68	0.6
Exp 113 (610°C)	Inert	55	0.7
TOSCO-II	Inert	93	0.6
LLNL L-1	Combustion	72	1.4
LLNL L-4	Combustion	85	1.3
LETC R-14	Combustion	43	1.8
Oxy No. 6	Combustion	40[a]	2.2
Rock Springs No. 9	Combustion	<10[a]	2.0
Dinneen 650°C	Inert	51	1.1
Dinneen 815°C	Inert	53	2.0
Dinneen 925°C	Inert	39	50

[a] These yields include losses resulting from poor sweep and
inefficient collection.

temperatures, the severe cracking conditions completely convert
the long-chain hydrocarbons to gases so that essentially no long-
chain alkenes are formed. As a result, the only significant
product of the severe cracking conditions associated with
combustion are aromatics, most of which are dealkylated. These
aromatics are carried in the gas stream to mix with uncracked oil
downstream. In this way, the recovered oil contains aromatic
compounds indicative of oil combustion while retaining the
original information about heating rate (and hence coking)
contained in the 1-alkene/n-alkane ratios.

Discussion

We can devise the general mechanism for oil generation and
destruction by combining the information about shale oil cracking
with previously published information about coking (Figure 10).
The rate constants for the indicated reactions are given in
Table IV. Oil generation from kerogen and bitumen precursors can
be described under most circumstances by a single first-order
rate constant, k_d (12).
The generated oil exists in three physical states: gaseous
oil (components whose boiling points are less than the generation
temperature), liquid oil (oil whose boiling point is greater than
the generation temperature), and oil vapor (gaseous oil in
equilibrium with the liquid phase). Oil gases and vapors are

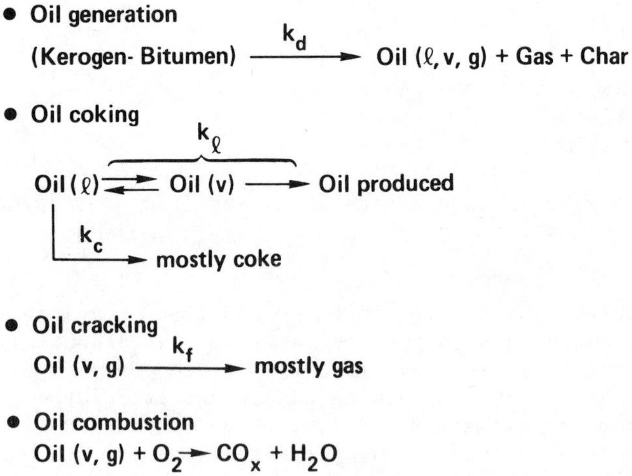

- Oil generation

  (Kerogen- Bitumen) $\xrightarrow{k_d}$ Oil (ℓ, v, g) + Gas + Char

- Oil coking

  $$\overbrace{\text{Oil}(\ell) \rightleftharpoons \text{Oil (v)}}^{k_\ell} \longrightarrow \text{Oil produced}$$

  $\big\downarrow k_c \longrightarrow$ mostly coke

- Oil cracking

  Oil (v, g) $\xrightarrow{k_f}$ mostly gas

- Oil combustion

  Oil (v, g) + $O_2 \rightarrow CO_x + H_2O$

Figure 10. Mechanism for oil generation and degradation developed at LLNL. Oil coking occurs inside the particles whereas oil cracking and combustion occur mostly outside the particles.

Table IV: Summary of rate constants for proposed mechanism
oil generation and destruction shown in Figure 10.[a]

Reaction	Rate Expression
(Kerogen-Bitumen) $\xrightarrow{k_d}$ [1-x(T)]•oil$^\ell$ + x(T)•oil^g	$k_d(s^{-1}) = 2.8 \times 10^{13} \exp(-26370/T)$ x(T) = 0.38 + (T-325)•0.0035, $T > 217°C$ = 1.00, $T \geq 500°C$
Oil$^\ell$ $\xrightarrow{k_c}$ 0.75 coke + 0.20 CH$_4$ + 0.05 H$_2$	$k_c(s^{-1}) = 3.1 \times 10^7 \exp(-17615/T)$
Oil$^\ell$ $\xrightarrow{k_\ell}$ oil produced	$k_\ell(s^{-1}) = 0.12°C^{-1}$•heating rate
Oil^g $\xrightarrow{k_g}$ oil produced	$k_g \gg k_d, k_c, k_\ell$
Oil^g $\xrightarrow{k_f}$ 0.31 coke + 0.02 H$_2$ + 0.03 CO + 0.11 CH$_4$ + 0.53 C$_x$H$_y$	$k_f(s^{-1}) = 4.8 \times 10^8 \exp(-19340/T)$

[a] Stoichiometries are given on a mass basis.

swept out of the oil shale particle by co-generated low-molecular-
weight gases. Liquid oil is subjected to condensation and
polymerization reactions (characterized by k_c) in which
aromatic nitrogen compounds form mostly solid products (coke).
These reactions cause a decrease in nitrogen content of the oil
as yield decreases (8).
     Oil coking can be minimized by decreasing the liquid-phase
residence time, which, in turn, can be accomplished by using high
pyrolysis temperatures and/or an inert sweep gas (9). Because
1-alkene/n-alkane ratios depend on pyrolysis temperature and
heating rate, they are good indicators of oil coking (16, 25,
26). However, if the temperature becomes too high, gas-phase oil
cracking reactions occur (characterized by k_f). In these
reactions, long-chain hydrocarbons are converted to low-molecular-
weight hydrocarbons. Cyclic compounds are dehydrogenated to form
aromatics. Aromatic nitrogen compounds are concentrated in the
remaining oil, causing an increase in nitrogen content. Under
the severe cracking conditions associated with combustion, alkyl-
substituted aromatics are dealkylated. This results is a
relationship between naphthalene content in the oil and the
amount of oil burning in a combustion retort containing Mahogany
Zone oil shale (16).

Summary

We have presented results for thermal cracking of shale oil
vapor over shale. Cracking temperatures of 504 to 610°C and
residence times of 2 to 11 seconds were studied. A first-order
Arrhenius rate expression and associated stoichiometry were given.
We also discussed changes in oil properties caused by
thermal cracking. Cracking increases nitrogen content and
decreases the H/C ratio and pour point of the recovered oil.
Spectroscopic evidence related the decrease in H/C ratio to an
increase in aromatic and alkene content of the oil. We
contrasted gas-phase oil cracking to liquid-phase oil coking as a
loss mechanism in oil shale retorting. We also compared our
results for oils prepared in the laboratory with oils prepared in
the TOSCO-II semi-works and in modified and true in-situ
combustion retorts. We demonstrated that the
naphthalene/2-methylnaphthalene ratio is a good indicator of
cracking temperature in an oil shale retort.

Acknowledgments

We appreciate the capillary GC work of J. Clarkson and the
helpful discussions with J. Campbell, J. Raley, and J. Carley.
Also gratefully acknowledged are M. Atwood of TOSCO and A. Harak
and D. Latham of LETC for supplying oil samples.
This work was performed under the auspices of the U.S.
Department of Energy by the Lawrence Livermore National
Laboratory under contract number W-7405-ENG-48.

Literature Cited

1. Robinson, W. E. "Kerogen of the Green River Formation" in
    Organic Geochemistry, G. Eglington and M. I. J. Murphy,
    Eds.; Springer-Verlag, New York, NY, 1969; p. 161.
2. Sohns, H. W.; Jukkola, E. E.; Cox, R. J.; Brantley, F. E.;
    Collins, W. G.; Murphy, W. I. R. "Entrained-Solids
    Retorting of Colorado Oil Shale: Equipment and Operation,"
    Ind. Eng. Chem. 1955, 47, 461.
3. Tihen, S. S.; Brown, J. F.; Jensen, H. B.; Tisot, P. R.;
    Melton, N. M.; Murphy, W. I. R. "Entrained-Solids Retorting
    of Colorado Oil Shale: Product Yields and Properties," Ind.
    Eng. Chem. 1955, 47, 464.
4. Hubbard, A. B.; Robinson, W. E. "A Thermal Decomposition
    Study of Colorado Oil Shale," Bureau of Mines, R.I. 4744,
    1950.
5. Allred, V. D.; "Kinetics of Oil Shale Pyrolysis," Chem.
    Eng. Progress 1966, 62, 55.

6.   Johnson, W. F.; Walton, D. K.; Keller, H. H.; Couch, E. J.
     "In-Situ Retorting of Oil Shale Rubble: A Model of Heat
     Transfer and Product Formation in Oil Shale Particles,"
     Colorado School of Mines Quart. 1975, 70, 237.
7.   Jensen, H. B.; Poulson, R. E.; Cook, G. L.
     "Characterization of a Shale Oil Produced by In-Situ
     Retorting," ACS Div. Fuel Chem. Preprint 1971, 15(1), 113.
8.   Stout, N. D.; Koskinas, G. J.; Raley, J. H.; Santor, S. D.;
     Opila, R. J.; Rothman, A. J. "Pyrolysis of Oil Shale:
     Effects of Thermal History on Oil Yields," Colorado School
     of Mines Quart. 1976, 71, 153.
9.   Campbell, J. H.; Koskinas, G. J.; Stout, N. D. "Oil Shale
     Retorting: Effects of Particle Size and Heating Rate on Oil
     Evolution and Intraparticle Oil Degradation," In-Situ 1978,
     2, 1.
10. Wallman, P. H.; Tamm, P. W.; Spars, B. G. "Oil Shale
     Retorting Kinetics," ACS Div. Fuel Chem. Preprint 1980,
     25(3), 70.
11. Bae, J. H. "Some Effects of Pressure on Oil-Shale
     Retorting," Soc. Petrol. Eng. J. Sept. 1969.
12. Campbell, J. H.; Koskinas, G. J.; Stout, N. D. "Kinetics of
     Oil Generation from Colorado Oil Shale," Fuel 1978, 57, 372.
13. Raley, J. H. "Monitoring Oil Shale Retorts by Off-gas
     Alkene/Alkane Ratios," Fuel 1980, 59, 419.
14. Burnham, A. K.; Taylor, J. R. "Shale Oil Cracking.
     1. Kinetics," Lawrence Livermore National Laboratory,
     Livermore, CA, UCID-18284 (1979).
15. Burnham, A. K.; Sanborn, R. H.; Crawford, R. W.; Newton,
     J. C.; Happe, J. A. "Shale Oil Cracking. 2. Effect on Oil
     Composition," Lawrence Livermore National Laboratory,
     Livermore, CA, UCID-18763 (1980).
16. Burnham, A. K.; Clarkson, J. E. "Determination of Process
     Yield for Oil Shale Retorting Using Oil Analysis by
     Capillary Column Chromatography," Proc. 13th Oil Shale
     Symp., J. H. Gary, Ed.; Colorado School of Mines Press:
     Golden, CO, 1980; p. 269.
17. Stout, N. D.; Koskinas, G. J.; Santor, S. "A Laboratory
     Apparatus for Controlled Time/Temperature Retorting of Oil
     Shale," Lawrence Livermore National Laboratory, Livermore,
     CA, UCRL-52158 (1976).
18. Campbell, J. H.; Koskinas, G. J.; Gallegos, G.; Gregg, M.
     "Gas Evolution During Oil Shale Pyrolysis I. Non-Isothermal
     Rate Measurements," Fuel 1980, 59, 718.
19. Dickson, P. F.; Yesavage, V. F. "The Utilization of Shale
     Oil as a Feedstock for Steam Pyrolysis and Petrochemical
     Intermediate Production," Quarterly Progress Report,
     December 1978 to February 1979; Colorado School of Mines,
     Golden, CO.

20. Burnham, A. K.; Ward, R. L. "A Possible Mechanism of
     Alkene/Alkane Production in Oil Shale Retorting," Lawrence
     Livermore National Laboratory, Livermore, CA, UCRL-84048,
     (1980); also ACS Div. Fuel Chem. Preprint, Fall 1980.
21. Nelson, W. L. "Petroleum Refinery Engineering"; McGraw-Hill,
     New York, NY, 1958.
22. Witcombe, J. A.; Vawter, R. G. "The TOSCO-II Oil Shale
     Process," in Science and Technology of Oil Shale, T. F. Yen,
     Ed.; Ann Arbor Science, Ann Arbor, MI, 1976; p. 47.
23. Hinds, G. P. "Effect of Heating Rate on the Retorting of
     Oil Shale," presented at 71st Annual Meeting of AIChE, Nov.
     1978.
24. Dinneen, G. U.; Smith, J. R.; Bailey, C. W. "High
     Temperature Shale Oil: Product Composition," Eng. Chem.
     1952, 44, 2647.
25. Coburn, T. T.; Bozak, R. E.; Clarkson, J. E.; Campbell,
     J. H. "Correlation of Shale Oil 1-Alkene/n-Alkane Ratios
     with Process Yield," Anal. Chem. 1978, 50, 958.
26. Evans, R. A.; Campbell, J. H. "Oil Shale Retorting: A
     Correlation of Selected Absorbance Bands with Process
     Heating Rates and Oil Yield," In-Situ 1979, 3, 33.

DISCLAIMER

RECEIVED January 14, 1981.

Hydrogen Sulfide Evolution from Colorado Oil Shale

A. K. BURNHAM, N. KIRKMAN BEY, and G. J. KOSKINAS

Lawrence Livermore National Laboratory, University of California, Livermore, CA 94550

Because traditional oil resources are declining, new-found attention is being focused on oil shale, coal, and oil sand as potential supplies of future energy. Unfortunately, extensive use of coal and oil shale could cause severe environmental problems. For example, oil shale retorting produces significant amounts of hydrogen sulfide and other gaseous sulfur species, e.g., 1.3 g H_2S/100 g shale oil (1). In addition, evolution of H_2S from oil shale retorted in the presence of steam is greater than in other gas environments (2).

In our study, we have measured the dependence of H_2S evolution on gas atmosphere. The gas environments used were argon, autogenous (self-generated), and steam-argon mixtures, all at atmospheric pressure. The samples used in these experiments were Green River oil shale from Colorado. In Green River oil shale, sulfur occurs in both inorganic and organic combinations. According to Smith et al. (3), the Green River oil shale rocks are basically siliceous dolomite that contain varying amounts of organic matter. They suggest that H_2S was generated by bacterial attack on the organic matter. Pyrite (FeS_2) then formed by the low-temperature reaction of iron and H_2S. Smith et al. (3) and Young (4) have shown that 70 to 85% of the sulfur is present as pyrite; most of the remaining sulfur is present as organic sulfur. The iron sulfide minerals have a median particle size of about 20 μm (5). Atwood et al. (6) found a correlation (r = 0.95) between oil shale grade and pyritic sulfur.

During pyrolysis, H_2S could be formed from the reaction of pyrite with hydrocarbons, hydrogen, or water, and from cracking of organosulfur compounds. Our objective was to determine the importance of these various reactions and to report the amounts of H_2S evolved from oil-shale samples obtained from locations in Colorado.

0097–6156/81/0163–0061$05.00/0

Experimental

     Sample Preparation and Apparatus. The oil-shale samples
used in this study were taken from the Anvil Points mine, Tract
C-a, Logan Wash, and the Colony mine. Table I gives the
properties of the shale samples. The shale samples were crushed
and sieved to less than 841 μm diam. A portion of Sample AP22
was doped with 1 wt% finely ground (<53 μm) pyrite. The
sample was mixed thoroughly for several days on a rotating
tumbler.
     For each experiment in an argon atmosphere, a small oil-shale
sample (about 0.20 to 0.55 g) was removed from the sample bottle
by spatula and transferred into a reactor vessel containing
silica wool as a support. A Chromel-Alumel thermocouple was
placed into the sample region. In the initial experiments, the
thermocouple was fastened to the outside of the reactor, and
subsequent measurements showed these temperatures were within a
few degrees Celsius of the measurements within the sample. The
ends of the furnace around the reactor vessel were packed with
Fiberfax to reduce heat loss. The furnace was heated at a nearly
constant rate (4.8°C/min). The furnace was controlled by a Data-
trac 5300 programmer and Lindberg 59344 controller (power supply).
The largest power input was near the ends of the furnace to give
a more uniform temperature profile. A gas flow of 1 litre/min
was used. The argon contained less than 10 ppm each of oxygen
and water vapor. About half of the gas was pumped through an
Interscan LD-17 H_2S monitor, which was used as the detector.

Table I. Properties of oil-shale samples used in this study.

Sample	Source[a]	Grade		Org. C	Acid CO_2
		litre/Mg	gal/ton	(wt%)	(wt%)
AP9	I	38	9	4.7	21.2
AP22	I	91	21.8	9.9	22.2
AP25	I	104	25.0	10.4	17.5
AP61	I	255	61.1	27.0	12.3
CA19	II[b]	78	18.6	8.8	19.5
CA36	II[c]	152	36.4	17.3	15.8
LW15	III	62	14.8	5.2	19.1
TC32	IV	134	32.2	14.7	20.2

[a] I. Anvil Points Mine. II. Rio Blanco mine shaft on Tract C-a.
III. Logan Wash, Occidental Oil Shale, Inc. IV. TOSCO, Colony
Mine.
[b] 560 ft.
[c] 432 ft.

(The LD-17 is an electrochemical voltametric detector operating
under diffusion-controlled conditions.) The effluent H_2S
concentration never exceeded 250 ppm and was usually less than 50
ppm. Evolution profiles were recorded by a strip-chart recorder.
Figure 1 shows the schematic diagram of the H_2S evolution
system.

For the autogenous experiments, the sample procedure was the
same as with argon except that the aliquot was transferred into a
6 by 15-mm quartz capsule. The capsule was covered by a loose
cap to allow gases from the reaction to escape. The capsule was
placed inside the reactor vessel and supported by silica wool.
The evolved autogenous gases were swept through the reactor vessel
by a constant flow of argon (1 litre/min). The remaining
procedure is the same as that used in the argon and hydrogen
experiments.

In the experiments using steam as the gas environment, the
sample was supported as in the argon and hydrogen experiments.
Steam was generated in a coiled stainless-steel tube placed
inside the reactor vessel. The tube was connected to a Masterflex
peristaltic pump that regulated the water flow at 0.4 or 0.45
cm^3/min. The steam was swept through the reactor vessel by
argon flowing at 1 litre/min. The reactor was heated to 200°C
before the water flow was started. The temperature was allowed
to stabilize before the linear heating began. The average
heating rate in the steam experiments was 5.5°C/min.
Temperatures were again measured by a thermocouple in the sample
region. The effluent water was acidified with dilute sulfuric
acid (0.1 M) to prevent the H_2S from dissolving. The part of
the apparatus enclosed by the dashed line was altered for the
steam experiments.

Results

Argon. The rate of H_2S evolution from Sample AP61 is
shown in Figure 2. The maximum rate of H_2S evolution occurs at
about 400°C before substantial amounts of hydrocarbons have been
evolved. A second H_2S peak is observed between 450 and 475°C,
about the same temperature that oil and gas evolution peak. A
third peak, the smallest, is observed between 500 and 525°C.
Similar H_2S evolution profiles were also observed for Samples
AP9, AP22, and LW15. In general, the total amount of H_2S
evolved was proportional to the grade of the shale.

Two samples from Tract C-a were also investigated (CA19 and
CA36). These samples evolved substantially more H_2S than samples
of similar grade from other locations. Moreover, Sample CA19 was
the only sample investigated that evolved a large fraction of its
H_2S between 480 and 550°C (Figure 3). The same behavior was observed, however, for Sample AP22 doped with finely divided pyrite.
Figure 4 shows that most of the increase in H_2S evolution resulting
from addition of finely divided pyrite comes at about 500°C.

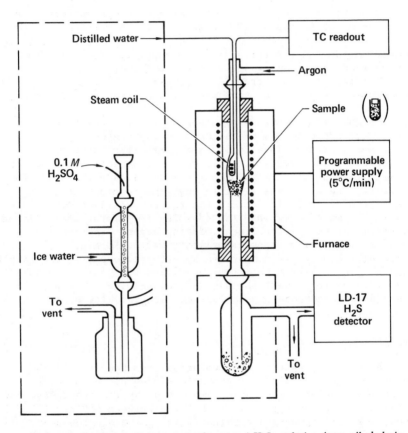

Figure 1.   Apparatus used to measure the rate of H_2S evolution from oil shale in argon, autogenous, and steam atmospheres.   For the autogenous experiments, the sample was contained in a capsule.   In the argon experiments, the sample was suspended in the silica wool for good gas–solid contact.   The part of the apparatus enclosed by the dashed line was changed for the steam experiments.   The steam was generated in a coil within the reactor; 0.1M sulfuric acid was added to the condensing effluent to prevent the H_2S from dissolving.

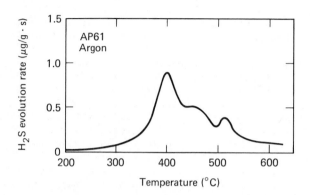

Figure 2. Rate of H₂S evolution from a powdered sample of 61-gal/ton Anvil Points oil shale (AP61) in an argon atmosphere. A gas flow of 1 L/min and a heating rate of 4.8°C/min were used.

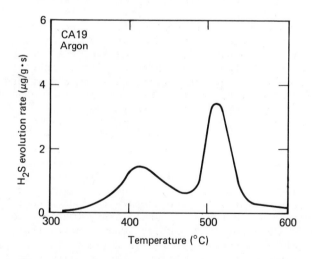

Figure 3. Rate of H₂S evolution from a 19-gal/ton Tract C-a sample of oil shale heated at 4.8°C/min in an argon atmosphere

Autogenous. Figure 5 shows the rate of H_2S evolution in an autogenous atmosphere from Anvil Points samples of 9-, 22-, 25-, and 61-gal/ton oil shale. The maximum rate of H_2S evolution occurs between 440 and 475°C, depending on the grade of the shale. The gas evolves at a lower temperature for the richer oil shale samples. This general profile of H_2S evolution in the autogenous atmosphere was also observed for Samples CA19, CA36, LW15, and TD32.

Figure 6 shows the increase in H_2S evolution from oil shale to which finely divided pyrite was added when heated in an autogenous atmosphere. In contrast to the results shown in Figure 4, only the magnitude (and not the profile) of the H_2S evolution changes. Comparing the results for Sample AP22 (both with and without added pyrite) in Figures 4 and 6 shows that the three-peaked evolution observed in an argon atmosphere merges into a single peak in the autogenous atmosphere at a temperature between the first two peaks in an argon atmosphere. The same observation can be made for Sample AP61 by comparing the results in Figures 2 and 5.

Steam. The H_2S evolution in a steam environment is much greater than that seen in an argon and/or autogenous gas environment. In Figures 7 through 10, the H_2S evolution in argon and in a 40%-steam atmosphere are compared for Samples AP22, AP61, CA36, and CA19. The largest increase in 40% steam comes at temperatures over about 475°C. In each case, the H_2S evolution rate in steam peaks at about 500°C. In Figure 11, we see the increase in H_2S evolution from Sample AP22 with the addition of 1 wt% of pyrite. These results demonstrate that the major source of increase in H_2S in the steam atmosphere is the reaction of steam with pyrite. We also note that upon closer examination, the samples with loosely held pyrite (CA19 and doped AP22) appear to have two peaks near 500°C. This may indicate that the loosely held pyrite is somewhat more reactive towards steam than pyrite intimately mixed with the kerogen.

Total Evolved H_2S. Table II summarizes the total amount of H_2S evolved from oil shale in argon, autogenous, and 40%-steam atmospheres. We can compare our autogenous H_2S results with TOSCO-Material-Balanced Assay (TMBA) results in three cases. For the TC32 sample, TOSCO reports that 28% of the original sulfur is evolved as H_2S in a TMBA. This compares favorably with the 24% we obtained. We can also compare our results on Tract C-a shales indirectly with TMBA data obtained from Rio Blanco Oil Shale Company. Figure 12 shows the distribution of the total sulfur in the gaseous (essentially H_2S), liquid, and solid products of the TMBA. Our results (■) for H_2S evolution fall generally on the curve relating the fraction of sulfur in the gas to the organic carbon content of the raw shale.

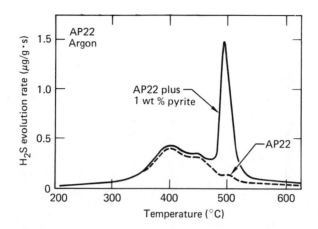

Figure 4.   Demonstration of the effect of added pyrite on the H_2S evolution from Sample AP22 heated at 4.8°C/min in an argon atmosphere. The additional H_2S evolution occurs mainly near 500°C.

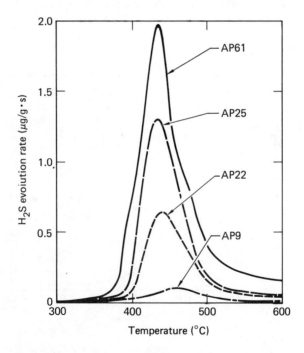

Figure 5.   Rate of H_2S evolution from Anvil Points (AP) samples of varying grades (e.g., Sample AP61 is 61 gal/ton). The samples were heated in an autogenous atmosphere at 4.8°C/min. The temperature of the peak evolution rate increases as grade decreases.

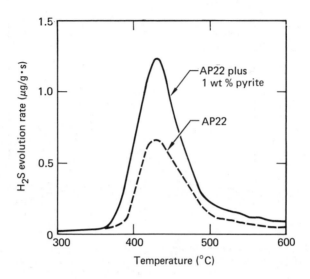

Figure 6.   Demonstration of the increase in H_2S evolution in an autogenous atmosphere with added pyrite

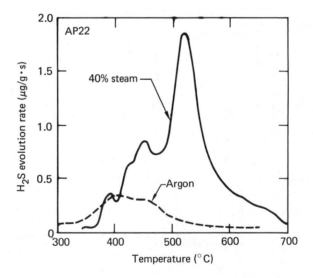

Figure 7.   Comparison of H_2S evolution from Sample AP22 heated in argon and 40% steam atmospheres. The fraction of total sulfur evolved as H_2S increases from 20% in the argon atmosphere to 76% in the 40% steam atmosphere. The H_2S evolution in argon shown here is from a different run than that shown in Figure 4.

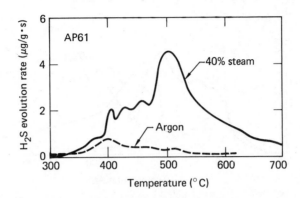

Figure 8.   Comparison of H₂S evolution rate from Sample AP61 heated in argon and 40% steam atmospheres. The fraction of total sulfur evolved as H₂S increased from 12% to 76%.

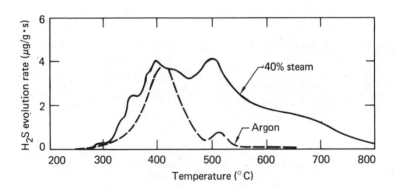

Figure 9.   Increase in H₂S evolution in the presence of steam for Sample CA36 (Tract C-a, 36 gal/ton). The fraction of total original sulfur evolved as H₂S increased from about 60% to nearly 100%.

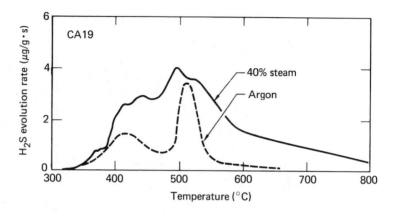

Figure 10.   A comparison of the H_2S evolution from Sample CA19 in argon and 40% steam atmospheres. The fraction of total sulfur evolved as H_2S increased from 19% to 49%.

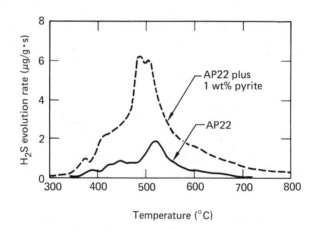

Figure 11.   Demonstration of the importance of the pyrite–steam reaction for oil shale heated at 5.5°C/min in a 40% steam, 60% argon atmosphere. The general increase in the H_2S evolution profile indicates that the steam–pyrite reaction is a major source of H_2S. The total amount of H_2S evolved demonstrates that the reaction goes significantly beyond the FeS state.

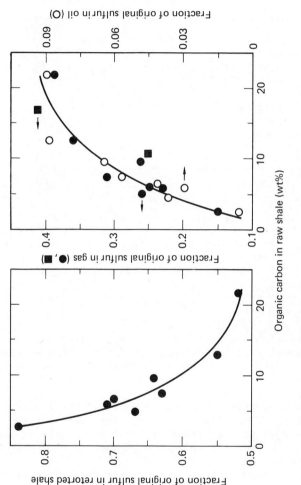

Figure 12. Dependence of the final distribution of sulfur in solid, gas, and liquid products as a function of organic carbon in the shale. The results come from TMBA data supplied by Rio Blanco Oil Shale Company on Tract C-a shales.

Table II.   Dependence of total evolved H_2S on gas atmosphere.

Sample	Total S (wt%)	Percent of total S evolved as H_2S		
		Argon	Autogenous	Steam
AP9	0.26	7	5	--
AP22	0.31	20	20	76
AP22[a]	0.84	12	13	99
AP25	0.66	12	16	--
AP61	0.98	12	19	76
CA19	1.70	19	24	49
CA36	1.05	61	41	100
LW15	0.40	11	10	--
TC32	0.82	--	24	--

[a] 1% added pyrite.

The amount of H_2S evolved in argon and autogenous atmospheres is comparable, although the evolution profiles are different. The amount of H_2S evolved in the presence of steam is substantially greater. Within the accuracy of the results, we conclude that $75 \pm 25\%$ of the initial sulfur ends up as H_2S in a steam atmosphere.

Discussion

Several reactions can produce H_2S. H_2S may evolve during pyrolysis of sulfur-containing portions of the kerogen or during secondary pyrolysis of evolved organosulfur compounds. H_2S may also arise from the reaction of pyrite with kerogen, liquid and gaseous hydrocarbons from kerogen pyrolysis, carbonaceous residue from kerogen pyrolysis, water from kerogen pyrolysis or dehydration of analcime and clays, or hydrogen from pyrolysis of kerogen and carbonaceous residue. All these sources together provide for the possibility of H_2S production from room temperature to 1000°C.

In an autogenous atmosphere, the temperature of the peak evolution rate varies from 440 to 475°C. The peak temperature increases with a decrease in sample grade (Figure 5). A possible explanation for this effect is that the greater availability of hydrocarbons in the rich shale enables the pyrite to react at a lower temperature.

A related trend has been found in TMBA results for Tract C-a shale, which were made available by Rio Blanco Oil Shale Company. In Figure 12, the fate of sulfur in a TMBA is shown as a function of the organic carbon (hence, grade) of the shale. In general,

the fraction of the original total sulfur remaining in the spent
shale decreases with increases in grade and the fraction evolved
in liquid and gaseous (essentially H_2S) products increases with
increases in grade. Our two H_2S results on Tract C-a shales
agree reasonably well with the TMBA results.

At very high grades, the fraction remaining in the spent
shale reaches a lower limit of about 50%. Since most of the
original sulfur is in the form of pyrite, this corresponds
qualitatively to the limit under assay conditions of

$$FeS_2 + 2H \rightarrow FeS + H_2S \ , \tag{1}$$

where the source of hydrogen is not well-characterized. This is
consistent with previous knowledge that it is very difficult to
remove the second sulfur in a reducing atmosphere (7). Actually,
the limiting product is probably pyrrhotite ($Fe_{0.9}S$) according
to Mössbauer studies (8). In addition, we never observed a
significant amount of $\overline{H}_2S$ evolved in an autogenous atmosphere
at temperatures from 550 to 950°C, even though hydrogen evolution
continues to above 900°C (9). This indicates that if any further
iron sulfide reactions occur, they probably lead to sulfate
formation (10).

Another comparison can be made with the Mössbauer
spectroscopy results of Williamson et al. (8). For "TOSCO-II
shale" with a grade of 40 gal/ton, they report that about 75% of
the pyrite is converted to pyrrhotite during Fischer assay.
Considering that some of this sulfur may be incorporated into the
oil and that some H_2S is produced by kerogen pyrolysis, this
result agrees with the results shown in Figure 12.

The H_2S evolution in an argon atmosphere is more complex.
H_2S is evolved at a lower temperature than in an autogenous
atmosphere. Perhaps this results from inhibition of H_2S-
producing reactions in the autogenous atmosphere because the
product H_2S is not removed rapidly enough by other evolved
gases. We do not know why the rate of H_2S evolution decreases
above 400°C in an argon sweep. It could be attributable to
either disappearance of a reactant or a decrease in the
reactivity of the partially reacted pyrite. Several authors
(11-14) have noted that the reduction of FeS_2 to FeS is
characterized by a fast (low-temperature) rate process and a slow
(high-temperature) rate process. The pronounced H_2S evolution
between 475 and 525°C from oil shale in the argon sweep probably
results from the reaction of partially reduced pyrite with
hydrogen from the carbonaceous residue remaining after kerogen
pyrolysis. This is especially apparent for samples containing
pyrite that is not associated with the kerogen.

For Sample CA36, our results indicate that 61% of the sulfur
is evolved as H_2S. On the surface, this appears inconsistent
with Reaction (1). However, if 20% of the original sulfur is
organic and is completely removed during pyrolysis, as suggested

by Mössbauer studies ($\underline{8}$), more than half the sulfur could be evolved as H_2S without reducing FeS. In addition, the difference between 50 and 60% of the sulfur forming H_2S is on the border of experimental error.

Although the organic matter in oil shale, particularly in rich samples, produces H_2S by reducing a substantial quantity of the initial pyrite to pyrrhotite, steam can potentially increase H_2S production from an oil shale retort by oxidizing both iron sulfides. While investigating the steam-carbon reaction in spent oil shale ($\underline{15}$), a noticeable amount of H_2S was evolved near and below 500°C. In addition, H_2S emissions from LLNL Retort Run L-2 (50% steam; 50% air) were about three times higher than from LLNL Retort Run L-1 (100% air) ($\underline{2}$). These two runs used similar grades of Anvil Points shale.

Although there are numerous possible reactions involving steam and pyrite, one that produces H_2S and FeS is

$$H_2O + FeS_2 + C \rightarrow H_2S + FeS + CO. \tag{2}$$

Reaction (2) is basically the production of hydrogen from carbon gasification followed by Reaction (1). The water-gas shift reaction may provide additional hydrogen. At 427°C, the equilibrium constant calculated from thermodynamic information in the JANAF tables ($\underline{16}$) is $K_2 = 2.6 \times 10^{-2}$ atm, where K_2 is the equilibrium constant for Reaction (2). Assuming unit solid activities and typical retort gas compositions, we find that

$$\frac{\left(P_{H_2S}\right)\left(P_{CO}\right)}{\left(P_{H_2O}\right)} \approx \frac{(0.01)^2}{0.5} = 2 \times 10^{-4} \text{ atm.}$$

Because this value is substantially smaller than K_2, the reaction is allowed thermodynamically (but not necessarily kinetically) in 50% steam if the products are removed.

The possibility also exists for producing more H_2S from the FeS. Depending on the effective partial pressure of oxygen determined by the steam/hydrogen ratio, the iron may be oxidized to FeO, Fe_3O_4, or Fe_2O_3 ($\underline{17}$). The reactions are:

$$FeS + H_2O \rightarrow FeO + H_2S , \tag{3}$$

$$FeS + \frac{4}{3} H_2O \rightarrow \frac{1}{3} Fe_3O_4 + H_2S + \frac{1}{3} H_2 , \tag{4}$$

$$FeS + \frac{3}{2} H_2O \rightarrow \frac{1}{2} Fe_2O_3 + H_2S + \frac{1}{2} H_2 . \tag{5}$$

Reactions (4) and (5) have free energy changes at 427°C of 10.35 and 12.97 kcal/mol FeS, respectively (6). At this temperature, FeO decomposes to Fe_3O_4 and Fe. These free energies result in equilibrium constants of 6×10^{-4} and 9×10^{-5}. Under the conditions of our experiments, the iron could be oxidized to Fe_2O_3. Using approximate concentrations of 100 ppm H_2 and 10 ppm H_2S, which are typical for our experiments, we find

$$\frac{\left(P_{H_2S}\right)\left(P_{H_2}\right)^{1/2}}{\left(P_{H_2O}\right)^{3/2}} \approx \frac{(10^{-5})(10^{-4})^{1/2}}{(0.4)^{3/2}} \approx 4 \times 10^{-7} .$$

Because 4×10^{-7} is substantially smaller than the equilibrium constant ($K_5 \approx 10^{-4}$), conversion of the second pyrite sulfur to H_2S and the accompanying oxidation of iron are thermodynamically allowed for our experimental conditions. The fact that we see most of the sulfur evolved as H_2S implies that these reactions are also allowed kinetically.

The next question is whether this reaction proceeds in a retort. Since the gas compositions change with location in the retort, this question is not answered easily. If we use a typical offgas composition with steam dilution of 40% steam and 5% hydrogen, we find, using the expression for K_4, that P_{H_2S} must be less than 500 ppm. This indicates that the reaction would be severely limited thermodynamically. At 727°C, ΔG for Reaction (4) is 11.71 kcal/mol, which results in $K_4 = 3 \times 10^{-3}$. Again, using 40% steam and 5% hydrogen, we find that P_{H_2S} must be less than 0.3%. This is a small but significant contribution. In addition, the hydrogen concentration is less at this point in the retort than at the exit because the kerogen pyrolysis contribution enters the gas downstream. This implies that P_{H_2S} may reach levels greater than 0.3% at 727°C. However, it does appear quite possible that thermodynamic limitations cause Reactions (3) through (5) to be less important than Reaction (2). Further work must be done to characterize the specific reactions that are occurring. In addition, oxidation reactions leading to COS, SO_2, and sulfate formation will require further characterization.

Summary

Most of the sulfur in oil shale occurs in pyrite and a smaller amount is contained in the kerogen. The major source of H_2S during oil shale pyrolysis appears to be the reaction of pyrite with organic matter. In an autogenous atmosphere, most of the H_2S evolves between 400 and 500°C. Addition of finely ground pyrite increases the amount of H_2S evolved but does not change the evolution profile. In an argon atmosphere, however, added pyrite causes a substantial increase in H_2S evolution

only between 475 and 525°C. Similar reaction characteristics
were observed with large-grained natural pyrite in Tract C-a
shale. The argon results demonstrate the importance of intimate
contact between the pyrite and organic material. In a steam
atmosphere, pyrite is oxidized to iron oxides and the H_2S
evolution increases substantially. In some samples, essentially
all the initial sulfur is evolved as H_2S at temperatures below
800°C. However, thermodynamics may limit the amount of H_2S
produced from pyrrhotite under retort conditions.

Acknowledgments

We thank Rio Blanco Oil Shale Company for providing the TMBA
results on Tract C-a shale, R. Ward for his help in setting up
the H_2S detector, and J. Huntington of TOSCO for providing
information concerning the TOSCO shale.

This work was performed under the auspices of the U.S.
Department of Energy by the Lawrence Livermore National
Laboratory under contract number W-7405-ENG-48.

Literature Cited

1. Goodfellow, L.; Atwood, M. T. "Fischer Assay of Oil Shale
    Procedures of the Oil Shale Corporation," Proc. 7th Oil
    Shale Symposium, Quart. Colo. School Mines 1974 69, 205.
2. Unpublished results from LLNL pilot retorts.
3. Smith, J. W,; Young, N. B.; Lawlor, D. L. "Direct
    Determination of Sulfur Forms in Green River Oil Shale,"
    Anal. Chem. 1964 36, 618.
4. Young, N. B.; Laramie Energy Technology Center, private
    communication, 1980.
5. Cole, R. D.; Liu, J. H.; Smith, G. V.; Hinckley, C. C.;
    Saporoschenko, M. "Iron Partitioning in Oil Shale of the
    Green River Formation, Colorado: A Preliminary Mössbauer
    Study," Fuel 1978, 57, 514.
6. Atwood, M. T.; Goodfellow, L.; Kauffman, R. K. "Chemical
    and Physical Properties of Oil Shale Dust and Correlations
    with Laboratory Fire and Explosivity Test Results," in Proc.
    12th Oil Shale Symp., J. H. Gary, Ed.; Colorado School of
    Mines Press: Golden, CO, 1979; p. 299.
7. Attar, A. "Chemistry, Thermodynamics, and Kinetics of
    Reactions in Coal-Gas Reactions: A Review," Fuel 1978, 57,
    201.
8. Williamson, D. L.; Melchior, D. C.; Wildeman, T. R.
    "Changes in Iron Minerals During Oil-Shale Retorting," Proc.
    13th Oil Shale Symp., J. H. Gary, Ed.; Colorado School of
    Mines Press: Golden, CO, 1980; p. 337.
9. Campbell, J. H.; Koskinas, G. J.; Gallegos, G.; Gregg, M.
    "Gas Evolution During Oil Shale Pyrolysis: Part 1.
    Nonisothermal Rate Measurements," Fuel 1980, 59, 718.

10.   Smith, J. W.; Robb, W. A.; Young, N. B. "High Temperature
      Reactions of Oil Shale Minerals and Their Benefit to Oil
      Shale Processing in Place," Proc. 11th Oil Shale Symp.,
      J. H. Gary, Ed.; Colorado School of Mines Press: Golden, CO,
      1978; p. 100.
11.   Schwab, G. M.; Philnis, J. "Reactions of Iron Pyrite: Its
      Thermal Decomposition, Reduction by Hydrogen, and Air
      Oxidation," J. Amer. Chem. Soc. 1947, 69, 2588.
12.   Vdinterva, V. C.; Tchuparoff, G. I. Zh. Prikl. Khim. 1941,
      14(1), 3.
13.   Yergey, A. L.; Lampe, F. W.; Vestal, M. L.; Day, A. G.;
      Fergusson, G. J.; Johnston, W. H.; Snyderman, J. S.;
      Essenhigh, R. H.; Hudson, J. E. "Nonisothermal Kinetic
      Studies of the Hydrodesulfurization of Coal," Ind. Eng.
      Chem. Process Des. Dev. 1974, 13, 233.
14.   Maa, P. S.; Lewis, C. R.; Hamrin, C. E., Jr. "Sulfur
      Transformation and Removal for Western Kentucky Coals," Fuel
      1975, 54, 62.
15.   Burnham, A. K. "Reaction Kinetics Between Steam and
      Oil-Shale Residual Carbon," Fuel 1979, 58, 719.
16.   "JANAF Thermochemical Data"; Dow Chemical Company: Midland,
      MI; 1977.
17.   Fast, J. D. "Interaction of Metals and Gases"; Academic
      Press: New York, NY, 1965; p. 67.

DISCLAIMER

RECEIVED January 14, 1981.

A Possible Mechanism of Alkene/Alkane Production

A. K. BURNHAM and R. L. WARD

Lawrence Livermore National Laboratory, University of California,
Livermore, CA 94550

Alkene/alkane ratios have been used extensively as indicators of oil-shale retorting conditions. Jacobson, Decora, and Cook (1) developed a retorting index that relates the ethene/ethane ratio to temperature, and Campbell and coworkers related ethene/ethane and propene/propane ratios (2), C_7 to C_{12} 1-alkene/n-alkane ratios (3), and total 1-alkene/n-alkane ratios (4) to the logarithm of the heating rate during retorting. In addition, Raley (5) worked out a relationship between the ethene/ethane and propene/propane ratios and the yield loss in the combustion retorts at Lawrence Livermore National Laboratory (LLNL). Uden et al. (6) reported how the C_2 to C_5 alkene/alkane ratios change with a change in the amount of the oxygen present during retorting. Finally, Burnham (7) demonstrated that the ethene/ethane ratios are related to the oil-cracking temperature.

Our objective was to clarify the reaction mechanisms that determine the observed alkene/alkane ratios under various conditions, and the results are reported here. When oil shale is pyrolyzed either isothermally or nonisothermally, the hydrocarbon and hydrogen concentrations are all time dependent. To determine if the alkene-alkane-hydrogen system is at equilibrium, we heated oil shale at a constant rate and measured the C_1 to C_3 hydrocarbons and hydrogen over time. We also measured the effect of an inert sweep gas on the time-dependent ethene/ethane and propene/propane ratios and the integral 1-alkene/n-alkane ratios in the oil. We determined that the C_2H_4-C_2H_6-H_2 system is not at thermal equilibrium and interpret our results in terms of a nonequilibrium free-radical mechanism proposed by Raley (8).

Pyrolysis of both kerogen and shale oil breaks larger molecules into smaller ones. For the alkene-alkane-hydrogen system to be at equilibrium, the reactions that lead to this equilibrium must be faster than those producing the smaller molecular fragments. To reach equilibrium, the ethene/ethane ratio must satisfy the condition:

0097–6156/81/0163–0079$05.00/0

$$\frac{\left(P_{C_2H_6}\right)}{\left(P_{C_2H_4}\right)\left(P_{H_2}\right)} = K_{eq} .$$

Because the enthalpy change for the C_2H_4 plus H_2 reaction is 34 kcal/mol (9), the ethene/ethane ratio must be a function of temperature when other conditions are constant. In addition, the ratio should be proportional to the amount of inert diluent when the system is at or near equilibrium, because the equilibrium expression has units of reciprocal pressure.

More generally, a ratio of alkene to alkane is determined by the relative production rate of each. During free-radical cracking, pyrolysis of alkanes yields either alkenes by unimolecularly decomposing free radicals, alkanes by free radicals abstracting a hydrogen from another source, or both. For example, ethene can be formed by decomposition of primary radicals (including ethyl),

    R-C-C• → R• + C=C

and

    C-C• → H• + C=C ,

and ethane from ethyl radicals by hydrogen abstraction,

    C-C• + R → C-C + R• .

Similarly, propene can form by decomposition of primary propyl radicals and secondary free radicals. Propane can form by propyl radicals abstracting hydrogen from another source.

The free-radical hypothesis leads to two interesting predictions:

a) The alkene/alkane ratios depend on total organic concentration, because alkene formation is a unimolecular reaction and alkane formation a bimolecular reaction. An inert sweep gas increases the alkene/alkane ratios by diluting the organic content of the gas phase.

b) The alkene/alkane ratios depend on retorting temperature, because the activation energies for alkene formation are greater than those for alkane formation. Alkene formation is favored at higher temperatures.

Therefore, both the equilibrium and free-radical hypotheses predict that the ethene/ethane ratios depend on pyrolysis temperature and inert diluent. However, the predictions are quantitatively different and can be tested.

Experimental

    Our starting material was oil shale from the Anvil Points
Mine near Rifle, Colorado, that had been ground and sieved to
<0.84 mm diam. This was then assayed and found to have an oil
content of 22 gal/ton. The samples used in our experiments were
pyrolyzed and analyzed in the apparatus diagrammed in Figure 1.
A sample, ranging in weight from 14 to 40 g, was placed in a
stainless steel can with a porous frit in the bottom that allowed
gas and oil to escape. It was then heated at a constant rate of
1.0 or 1.5°C/min in a programmable furnace. A constant flow of
nitrogen or argon entered the system either near the bottom or
through the top of the sample can. The retorting occurred under
a self-generated atmosphere (autogenous conditions) if the sweep
gas entered from below. The sweep gas passed directly through
the sample if the inert gases entered from the top. Hydrocarbons
were detected with a flame-ionization gas chromatograph; hydrogen,
nitrogen, and carbon monoxide were detected using a thermal-
conductivity gas chromatograph. Two traps (ice water and Dry
Ice-isopropanol) preceded the chromatographs.

Results

    The rates of ethene and ethane evolution, the ratio of
ethene to ethane, and the partial pressure of hydrogen (relative
evolution rate of hydrogen to total gas) are shown in Figure 2
for oil shale heated at 1.5°C/min under an autogenous atmosphere.
The ethene/ethane ratio reaches a first minimum before the peak
rate of C_2 evolution. It then increases slightly before
reaching a second minimum at about 540°C. A more pronounced
variation in the propene/propane ratio was observed at 1°C/min
(Figure 3).
    If the ethene/ethane ratios are combined with the hydrogen
partial pressures, we can demonstrate that the ethene-hydrogen-
ethane system is far from thermal equilibrium under the conditions
of the experiment shown in Figure 2. The experimental value of
$(P_{C_2H_6})/(P_{C_2H_4})(P_{H_2})$ is compared in Figure 4 with the value of
K_{eq}. Only at temperatures near and above 600°C, at which the
C_2 evolution rate is negligible, does the ethene/ethane ratio
approach equilibrium. Therefore, a nonequilibrium explanation of
the observed alkene/alkane ratios is required.
    The free-radical mechanism also predicts that the
ethene/ethane ratio should increase if inert diluent is added
(Figure 5). The addition of an inert sweep causes both the
instantaneous values above 450°C and the integral values of the
ethene/ethane ratio to increase. The integral value of the
ethene/ethane ratio increased from 0.21 under autogenous
conditions to 0.29 in the slow-sweep experiment and to 0.33 in
the fast-sweep experiment. We determined a value of 0.34 at

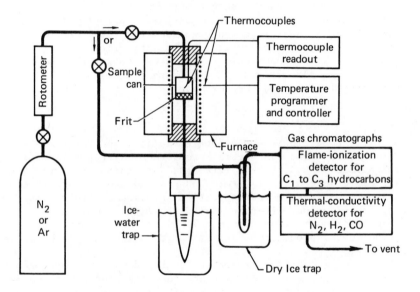

Figure 1.   Apparatus used to measure the rate of evolution of gases from oil shale during retorting at a constant heating rate

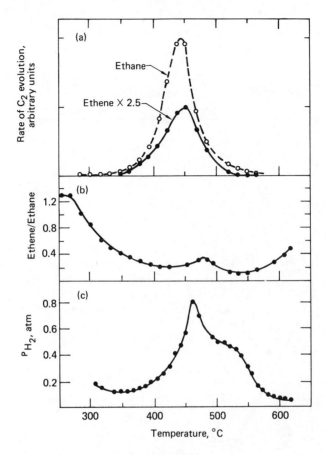

Figure 2. Product measurements for oil shale heated at 1.5°C/min under an autogenous atmosphere: (a) rate of C_2 evolution; (b) ethene/ethane ratio; (c) partial pressure of hydrogen released.

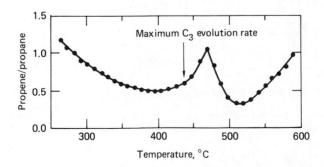

Figure 3. Propene/propane ratios for oil shale heated at 1°C/min under an autogenous atmosphere

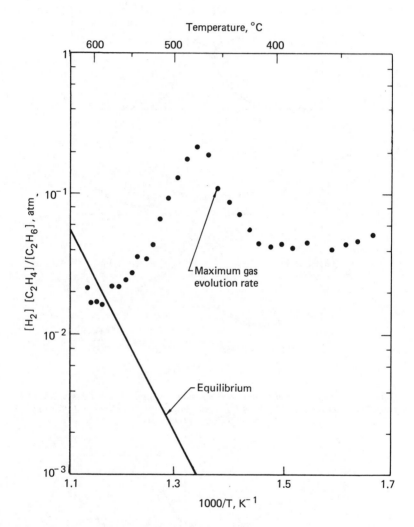

*Figure 4. Arrhenius plot for the time and temperature dependence of $[H_2][C_2H_4]/$
$[C_2H_6]$ evolved from 22 gal/ton oil shale heated at 1.5°C/min under an autogenous
atmosphere. The maximum rate of gas evolution, which corresponds to the minimum residence time, is shown.*

infinite dilution by plotting the ethene/ethane ratios against the sample-size/sweep-rate ratio and extrapolating to zero.

The 1-alkene/n-alkane ratios in the oil, measured by capillary-column gas chromatography/mass spectroscopy, also increase with the addition of inert diluent (Figure 6). This effect and the previously demonstrated dependence on heating rate are consistent with a free-radical mechanism. In addition, we noted that alkene/alkane ratios for even-numbered hydrocarbons are significantly higher the ratios for odd-numbered ones. We do not understand this effect at this time but suspect that it is related to the structure of kerogen and the mechanism of its pyrolysis.

Discussion

To form an alkane by the free-radical mechanism, there must be a source of reactive hydrogen. If this source is constant, the ethene/ethane ratio would increase continuously with temperature. However, the compositions of the gas and the solid are continuously changing, which makes the problem more difficult. The first minimum in the ethene/ethane ratio occurs before the maximum oil evolution but near the temperature of maximum hydrogen sulfide evolution (10). Hydrogen sulfide is a good donor of hydrogen to free radicals (11). The second minimum observed in the alkene/alkane ratios occurs at about the same temperature as the maximum rate of hydrogen evolution from secondary char pyrolysis (2). The second minimum may occur because either ethyl radical or ethene undergoes additional reaction with labile hydrogen in the char or because the temperature is high enough for the gas-phase reaction of ethene and hydrogen to proceed rapidly.

The general observation that temperature and inert diluent affect the ethene/ethane ratio is useful for correlating various data in the literature. In Figure 7, we show ethene/ethane results from a series of shale-oil cracking experiments (7). The ethene/ethane ratio is plotted against the cracking conversion and the logarithm of the ethene/ethane ratio against the reciprocal cracking temperature (Arrhenius plot). In the Arrhenius plot, we note a higher correlation, indicating that temperature rather than conversion is the controlling factor. From its slope, we calculate an effective activation energy of 12.4 kcal/mol.

In a related matter, Campbell and coworkers found that the ethene/ethane ratio (2) and higher alkene/alkane ratios (3, 4) produced during kerogen pyrolysis could be correlated with the logarithm of the heating rate in a nonisothermal pyrolysis experiment. This can be understood if we consider the transformation of kerogen to oil and gases as a thermal cracking reaction. A change in the heating rate, D, causes a change in

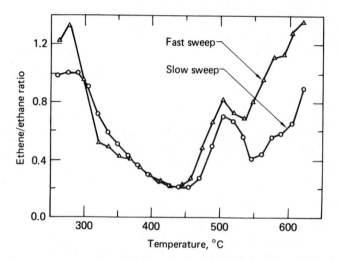

Figure 5. Effect of inert sweep gas on the time-dependent ethene/ethane ratio for oil shale heated at 1.5°C/min under autogenous conditions. The slow-sweep sample size and flow rate were 28 g and 50 cm³/min, respectively. The fast-sweep sample size and flow rate were 14 g and 100 cm³/min, respectively. Most of the ethene and ethane was evolved between 400° and 500°C.

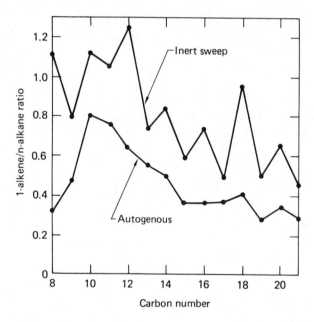

Figure 6. Effect of inert sweep gas during retorting on the 1-alkene/n-alkane ratios in shale oil. The ratios at the peaks were determined on samples from capillary column GC by total-ion MS.

the average temperature at which the reaction occurs. The
reaction rate is given by

$$- \frac{dc}{dt} \approx Ac_0 \exp\left[- \frac{E}{RT} - \frac{ART^2}{DE} \exp(-E/RT) \right] . \qquad (1)$$

The reaction rate initially increases with time as the temperature
increases, and then peaks and drops to zero as the reactant is
consumed. The temperature at the maximum reaction rate, T_p, can
be used as the effective temperature for the reaction. We can
calculate T_p from the rate parameters by differentiating the
right-hand side of Equation (1) with respect to T, setting the
derivative equal to zero, and finding the roots of the resulting
equation

$$0 = \frac{DE}{ART_p^2} + \left(1 - \frac{2RT_p}{E} \right) \exp(-E/RT_p) . \qquad (2)$$

     The root was found iteratively on a programmable hand
calculator using the rate parameters described by Campbell et al.
(12). We plotted the ethene/ethane ratio as a function of yield,
the logarithm of the heating rate, and an Arrhenius plot using
T_p (Figure 8). The straight line in the Arrhenius plot
(Figure 8c) again indicates that pyrolysis temperature is an
important factor for determining alkene/alkane ratios.
     We combined the results shown in Figures 7b and 8c with
other data (1, 13) on a single Arrhenius plot (Figure 9). From
this plot we can see the dependence of the ethene/ethane ratio on
both temperature and sweep gas. The ratio from all retorting and
cracking experiments under autogenous, or nearly autogenous,
conditions can be predicted to within 20% by a single Arrhenius
expression having an activation energy of 11 kcal/mol. This
energy is substantially lower than the enthalpy of the ethane-
hydrogen-ethene reaction, i.e., 34 kcal/mol.
     The ethene/ethane ratios obtained by Sohns et al. from an
entrained-solids (steam) retort (13) are two to three times
larger than the ratios from autogenous experiments at the same
temperature. We do not agree with the original interpretation of
Jacobson et al. (1) that longer residence times and more secondary
cracking cause this effect. We showed in Figure 7 that the
ethene/ethane ratio produced during cracking at constant
temperature depends only slightly on residence time and extent of
cracking. Instead, the elevated ethene/ethane ratios in the
entrained-solids retort are most likely caused by the steam
diluent, as implied by Prediction (a) above. To confirm our
explanation, the ethene/ethane ratio from the infinite dilution
extrapolation of our nitrogen-sweep experiments is roughly
consistent with an extrapolation of the entrained-solids data to
low temperature (the black circle in Figure 9).

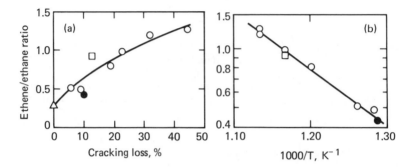

Figure 7. Effect of cracking on the ethene/ethane ratios of the total evolved gases, shown as a function of (a) cracking losses and (b) cracking temperature. The result indicated by △ is for a Fischer assay. The other points indicate cracking over burnt shale (○), retorted shale (●), and in an empty reactor (□). The ratios correlate better with the cracking temperature than with the cracking losses.

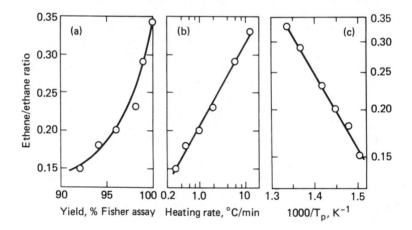

Figure 8. Ethene/ethane ratio as a function of (a) yields as a percentage of Fischer assay (FA), (b) the logarithm of the heating rate, and (c) an Arrhenius plot using T_p.

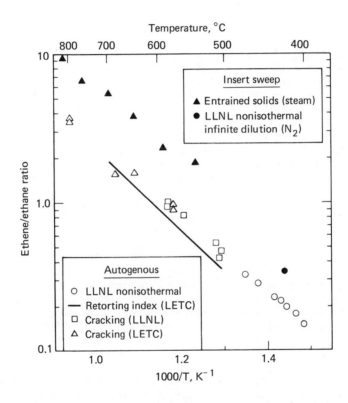

Figure 9. Effect of temperature and inert sweep gas on the ethene/ethane ratio from retorting oil shale. Results are shown for work at LLNL and LETC. The temperature dependence of the ethene/ethane ratio can be characterized by an activation energy of about 11 kcal/mol.

These findings have certain implications for using ethene/ethane ratios as indicators of retorting conditions. The retorting index of Jacobson et al. (1) should work well for retorting under autogenous conditions, as in either a TOSCO-II or Lurgi process (14). It does not work where inert diluent is added, as in a fluidized bed. Here, the relationship between retorting temperature and ethene/ethane ratio probably depends on both gas-to-solid ratios and particle size.

The situation is more complicated in a combustion retort. For particle sizes greater than 2 or 3 cm, retorting occurs under autogenous conditions, regardless of sweep, because there are diffusion limitations. When oil combustion occurs, shale-oil cracking also occurs in the gas stream at the interface of the combustion and kerogen pyrolysis zones. This produces locally high ethene/ethane ratios resulting from high temperatures, inert diluent, and, perhaps, oxidative dehydrogenation. The ethene/ethane ratio at the exit depends on the amount of C_2 hydrocarbons produced by both kerogen pyrolysis and shale-oil cracking in the gas stream and on the conditions existing at each location. Low ethene/ethane ratios produced when heating rates are slow and intraparticle coking occurs can be overshadowed by high ratios produced during oil cracking in the gas stream. Therefore, any empirical relationship between oil destruction in a combustion retort and the ethene/ethane ratio must be used with caution when both coking and cracking occur.

Summary

When oil shale is heated at a constant rate, the alkene/alkane ratios in the evolved hydrocarbon gases change with time. In addition, the alkene/alkane ratios in both the gas and the oil are affected by an inert sweep gas. The ethene/ethane ratio is not determined by equilibrium with hydrogen, and we interpret this phenomenon in terms of a free-radical cracking mechanism. The implication is that alkene/alkane ratios, especially the ethene/ethane ratio, can be used as an indicator of retort performance only if the correct relationships are used for each set of retort conditions.

Acknowledgments

We thank J. H. Raley for his many helpful discussions concerning this work and R. W. Crawford for the gas chromatography/mass spectroscopy results.

This work was performed under the auspices of the U. S. Department of Energy by the Lawrence Livermore National Laboratory under contract number W-7405-ENG-48.

Literature Cited

1.   Jacobson, I. A., Jr.; Decora, A. W.; Cook G. L. "Retorting
     Indexes for Oil Shale Pyrolysis from Ethene/Ethane Ratios of
     Product Gases," in Science and Technology of Oil Shale, T. F.
     Yen, Ed.; Ann Arbor Sciences Publishers: Ann Arbor, MI, 1976;
     p. 103.
2.   Campbell, J. H.; Koskinas, G. J.; Gallegos, G.; Gregg, M.
     "Gas Evolution During Oil Shale Pyrolysis: Part 1.
     Nonisothermal Rate Measurements," Fuel 1980, 59, 718.
3.   Coburn, T. T.; Bozak, R. E.; Clarkson, J. E.; Campbell,
     J. H. "Correlation of Shale Oil 1-Alkene/n-Alkane Ratios
     with Process Yield," Anal. Chem. 1978, 50, 958.
4.   Evans R. A.; Campbell, J. H. "Oil Shale Retorting: A
     Correlation of Selected Absorbance Bands with Process
     Heating Rates and Oil Yield," In-Situ 1979, 3, 33.
5.   Raley, J. H. "Evaluation of Retort Performance from Gas
     Data," in 12th Oil Shale Symposium Proceedings, J. H. Gary,
     Ed.; Colorado School of Mines Press: Golden, CO, 1979;
     p. 342.
6.   Robillard, M. V.; Siggia, S.; Uden, P. C. "Effect of Oxygen
     on Composition of Light Hydrocarbons Evolved in Oil Shale
     Pyrolysis," Anal. Chem. 1979, 51, 435.
7.   Burnham, A. K.; Taylor, J. R. "Shale Oil Cracking.
     I. Kinetics," Lawrence Livermore National Laboratory,
     Livermore, CA, UCID-18284 (1979).
8.   Raley, J. H. "Monitoring Oil Shale Retorts by Off-Gas
     Alkene/Alkane Ratios," Fuel 1980, 59, 419.
9.   American Petroleum Institute, Research Project 44, (Carnegie
     Institute of Technology, Pittsburgh, PA, 1952).
10. Burnham, A. K.; Kirkman Bey, N.; Koskinas, G. J. "Hydrogen
     Sulfide Evolution from Colorado Oil Shale," in Proceedings
     of Symposium on Oil Shale, Tar Sands, and Related Materials,
     ACS Symposium Series; American Chemical Society: Washington,
     DC, 1981.
11. Trotman-Dickenson A. F.; Milne, G. S. "Tables of
     Bimolecular Gas Reactions"; National Bureau of Standards,
     Gaithersburg, MD, NSRDS-NBS 9 (1967).
12. Campbell, J. H.; Koskinas, G. J.; Stout, N. D. "Kinetics of
     Oil Generation from Colorado Oil Shale," Fuel 1978, 57, 372.
13. Sohns, H. W.; Jukkola, E. E.; Murphy, W. I. R. "Development
     and Operation of an Experimental, Entrained-Solids,
     Oil-Shale Retort"; U. S. Bureau of Mines, Washington, DC,
     Report of Investigations 5522 (1959).
14. Baughman, G. L., Ed. "Synthetic Fuels Data Handbook,"
     2nd ed.; Cameron Engineers, Inc.: Denver, CO, 1978; p. 81.

DISCLAIMER

This document was prepared as an account of work sponsored by an agency of the United States Government. Neither the United States Government nor the University of California nor any of their employees, makes any warranty, express or implied, or assumes any legal liability or responsibility for the accuracy, completeness, or usefulness of any information, apparatus, product, or process disclosed, or represents that its use would not infringe privately owned rights. Reference herein to any specific commercial products, process, or service by trade name, trademark, manufacturer, or otherwise, does not necessarily constitute or imply its endorsement, recommendation, or favoring by the United States Government or the University of California. The views and opinions of authors expressed herein do not necessarily state or reflect those of the United States Government thereof, and shall not be used for advertising or product endorsement purposes.

RECEIVED January 14, 1981.

Oil Shale Retorting Kinetics

P. H. WALLMAN, P. W. TAMM, and B. G. SPARS

Chevron Research Company, 576 Standard Avenue, Richmond, CA 94802

Several aboveground oil shale retorting processes are
characterized by rapid heating of the shale followed by
pyrolysis of the kerogen at essentially isothermal conditions. The objective of this study is to investigate the
retorting kinetics applicable to processes characterized both
by rapid heating of relatively small particles and by rapid
sweeping of the produced hydrocarbon vapors out of the
retort. Rather surprisingly, accurate kinetics for these conditions are not available in the literature.

Several previous investigators have taken an isothermal
approach but have failed to eliminate significant heatup
effects in the measured kinetics. The important investigation
by Hubbard and Robinson (1) is in this category. Attempts were
made to correct the Hubbard and Robinson data for the heatup
effects by Braun and Rothman (2) and Johnson et al. (3).
Allred (4) took new isothermal data with increased accuracy,
but his results also suffered from interfering heat-transfer
dynamics. Weitkamp and Gutberlet (5) used both isothermal and
nonisothermal techniques but covered only low temperatures and
presented no kinetic model.

A frequent characteristic of past investigations is excessive complexity of the proposed kerogen pyrolysis models. The
works of Fausett et al. (6) and Johnson et al. (3) belong in
this category. A goal of the present investigation is to keep
the model as simple as possible.

One previous investigation that deserves special attention
is that by the Lawrence Livermore Laboratory (LLL) described in
Campbell et al. (7) and Campbell et al. (8). The LLL group
determined retorting kinetics by both isothermal and

0097–6156/81/0163–0093$05.25/0
© 1981 American Chemical Society

nonisothermal experiments with reasonable agreement between the
two approaches. However, the LLL work was directed toward
in-situ retorting where heating rates are inherently low. Low
heating rates were found to decrease the oil yield below
Fischer Assay levels by increasing coke formation. For small
particles, the detrimental effect of slow heating could be
eliminated by sweeping the sample with an inert gas implying
that the coking was associated with holdup in a liquid state.
Such coking is not of importance in the present investigation
where the sample is well swept, and heatup rates are three
orders of magnitude higher than typical in-situ rates.

The LLL kinetic model predicts that the maximum achievable
oil yield is that of Fischer Assay and that the coke associated
with Fischer Assay is stoichiometrically related to the kerogen. This assumption may be appropriate for in-situ retorting,
but it is not applicable to the present conditions where oil
yields higher than Fischer Assay are measured. Oil yields as
high as 110% of Fischer Assay have been reported for high
heating rates (Hinds, 9). Therefore, another objective of this
work is to extend the kinetics of oil production beyond the
Fischer Assay limit.

Experimental Technique

A bench-scale fluidized bed reactor shown in Figure 1 was
used to retort small samples of oil shale particles. The glass
reactor held a bed of inert solids such as glass beads or sand
that was continuously fluidized by a controlled flow of helium
or any other gas. A weighed sample of shale in an amount no
greater than 2% of the bed was dropped into the preheated
reactor, producing a negligible drop in bed temperature. Heat
transfer in the fluidized bed was very rapid, and the volatile
products were rapidly swept out by the fluidizing gas. The
vapor residence time in the reactor was typically 3 seconds. A
small sample stream was diverted to a flame ionization detector
(FID in Figure 1). The FID produced a signal proportional to
the concentration of total hydrocarbon. Heteroatom content of
evolved products was assumed constant with time. Since the
hydrocarbon concentration dropped to very low levels at the end
of the retorting reaction, the sensitivity of the detector had
to be increased by at least a factor of ten as the retorting
progressed. This increased sensitivity made it possible to

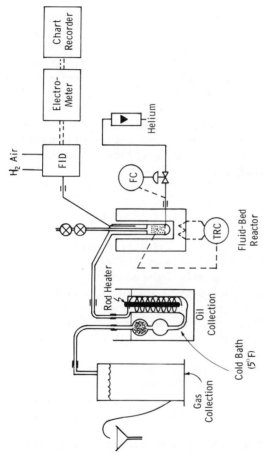

Figure 1.   Fluid-bed reactor system for oil shale retorting

record the full product-evolution curve including the long
"tail" which contains information on the kinetics at high conversion levels. Attempts were made to use the FID for quantitative determination of volatile hydrocarbon yields, but the
results were of insufficient accuracy. The area under the
curve did, however, give an approximate yield which was used as
an experimental check.

   Oil and gas yields were obtained from another branch of
the apparatus shown in Figure 1. The oil was condensed in a
cold trap, and the gases were collected in a gas cylinder by
liquid displacement. The amount of oil was determined gravi-
metrically, and the amount of hydrocarbon gas was determined
from the total volume of gas collected and the gas composition. The oil was recovered by CS_2 extraction and subjected to
GC analysis, standardized against n-paraffins. Finally, to
close the hydrocarbon balance, the entire bed consisting of
inert particles and retorted shale was recovered and its hydrocarbon content determined by burning off the organic matter and
measuring the amount of oxygen consumed.

   The oil collection trap shown in Figure 1 proved to be a
critical part of the apparatus. The product oil tended to form
a stable aerosol making it difficult to collect. This problem
was overcome by a trap design where the condensation occurred
under a steep thermal gradient. The inside wall of the cold
trap was kept at 300°F while the opposite wall was in contact
with a bath at 5°F. A thermally induced outward radial flow
promoted film condensation on the cold wall. Interestingly,
this design eliminated aerosol formation when using helium as
the fluidizing gas; but with heavier gases such as argon,
nitrogen, and even methane, aerosol formation still occurred.
The cause of this effect was not investigated, but it could be
related to differences in conductivity between the gases. The
selected bath temperature of 5°F proved practical because no
butanes condensed, and only a small portion of light oil
(C_5-C_7) was lost to the gas. This light oil was accounted for
by use of the gas analysis.

   Another area of experimental difficulty was gas analysis. At low temperatures requiring long reaction times, large
amounts of helium were necessary; and the hydrocarbon products
were in very low concentration. This difficulty was overcome
by recycling the gas back into the fluidized bed and thereby
allowing the hydrocarbon concentration to build up. Some oil
vapor was undoubtedly recycled increasing the possibility of
thermal cracking.

The shale samples used in this work were obtained by
screening from a single bulk sample of Colorado oil shale
(Anvil Points Mine, courtesy of Development Engineering
Incorporated and the U.S. Department of Energy). The Fischer
Assay oil yield was 10.5 wt % based on fresh shale (27.5
gallons/ton) for the larger particles and somewhat lower for
the finer size cuts, for example, 10.15 wt % for 100 µm
particles.

Yield Results

Experiments were conducted to determine the effect of oil
shale particle size on product yields at 930°F. The yields
obtained for particles of six different sizes are compared with
Fischer Assay yields in Figure 2. It is apparent that oil
yields higher than Fischer Assay are obtained for small particles; whereas large particles produce Fischer Assay yield. The
incremental oil produced from small particles is balanced by a
decreased coke make while the gas make remains constant. The
oil yield appears to have a limit at about 110 wt % Fischer
Assay, but this may be entirely due to the limited range of
particle sizes investigated. It is possible that the oil yield
would increase further for, say, 10 µm or 1 µm particles.
However, particles of this size could not be studied in the
apparatus of this work.

Not only do smaller particles produce more oil, but there
is also a change in the oil composition. The concentration of
C_{29+} components in the product oil is shown in Figure 3.
Increased oil yields are accompanied by increased heavy ends.
Hence, the conclusion is that the incremental oil obtained from
small particles is of higher molecular weight.

The effect of retorting temperature on the yields obtained
from 0.4 mm particles and the accompanying change in oil composition are shown in Figures 4 and 5. The important findings
here are that coke yield is unaffected by retorting temperature
and that oil yield is increased due to decreased gas make at
the lower temperatures. This second finding suggests decreased
cracking since Figure 5 shows that a lighter oil product is
obtained at the higher temperatures. It will also be noted
that the data set shown in Figure 4 has some "extra" cracking
in comparison with the data of Figure 2. This is due to the
fact that the results of Figure 4 were obtained in the recycle
gas mode where recycling of a small portion of the oil

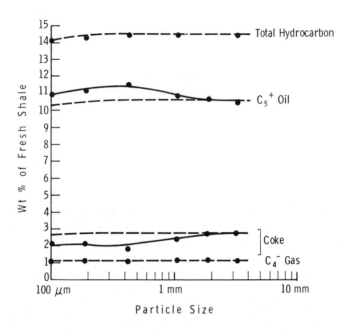

*Figure 2.   Particle-size effect on hydrocarbon yields at 930°F: fluidized-bed retort
(●); Fischer assay retort (– – –).*

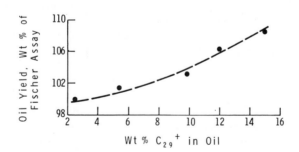

Figure 3.   Correlation between oil yield and oil composition

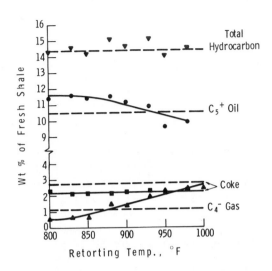

Figure 4. Temperature effect on hydrocarbon yields for 0.4-mm particles: Fischer assay (– – –).

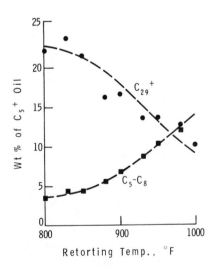

Figure 5. Oil composition as a function of retorting temperature

occurred. In general, the gas make was found to be very sensitive to equipment conditions such as the temperature of the product line leading to the condenser.

Kinetic Results

The kinetic complement to the yield results discussed above was obtained from the FID response curve. Integration of this curve gave the fractional conversion. Figure 6 shows the results of the particle-size effect experiments plotted as the logarithm of the fraction unconverted hydrocarbon versus time. It appears that the results can be described by a pair of first-order processes since the curves can be approximated by two straight-line segments. By comparing the slopes of the two segments, the rates of the two processes are found to differ by a factor of ten. This is an important finding with consequences for the pyrolysis model to be proposed in a subsequent section.

The small differences between the initial segments of the kinetic curves is due to differences in heatup time for the different particle sizes. However, heatup time is relatively unimportant even for the 3 mm particles because the straight-line segment extrapolates to only 15 seconds on the time axis. This "experimental" heatup time is about what one would calculate using a heat transfer coefficient of 100 Btu/hr ft^2 °F.

An important feature of the results shown in Figure 6 is that the slope of the latter segment of the curve changes for particles of different size. The process corresponding to this segment appears to be slower for the small particles than for the large ones. This unexpected characteristic is at first surprising. It is, however, a consequence of the different yields for different particle sizes shown in Figure 2. The yield differences do not enter the kinetic results of Figure 6 because the ordinate is normalized by the total hydrocarbon evolved (this type of plot is required for determination of the rate constants).

The kinetic and yield data are combined in Figure 7 for the 0.4 mm and 3 mm particles. This figure shows that the hydrocarbon evolution is essentially independent of particle size up to 100% Fisher Asay oil yield. At this level the oil production stops for large particles, whereas it continues for small particles at a reduced rate.

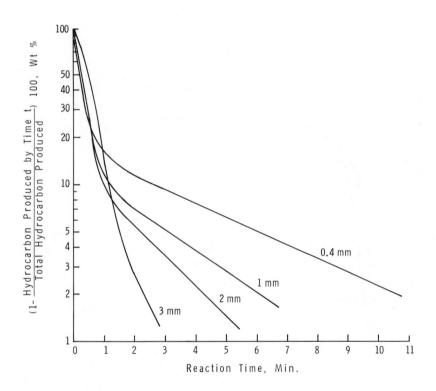

Figure 6.   Particle-size effect on retorting kinetics at 930°F

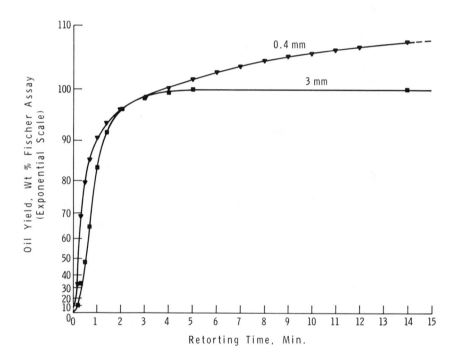

Figure 7.   Oil production kinetics at 930°F

The effect of temperature on the retorting kinetics is shown in Figure 8 for the 1 mm particles. Both processes respond to temperature but the fast one more so than the slow one.

Table I

Rate Expressions for Hydrocarbon
Production from Kerogen
(C_o Initial Kerogen Content)

Light Hydrocarbon Production:

$$\text{Rate} = f_1 \cdot k_1 \cdot C_o \cdot e^{-k_1 t}$$

$$\text{Amount} = f_1 \cdot C_o \cdot (1 - e^{-k_1 t})$$

Primary Heavy Oil Production:

$$\text{Rate} = f_2 \cdot k_2 \cdot C_o \cdot e^{-(k_2 + k_c)t}$$

$$\text{Amount} = f_2 \frac{k_2}{k_2 + k_c} \; C_o \cdot [1 - e^{-(k_2 + k_c)t}]$$

Intraparticle Coke Production:

$$\text{Rate} = f_2 \cdot f_c \cdot k_c \cdot C_o \cdot e^{-(k_2 + k_c)t}$$

$$\text{Amount} = f_2 \cdot f_c \frac{k_c}{k_2 + k_c} \; C_o \cdot [1 - e^{-(k_2 + k_c)t}]$$

Kerogen Pyrolysis Model

The combined kinetic and yield data can be correlated with the pyrolysis model shown in Figure 9. Here kerogen decomposes into a "light" hydrocarbon product and a heavy intermediate product, "bitumen." The light product is largely a vapor at retorting conditions and is, therefore, produced rapidly without significant secondary reactions. The bitumen, on the other hand, is of high boiling range and remains in the particle for significant periods of time. It becomes subject to two competing processes: (1) heavy oil production and (2) intraparticle (liquid-phase) coking. The released heavy oil is further

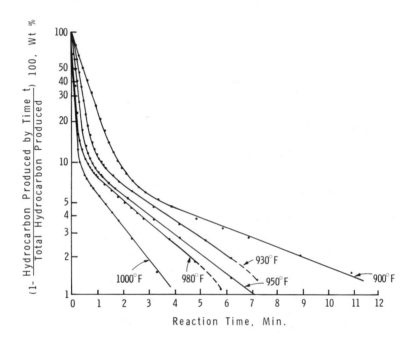

Figure 8.   Temperature effect on retorting kinetics for 1-mm particles

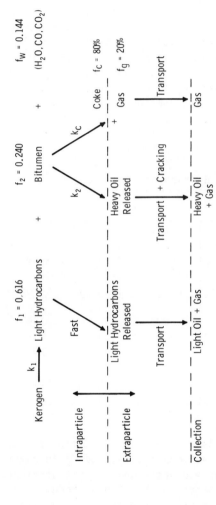

Figure 9. Proposed kerogen pyrolysis model

subjected to thermal cracking in the vapor phase surrounding
the particles.

First-order rate expressions are proposed in Table I for
the three principal steps: light hydrocarbon production
(equals kerogen decomposition), primary heavy oil production,
and coking.

The model accounts for the dramatic change in oil production rate which is observed. The fast initial rate is governed
by the rate constant k_1 (first order in kerogen content). The
latter slow rate is governed by the sum of the two bitumen
reactions, which are assumed first order in the intraparticle
bitumen content and have rate constants k_2 and k_c. At the
temperatures of interest, k_1 is much greater than $k_2 + k_c$ so
that the first step of the reaction goes virtually to completion before there is any appreciable conversion of the bitumen.

Table II

Light Hydrocarbon Fraction, f_1

Particle Size, mm	Total Volatile-Hydrocarbon Yield, % of Kerogen	Light Hydrocarbon Yield, % of Total Volatile Hydrocarbon	Light Hydrocarbon Yield, % of Kerogen
3	68.8	90	61.9
2	70.0	87	60.9
1	71.1	87	61.9
0.4	74.4	83	61.8
			Avg = 61.6

The relative yields of the kerogen decomposition products
are expressed as the fractions f_1, f_2, and f_w in Figure 9. The
(H_2O, CO, CO_2) fraction was set equal to that of Fischer Assay
because the amount of water in the liquid product could not be
easily determined in the yield experiments. The light hydrocarbon fraction, f_1, was determined by a combination of the
yield and the kinetic data. The light hydrocarbon yields as

fractions of total volatile hydrocarbon were obtained by extrapolating the slow reaction segments of Figure 6 to zero time
and reading the fractions off the ordinate. The results are
shown in Table II. The values of f_1 obtained for the four particle sizes are sufficiently constant to justify an average
value of 61.6%. The light hydrocarbon yield fraction f_1 is
also seen to be approximately independent of temperature from
Figure 8 where all the slow reactor segments extrapolate back
to approximately the same point on the ordinate, namely 87%
light hydrocarbon. The bitumen fraction f_2 in Figure 9 is
obtained by difference and equals 24%. Hence, f_2 is constant
with both particle size and temperature at least in the range
of 900-1000°F. Finally, a ratio between coke and gas in the
coking reaction of 80:20 was set on the assumption that the gas
yield at 800°F in Figure 4 is the result of coking alone.
Campbell et al. (8) used essentially the same coke-gas ratio
for a similar reaction in their reaction sequence.

In addition to the coking reaction, vapor-phase cracking
of the heavy oil released from the particle is a source of
gas. Cracking of the light hydrocarbon fraction is also possible; but because it occurs to a lesser extent, it has been
assumed to be zero. The kinetics of the cracking reaction lie
outside the scope of the present investigation, but this important reaction has been studied by Burnham and Taylor (10). A
third source of gas is the initial decomposition of kerogen
itself. However, the contribution of each gas-generation step
cannot be determined in the present investigation because of
the inability of the FID detector to distinguish between gas
and oil.

The kerogen decomposition rate constant, k_1, and the
bitumen disappearance rate constant $(k_2 + k_c)$ are obtained
directly as the slopes of the two straight-line segments of
Figures 6 and 8 (and similar graphs for the other particle
sizes). Figure 10 shows the temperature dependence of these
rate constants. It is also seen that k_1 is independent of
particle size. This implies that there is no significant
resistance to the transport of light hydrocarbons from the
interior of the particle into the bulk of the carrier gas.
This condition is a consequence of the high vapor pressure of
the light hydrocarbon fraction. Because of the rapid transport
out of the particle, this fraction has no possibility to
coke. The bitumen, on the other hand, is viewed as a high
boiling liquid which can undergo intraparticle coking. The

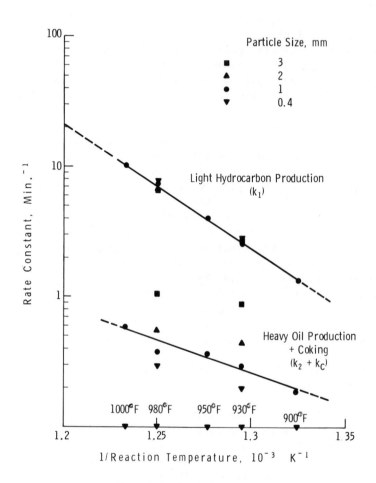

Figure 10.   Pyrolysis rate constants

particle size dependence of $(k_2 + k_c)$ in Figure 10 suggests that a diffusional resistance may come into play in the heavy oil production step. Also, the activation energy for the reactions governing bitumen disappearance is only 22.6 kcal/mole as compared to 43.6 kcal/mole for the kerogen decomposition reaction.

In order to determine k_2 and k_c individually, the kinetically determined values for the sum $(k_2 + k_c)$ must be used in consort with the expression for the coke yield $0.8 \cdot f_2 \cdot k_c/(k_2+k_c)$. The calculated values of the ratio $k_c/(k_2+k_c)$ together with the kinetically obtained values of $(k_2 + k_c)$ are given in the Appendix. The resulting k_2 and k_c values show some interesting characteristics: k_2 is independent of particle size whereas k_c is proportional to particle size. Both have the same temperature dependence because the coke yield is constant with temperature. The temperature dependence and the particle size dependence of k_c are shown explicitly in Table III. k_c is seen to dominate over k_2 even for the 0.4 mm particles. For the 3 mm particles, k_2 is insignificant in relation to k_c implying complete coking of the bitumen.

Table III

Rate Constants (Min.$^{-1}$)

Kerogen Decomposition:
$$k_1 = 5.78 \cdot 10^{12} \exp \left(- \frac{43.6 \text{ kcal/mole}}{R \cdot T} \right)$$

Heavy Oil Production:
$$k_2 = 1.8 \cdot 10^5 \exp \left(- \frac{22.6 \text{ kcal/mole}}{R \cdot T} \right)$$

Coking:
$$k_c = A_c \cdot \exp \left(- \frac{22.6 \text{ kcal/mole}}{R \cdot T} \right)$$

where	A_c	Particle Size, mm
	$18 \cdot 10^5$	3
	$9 \cdot 10^5$	2
	$5 \cdot 10^5$	1
	$3 \cdot 10^5$	0.4

Discussion

As part of this investigation, kerogen pyrolysis models different from the one proposed here were considered. One such model of theoretical appeal is similar in structure to the one given in Figure 9 but with a pure diffusion process for the heavy oil production. However, this alternative model is incompatible with some experimental findings: It predicts lower coke concentrations on the surface of the particle than in the interior, whereas microprobe results indicate a uniform coke distribution. Further, this diffusion model predicts zero coke yield for infinitely small particles, whereas the limited amount of data available for small particle sizes suggest a leveling-off of the coke yield below a particle size of 0.4 mm.

The approach to Fischer Assay yield structure with increasing particle size is accounted for in the proposed model by complete coking of the bitumen fraction. The model predicts a coke yield of 19% of the kerogen when the bitumen is completely coked, well within Fischer Assay range. Therefore, fluid-bed and Fischer Assay retorting give different yields for small particles only. The interpretation of this is that in a Fischer Assay retort small particles produce the same amount of coke as large particles because there is no sweep gas to facilitate oil removal from the small particles. The fluid bed retorting experiments have shown that additional oil can indeed be produced from small particles.

The proposed model can be compared with both the model of Allred (4) and that of Campbell et al. (8). Allred's model does not have the feature of competing parallel reactions that is essential to the pyrolysis model proposed here. It does, however, have the intermediate product bitumen which reaches a maximum level almost identical to the one in this work. Allred postulates that all kerogen decomposes into bitumen, whereas bitumen in the present work is the remainder of the kerogen after the light hydrocarbon fraction has been stripped off.

There are some interesting similarities and contrasts between the present model and the Lawrence Livermore Laboratory (LLL) model of Campbell et al.(8) The activation energy of the initial decomposition is similar in both models, 48-54 kcal/mole in the case of LLL and 44 kcal/mole here. Bitumen is treated merely as an intermediate in the kerogen decomposition by LLL; whereas, here it is one of several decomposition products. Coking steps are included in both models,

but the material involved is different. The coking kinetics
accounted for by LLL only apply to the light hydrocarbon of the
present model, and this coking reaction does not occur here
because of the high heating rate and the sweep gas. The coking
considered in the present model involves the intermediate
bitumen product and the coking rate depends on particle size.
Small particles produce less coking and; consequently, oil
yields higher than Fischer Assay.

Both Allred (4) and Weithamp and Gutberlet (5) observed
the slow oil production regime. Calculating a rate constant
for this slow production regime at 856°F from the results of
the latter investigators gives a value of 0.12 min.$^{-1}$ identical
to $(k_2 + k_c)$ of this work.

A practical implication of the results of this work is
that Fischer Assay yield is probably a reasonable upper limit
for any retorting process. This work has shown that a very
small particle size increases oil yield and decreases coke
yield, but long reaction times are necessary. Also, low coke
yields may not be desirable from overall heat balance considerations if the coke is to be used as an energy source for the
process. Lowering the temperature also increases oil yield but
at the expense of the gas yield and with the requirement of
long reaction times.

This work has added to the understanding of the very
complex phenomena occurring during oil shale retorting. The
simple kerogen pyrolysis model will be useful in modeling product yields from retorting processes handling small size particles at high retorting rates.

Abstract

An isothermal fluid-bed reactor was used to retort small
samples of 0.1-3 mm oil shale particles. The rate of volatile
hydrocarbon evolution was measured by a flame ionization
detector. Yields of oil, gas, and residual coke were determined and the boiling range of the product oil and the composition of the gas were measured.

Higher oil yields and lower coke yields are obtained for
smaller particles. Retorting temperature in the range 800-
1000°F does not affect coke yield but has an effect on the
relative yield of oil and gas. The experimental data are correlated by a simple empirical pyrolysis model where kerogen
decomposes by a first-order reaction into a light hydrocarbon
product and a heavy intermediate product, "bitumen." Subsequently, the bitumen is subject to two competing processes:

(1) heavy oil production and (2) intraparticle (liquid-phase) coking. Both of these processes are modeled as first-order reactions. The produced oil is also subject to thermal cracking in the vapor phase surrounding the particles. The rate constants for the disappearance of bitumen by reactions (1) and (2) are an order of magnitude smaller than the kerogen decomposition rate constant which ranges from 1 to 10 min.$^{-1}$ over a temperature range of 900–1000°F.

Literature Cited

1. Hubbard, A. B.; Robinson, W. E. "A Thermal Decomposition Study of Colorado Oil Shale," Report of Investigation 4744, Bureau of Mines, Washington, D.C., 1950.

2. Braun, R. L.; Rothman, A. J. Fuel, 1975, 54, 129.

3. Johnson, W. F.; Walton, D. K.; Keller, H. H.; Couch, E. J. Quarterly of the Colorado School of Mines, 1975, 70 (3), 237.

4. Allred, V. D. Chem. Eng. Progr., 1966 62, (8), 55.

5. Weitkamp, A. W.; Gutberlet, L. C. Ind. Eng. Chem. Process Des. Develop., 1970, 9 (3), 386.

6. Fausett, D. W.; George, J. H.; Carpenter, H. C. "Second-Order Effects in the Kinetics of Oil Shale Pyrolysis," Report of Investigation 7889, Bureau of Mines, Washington, D.C., 1974.

7. Campbell, J. H.; Koskinas, G. H.; Stout, N. D. "The Kinetics of Decomposition of Colorado Oil Shale: I. Oil Generation," Report UCRL-52089 Prepared for the U.S. Energy Research and Development Administration, Lawrence Livermore Laboratory, June 1976.

8. Campbell, J. H.; Koskinas, G. H.; Coburn, T. T.; Stout, N. D. "Oil Shale Retorting: The Effects of Particle Size and Heating Rate on Oil Evolution and Intraparticle Oil Degradation," Report UCRL-52256 Prepared for the U.S. Energy Research and Development Administration, Lawrence Livermore Laboratory, April 1977.

9. Hinds, G. P., "Effect of Heating Rate on the Retorting of Oil Shale," Paper Presented at the 71st Annual Meeting of the AIChE, Miami Beach, Florida, November 1978.

10. Burnham, A. K.; Taylor, J. R. "Shale Oil Cracking. 1. Kinetics," Report UCID-18284 Prepared for the U.S. Energy Research and Development Administration, Lawrence Livermore Laboratory, October 1979.

A P P E N D I X

HEAVY OIL PRODUCTION AND COKING RATE CONSTANTS, k_2 AND k_c (RATE CONSTANTS IN MIN.$^{-1}$, COKE YIELDS IN WT % KEROGEN)

Particle Size, mm		900°F	930°F	950°F	980°F	1000°F
3	$k_2 + k_c$		0.887	1.04		
	Coke Yield		16.8	16.8		
	$k_c/(k_2 + k_c)$		0.875	0.875		
	k_c		0.776	0.908		
	k_2		0.111	0.130		
2	$k_2 + k_c$		0.442	0.545		
	Coke Yield		15.6	15.6		
	$k_c/(k_2 + k_c)$		0.813	0.813		
	k_c		0.359	0.443		
	k_2		0.083	0.102		
1	$k_2 + k_c$	0.186	0.292	0.367	0.378	0.587
	Coke Yield	14.5	14.5	14.5	14.5	14.5
	$k_c/(k_2 + k_c)$	0.755	0.755	0.755	0.755	0.755
	k_c	0.140	0.220	0.277	0.285	0.443
	k_2	0.046	0.072	0.090	0.093	0.144
0.4	$k_2 + k_c$		0.197	0.296		
	Coke Yield		11.2	11.2		
	$k_c/(k_2 + k_c)$		0.583	0.583		
	k_c		0.115	0.173		
	k_2		0.082	0.123		

RECEIVED January 19, 1981.

Kinetics of Oil Shale Char Gasification

W. J. THOMSON[1], M. A. GERBER, M. A. HATTER, and D. G. OAKES

Department of Chemical Engineering, University of Idaho, Moscow, Idaho 83843

During oil shale retorting, whether it be by in-situ or sur-face techniques, a certain fraction of the organic carbon is left behind on the retorted shale. This "char" contains a significant fraction of the available energy in the raw shale and can actually supply all the energy for the retorting process for shales assayed at 20 gallons/ton or greater[1]. To recover this energy, the char can be burned in air or gasified in oxygen-steam environments; the latter in order to produce a low to medium BTU gas which can be burned elsewhere in the plant. Consequently we have been conduc-ting kinetic studies of the reactions of oil shale char in an on-going research program. Earlier we reported on the results of our oxidation experiments[2] and here we will discuss our work with CO_2 and steam gasification of the char.

It should be noted that there has been some previously pub-lished work dealing with these reactions. Studies at Union Oil Research in the early 1970's appear to be among the first to at-tempt the exploitation of the steam-char reaction and led to the development of the SGR retorting process[3]. Later, Burnham at Lawrence Livermore Laboratories[4,5,6] conducted both non-isothermal and isothermal experiments and obtained reaction rate expressions for the rate of char consumption due to both reac-tions

$$CO_2 + C \rightarrow 2CO \tag{1}$$
$$H_2O + C \rightarrow CO + H_2 \tag{2}$$

They observed, as did the earlier researchers at Union Oil that the water gas shift reaction

$$CO + H_2O \rightleftarrows CO_2 + H_2 \tag{3}$$

[1] Current address: Department of Chemical Engineering, Washington State University, Pullman, WA 99164.

0097–6156/81/0163–0115$05.00/0

also occurred at a rapid rate so that the primary gaseous products were essentially H_2 and CO_2.

Since we will be comparing our current results with those measured by Burnham at Lawrence Livermore Laboratories (LLL), it is appropriate to repeat them here. Burnham was best able to fit his data by assuming the presence of two separate carbon species which reacted in parallel and suggested the following rate expression

$$r_{CO_2} = (k_1 C_{c_1} + k_2 C_{c_2})(P_{CO_2})^{0.2} \qquad (4)$$

where C_{c_1} and C_{c_2} initially represented 75% and 25%, respectively, of the total organic carbon. The C_1 species had a higher activation energy (205 kilojoules/mole vs 134) and was thus more sensitive to increases in temperature. Their steam gasification data were also fit to a parallel reaction rate expression

$$r_{H_2O} = k_3 C_{c_1}{}'(P_{H_2O})^{0.5} + k_4 C_{c_2}{}' \qquad (5)$$

but in this case $C_{c_1}{}'$ accounted for 57% of the initial organic carbon and again had a higher activation energy (184 kilojoules/mole vs 134).

The empirical nature of these expressions is apparent and thus a major goal of our work was to attempt to derive rate expressions more typical of what would be expected for char gasification reactions based on the coal literature[7]. Another goal was to be able to predict make-gas compositions and thus a separate determination of the water-gas shift reaction rate was also undertaken. Finally, because of evidence that the iron present in the shale acted to catalyze the shift reaction, a number of oxidation/reduction experiments were run in order to assess the ability of the reacting gases to affect the oxidation state of the iron.

Since some of the minerals indigenous to the shale can act as catalysts, it is relevant to list the pertinent mineral reactions which can take place:

$$CaMg(CO_3)_2 \rightarrow CaCO_3 + MgO + CO_2 \qquad (6)$$
$$CaCO_3 \rightleftarrows CaO + CO_2 \qquad (7)$$
$$CaCO_3 + SiO_2 \rightarrow Silicates + CO_2 \qquad (8)$$
$$CaFe(CO_3)_2 \rightarrow FeO + CaCO_3 + CO_2 \qquad (9)$$

Equation (6), "dolomite decomposition," is irreversible and takes place at $T > 875K$. Equation (7), "calcite decomposition," is reversible and can be prevented if there is a sufficient CO_2 overpressure. Equation (8), "silication," is irreversible and takes place at higher temperatures (>1050K) provided that calcite decomposition is prevented. Equation (9) occurs at lower temperatures and is significant because the iron oxides that result can act as catalysts depending on the valence state of iron, and this can be influenced by the temperature and concentration of the surrounding gases.

Experimental Equipment and Procedures

Equipment. All of the gasification experiments were conducted with the same apparatus employed in the earlier oxidation work and has been described in detail elsewhere(2). The technique involved simultaneous measurements of mass loss (TGA) and exit gas compositions (gas chromatograph) in a vessel which behaved as an ideal back-mix reactor. All experiments were run under isothermal conditions. As before, powdered shale samples (200 mesh) of previously retorted oil shale from the Parachute Creek member in Colorado were suspended from an electrobalance and placed in a furnace. In this way continuous gravimetric readings were available to monitor the consumption of the char. The off-gases were analyzed on a Carle gas chromatograph equipped with a Carbosieve B column.

Procedures. Since the char reactions can be accompanied by mineral decomposition reactions, some of which are catalytic, every attempt was made to isolate the pertinent reactions. Of course there is always the possibility that significant interactions will be missed by this procedure and thus it is important to state the procedures which were employed.

CO_2 - *Gasification*. The previously retorted shale (see (8) for details) was first raised to 900K in a helium atmosphere to allow irreversible dolomite decomposition to take place. For those experiments in which CO_2 was the only species in the feed gas, the rate of CO_2 gasification was followed by monitoring the rate of production of CO; i.e., from G.C. measurements. However this was not accurate in those experiments which had CO in the inlet gas, and in these cases the rate was determined solely by gravimetric measurements. A further complication during these experiments was the fact that the presence of even small quantities of CO retarded the CO_2 gasification rate to the point where silication rates were on the same order of magnitude. Consequently the sample was purposely pretreated by allowing complete silication to take place. This was achieved by exposing the sample to a 40% CO_2-30% CO mix at 1100K for 8-12 hours. The CO_2 prevented calcite decomposition (equation (7)) and the high CO concentration retarded CO_2 gasification so that only 5-10% of the carbon was consumed during the pretreatment.

Steam Gasification. Because of the temperatures required for steam gasification (>950K), significant CO_2 pressures would be required to prevent calcite decomposition. Since we were attempting to study the H_2O + C reaction in the absence of CO_2 gasification, we decided to allow the calcite to decompose completely to the oxides. This was done in a helium purge stream at 975K. The decomposition time and purge rate were such that at this tempera-

ture only about 10% of the carbon was consumed due to CO_2 gasification. Although the kinetic data were taken in the presence
of oxides, a few runs were also conducted with shale samples subjected to acid leaching(9).

   Water Gas Shift Reaction (WGSR). The WGSR was studied over
shale samples which had been previously decharred and silicated.
After de-charring at 700K in a 10% O_2 stream, the sample was exposed to 40% CO_2 at 1100K for 12 hours. Upon completion of
silication the temperature was adjusted to the desired value and
the shale was either oxidized (in air or CO_2) or reduced (in H_2
or CO). This was followed by WGSR experiments in which various
concentrations of CO, H_2O, CO_2 and H_2 were fed to the reactor.

   Variables. CO_2 gasification data were obtained up to P_{CO_2} =
100 kPa and at temperatures between 975K and 1100K. Steam gasification was studied at H_2O pressures between 15 and 75 kPa and
at temperatures between 975K and 1150K. The kinetics of the WGSR
were also studied over this same temperature range and with various feed gas compositions consisting of H_2O, CO, CO_2 and H_2. In
order to remain on the left hand side of the WGSR equilibrium,
the maximum pressures of CO_2 and H_2 were 30 kPa. The oil shale
was from the Parachute Creek Member in Colorado and assayed at
50 gallons/ton. Our earlier work(2) had indicated that there was
no effect of assay on the char oxidation kinetics.

Results

   CO_2 Gasification. The rate expression which results from an
analysis of the CO_2 gasification data is given in equation (10).

$$\frac{r_{CO_2}}{C_c} \quad \frac{k_5 P_{CO_2}}{1 + K_1 P_{CO_2} + K_2 P_{CO}} \quad (10)$$

where

$$k_5 = 7.83 \times 10^4 \exp(-184/RT) \ (kPa\text{-}sec)^{-1}$$
$$K_1 = 0.0495 \ (kPa)^{-1}$$
$$K_2 = 5.0 \ (kPa)^{-1}$$

This form of the rate expression is typical of that used to correlate much of the early gasification data on coal. The parameters themselves were obtained from a. multiple regression
analysis of the reciprocal of equation (5). An initial value of
the activation energy was obtained from a power law fit and was
then adjusted by tiral and error until it was compatible with the
best fit from the regression. Figure 1 gives some idea of the
ability of the equation to fit the data over a wide CO_2 pressure
range. Of particular significance is the fit to the data corres-
poinding to the dashed line which were obtained during mineral
decomposition. That is, the only source of CO_2 was that released

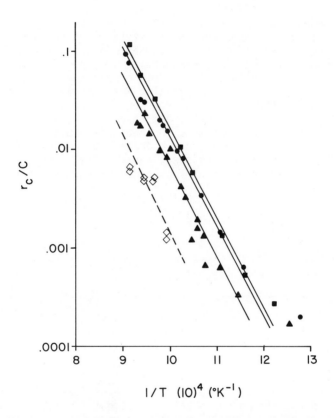

Figure 1.   *Arrhenius plot for CO_2 gasification: 1.0 atm CO_2 (■); 0.5 atm CO_2 (●); 0.1 atm CO_2 (▲); 0.016 atm CO_2 (◇).*

during mineral decomposition and, since the helium sweep gas
rate was high, this resulted in very low CO_2 pressures.

The similarity between this expression and rate equations
which have been derived from coal char gasification data[7] in the
absence of CO is striking. Although the value of K_1 is almost
identical to the value reported by Smoot and Prath[7] for the CO_2
gasification of char, the value of K_2 for oil shale char is ten
times greater. Consequently, even low pressures of CO will have
a strong inhibiting effect on CO_2 gasification. During the deri-
vation of equation (10) we also attempted to fit our data to the
expression suggested by Ergun and Menster[10] which is similar to
equation (10) except that $K_1 P_{CO_2}$ and $K_2 P_{CO}$ are taken to be much
greater than 1.0. When this was done, a very poor fit was obtained and it was concluded that their expression is not appropriate for oil shale char. It is also interesting to compare
equation (10) to the expression proposed by Burnham, equation (4).
Because of the high value of K_1, the reaction rate is certainly
fractional order with respect to CO_2 and this explains his reaction order of 0.2. Table I shows a comparison of our initial
rates with his and, as can be seen, equation (4) consistently
predicts a rate which is about four times higher than ours.

TABLE I

RATES OF CO_2 GASIFICATION

T (K)	P_{CO_2} (kPa)	P_{CO} (kPa)	Rate x 10^4 (sec^{-1})		
			This Work Eq. (10)	Reference 5 Eq. (4)	Charcoal Ref. (7)
975	10	0	0.75	3.1	0.0076
975	10	1.0	0.17	-	0.0027
975	40	0	1.0	4.1	0.0268
1100	10	0	9.8	53	0.19

Note also that even with a low CO pressure of 1 kPa, the CO_2
gasification rate drops by a factor of almost five. Recall that
Burnham proposed two parallel reactions, presumably due to two
separate carbon species of different activity. Since carbon
species '1' is more active, one explanation could be the fact that
we lost 5-10% of the carbon during pretreatment and the most active carbon would be expected to gasify under those mild conditions. However this is substantially less than the 75%
assigned to species '1' by Burnham and in our opinion the differences are more likely due to the statiscal analyses of rate
data which are difficult to measure. At higher carbon conversions
the two rate expressions are closer due to the lower activity of
carbon species '2' in equation (4).

Steam Gasification. The rate expression for steam gasification is given in equation (11).

$$\frac{r_{H_2O}}{C_c} = \frac{k_6 P_{H_2O}}{1 + K_3 P_{H_2O} + K_4 P_{H_2}} \qquad (11)$$

where

$$k_6 = 6.62 \exp(-100.7/RT) \ (kPa\text{-}sec)^{-1}$$
$$K_3 = 0.20 \exp(-17/RT) \ (kPa)^{-1}$$
$$K_4 = 0.15 \ (kPa)^{-1}$$

Again the reaction rate is first order with respect to char and the remaining parameters were determined as described above for CO_2 gasification. It is interesting that the value of K_3 is such that it is effectively one-half order with respect to H_2O, consistent with the first of the two reaction rate expressions given by Burnham(6).

Table II shows a comparison of the rates predicted by equation (11) with those predicted by equation (5) and with charcoal as reported by Smoot and Prath(7). Again Burnham's rate expression predicts higher rates but, in this case, the discrepancy is almost a factor of 20 at the higher temperature. The latter is due to the very high activation energies reported by Burnham which are 30-80% higher than our values. One possible explanation is that Burnham based his rate expression on the rate

TABLE II
RATES OF STEAM GASIFICATION
Rate x 10^4 (sec^{-1})

T (K)	P_{H_2O} (kPa)	P_{H_2} (kPa)	This work Eq. (11)	Reference 6 Eq. (5)	Char Ref. (7)
975	30	0	4.64	15.8	0.75
975	30	10	2.50	-	0.21
975	70	0	5.6	19.5	1.33
1150	30	0	26.5	474	53.3

of H_2 production in the make-gas. As mentioned earlier, the water gas shift reaction is very fast over retorted oil shale and this would result in additional H_2 than that produced by the steam-char reaction. What is more, the CO_2-char reaction would also take place under these conditions and, in the non-isothermal experiments employed by Burnham, it is difficult to distinguish between them. Equation (11) on the other hand, is based solely on initial rate data so that it applies strictly to the steam-char reaction. In comparing our results to those for the steam gasification of charcoal, it is seen that the steam gasification

rates for oil shale are 5-10 times higher at the lower temperature
but lower by a factor of two at the higher temperature. It is
interesting that this is quite different from CO_2 gasification
where the rates for oil shale char were almost two order of
magnitudes higher.

Recall that equation (11) is based on data collected for
steam gasification in the presence of CaO; i.e., a thermally
decarbonated shale sample. Figure 2 is a first order plot which
compares the rate of char consumption for samples which were
leached in acid with a thermally decarbonated sample under the
same conditions. The fact that the leached samples have significantly lower rates is apparently due to changes induced in the
mineral matrix as a result of the acid leaching. This is better
understood when the results for gasification in the presence of
CO_2-H_2O mixtures are analyzed. Figures 3 and 4 show the predicted and experimental results for two experiments conducted
under similar gas compositions but at two different temperatures.
The results shown in Figure 3 are at a temperature of 980K and,
at this temperature, a CO_2 pressure of 10 kPa is sufficient to
prevent calcite decomposition. The predicted rate of char consumption is based on a dynamic mathematical model which incor-
porates equations (10) and (11). Note that the actual rate is
much slower than that predicted by equations (10) and (11). The
data shown in Figure 4 were also obtained at P_{CO_2} = 10 kPa but at
a higher temperature of 1040K. In this case approximately one-
half of the available $CaCO_3$ had decomposed to CaO and, as can be
seen, the predicted char consumption rates are close to those ...
measured. Given these results and the lower rates measured with
acid leached shale (where all the calcium is removed), it is
apparent that CaO catalyzes the steam-char reaction. This of
course is no surprise to those familiar with the literature on
coal gasification where alkaline earth oxides have been known to
catalyze these very same reactions(11,12).

Water Gas Shift Reaction (WGSR). As described earlier, the
WGSR was studied over decharred and totally silicated shale samples. Early in the course of this phase of the study we discovered that the iron present in the shale could be reversibly
oxidized or reduced, depending on the gas composition and temperature. Although the WGSR rates were determined only for samples
which had been subjected to reduction in H_2, a limited number of
oxidation/reduction experiments were also conducted. Again, these
were accomplished in the TGA apparatus mentioned above. The
procedure was to initially reduce the sample in flowing H_2
(100 kPa) prior to exposing it to an oxidizing atmosphere (CO_2 or
air) and to record the weight gain as a function of time. Prior
to reduction experiments the sample was completely oxidized in
100 kPa air and then exposed to a reducing atmosphere (H_2 or CO).
The oxidation/reduction rates were found to be first order with
respect to the gas concentration as well as to the quantity of
unconverted iron present in the shale. Table III gives the values

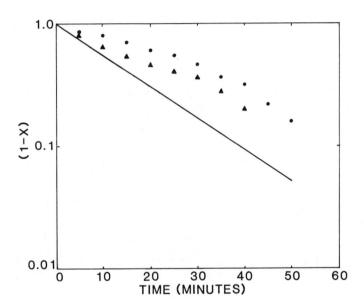

Figure 2. Steam gasification rates for leached and unleached shale: 1033 K; P_{H_2O} = 37 kPa; HCl leached (●); H_2SO_4 leached (▲); unleached (——).

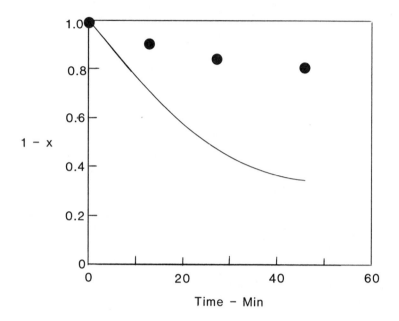

Figure 3.   Mixed gasification–No CaO ($P_{H_2O} = 50$ kPa, $P_{CO_2} = 10$ kPa, T = 980 K) predicted (——); experimental ($\bullet$).

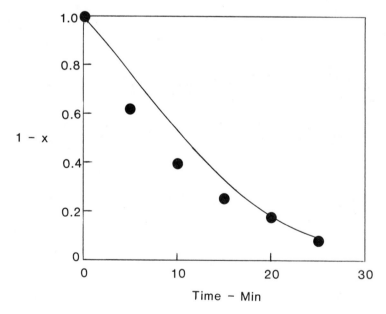

Figure 4.   Mixed gasification–CaO present ($P_{H_2O} = 37$ kPa, $P_{CO_2} = 10$ kPa, T = 1040 K) predicted (——); experimental data ($\bullet$).

TABLE III
FIRST ORDER RATE CONSTANTS FOR THE
OXIDATION/REDUCTION OF IRON

Rate Constant (sec^{-1})

	CO_2	AIR	H_2	CO
Oxidation (T = 980K)	0.07	3.18	-	-
Reduction (T = 1040K)	-	-	0.22	0.20

of the first order rate constants obtained at two different temperatures for oxidation in the presence of 10 kPa of air and CO_2
and for reduction at 10 kPa of CO and H_2. As would be expected,
the rate of oxidation in air is more than an order of magnitude
higher than oxidation in CO_2 whereas the CO and H_2 reduction rates
are comparable.

Equation (12) is an expression for the WGSR rate. The data
were purposely fit to the elementary reaction rate expression
given in brackets so that the rate would go to zero as equilibrium was approached.

$$r_{WGSR} = \frac{k_7 [P_{CO} P_{H_2O} - 1/K_E P_{CO_2} P_{H_2}]}{1 + K_5 P_{CO_2} + K_6 P_{H_2O}} \quad (12)$$

k_7 = 4.16 X 10^{-3}exp[-82.1/RT] moles/g-kPa^2-sec
K_5 = .0278 (kPa)$^{-1}$
K_6 = .0492 (kPa)$^{-1}$

It should be noted that equation (12) predicts an inhibitory
effect of CO_2 on the reaction rate. However just the opposite
was observed for CO_2 pressures less than 10 kPa and consequently
equation (12) is only valid for $P_{CO_2} > 10$ kPa

Catalytic Effects. Although it is yet to be proven, we believe that the anomalous behavior of CO_2 on the WGSR rate is due
to its influence on the oxidation state of iron. In fact during
the WGSR rate experiments we observed changes in the mass of the
shale sample as the gas composition was varied. Consequently a
complete understanding of the WGSR is dependent on a quantitative
knowledge of how the catalytic activity of iron varies with its
oxidation state. Once this is known, reaction rate expressions
for the oxidation/reduction of iron could be combined with WGSR
rate expressions to provide a more accurate prediction of the
make-gas compositions.

The role of CaO as a catalyst for the steam-char reaction can be inferred from the results obtained during mixed CO_2-H_2O gasification (figures 3 and 4). In many respects it is desirable to prevent the decomposition of $CaCO_3$ to CaO because of the high endothermic heats of reaction associated with this reaction. However, as we have shown, the steam gasification of oil shale char is about ten times slower when CaO is not present. A better evaluation of the importance of CaO requires a knowledge of the dependence of the reaction rate on the quantity of CaO present.

Nomenclature

C_c - char concentration, moles/g shale
k - rate constants
K - adsorption constants, kPa^{-1}
K_E - equilibrium constant
Pi - partial pressure of i, kPa
r - reaction rates, moles char reacted/s-g shale
R - gas constant, 0.008324 kjoules/mole-°K
T - temperature, °K

Abstract

The kinetics of oil shale char gasification have been studied for Colorado oil shale from the Parachute Creek member. Reaction rate expressions similar to those previously reported for coal char were obtained for the H_2O-char, CO_2-char and water gas shift reactions. Evidence is presented to suggest that CaO, a product of mineral decomposition, catalyzes the H_2O-char reaction and that indigeneous iron catalyzes the water gas shift reaction. The latter reaction proceeds rapidly so that the make-gas consists primarily of H_2 and CO_2.

Literature Cited

1. Dockter, L., paper presented at 68th Annual Meeting of AIChE, Los Angeles, Ca., November 20, 1975.
2. Soni, Y.; Thomson, W. J., I&EC PROC. DES. & DEV., 1979, 18, 661.
3. OIL & GAS JOURNAL, June 17, 1974, p.26.
4. Burnham, A. K., FUEL, 1979, 58, 285.
5. Burnham, A. K., FUEL, 1979, 58, 713.
6. Burnham, A. K., FUEL, 1979, 58, 719.
7. Smoot, L. K.; Prath, D. T., "Pulverized Coal Combustion and Gasification," PLENUM PRESS, N.Y., 1979.
8. Soni, Y.; Thomson, W. J., "PROC 11TH OIL SHALE SYMP," Colorado State Univ. Press, Golden, CO., 1978.
9. Thomson, W. J., paper presented at National Meeting of AIChE, Houston, TX., March 30, 1979.

10. Ergun, S.; Menster, M., in "Chemistry and Physics of Carbon," Vol. 1, (ed. P. L. Walker, Jr.), Marcel Dekker, N.Y., 1965, p.203.
11. Lewis, W. K.; Gilliland, E. R.; Hipkin, H., IND & ENG CHEM, 1953, 45, 1697.
12. Eakman, J. M.; Wesselhoft, J. J.; Dunkleman, J. J.; Vadovic, C. J., paper No. 63d, presented at 72nd Annual Meeting of AIChE, San Francisco, November 1979.

RECEIVED January 19, 1981.

A Comparison of Asphaltenes from Naturally Occurring Shale Bitumen and Retorted Shale Oils: The Influence of Temperature on Asphaltene Structure

FENG FANG SHUE and TEH FU YEN

School of Engineering, University of Southern California, Los Angeles, CA 90007

The majority of the organic material in oil shale is known as kerogen (organic solvent-insoluble fraction). Bitumen (organic solvent-soluble fraction) generally comprises only a small part of the total organic matter in oil shale. During retorting of the oil shale, kerogen and bitumen undergo thermal decomposition to oil, gas and carbon residue. According to a number of investigators (1,2,3), the mechanism for thermal cracking of oil shale is by decomposition of kerogen to bitumen and subsequently decomposition of bitumen to oil, gas and coke. Since bitumen is the intermediate formed from kerogen during thermal cracking, it may be accepted as representative of the natural-occuring organic matter in oil shale.

According to the solvent fractionation scheme for the fossil fuel products, asphaltene is defined as the pentane-insoluble and benzene-soluble fraction. The role of asphaltene is significant (4). Asphaltene is suggested to be the "transitional stage" in the conversion of fossil to oil (5). Therefore the structures of asphaltene fractions produced at various temperatures may be useful indicators of the severity of temperature effects during processing. In this research, the asphaltene fractions produced from natural-occuring shale bitumen and shale oils retorted at 425 and 500°C were compared to investigate structural changes during thermal cracking. Due to the complexity of the asphaltene structure, an approach using the so called "average structural parameters" (6,7) was used to characterize the gross structural features. The average structural parameters were calculated principally from proton and carbon-13 NMR data (8-14). Comparisons of the relative values of these structural parameters clearly indicate the effects of thermal treatment on asphaltene structures.

Experimental

Solvent Extraction. A sample of the Green River oil shale from Anvil Points, Colorado was crushed to 8-20 mesh size prior

0097–6156/81/0163–0129$05.00/0

to solvent extraction or retorting. Bitumen was extracted from
the shale by exhaustive Soxhlet extraction with 10% methanol in
benzene for 72 hrs. Total bitumen yield was 2.1% by weight.

Shale Retorting. The retort chamber was a cylindrical quartz
column, 47 mm in diameter and 300 mm in length with a screen of
20 mesh size welded to the bottom. Heat was transfered to the
shale through the quartz wall wrapped with two heating wires connected to a transformer. A stainless steel sheathed chromel-alumel (type k) thermocouple was inserted in the center of the retort chamber. The temperature was raised rapidly to 425°C in one
experiment and to 500°C in another, and maintained there for three
hours. Air entered through the top of the chamber at a flow rate
of 1 cc/sec and moved downward together with the product oil
through the cooling column. The product oil was collected into
the receiver and then seaprated from the water phase. The yields
of shale oils were 10.0% at 425°C and 12.5% at 500°C. Gas and
coke were not analyzed.

Isolation of Asphaltene. Asphaltenes were isolated by pre-
ciptating with a 20-fold volume of n-pentane. The oil/resin
fraction was separated from the preciptate by filtration through
the thimble followed by Soxhlet extraction with n-pentane. The
asphaltene fraction was obtained by Soxhlet extraction of the
residue with benzene. In the following text, the three asphaltenes will be abbreviated as Bitu, R_{425} and R_{500} representing
bitumen asphaltene and asphaltenes derived from shale oils retorted at 425 and 500°C respectively.

Physical and Chemical Analysis. Elemental analyses were done
by Elek Microanalytical Laboratories, Torrance, California. Molecular weights were determined on a Mechrolab Model 301A Vapor
Pressure Osmometer using THF as the solvent at 40°C. IR spectra
were recorded at a concentration of 25 mg/ml in CH_2Cl_2 using 0.5
mm NaCl cells on a Beckman Acculab 6 instrument. Proton and
carbon-13 NMR spectra were obtained on a Varian XL-100 spectrometer operating at 100.1 MHz for proton or 25.2 MHz for carbon.
Proton NMR was measured in CD_2Cl_2 (central residue peak at 5.3
ppm). Carbon-13 NMR was measured in $CDCl_3$ (central peak at 77.1
ppm). A sample of asphaltene (0.5 g) was dissolved in 2.5 ml of
$CDCl_3$ with 35 mg of $Cr(acac)_3$ added to it. To obtain reliable
quantitative results, a delay time of 4 sec after each 35° pulse
and 0.68 sec acquisition time was used in the gated decoupling
sequence. All chemical shifts were reported in ppm downfield
from TMS.

Results and Discussion

Fractionation of the three samples afforded the asphaltene
fractions constituting 7.3%, 0.39% and 0.74% by weight for the
shale bitumen, shale oils retorted at 425 and 500°C respectively.

Elemental Composition. Elemental analysis data for the three
asphaltene samples are presented in Table I.

Table I. Elemental Compositions of Green River Asphaltenes

	Bitu	R_{425}	R_{500}
wt. % C	74.53	76.50	78.22
wt. % H	8.86	7.97	7.02
wt. % N	2.71	4.49	5.03
wt. % S	1.80	1.37	1.08
wt. % O[a]	10.32	8.01	7.71
wt. % Ash	1.78	1.59	0.94
H/C	1.42	1.25	1.08
N/C	0.031	0.050	0.055
S/C	0.009	0.0067	0.0052
O/C	0.104	0.079	0.074
Molecular[b] Weight	1100	660	620

a   by difference

b   by VPO in THF

The results of the elemental analysis show that asphaltenes
derived from retorted shale oils have smaller values of H/C ratio
and smaller oxygen and sulfur contents, but greater nitrogen content than that derived from shale bitumen.

Infrared Data. Infrared spectra of the three asphaltene samples are presented in Figure 1. A number of well defined bands
were used for comparison: O-H streching of phenols (3600 cm^{-1}),
N-H streching of pyrroles (3460 cm^{-1}), C-H streching of aliphatic
alkyl groups (2925 and 2860 cm^{-1}), C=O streching of carbonyl compounds (1800 - 1650 cm^{-1}), C-C streching of aromatics ($\approx$1600 cm^{-1})
and C-O streching of aromatic ethers and phenols (1320 - 1200

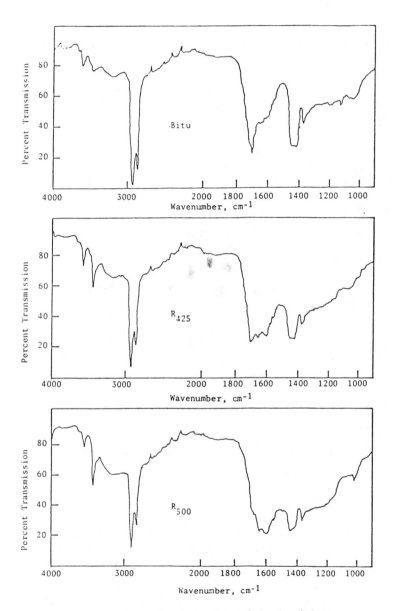

Figure 1.   IR spectra of shale oil asphaltene

cm^{-1}). R_{425} and R_{500} have stronger absorption intensities for phenolic O-H and pyrrolic N-H groups and C-O streching of aromatic ethers and phenols. As the processing temperature increases, the aliphatic C-H absorptions decrease and the aromatic C-C absorption increases. Band shapes for the carbonyl streching region of the three samples also show remarkable differences. Bitu has very strong carbonyl absorption at 1700 cm^{-1}. For R_{425} and R_{500}, carbonyl absorptions were shifted toward lower frequencies. Since it is well known that either hydrogen bonding or conjugation with an olefinic or phenyl group causes a shift of the carbonyl absorption at lower frequencies, the result seems to indicate a relatively greater proportion of hydorgen-bonded and/or conjugated carbonyl groups for R_{425} and R_{500} than for Bitu.

<u>^{1}H NMR Data</u>. Proton NMR spectra of Bitu, R_{425} and R_{500} are shown in Figures 2-4. If contributions from acidic protons (i.e. O-H and N-H, such protons show very broad chemical shift ranges (<u>15</u>)) are neglected, the spectra can be divided into different proton groups based upon chemical shift ranges. Proton type distributions are defined as follows: H_A(9.0-6.0 ppm), protons on aromatic rings; H_α(4.5-1.9 ppm), alpha alkyl protons; H_β(1.9-1.0 ppm), beta alkyl protons plus methine and methylene protons in the gamma positions or further from aromatic rings; H_γ(1.0-0.4 ppm), methyl protons in the gamma positions or further from aromatic rings. The integrated proton intensities for each specific group were obtained directly from integration curves. Normalized proton type distributions are given in Table II. A specific group of protons with chemical shifts in the range of 4.5-3.3 ppm, assigned as protons on carbons alpha to two aromatic rings, were observed in the NMR spectra of Bitu and R_{425}. The result seems to indicate that diphenyl methane type of structure remains stable at 425°C but is cleaved at 500°C.

<u>Carbon-13 NMR Data</u>. Carbon-13 NMR data were fractionated into groups based upon chemical shift ranges: carbonyl carbons (220-168 ppm); aromatic carbons joined to oxygens, i.e., aromatic ethers and phenols (168-148 ppm); aromatic carbons not joined to oxygens (148-100 ppm) and aliphatic carbons (60-9 ppm). Aromaticity was calculated as fraction of aromatic carbons (168-100 ppm) over total carbons. For simplicity, carbons associated with nitrogens were discounted in the above scheme due to the relatively small percentage of nitrogen present in the samples. Carbon group distributions and aromaticities of three asphaltene samples are compared in Table III. We have observed very poor agreement between the oxygen contents determined by ultimate analysis (see Table I) and by ^{13}C NMR (see Table III) for all three samples. For Bitu, O/C = 0.104 by elemental analysis but O/C =0.024-0.037 by ^{13}C NMR. We think quantitative analysis of carbonyl carbons by ^{13}C NMR is difficult for two reasons: 1) carbonyl carbons generally have very long relaxation times (<u>16</u>) and are quantitatively underestimated even under current conditions; 2) the disappearance of a large number of carbonyl absorptions in the noise is accen-

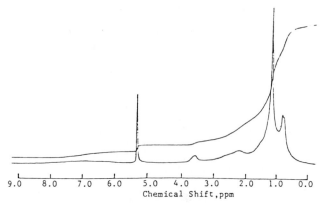

Figure 2.   H-1 NMR spectrum of asphaltene from shale bitumen

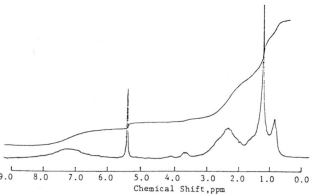

Figure 3.   H-1 NMR spectrum of asphaltene from shale oil retorted at 425°C

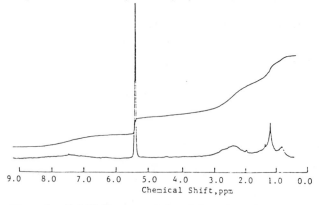

Figure 4.   H-1 NMR spectrum of asphaltene from shale oil retorted at 500°C

(^{1}H and ^{13}C NMR are being used only to characterize the hydrocarbon portion and, thus, the contribution from heteroatom portions of the molecule have been minimized.)

Table II. Fractional Proton Distributions of Green River Asphaltenes by ^{1}H NMR

Proton Type	Bitu	R_{425}	R_{500}
H_A (9.0-6.0 ppm)	0.046	0.145	0.179
H_α (4.5-1.9 ppm)	0.204	0.337	0.402
H_β (1.9-1.0 ppm)	0.525	0.389	0.330
H_γ (1.0-0.4 ppm)	0.225	0.129	0.089

Table III. Percentage Carbon Group Distributions of Green River Asphaltenes by ^{13}C NMR

Carbon Type	Bitu	R_{425}	R_{500}
carbonyl carbons (220-168 ppm)	1.3	-	-
aromatic carbons joined to oxygens (168-148 ppm)	1.1	2.4	2.8
aromatic carbons not joined to oxygens (148-100 ppm)	23.0	48.7	56.8
aliphatic carbons (60-9 ppm)	74.6	49.9	40.4
Aromaticity	0.24	0.51	0.60

tuated due to the inefficient number of scans and the broader
range of carbonyl resonance for a sample containing many components. A conversion of C=O functions into CHOH or CH_2 groups by
reduction would benefit their detection by ^{13}C NMR. Indeed we
have observed new absorption in the aliphatic ether and alcohol
region (75-60 ppm) and increased absorption in the aliphatic
amine region (60-50 ppm) in the ^{13}C NMR spectrum of Green River
Bitumen asphaltene reduced by $LiAlH_4$ (17). Reductions of carboxylic acids and ketones to alcohols, esters to ethers and amides
to amines by $LiAlH_4$ are well known reactions (18). Further evidence for the presence of carbonyl functions in these samples was
discussed earlier from infrared data.

Structural Parameters. Average structural parameters include:
aromaticity (f_a), degree of substitution of the aromatic sheet(σ),
number of carbon atoms per alkyl substituent (n), ratio of peripheral carbons per aromatic sheet to total aromatic carbons
(Haru/Car) and aliphatic H/C ratio can be calculated according to
Eq. (1)-(5)

$$f_a = \frac{C/H - (H_\alpha/X + H_\beta/Y + H_\gamma/3)}{C/H} \quad \ldots\ldots\ldots\ldots (1)$$

$$\sigma = \frac{H_\alpha/X}{H_A + H_\alpha/X} \quad \ldots\ldots\ldots\ldots\ldots (2)$$

$$n = \frac{H_\alpha/X + H_\beta/Y + H_\gamma/3}{H_\alpha/X} \quad \ldots\ldots\ldots\ldots\ldots (3)$$

$$\frac{Haru}{Car} = \frac{H_A + H_\alpha/X}{C/H - (H_\alpha/X + H_\beta/Y + H_\gamma/3)} \quad \ldots\ldots\ldots\ldots (4)$$

$$aliphatic \; \frac{H}{C} \; ratio = \frac{H}{C} \times \frac{1-H_A}{1-f_a} \quad \ldots\ldots\ldots\ldots (5)$$

where X and Y are the assumed atomic H/C ratios for H_α and H_β
fractions. Assuming X=Y, these values were chosen to give f_a
(aromaticity) values consistent with those measured directly by
^{13}C NMR. The calculated values of X or Y were 1.60 for Bitu,
2.08 for R_{425} and 2.15 for R_{500} respectively. Calculated average
structural parameters are presented in Table IV. These structural
parameters highlight the differences among the three asphaltene
samples. As the temperature of treatment increases, the aromaticity also increases but average alkyl chain length, degree of substitution and degree of condensation of the aromatic system decrease. The overall aliphatic H/C ratio for Bitu was 1.8, implying a significant amount of condensed naphthenic ring structure.
The aliphatic H/C ratio for R_{425} or R_{500} was above 2, implying
the growing number of methyl groups upon heating. Although
assumptions were made in calculations of these structural parameters, the trend of changes in structure with temperature was
clearly indicated.

Table IV. Average Structural Parameters of
           Green River Asphaltenes

Strutural Parameter	Bitu	R_{425}	R_{500}
f_a	0.24	0.51	0.60
σ	0.73	0.53	0.51
n	4.16	2.42	1.98
Haru/Car	0.99	0.75	0.66
aliphatic H/C ratio	1.80	2.18	2.22

Summary

A structural comparison of asphaltenes derived from shale
bitumen and retorted shale oil has been undertaken in order to
investigate structural changes during thermal cracking. The
results of elemental analysis indicate that asphaltene derived
from retorted shale oil has lower H/C ratio and less oxygen and
sulfur contents, but more nitrogen content than that derived
from shale bitumen. Heteroatom functional groups have also been
investigated for these asphaltenes. The retorted shale oil
asphaltene has more O-H and N-H functional groups as indicated
in the IR spectra. Retorting processes also increase the aromaticity, decrease the degrees of substitution and condensation of
the aromatic sheet and shorten the chain length of the alkyl substituent.

Acknowledgement

This work has supported by U.S. Department of Energy, Office
of Environment under Contract No. 79EV10017,000.

Literature Cited

1. Allred, V.D., Quart. Colorado School of Mines, 1967, 62 (3),
    91.

2. Hubbard, A.B. and Robinson, W.E., "A Thermal Decomposition
    Study of Colorado Oil Shale," U.S. Bureau of Mines, 1950, R.I.
    4744.

3. Wen, C.S. and Yen, T.F., Chem. Eng. Sci., 1977, 32, 346.

4. Yen, T.F., "The Role of Asphaltene in Heavy Crudes and Tar
    Sands," Proceeding of the First International Conference on
    the Future of Heavy Crude and Tar Sands, paper 54, UNITAR,
    1979.

5. Weller, S., Pelipetz, M.G. and Friedman, S., Ind. Eng. Chem.
    1951, 43, 1572.

6. Williams, R.B., Sym. on Composition of Petroleum Oils, Deter-
    mination and evaluation, ASTM Spec. Tech. Publ., 1958, 224,
    168.

7. Brown, J.K. and Ladner, W.R., Fuel, 1960, 39, 87.

8. Bartle, K. D., Martin, T.G. and Williams, D. F., Fuel 1975,
    54, 226.

9. Cantor, D. M., Anal. Chem., 1978, 50, 1185.

10. Wooton, D. L., Coleman, W. M., Taylor, L. T. and Dorn, H. C.,
    Fuel, 1978, 57, 17.

11. Dereppe, J. M., Moreaux, C. and Castex, H. Fuel, 1978, 57,
    435.

12. Bartle, K. D., Ladner, W. R., Martin, T. G., Snape, C. E. and
    Williams, D. F., Fuel, 1979, 58, 413.

13. Ladner, W. R., Martin, T. F. and Snape, C. E., ACS Div. Fuel
    Chem. Preprints, 1980, 25(4), 67.

14. Dickinson, E. M., Fuel, 1980, 59,290.

15. Jackman, L. M. and Sternhell, S., "Applications of Nuclear
    Magnetic Resonance Spectroscopy in Organic Chemistry,"
    Pergamon Press, 1969, p.215.

16. Levy, G. C. and Nelson, G. L., "Carbon-13 Nuclear Magnetic
    Resonance for Organic Chemists", Wiley-Interscience, 1972.

17. Shue, F. F. and Yen, T. F., unpublished work.

18. House, H. O., "Mordern Synthetic Reactions", W. A. Benjamin,
    Inc., 1972.

RECEIVED March 19, 1981.

Beneficiation of Green River Oil Shale by Density Methods

OLAF A. LARSON

Gulf Research & Development Company, Pittsburgh, PA 15230

C. W. SCHULTZ and ELLERY L. MICHAELS

Institute of Mineral Research, Michigan Technological University, Houghton, MI 49931

Green River oil shale, found in Colorado, Utah, and Wyoming is an extremely complex and challenging resource. The C-a tract in Colorado has been Gulf's main interest in oil shale since about 1974. Initial plans called for the use of an open pit mine with conventional surface retorting.

From a process point of view, the most important property of much of the oil shale throughout the Green River formation is its low organic content. For example, the integral average of shale on the C-a tract, measured from the top of the Mahogany Zone through the Blue Marker (over a 1,000-foot interval) is about 23 GPT. This corresponds to an organic concentration of 14.7% by weight.

Retorting of shale is the most commonly considered method for oil recovery from the rock. Despite the apparent simplicity of retorting, it is a complex process. This complexity is due to the lean nature of the ore, the requirement to add heat at high temperature, and the chemical and physical changes which take place in retorting.

There are two principal reasons for the beneficiation of oil shale. First, a reduction in solids handling intensity of lean shale movement and retorting may be possible. Secondly, beneficiation to higher concentration levels might allow the substitution of alternate technology for retorting. Overall, the incentive is to reduce costs and improve thermal efficiency of the conventional mining and process routes.

A survey of the literature indicated that little information had been published on oil shale beneficiation. Dismant (1) reviewed the potential for various beneficiation methods. A density method has been used in the industry, mainly as an analytical tool, to prepare organic-rich concentrates (2). Most recently, Fahlstrom (3) has described fine-grinding and froth flotation on Green River and Kvarntorp (Sweden) oil shales. After reviewing the problem, we decided to focus on

0097–6156/81/0163–0139$05.00/0

what kinds of separation are possible using coarse size
fractions. Avoidance of fine grinding and hydro—metallurgical
circuits seemed most desirable to reduce complexity and cost.

Access to shale at the C—a tract was not possible when this
study was started. The Mahogany Zone shale from the Anvil
Points Mine was used in this study.

Experimental

Shale Sampling. Oil shale used in this work was from the
Mahogany Zone of the Green River formation. The Bureau of Mines
room—and—pillar mine at Anvil Points has access to the Mahogany
Zone shale in the U.S. Naval Oil Shale Reserve. Figure 1 shows
a (72—foot) interval of shale which is mined at Anvil Points.
The histogram plot of a typical core is adapted from the Bureau
of Mines report (4). The average Fischer Assays of the various
beds of shale have been noted in Figure 1. Additional reference
can be made to the Bureau of Mines' reports for characteristics
of the mine (5). The mineable beds labelled A through J
correspond to the original designations of the Bureau of Mines.

During our sampling period, shale was being mined mainly
from beds A through F as a part of the Paraho demonstration
program. The normal floor level in the mine is at —20 feet
below the Mahogany marker. The relatively lean shale in Beds A,
C, and D results in a low grade of shale as run—of—mine
material. The Mahogany marker itself is a thin bed
approximately 4 to 6 inches in thickness, which contains little
organic matter. The integration of all of the zones from A
through F give a shale averaging about 26 GPT. As will be shown
later, our assay results were consistent with this value, which
verified that the mine blasting and blending procedure was in
good control.

A second objective of sampling at the Anvil Points mine was
to obtain a representative sample of a full 60—foot interval.
The zone selected was from 20 feet above the Mahogany marker to
40 feet below. This procedure gave us samples of shale from
beds G and H, which show a highly cylical grade change with
depth in the core analysis histograms.

Every effort was taken to assure uniform and accurate
sampling in the mine. Careful measuring was done by driving a
steel pin into the face at the upper edge of the Mahogany
marker. Vertical intervals were measured from the reference
points and marked with spray paint. Samples were broken from
the face using a hammer and rock chisel. Ten to twelve pounds
of sample were taken from each one—foot interval.

Samples for the interval from 2 feet below the Mahogany
marker to 20 feet above the marker were taken from the face of G
(George) drift, approximately 20 feet south of number 11 cross—
cut. The strata from 2 feet to 20 feet below the Mahogany
marker were taken at the intersection of A (Able) drift and

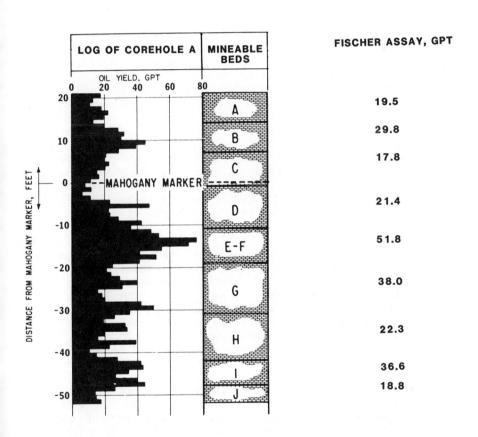

Figure 1. Core intervals and mineable beds at Anvil Points mine, Rifle, CO

142   OIL SHALE, TAR SANDS, AND RELATED MATERIALS

number 11 crosscut. The only location in the mine where the
strata from 20 feet to 40 feet below the marker is exposed is at
the north end of the A drift. At number 11 crosscut, A drift
declines to -40 feet at the number 13 crosscut. The samples for
the lower zone were taken from this location.

Sample Preparation. The mine-run sample was received in a
nominal crushed form of 3 inch by 1/4 inch. An aliquot portion
of a 470 pound lot was screened again over a 1/4-inch screen.
Only about 0.5% was recovered as fines, which indicated good
screening at the mine site. The +1/4 inch material was divided
into two portions. The first portion was reserved for heavy
media tests. The other half of the 3 inch by 1/4 inch material
was crushed to pass a 3/4-inch screen. This sample was then
screened through a 1/4-inch screen and 19% of the sample was
recovered as fines. The remaining 3/4 inch by 1/4 inch material
was reserved for heavy media tests.

Each individual hand-picked sample was stage crushed to
pass a 2-inch screen and was screened at 1/4 inch to remove
fines. Three composites were made from the 60 interval
samples. The first composite was from 0 to +20 feet above the
Mahogany marker. The other two samples were from 0 to -20 feet
below the marker and from -20 to -40 feet below the marker.
Each composite consisted of an equal weight of each one-foot
interval.

Heavy Media Tests. The general test procedure is
illustrated schematically in Figure 2. Heavy media suspensions
were made by adding magnetite (-65 mesh) to water in a stirred
separating vessel. The first separating gravity was 1.8. The
pre-wetted shale sample was introduced into the vessel with
constant stirring. After removal of the float product, the sink
material was removed and rinsed of all adhering media. The
process was repeated at specific gravities of 1.95, 2.10, 2.25,
and 2.40. A mixture of 75% by weight magnetite and 25% by
weight ferrosilicon was used to prepare the 2.40 specific
gravity suspension.

All products from the laboratory heavy media separation
were thoroughly rinsed to remove adhering medium and were air
dried at 90°C. Representative samples were crushed to -10
mesh. Specific gravities were obtained with an air pycnometer
and standard Fischer Assays were run.

Results

The heavy media separation procedure resulted in six
separate fractions for each composite. Table I shows the yield
results, specific gravity, and Fischer Assay results for the
mined composite of 3 inch to 1/4 inch material. Similarly,
Table II gives the results for the 3/4 inch by 1/4 inch crushed
material.

Table I
Rifle Mine
(Mined Composite, -3 inch + 1/4 inch)

Product	Specific Gravity	Weight % Yield	Fischer Assay, GPT
Float (1.80)	1.76	3.07	70.1
Sink (1.80), Float (1.95)	1.98	7.67	49.4
Sink (1.95), Float (2.10)	2.14	22.53	35.2
Sink (2.10), Float (2.25)	2.28	34.45	22.7
Sink (2.25), Float (2.40)	2.44	30.06	13.6
Sink (2.49)	2.62	2.22	(~5.0) est.
Total	2.265	100.00	25.8

Table II
Rifle Mine
(Mined Composite, -3/4 inch to +1/4 inch)

Product	Specific Gravity	Weight % Yield	Fischer Assay, GPT
Float (1.80)	1.74	2.74	70.4
Sink (1.80), Float (1.95)	2.04	13.96	36.0
Sink (1.95), Float (2.10)	2.18	31.33	29.0
Sink (2.10), Float (2.25)	2.38	45.33	17.4
Sink (2.25), Float (2.40)	2.50	6.25	10.7
Sink (2.40)	2.72	0.39	(0.0) est.
Total	2.261	100.00	24.6

Some shift in the yields of each density fraction can be noted in comparing results in Tables I and II. For example, nearly 65% of the material is collected in the two fractions averaging about 18 GPT for the coarse sample. After crushing to 3/4 inch, only about 50% of the total is found in these fractions, and the average grade was decreased slightly from 18 GPT. However, very little rich material has been liberated through the crushing to finer size.

The effect of crushing can be seen in Figure 3. The cumulative weight fraction of shale, when plotted versus density, shows a shift to lower specific gravity upon crushing. However, the steep slope of the curve between specific gravity of 1.95 and 2.10 shows that most of the material is found between these two extremes. When it is noted that 19% of the coarse shale was removed as -1/4 inch fines, it is apparent that crushing the shale to the finer size had very little effect in liberation of rich material. Crushing appears to have shifted the curve without changing its shape significantly in the richer fractions.

The results for each of the hand-picked composites are given in Tables III, IV, and V. The interval for 20 feet above the Mahogany marker, shown in Table III, has a behavior similar

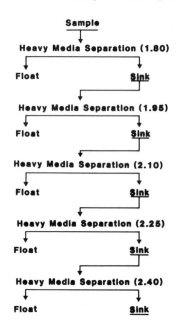

Figure 2.   Heavy-media test flowsheet

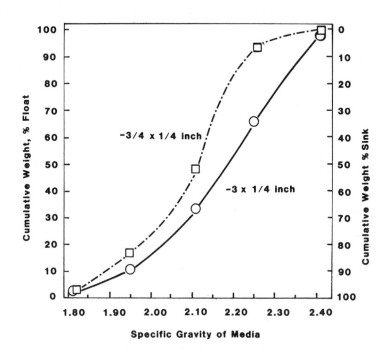

Figure 3.   Weight recovery vs. specific gravity for mine-run composites

to the run-of-mine material. For example, about 61% of the material falls in two fractions, averaging about 18 GPT. Moreover, only a little material is found in the rich fractions above 40 GPT.

Table III
Rifle Mine
Hand Picked Composite, 0 to +20 Feet

Product	Specific Gravity	Weight % Yield	Fischer Assay, GPT
Float (1.80)	1.85	2.9	53.1
Sink (1.80), Float (1.96)	2.02	7.8	38.5
Sink (1.96), Float (2.12)	2.22	21.3	27.0
Sink (2.12), Float (2.26)	2.32	33.2	21.6
Sink (2.26), Float (2.41)	2.43	28.0	14.4
Sink (2.41)	2.58	6.8	8.6
Total	2.31	100.00	22.1

Table IV
Hand Picked Composite, 0 to -20 Feet

Product	Specific Gravity	Weight % Yield	Fischer Assay, GPT
Float (1.79)	1.76	21.3	65.6
Sink (1.79), Float (1.95)	1.93	16.2	43.6
Sink (1.95), Float (2.11)	2.12	19.2	33.1
Sink (2.11), Float (2.25)	2.31	22.3	22.9
Sink (2.25), Float (2.40)	2.48	18.8	12.0
Sink (2.40)	2.54	2.2	5.8
Total	2.132	100.00	34.9

Table V
Hand Picked Composite, -20 to -40 Feet

Product	Specific Gravity	Weight % Yield	Fischer Assay, GPT
Float (1.78)	1.81	13.8	58.9
Sink (1.78), Float (1.95)	1.93	12.5	46.7
Sink (1.95), Float (2.11)	2.13	15.6	32.3
Sink (2.11), Float (2.25)	2.29	31.6	23.4
Sink (2.25), Float (2.39)	2.43	25.4	16.2
Sink (2.39)	2.53	1.1	9.2
Total	2.192	100.00	30.6

The richest material sampled is that in the 20-foot interval below the Mahogany marker. These results are summarized in Table IV. About 38% of the material averages about 55 GPT. Also, only about 20% of the total material is in the leanest fractions.

The lowest interval sampled, from 20 feet to 40 feet below the Mahogany marker, is summarized in Table V. In one respect, this interval is similar to the interval above it. For instance, a significant fraction of the samples is contained in the richer fractions. However, the degree of enrichment is not quite as good as in the upper zone. This can be noted in that the richest fraction was 58.9 GPT. In contrast, a larger fraction of richer material (65.6 GPT) was obtained in the upper interval.

Discussion

Liberation by Fine Grinding. Two samples shown in Table I (49.4 GPT, specific gravity of 1.98) and (13.6 GPT, specific gravity of 2.44) were examined further for liberation of organic matter by fine grinding to a particle size of less than 45 microns. The samples were sent to H. Tinsley and Company in London for a Micro Vibratory Sluice separation.

After separation at less than 45 microns, the rich sample (49.4 GPT) contained most of the fine particles below 2.00 gravity. Moreover, less than 10% of the material was contained between 2.0 and 2.20 and less than 5% over 2.2 specific gravity. The lean sample (13.6 GPT) had a main band at 2.33 gravity and other bands at 2.40 and 2.46 gravity. In the lean sample, about 90% of the material was between 2.20 and 2.47, with about 40% below 2.30 specific gravity.

These finely ground samples represent narrow specific gravity distributions. It is apparent that little additional organic and mineral separation is possible by fine grinding down to about 45 microns.

Geochemical Basis. The existence in Green River shale of the minute seasonal pairs of lamina called varves is important to the understanding of beneficiation potential. The most classic work in the areas of geology and geochemistry is by Bradley (6, 7).

Bradley estimated that rich shale of about 35 GPT required 8,200 years per foot of accumulation. Lean shale of 10-14 GPT required about 2,000 years per foot with other shale intermediate to these extremes. Accordingly, the annual thickness of the layer pairs range from about 150 microns for lean shale to about 25-35 microns for rich shale. Moreover, Bradley found that the thickness of the rich shale (designated oil shale) and the thickness of the lean shale (designated marlstone) followed quite precise rhythmical changes. The length of the cycle over the entire depth averaged about 22,000 years. Bradley pointed out that the average of the precession cycle and eccentricity cycle in the earth's orbit would give a resultant cycle of about 21,000 years. Most of the lean marlstone beds are about 6 feet thick, though the range was from 3.8 to 8.8 feet. The richer oil shale beds range from 0.6 to

3.0 feet. These rhythmic cycles can easily be visualized by examining Figure 1. Bradley's observations of more than 50 years ago are remarkable. Recent modeling of climatic responses to orbital variations seems to suggest a general relationship in all organic sediments (8). Accordingly, the cyclical ups and downs of shale grade in the Green River are due to changes in weather cycles which, in turn, were due to changes in the earth's orbit.

Correlation of Grade with Specific Gravity. Correlation between density of oil-shale rock and the rock's organic content have been known for some time. For example, Frost and Stanfield (2), and Smith and co-workers (9, 10, 11) have published data specifically for Green River shale. An empirical expression has been developed between oil-shale density and oil yield:

(1)   Oil Yield (GPT) = $31.563 \ D_R^2 - 205.998 \ D_R + 326.624$

where D_R is the rock density in gm/cm^3. This is a parabolic function, which is strongly curved, particularly in rich shale above 35 GPT. It has been generally recognized that the Fischer Assay is a relatively poor measure of the grade or quality of shale. The quality and quantity of liquid can vary, highly dependent on the elemental and minerals analysis and how the retorting is carried out.

The Fischer Assay results and specific gravity obtained in this study have been plotted in Figure 4. The correlation shown above has been plotted in Figure 4 to see how it compares. Between a specific gravity of 1.95 and 2.05, the agreement is quite good. However, the heavy media samples of lean shale between specific gravities of 2.20 and 2.50 seem to contain more organic matter than the Smith correlation would indicate. This difference is not surprising. The Smith correlation was developed by averaging core data of long intervals for the entire Green River formation, while the data in Figure 4 are specific, small particle results for extremely narrow specific gravity fractions.

Volume percent of organic matter is a linear function of rock density. Smith (6) has also shown that

(2) $V_0 = 100 \ (D_M - D_R)/(D_M - D_O)$

where V_0 is volume percent of organic.

Using an average density of mineral matter, D_M of 2.72 and 1.07 for organic density, D_O, the equation reduces to:

(3) $V_0 = 164.85 - 60.61 \ D_R$

where D_R is the density of the shale.

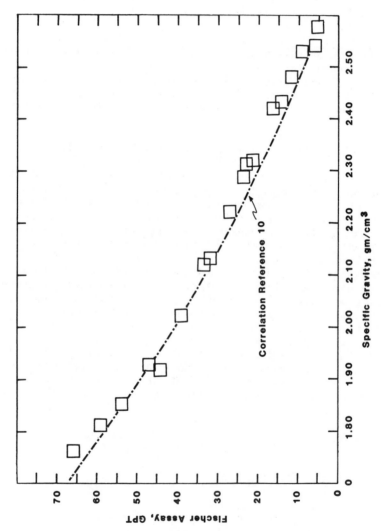

*Figure 4. Fischer assay results for separated fractions: correlation based on specific gravity
(– · –) (10).*

Equation (3) is the standard form recommended for Mahogany Zone shale.   However, several linear plots are shown in Figure 5.   The specific gravity for the mineral matter has been varied from 2.66 to 2.78.   Also, the organic gravity has been varied from 1.02 to 1.12 gm/cm^3.   It is clear that the lean shale particles show an extreme sensitivity to variations in the mineral density and organic density.   For example, a particle of 2.60 specific gravity shows a range from 4.0 volume % organic to 10.0% for the different densities chosen.   Moreover, the calculated organic content of rich shale particles show much lower sensitivity to the densities of the mineral and organic components.   Accordingly, the density correlation developed by Smith must be used with caution for lean shale particles.   For lean shale particles, the density of the organic phase is lower than average while the mineral phase is higher than average.   In comparison, in the rich shale particles, the organic phase is higher than average while the mineral phase is lower than average.   These effects are masked by the average values of Smith (10, 11).

Bi-Modal Nature of Shale Deposits

Our results indicate that the organic concentration and stratigraphy of shales fall into two distinct classes.   These classes are shown by the data in Tables III, IV, and V.   The shale interval above the Mahogany marker contains very little rich shale which can be freed by crushing to about 1 inch in size.   In contrast, the two intervals below the marker contain much rich material which is separable at coarse size fractions.

The bi-modal nature of the shale over the full 60-foot zone is shown more clearly in Figures 6, 7, and 8.   The weight percent of organic material present in each fraction has been calculated from Fischer Assay using the Smith (11) correlations.   The distribution of organic material in each fraction is plotted as histograms for each of the three sub-zones.   The upper and lower zones of shale shows a relatively sharp maximum at about 25 GPT.   The middle zone, immediately below the marker, does not show this maximum (Figure 7).   The two zones below the marker show a trend toward a second maximum in the range of 60-70 GPT.   Our lowest separation gravity was at 1.80, so there is no way of defining the second maximum precisely.   Since the intervals of organic level in the richer zones above 30 GPT are somewhat broader, this adds to the imprecision in defining the second maximum.

This bi-modal nature of Mahogany Zone shale is consistent with the observations of Bradley (6).   In this classic work Bradley noted the distinct cyclic behavior of accumulations of a lean marlstone and a rich oil shale.   As previously noted, the cyclic accumulations were correlated with the earth's orbit and subsequent weather cycles.   Since the cycles were detected at

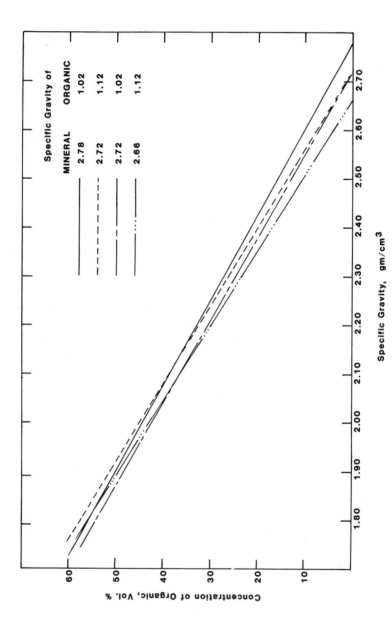

Figure 5. Dependence of calculated organic volume on organic and mineral specific gravity

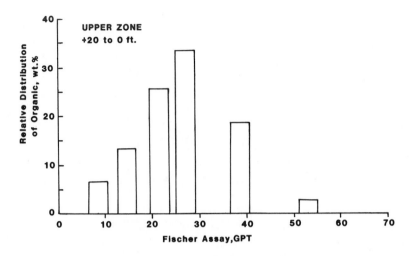

Figure 6.   Distribution of organic matter in Mahogany zine shale, Anvil Points mine, upper zone, + 20 ft to Mahogany marker

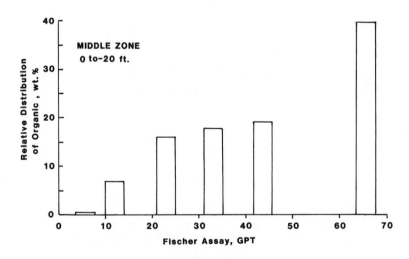

Figure 7.   Distribution of organic matter in Mahogany zone shale, Anvil Points mine, middle zone, Mahogany marker to − 20 ft

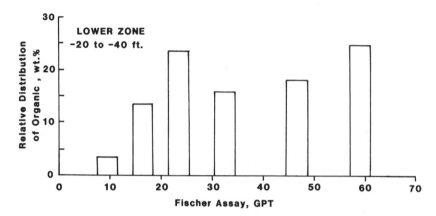

Figure 8.   Distribution of organic matter in Mahogany zone shale, Anvil Points mine, lower zone, −20 to −40 ft

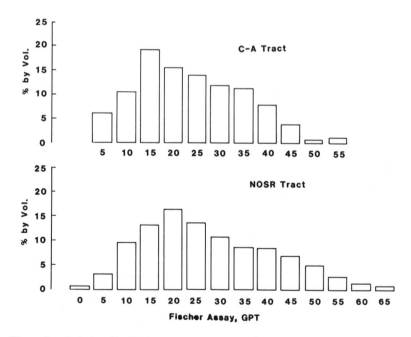

Figure 9.   Relative distribution of shale grade on C-a tract and Mahogany zone, Anvil Points :(upper figure) based on CE-205 core, 2-ft increments, 1050-ft interval; (lower figure) based on A-core, 1-ft increments, 73-ft interval.

intervals of about 1-9 feet, consistent with the frequency of 21,000 years, there is every reason to believe this cycle would be detected at our dimensions of 1/4 to 3 inches. As noted by Bradley, the clastics-rich (lean marlstone) portions have varve thicknesses of about 150 microns. Accordingly, a lean particle averaging 1.18 inches (3 cm) in dimension perpendicular to the varves would represent a 20-year interval. In contrast, an extremely rich particle of about 65 GPT with similar dimensions would represent an interval of at least 100 years. Finally, it can be noted that the fine crushing of shale down to about 45 microns failed to change the density distribution of the particles significantly. Accordingly, it can be concluded that the histograms shown in Figure 6 would not change significantly if the material were separated at these smaller sizes.

Application to Other Shale Zones

The results described in this study were on shale from the Mahogany Zone in the southern Perimeter of the Piceance Basin. Given the relatively constant stratigraphy, it may be assumed that the results are at least qualitatively applicable to the Mahogany Zone. For example, Curry (12) demonstrated the precise match of individual tiny annual varves in two core sections taken 8-1/2 miles apart. Smith and Robb (13) have also remarked on the similarity in mineral character and organic character throughout the shale measures in the Green River formation. Yet, caution should be exercised in extrapolating these results to the deeper shale. For example, nahcolite and dawsonite are found in the Saline Zone, while dawsonite is much more common in the Leached Zone. Also, the specific gravity of the organic matter is known to change with depth.

We were generally interested in comparing the distribution of rich and lean zones of shale throughout the C-a tract relative to the Mahogany Zone on the southern perimeter. Accordingly, the Fischer Assay results for one core in the central portion of tract C-a have been compared with the results from a core in the southern Mahogany Zone. This comparison is shown in Figure 9. The data are based on a 2-foot interval sampling on C-a tract versus a 1-foot interval in the southern perimeter shale. Several interesting comparisons are noted. The C-a tract shale shows a peak at 15 GPT instead of 20 GPT. Also, the C-a shale interval shows more of the material in the medium-grade interval of 25-35 GPT. It is also apparent that intervals of 40 GPT and richer shale blocks are a much lower percentage on the C-a tract.

Nevertheless, it seems apparent that the paleo-limnology and paleo-climatology of the Green River Lakes, which was so beautifully analyzed by Bradley, has a dominant effect in predicting results.

Acknowledgements

    The authors are indebted to J. F. Patzer and P. S. Sundar
for their assistance, discussions, and their reviews.

Literature Cited

1. Dismant, John H. The Mines Magazine March, 1961, pages 15-
    22.

2. Frost, I.C. and Stanfield, K. E. Anal. Chem. March, 1950,
    22, pages 491-492.

3. Fahlstrom, P. H., Proceedings of 12th Oil Shale Symposium,
    Colorado School of Mines, 1979.

4. Stanfield, K. E.; Frost I. C.; McAuley, W. S.; Smith, H. N.,
    Bureau of Mines, RI 4825, November, 1951.

5. East, J. H., Jr. and Gardner, E. D., Bureau of Mines,
    Bull 611, 1964.

6. Bradley, Wilmot H., U.S. Geological Survey, Professional
    Paper 158-E, 1929.

7. Bradley, W. H. Geological Society of America Bulletin 1948,
    59, pages 635-648.

8. Imbrie, John, and Imbrie, John Z. Science February 29, 1980,
    207, pages 943-953.

9. Smith, John Ward Chem. Eng. Data Series 1958, 3, No. 2,
    pages 306-310.

10. Smith, John Ward, Bureau of Mines RI-7248, 1969, 14 pages.

11. Smith, John Ward, LERC/RI-76/6, September, 1976.

12. Curry, H. D., Intermountain Assoc. Petrol. Geol., 13th Ann.
    Field Conf. Guidebook, 1964, pages 169-171.

13. Smith, John Ward and Robb, William A., Bureau of Mines
    RI-7727, 1973.

RECEIVED February 18, 1981.

Beneficiation of Green River Oil Shale by Pelletization

J. REISBERG

Shell Development Company, P.O. Box 481, Houston, TX 77001

Green River shale is a sedimentary, highly laminated, fine textured rock composed mainly of the minerals dolomite, calcite, quartz, feldspar, clay and frequently, pyrite. A minor portion, less than 50 percent by weight and averaging about 10 percent, consists of kerogen, a solid organic, highly cross-linked polymeric substance, polycyclic in nature, with an appreciable hetero-atom content. Oil shale, unlike tar sands and gilsonite, is largely insoluble in organic solvents. However, it exhibits a striking tendency to imbibe and swell in the presence of organic liquids. Kerogen can be converted by pyrolysis to liquid and gaseous fuels and to a carbonaceous residue.

The high mineral content of oil shale imposes a huge heat demand upon a thermal upgrading process and calls for very large processing facilities. A reduction in the mineral content of the feed by an ore beneficiation step can strongly influence the process economics and may also afford the ancillary advantage of a decreased volume of contaminated, possibly biologically harmful retort tailings. A process for the beneficiation of Green River shale was investigated which yields kerogen-enriched oleophilic pellets and a dispersion in water of most of the mineral matter.

BACKGROUND

There exist a number of familiar procedures for effecting mineral separations, including sink-float methods based on density differences and froth flotation based on wettability. Because of the tendency of kerogen to swell and soften in the presence of organic liquids and thus possibly to mobilize trapped mineral particles, and because most minerals are water-wetted and thus extractable with water, we investigated a liquid-liquid (oil-water) pelletization method.

Several related procedures for upgrading shales have been described in the literature. Generally these were developed as an adjunct to the chemical analysis of kerogen, the purpose being to reduce interference by minerals and to avoid the risk of oxidation of the organic matter by severe chemical deashing.

0097–6156/81/0163–0155$05.00/0

A South African shale, Torbanite,[1] was ground with water
in a porcelain ball mill. Oil (unspecified) was added in sufficient quantity to form a paste with the organic-rich fraction
and grinding was continued. Mineral matter became suspended in
the aqueous phase and this was discarded. The oily paste was
solvent washed, dried and analyzed. The ash content was reduced
from an original value of less than 40 percent to a value of
about 10 percent.

A new Brunswick oil shale containing 58 percent mineral
matter[2] was processed in a similar way except that it was
preground in a heavy gas-oil prior to the introduction of water.
Following a 16-hour grinding period, the dried, enriched material
had a mineral content of 34 percent.

Green River oil shale[3] was treated with 5 percent acetic
acid to remove carbonate minerals prior to grinding in a water,
n-octane system. The aqueous mineral suspension was removed and
replaced repeatedly with fresh water until no mineral matter was
observable in the water. Analysis of the residue indicated that
the mineral content was reduced from an initial 75 percent to 16
percent.

These procedures resemble the process for coal purification
described in 1922 by W. E. Trent.[4] It comprised grinding of
coal to a 100/200 mesh size, sufficient to detach the mineral
particles from the coal, then agitating with an organic, water
insoluble liquid possessing a "selective affinity" for the coal.
The process produced an "amalgam" of coal and organic liquid and
rejected the inorganic gangue as aqueous slurry.

Recently, similar methods have been applied to the separation of tar from Alberta tar sands.[5]

EXPERIMENTAL

Procedure. The laboratory work described here was performed
with two shale samples; one consisted of material from cores
taken at a depth of 1830-1860 feet from the Marathon lease and
the second in the form of rock fragments from the Colony mine
(Dow property).

For the beneficiation we used a 5.5 gallon porcelain ball
mill, and 1.5-inch grinding medium (Burundum, of cylindrical
form). The mill was charged with 10 pounds of grinding medium,
400-800 ml of water, 100-200 grams of shale (pulverized earlier
to pass through a 100 mesh screen) and 50-100 ml of organic
liquid binding agent (heptane). The mill was rotated for an
hour. Typically, after about 10 minutes of operation, a kerogen-
enriched fraction in the form of discrete flakes or pellets
began to separate. After a one-hour milling cycle, the aqueous
gangue dispersion was removed and replaced with fresh water. A
small sample, 0.2-0.3 grams, of the enriched pellets was recovered for analysis and the milling operation repeated for as many

cycles as deemed necessary. Both gangue and kerogen-enriched
pellets were dried under vacuum at 70°C-80°C (see Plate I). The
kerogen content was determined as weight loss by plasma ashing.
(We used two plasma ashing devices: International Plasma Corporation, Model 1003B-248AN and LFE Corporation, Low Temperatures
Asher, No. LTA-600.) Since the plasma combustion temperature
does not exceed 50°C we avoid the possibility of mineral decomposition (especially of carbonates) encountered during high
temperature combustion.

Results. The size of the enriched pellets is a function of
the quantity of added organic binding agent. An insufficient
quantity of binding agent yields pellets too small for easy
separation from the gangue suspension by means of coarse sieves.
An excess of binder results in the formation of a voluminous,
soft kerogen paste which entrains gangue. The optimum condition
described above yields pellets about 1 cm in diameter. The
result of a typical beneficiation experiment with Marathon lease
material is shown in Figure 1. This entailed four one-hour
milling cycles, the aqueous mineral dispersion being removed and
replaced with fresh water after each cycle. Kerogen contents
for both the organic-rich pellets (oleophilic) and the water
dispersible mineral gangue (hydrophilic) are shown. The figure
also shows the results of two single cycle experiments.

The Marathon sample was obtained from a depth of more than
1800 feet. Since an ore beneficiation step would be more appropriate for a minable, shallow formation, we also tested samples
from the Dow-Colony (Parachute Creek) mine. Starting with particles in the 8 to 10 sieve size range, this material was milled
in water until 90 percent passed through a 100 mesh screen.
Organic binder was added to the aqueous slurry and the process
was continued as described above. Results of duplicate experiments are shown in Figure 2. The beneficiation obtained with
this Dow-Colony shale is less favorable than that with Marathon
lease material.

Analysis of oil shale surfaces by the scanning electron
microscope prior to and following low temperature ashing reveals
that the mineral matter occurs in the form of fine, discrete
particles within a continuous kerogen matrix.

Figure 3 shows the size distributions of inorganic mineral
particles obtained by low temperature ashing of unprocessed oil
shales. These minerals have mean particle diameters (50 percent
frequency level) of 5-6 microns.

X-ray diffraction analysis of the products of the beneficiation of Dow-Colony shale is shown in Table I. It is clear that
the oleophilic extract (pellets) retains or concentrates the
calcium and magnesium carbonates (dolomite, calcite, aragonite),
particularly the dolomite. The hydrophilic gangue consists
mainly of feldspar and quartz. Since silica, silicates and
Ca/Ca-Mg carbonates, in a clean condition, are water wettable

Plate I.   Beneficiation products of Green River oil shale

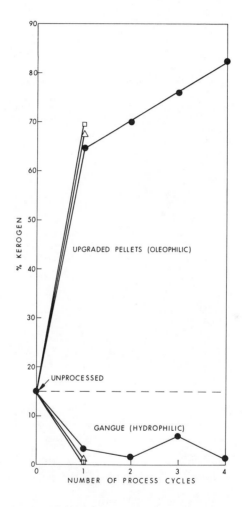

Figure 1. Recovery of Marathon Lease kerogen as a function of the number of beneficiation cycles. (Kerogen determined by weight loss on low-temperature ashing.)

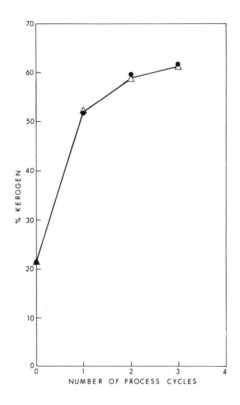

Figure 2.   Beneficiation of Dow–Colony shale

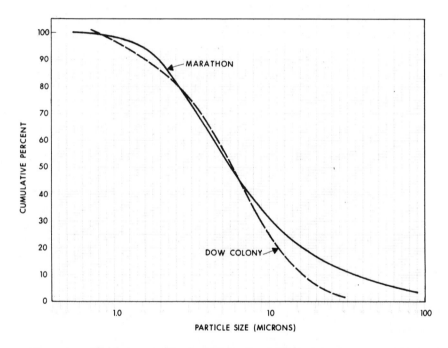

Figure 3. Cumulative particle-size distribution of the mineral constituents of oil shales (by low-temperature ashing). Particle size by Coulter counter.

the above results would indicate that the beneficiation procedure
renders at least a portion of the carbonates oil-wettable. The
mechanism for the wettability reversal of the carbonates may
reside in the adsorption of certain carboxylic constituents of
the shale, viz., the bitumens. Bitumens, the solvent-extractable
organic components of oil shale are rich in carboxylic functional
groups; they contain about 35 percent fatty acids, resinous
acids, polymer acids and benzenoid acids[6] (see below). Their
dissolution in the added organic binder would make them accessible
to adsorption by the carbonates. Carboxylic acids are a commonly
utilized "collector" for carbonate minerals in froth flotation
processes.[7] They adsorb strongly and decrease the water wettability of calcium carbonate thus facilitating its separation
from a hydrophilic gangue with the gas phase. Similarly, in
this pelletization process, the action of the adsorbed bitumen
constituents on the Ca/Ca-Mg carbonate mineral particles renders
them largely inseparable from the oleophilic, oil swollen kerogen.
Where pyrite is present, one would expect that, due to its
inherent oil wettability, it too would accumulate in the oleophilic pellets.

TABLE I.   MINERAL DISTRIBUTION FOLLOWING BENEFICIATION STEPS
DOW-COLONY SAMPLE
(Estimated Weight Percent in Crystalline
Portion by X-ray Diffraction)

	Untreated	Kerogen Extract (Oleophilic Pellets)	Gangue (Hydrophilic)
Calcite	10	10	5
Dolomite	65	83	20
Aragonite	5	5	–
Quartz	10	1	20
Feldspar	10	1	52
Dawsonite	–	–	3

Samples of pulverized Dow-Colony oil shale were extracted
both at room temperature and by Soxhlet refluxing with n-heptane
and with toluene. Solvent was stripped from the extract under
vacuum and the acid numbers of the tar-like residual bitumens
were determined. Results for duplicate samples are shown in
Table II. We note that significant quantities of carboxylic
acids are indeed extracted.

In view of the above, one would anticipate difficulty in
upgrading by this method, shales containing large quantities of
carbonate mineral (dolomite, calcite, aragonite) and/or pyrite
(FeS_2). In Table III we show the mineral distributions, determined by X-ray diffraction, of samples from the Marathon and

TABLE II.   EXTRACTION OF BITUMEN FROM DOW-COLONY SHALE

Solvent	Bitumen Recovered % of Shale	Acid Number, MgKOH/gram
Toluene, Room Temp.	0.7	9.2, 9.5
Heptane, Room Temp.	0.9	3.6, 2.6
Toluene, Soxhlet	1.5	12.7, 18.8
Heptane, Soxhlet	1.6	19.2, 13.1

Dow-Colony leases. The sums of the weight percent of the Ca/Ca-Mg carbonates and pyrites in the Marathon samples lie between 30 and 35 percent whereas in the Dow-Colony samples, they lie between 47 and 80 percent. This observation supports the finding that the superior upgrading of the Marathon lease shale is due to its lower carbonate/pyrite content.

TABLE III.   MINERAL CONSTITUENTS OF MARATHON LEASE
AND DOW-COLONY MINE SHALE SAMPLES
(Estimated Weight Percent in Crystalline Portion)

	Marathon Lease		Dow-Colony		
Calcite	–	–	10	10	10
Dolomite	35	30	27	40	65
Aragonite	–	–	–	–	5
Pyrite	–	–	10	10	–
Quartz	15	20	12	10	10
Feldspar	15	20	25	15	10
Analcite	–	–	3	10	–
Dawsonite	20	15	5	–	–
Nahcolite	10	10	–	–	–
Clay	–	–	5	–	–
Unidentified	5	5	3	5	–

In an effort to improve the ore upgrading process by increasing the level of carbonate minerals rejection, we studied the effect of the chemical additives shown below.

1. Flotation depressants: It was indicated earlier that the release of oil soluble carboxylic acids may be responsible for the retention of Ca/Ca-Mg carbonates by the kerogen-organic binder pellets. Chemical flotation depressants are sometimes applied to overcome the collecting tendency of fatty acids and thus to increase the water wettability of the carbonate particles in the presence of carboxylin acids.[7] The introduction of such flotation depressants, including sodium oxalate, chromium nitrate, copper nitrate, ferric sulfate and aluminum nitrate failed to improve the beneficiation process described here.

2. Sodium bicarbonate: Marathon lease samples which exhibit
high levels of beneficiation also contain nahcolite ($NaHCO_3$).
The beneficiation process thus operates at an elevated pH.
To investigate the effect of high pH on Dow-Colony shale, experiments were performed with added sodium bicarbonate and sodium
hydroxide. No improvement in kerogen enrichment was obtained.
3. Surfactants: A selection of typical commercial surface
active agents, both anionic and nonionic, were tested to determine
whether beneficial interfacial or wetting conditions could be
obtained. These agents included:

      Triton X-100 (nonionic, ethoxylated octyl phenol)
      Pluronic F68 (nonionic, ethylene oxide - propylene
oxide condensation product)
      NEODOL® 25-7, 25-9, 25-30, 25-45 (nonionic, linear
primary alcohol ethoxylates)
      NEODOL 25-3S (anionic, sulfated form of NEODOL 25-3).

The effects of several dispersants were also examined; they
included:

      Marasperse N22 and CB (lignosulfonates)
      Guartec (industrial grade guar gum)
These approaches were also unrewarding.

Product Assay. Fischer Assays were performed with samples
of Marathon lease material, with both raw shale and with the
beneficiated pellets. Spent shale (char) from the assay was
subjected to heat value (Btu content) analysis. Results are
shown in Table IV.

TABLE IV.   FISCHER ASSAYS, MARATHON LEASE SHALE

	Raw Shale	Beneficiated Product
Oil, gal/ton	44.3	154.2
Oil, % by weight	16.6	57.4
Water, gal/ton	6.4	2.5
Water, % by weight	2.7	1.0
Spent Shale (char), % by weight	74.4	33.0
Gas + Loss, % by weight	6.3	8.6
Btu/lb of char	693.0	5,352.0

DISCUSSION

Kerogen, as noted earlier, is a polymeric substance that can
imbibe large quantities of organic liquids. This is accompanied

by swelling and a slight softening of the matrix. Such gross
swelling, as well as exfoliation, under the influence of various
organic liquids can be observed visually with raw oil shale. We
suggest that this swelling and softening of the kerogen is a key
element in the beneficiation scheme described here. During the
milling process the inorganic mineral particles are not ejected
via comminution of a brittle matrix (chopped out of the kerogen,
so to speak) but are instead worked out of the softened kerogen
mass by a deforming and kneading process. The kerogen particles
become fused rather than bridged by pendular rings of binding
agent as in coal pelletization. After drying, the gangue dis-
integrates into its component small particles but the kerogen
pellets dry to a hard brittle mass exhibiting no evidence of the
presence of discrete small particles.

Two shale samples were studied; one from the Marathon lease
(cores) and the other from the Dow-Colony mine. Clearly, the
latter is the more relevant to an ore beneficiation process.
The results obtained with this material are less favorable than
those achieved with the Marathon cores. Still the increase in
kerogen content from a value of 21 percent for the raw material
to 62 percent for the upgraded pellets represents a rejection of
83 percent of the mineral matter (neglecting a small loss of
kerogen to the gangue). This upgrading can represent a sizable
decrease in the heat demand of a retorting process. There may
also be an ancillary environmental benefit. The rejected inorganic gangue contains only a small residue of kerogen, in unmodified
form. This is no more damaging than the kerogen in the original
oil shale. The residual char from the retorting of the enriched
pellets has a sufficiently high Btu content (Table IV) and low
minerals content to be itself useful as a process fuel. Its ash
would be free of organic matter and low in silica dust. Thus
the material returned to the environment from a process involving
ore beneficiation, retorting of the kerogen-enriched pellets and
char burning would be free of organic pyrolysis products.

The laboratory experiments were performed batchwise in small
ball mills. A larger scale operation would call for continuous
processing, probably in a rod mill. At present the procedure
does not appear to be economically feasible. A major cost is
that of the initial comminution of the shale. Because the
material possesses a very unfavorable grindabiilty work index,
this step requires an excessive power outlay. Furthermore, the
process calls for a large quantity of organic binding agent, the
recovery of which is also very costly. Whether or not means can
be devised for improving the economics must await further investigation.

ABSTRACT

A procedure is described for the beneficiation of Green
River oil shale, based on the wettability contrast between the

organic kerogen and its inorganic minerals. It entails the milling of the shale in a mixture of water and a liquid hydrocarbon binding agent followed by the separation of kerogen-enriched pellets and the rejection of an aqueous dispersion of hydrophilic mineral particles. A portion of the calcite and dolomite is rendered oleophilic and inseparable from the hydrocarbon-swollen kerogen pellets. This is brought about by the adsorption of oil soluble carboxylic constituents contained in the bitumens. Certain shale samples were upgraded from an initial kerogen content of 15 percent to a kerogen content in excess of 80 percent.

LITERATURE CITED

1. Quass, F. W., The Analysis of the Kerogen of Oil Shales, Inst. Pet. J., 1939, 25, 813.
2. Himus, G. W. and Basak, G. C., Analysis of Coals and Carbonaceous Materials Containing High Percentages of Inherent Mineral Matter, Fuel, 1949, 28, 57.
3. Smith, J. W. and Higby, L. W., Preparation of Organic Concentrate from Green River Oil Shale, Anal. Chem., 1960, 32, 1718.
4. Trent, W. E., Process of Purifying Materials, U. S. Patent No. 1,420,164, 1922.
5. Puddington, I. E. and Farnard, J. R., Oil Phase Separation, U. S. Patent No. 3,999,765, 1968.
6. Investigation of Colorado Oil Shale, First Annual Report, Denver Research Institute, 1966, pp. 19-20.
7. Sutherland, K. L. and Wark, I. W., Principles of Flotation, Australasian Institute of Mining and Metallurgy, 1955, pp. 317-321.

RECEIVED January 19, 1981.

12

Shell Pellet Heat Exchange Retorting: The SPHER Energy-Efficient Process for Retorting Oil Shale

J. E. GWYN, S. C. ROBERTS, D. E. HARDESTY,
G. L. JOHNSON, and G. P. HINDS, JR.

Shell Development Company, P.O. Box 1380, Houston, TX 77001

Oil shales of primary interest for surface processing occur mainly in the Piceance Basin of western Colorado. These shales contain, typically, 10 to 20 percent weight of hydrocarbons recoverable by simple pyrolysis.

Process research and development in shale oil production has gone on for decades, but the once plentiful supply of low cost petroleum crudes made the economics of such processes very unfavorable. The recent shortages and cost escalation of petroleum crudes have renewed interests in "unconventional" raw material sources such as coal and oil shale.

Several processes for above ground retorting of oil shale, which have been under development for some time, include the TOSCO-II, PARAHO, and Union technologies.[1] Shell had particular interests in the first two. The TOSCO (The Oil Shale Company) process uses hot balls to heat preheated shale in a rotary kiln to retorting temperatures. The shale is preheated during staged, pneumatic transport using flue gas from the retort ball heater. The PARAHO retort is a vertical kiln employing a downward moving rock bed with upflowing recycle gas and combustion products which sweep retorted hydrocarbons from the vessel. The Union process is similar but utilizes an upward flow of crushed shale. Shale is introduced at the bottom of the retort and pushed upward by a mechanical "rock pump". Fluidized bed retorting of oil shale was proposed in the early fifties but was never developed to a commercial state.

The TOSCO-II process is capital intensive because it requires a large volume of heating gases and mechanically complex equipment; the PARAHO and Union processes are also capital intensive because they have long residence time requirements that entail massive hardware. The PARAHO and Union processes are, however, heat efficient as a result of countercurrent shale and gas flow. But the TOSCO process, although having some degree of heat recovery, uses heat relatively inefficiently.

The purpose of this work was to develop a new retorting process of relatively low capital cost that is mechanically simple, highly reliable, and uses heat efficiently. The process,[2] term SPHER for

0097–6156/81/0163–0167$05.00/0

Shell Pellet Heat Exchange Retorting, is a fluidization bed process conceived for the retorting of oil shale. The fluidization mode referred to in this discussion applies to a range of superficial gas velocities between those used for riser transport and dense bed operation in processes such as catalytic cracking. By this mode, shale can be made to flow upward, countercurrently to larger heat-carrier pellets that fall through the fluidized mixture. This counterflow of heat-carrier pellets and relatively coarse shale particles is the basic idea around which novel, small sized, thermally efficient and economically viable processes have been conceived. Other feedstocks to which SPHER may have potential applicability include numerous coals, lignite, wood and bark waste, agricultural residues, biotreater sludges, and industrial and municipal solid wastes. Some specific process descriptions, with some variations, are discussed below.

Brief Description of Process Applied to Oil Shale

The SPHER process as originally conceived is shown schematically in Figure 1. This conceptual design produces 55,000 bbl/day (7575 t/d)* of raw shale oil from 66,000 ton/day (60,000 t/d) of 35 gal/ton (13.6%w) oil shale. It can be seen that there are two loops for circulation of heat carrying balls. The cool ball loop carries heat from the heat recovery column to the preheater. The hot ball loop carries heat from the ball heater to the retort.

Shale is crushed or ground to a fluidizable size; preferably as large as is compatible with heat transfer requirements and ready separation from heat-carrying balls. Initial work indicates that 1/16-inch (1.6 mm) minus shale and 1/4 (6 mm) or 5/16 (8 mm) inch balls are desirable.

The shale is preheated in a fast-fluidized (entraining) bed by outer loop, heat-carrying balls that rain through the bed in countercurrent fashion (Figure 2). With air as the fluidizing medium, preheating is limited to about 600°F (315°C) because there is danger from auto-ignition, which is time, temperature, and oxygen dependent.[3] With other nonoxidizing gases, preheating is limited to about 650°F (343°C) by the onset of kerogen pyrolysis.

In a dense-bed fluidized bed the preheated shale is further heated to and held at the retorting temperature for sufficient time to complete the pyrolysis reactions (Figure 3). The total inventory of shale in the retorting vessel is determined by the required residence time for complete kerogen conversion and the shale throughput. The retort heat requirements are supplied by ceramic balls which circulate in the inner loop. They are reheated in a separate vessel which may operate as a moving bed, raining pellet bed, or entrained flow heater.

The spent shale is cooled in a fast-fluidized bed by the recirculated cool pellets from the preheater. In this manner, countercurrent flow of heat carriers and the shale assures efficient

*ton = 2000 pounds, t = metric ton = 1000 kg.

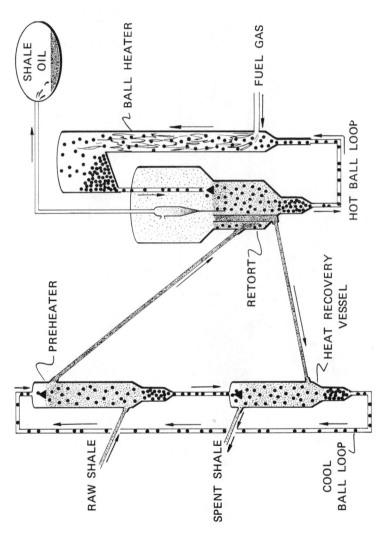

Figure 1. SPHER oil shale process

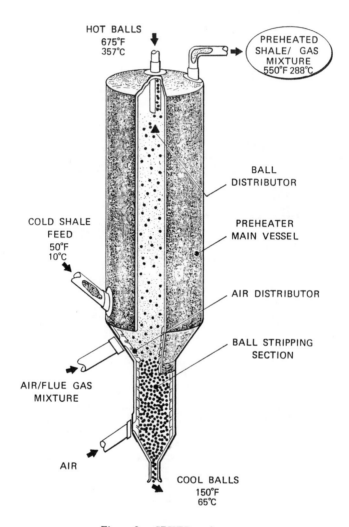

Figure 2.   SPHER preheater

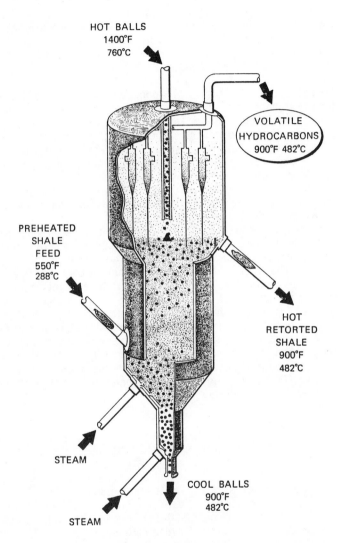

Figure 3.   SPHER retort

energy utilization. This characteristic is a prime advantage of the process.

Most conditions and features of the conceptual process are chosen to assure high throughputs (small equipment) and hence relatively low capital and fixed costs. These include the choice of flow regimes, heat carriers (density and heat capacity) and the solids-to-gas weight ratios. Attendant features of the process, such as baffle design and gas routing, are chosen to achieve operability and optimum operation.

Segregation of the two ball loops permits the tailoring of the ball material, shape and size to each specific task. Circulation of balls in the outer loop is a relatively low temperature operation and is dedicated to heat transfer. Therefore, desired ball properties include high heat capacity, small size or large heat transfer surface, erosion resistance, and low cost. Hence, a pea gravel may be suitable. Corrosion resistance may not be needed unless condensation occurs in the heat recovery section. The use of the smallest balls separable from the shale increases heat transfer and reduces the size of the exchange vessel required.

In contrast, circulation of balls in the inner loop involves the ball heater and retort where high temperatures and longer residence times are required. Reaction rate rather than heat transfer is expected to be the controlling factor in the retort design. In order to achieve the residence time needed for high conversion a pseudo plug-flow device such as a rotary kiln or a staged, dense-phase fluidized bed may be desirable. Since heat transfer is not controlling, the balls can be larger for easier separation from shale but they must still be small enough to permit pneumatic transport. These inner loop balls must also be resistant to thermal shock, chemical attack by the hot gases and spent shale and exposure to high temperatures. Thus, the choice of the inner loop balls is limited to materials such as ceramics.

Detailed Process Description

A more process oriented schematic of the process is shown in Figure 4.

Shale Feed Preparation. Shale preparation for SPHER requires more energy than it does for processes such as TOSCO-II in that the larger crushed shale used in TOSCO-II, e.g., 1/2-inch (13 mm) minus, must be reduced to a readily fluidizable size, e.g., 1/16-inch (1.6 mm) minus, for use in SPHER. Grinding by separating and recycling coarse shale is expected to produce a better size range with less fines than once-through grinding is for the same maximum particle size. Separation of shale with the desired size from oversized material may be accomplished by elutriation with gas or by screening. The recovered coarse shale is conveyed back to the grinder. Shale with the desired top size may then be pneumatically transported to a feed hopper or standpipe.

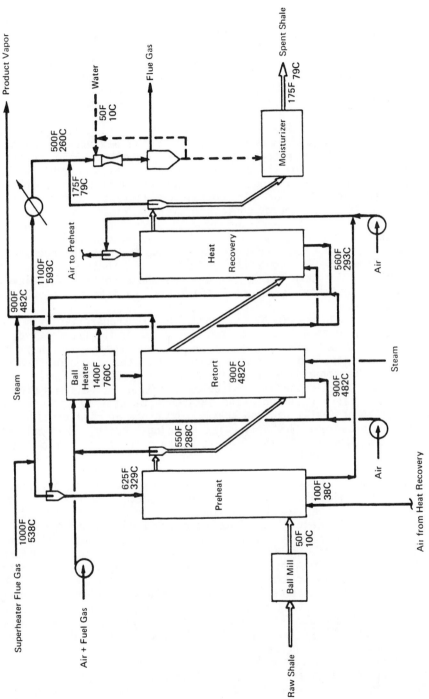

Figure 4. *Raining ball oil shale pyrolysis scheme*

Preheater.   Figure 2 is a schematic of the preheat section.
Ground raw shale is allowed to slide into or is pneumatically transported (a minimal volume flow) into the lower part of the preheater.
A standpipe of shale serves as a resistance seal to purging gas and
allows the preheater to be pressurized by transporting gas. Although
a slide valve near the bottom of the standpipe should provide adequate
flow control for the shale, a flapper valve, screw feeder, or rotary
lock may be considered as options.
    The shale is carried up, countercurrent to the raining pellets,
as a fast-fluidized bed by compressed gas (air or mixtures of air and
flue gas or recycle process gas).   The preheated shale is then
recovered at the top of the preheater in high-efficiency, high-load
cyclones.   Extremely fine dust may be carried by elutriation to the
ball heater when air or air containing mixtures are used for
conveying. Thus, the energy content of even the finest shale dust can
be recovered without requiring expensive dust-control equipment
during the preparation of shale for retorting. As conceived, the use
of standpipes and proper routing gas streams reduces the necessary
number of air and gas compressors and also aids in heat recovery. In
this fashion, pressure balance across the whole system is achieved
with sufficient extra pressure differential available for process
control.
    Warm ($\sim$625°F, $\sim$330°C) balls, pneumatically transported from the
heat recovery section, are recovered at the top of the preheater by a
cyclonic separator into a surge hopper.   From the hopper they are
admitted in controlled flow to the upper part of the preheater through
an appropriate control valve and steam purge system. A conical (or
other shaped) deflector is desirable to disperse the ball stream
uniformly.   Balls fall under the influence of gravity against the
rising steam of fast-fluidized shale. The range of conditions under
which countercurrent flow will exist is being studied. The smallest
balls, i.e., those with the highest surface-to-volume ratio, that
will fall sufficiently fast through the preheater at an economical
shale mass flux are desirable for effective heat exchange.
    Balls collecting at the bottom of the preheater in an appro-
priately dimensioned boot are stripped of shale particles by elutriating gas.   Under ideal conditions, the largest shale particles
that can be readily elutriated from between the pellets are about half
the size of the pellets. In practice the separation is more efficient
when the ball/shale size ratio is 4-5. Balls drop by controlled flow
into a transport line where they are pneumatically conveyed to the
shale heat recovery section.
    The countercurrent raining-ball/fast-fluidized flow regime must
be operated so that staging is effected, i.e., backmixing must be
effectively retarded. Temperature approaches were initially assumed
to be 75°F (42°C) at the top and 50°F (28°C) at the bottom of the
preheat vessel. Any increase in holdup of the balls in contact with
shale will reduce the height of vessel required. Increased staging
and holdup of balls are both accomplished by a system of baffles
and/or grid plates. With such designs it is important to avoid dead

hot spots where shale might accumulate because spontaneous ignition
of shale might occur if air is used as the transporting gas.

Due to vaporization of water in the preheater it may be desirable
to increase the diameter of the preheater with increasing height to
maintain relatively constant flow conditions. At proposed preheater
temperatures, the short residence time in the preheater should allow
air to be used as a transporting gas without spontaneous ignition and
with little shale degradation and yield loss. Dilution of transport
air with flue gas may be used to permit a higher preheating
temperature without ignition. The use of air as the entraining gas in
the preheater permits the finest oil shale dust and any prematurely
evolved hydrocarbons to be economically burned in the ball heater.
Thus, combustion air is also preheated in the shale preheater. By
operating the preheater in counterflow with a temperature approach
of ≤ 100°F (55°C), overheating of small particles is avoided.

Retort.   Figure 3 depicts the retort section of the raining
pellet process.

Shale entrained from the preheater is fed to the lower portion of
the retort through a high-load, high-efficiency separater and surge
hopper (with aeration).   The shale feed rate to the retort is
controlled in the same way as it is to the preheater.

Steam or gas injection is required at the bottom of the retort to
start the fluidization. However, some or all of this gas may be first
used in the ball stripping section. Vapor emitted by retorting adds
greatly to the volumetric flow of fluidizing gas as it rises up
through the retort.   The vessel cross-section is increased accordingly to maintain constant conditions for the dense fluidized
bed.

Hot heat carrying balls (at about 1400°F, 760°C) are added to the
top of the retort in the same manner as they are to the preheater, but
in separater streams to different levels in the retort. This avoids
overheating (and cracking) at the top of the retort.   The ball
diameters should be about 1/4-inch (6 mm) to assure a reasonable fall
velocity (0.25 fps, 0.087 m/s) through the dense-phase fluidized bed
of shale.

The balls collect in a boot at the bottom of the retort and are
stripped of shale fines in an elutriating section. Superheated steam
(1200°F, 650°C) provides both the stripping action and the feed shale
fluidizing action.   The cooled balls (900°F, 480°C) are then
recirculated pneumatically to the ball heater for reheating. Air for
the ball lift is combined with air from the preheater cyclones and
with a third air/fuel-gas stream to provide the desired fuel mixture
for the ball heater.

Processed shale is removed at the top of the retort. A cir-
cumferential weir is provided to maintain a constant bed height in the
upper stage. Entrained shale particles are removed from the product
vapor by high-efficiency cyclones located in the vapor disengagement
section. The dimensions of this top section area, in fact, determined
by the cyclone configuration. Superheated steam (1200°F, 650°C) is

injected in an effort to eliminate condensation coking in the vapor section.

Adsorbed and entrained vapors are removed from the retorted shale by steam in the spent shale stripper. Stripped shale is sent to the heat recovery section. The overhead products from the spent shale stripper are combined with the retort vapors and are further superheated with steam to reduce condensation coking and quenched with fractionator bottoms in a quench tower.

Staging of the retort can reduce the average residence time required for a given hydrocarbon yield. This staging could be achieved by adding restrictive horizontal grids spaced, for example, at ten-foot intervals of height. However, since staging may also introduce an unwanted temperature gradient across the retort, a single-stage design may be favored.

Pyrolysis data indicate that a relatively long (several minutes) residence time is required for the retorting reaction.[4] Hence, heat transfer is not limiting in the retort and larger balls with a lower surface-to-volume ratio may be used. Larger balls are desirable because, inter alia, their manufacturing cost is less. The maximum ball diameter is limited by the ability to transport them pneumatically and by their settling velocity through the fluidized bed of shale. Thermal shock could also be a factor that limits ball size. About 1/4-inch (6 mm) diameter balls may be a good compromise on size, as mentioned above.

Ball Heater. The ball heater can be a moving bed, a raining pellet or an entrained flow design. Preheated air from the ball lift pipe plus air from the preheater and supplemental air and fuel form the combustion mixture used to heat the balls. Ball heater flue gas is routed partly to a waste heat boiler to recover energy in the form of high-pressure steam and partly to other vessels in the process to serve as a transport gas. Cooled gases are then scrubbed to remove both particulates and any sulfur oxides. The particulate shale dust naturally absorbs sulfur oxides in the wet scrubber. Exiting hot balls return to the retort through several feed standpipes.

Heat Recovery. The heat recovery section is similar to the preheat sections.

Fast-fluidized retorted shale is cooled from 990°F (482°C) to about 175°F (79°C) by contacting it countercurrently with balls from the preheat section. Since the conveying (flue) gas is cooled and contracts as it rises, it may be desirable to reduce the vessel size accordingly in the upper portion to maintain the desired flow rate of gas.

Elutriated cooled shale is separated in a high-efficiency separator and routed to a moisturizer in preparation for disposal. Gas from the heat recovery unit is water washed in a venturi scrubber and excess water from the scrubber is used in the moisturizer. Little water vapor is generated in scrubbing the gas and wetting the spent shale because the outlet temperature of the heat recovery unit is low

($175^{\circ}F$, $79^{\circ}C$). Water usage in the SPHER process is, therefore, desirably low.

Problem Areas

Since SPHER represents the application of new regimes of fluidization to shale retorting, there are a number of questions that must be answered and factors that must be quantified. Some have been answered by simple experiments, the results of which would indicate either a "go" or a "no go" on future work, and some factors will eventually require demonstration plant operation under design conditions to prove the process. Factors of primary concern are discussed below.

Heat Transfer Rates. Process evaluations have used a rate coefficient of 90 Btu/sq ft/hr $^{\circ}F$ (0.51 kw/m^2/$^{\circ}C$), based upon the surface area of the balls. Literature data on transfer from fluidized beds to submerged objects indicate that even higher rates have been achieved, but these high rates are functions of bed density and the size of the fluidized particles. Data directly applicable to the SPHER system are required for final evaluations and designs.

Flow Regimes. The countercurrent flow of pellets relative to the fast-fluidized shale and its fluidizing gas suggests the existence of limiting or flooding velocities. The impingement of shale particles upon pellets (knockback effect) retards the upward flow of shale as well as the fall of the pellets. The size of the effect is different in dense-bed and fast-fluidized regimes. In dense beds, the falling velocity of pellets will be about 1/4 fps (0.08 m/s) while in the fast-fluidized bed the falling velocity is expected to be larger. Operational windows and pressure drop/holdup equations must be defined. These phenomena have been investigated on the 7-1/2-inch (19 cm) diameter cold-flow unit. Shale flux rates of 10 lb/sec/ft^2 (49 kg/sec/m^2) and ball flux rate of 15 lb/sec/ft^2 (73 kg/sec/m^2) were achieved at superficial gas velocities of 15 to 20 ft/sec (4.6 to 6.1 m/s).

Staging. Efficient use of heat and, to a lesser extent retorting yield, require some countercurrent staging to achieve the economic advantages expected for the SPHER process. About six stages are desired for the preheater, four in the heat recovery section and two or three stages may be desired in the retort.

Gas-fluidized beds are basically unstable and they tend to have a high degree of backmixing due to circulation patterns caused by rising gas bubbles. Beds with a large height-to-diameter ratio (L/D) tend to restrict this circulation and increase the staging of fluidized solids. For example, the Shell's Anacortes CCU regenerator (L/D $\cong$ 2.5) performs with about four solids mixing stages.

Pneumatic lift pipes (risers) for solids do not exhibit large eddy mixing currents but they do have radial velocity profiles that peak toward the center of the pipe. It is even possible (at lower velocities) for solids in risers to flow down along the wall. Catalytic cracking feed risers (L/D $\cong$ 20) exhibit four to six solids mixing stages. The velocity profile flattens (approaches plug flow) with increasing pipe diameter but becomes more peaked with increased solids loading and decreased velocity.

Determination of staging and mixing of solids in the raining pellet system may require large test facilities.

Agglomeration and Defluidization. Two possible problems arise: (1) ground shale containing a sizeable fraction of 1/16-inch-or-less (1.6 mm) particles will segregate into coarse and fine layers, even under moderate fluidization conditions, and (2) the ground shale might become tacky, due to the presence of liquids on the shale surface under retort conditions, and defluidize by agglomeration.

The question of agglomeration needs further resolution. Small scale experiments indicated direct vaporization of shale oil occurred during retorting and no agglomeration tendencies were noted. However, agglomeration could take place in cold spots where hydrocarbon condensation might occur. Two requirements of retort design are to avoid cold spots and to provide sufficient mixing of fresh shale with inerts (i.e., with spent shale) to prevent agglomeration.

Overheating and Ignition. Air was originally conceived as the preheater gas for transporting shale but use of an inert gas may be preferred. If shale is heated in air to a temperature where retorting proceeds, then a combustible mixture is formed and ignition can occur. At atmospheric pressure this occurs at about 630°F (332°C). Local stagnation zones of shale near the ball inlet should be avoided because they might lead to such a condition. Dilution with an inert gas or use of another gas as a carrier may be preferred because both will permit a broader range of operation without the possibility of shale ignition.

Pressure Balance - Operability. Overall operation, as in catalytic cracking, depends on use of standpipes to generate the pressure differentials necessary to cause shale and balls to flow into the process vessels. Excess pressures are taken out by slide valve control which also dampens the transfer of pressure surges between vessels.

The high permeability of the standpipe material, especially of the spheres or pellets, will allow appreciable gas leakage. Adequate purge gases in the standpipe will, therefore, be required.

Ball Separation and Recovery. The raining balls must be stripped free of shale before being removed from a vessel. This can be most readily done by use of a stripping gas at relatively high velocity ($\geq$ 10 fps, 3 m/s) in a ball-collection boot. This might be a large fraction of the fluidizing gas in a vessel and reduces the quantity of gas available for transferring shale into the vessel above the boot.

Generation of Fines and Entrainment of Shale.   Although retorting of shale does not, in itself, generate fines it does weaken the particles so that they are more readily attritable. Particle size distribution reported for a fluidized bed process is listed in Table 1. This potential generation of fines may not be serious for SPHER since operation will be once through for the shale and residence time in vessels with fluidized beds is only a few minutes.

Entrainment of shale in gas in the preheat and heat recovery sections is the basic mode of transport for shale. In the retort, excessive entrainment reduce the residence time below that needed for retorting and extra steps may be required for returning shale fines to the retort.

In all cases, high-load and high-efficiency (cyclone) separators will be required to prevent excessive carryover of shale in gas streams to other portions of the process. These recovered fines may need to be recycled to the appropriate vessels in order to insure the proper concentration of fines for smooth fluidization.

Choice of Ball Material.   The purpose of the balls is to provide a means of conveying and exchanging highly concentrated heat energy. Thus, they should have a high external surface area (i.e., a small diameter) and a high heat capacity. However, they must be large enough to be readily separable from the shale. For ease of separation they should have a high density. Table 2 lists some properties of candidate materials. Other factors to consider include cost and resistance to corrosion, abrasion and thermal shock. The quality of a material such as alumina is highly dependent upon its method of manufacture and the suitability of specific aluminas must be defined.

Erosion/Attrition/Thermal Shock.   The high velocities of balls in lift pipes and the turbulent nature of the fluidized beds lead to the possibility of erosion of the equipment and attrition or fracturing of the balls. Erosion can be reduced by using abrasion resistant refractory linings in pipes. Attrition and fracturing of balls can be reduced by proper design to reduce the effect of impaction at elbows and on deflection plates.

Breakage by thermal shock is reduced by countercurrent operation, which allows reduced temperature gradients, and by a small ball size, which reduces thermal stresses.

Conclusions

As with most newly conceived processes there is considerable development work to be done before SPHER is a mature process. This

TABLE 1. PARTICLE SIZE DISTRIBUTIONS OF SHALE RETORTED BY
          FLUIDIZED BED TECHNIQUES.

Fluidized Spent Shale[a]

Size Range, μ	Percent
0-20	<25
20-60	5-15
60-200	20-50
200-400	20-30
<400	< 5

a) See Reference No. 5

TABLE 2. PROPERTIES AND CIRCULATION RATES OF CANDIDATE MATERIALS
          FOR OUTER BALL LOOP.

Material	Density		Heat Capacity		
	lb/ft^3	t/m^3	Btu/Lb^{o}F	Btu/Ft^3 ^{o}F	Kcal/m^3 ^{o}C
High Density Alumina (ceramic balls used by Tosco)	231	3.70	0.22	50.8	814
Aluminum	168	2.69	0.23	38.8	622
Steel	487	7.80	0.12	58.4	935
Lead	686	10.99	0.03	20.6	330
Gravel	156	2.50	0.2	31.2	500

report serves to present the basic features of SPHER and to point up some areas requiring development work.

Abstract

The concept of a novel retorting process for the recovery of hydrocarbonaceous fluids from particulate solids, especially oil shale, is described. In this process, heat is transferred between fluidized shale and heat-carrier pellets, raining in countercurrent flow in a preheater, a retort, and a heat recovery vessel.

The desirability of this process results from a high heat flux and efficient countercurrent heat recovery from the spent shale. This, in turn, results in a thermally efficient plant of relatively small size and low capital expense.

The process is also adaptable to similar uses with other feed materials; for example, the devolatilization of coal and lignites.

New regions of fluidization technology and rapid pyrolysis are envisioned and some developments of these regions are covered. This report further discusses the basic features of the conceptual process and potential problem area.

References

1. Hendrickson, T. A., Quarterly of Colorado School of Mines 69(2):45 (1974).
2. U.S. Patent No. 4,110,193, dated August 29, 1978.
3. Allred, V. B., Quarterly of Colorado School of Mines 59(3):56 (1964).
4. Hinds, G. P. Jr., AIChE Annual Mtg., Miami, Nov. 1978.
5. U.S. Patent No. 2,717,869, dated September 13, 1955.

RECEIVED January 19, 1981.

Retorted Oil Shale Disposal Research

R. N. HEISTAND

Paraho Development Corporation, Box A, Anvil Points, Rifle, CO 81650

In the quest for alternate energy sources, oil shale appears particularly attractive because of the large domestic deposits and because the retorting process produces liquid and gaseous fuels directly. However, the retorting process also produces large quantities of retorted shale which could pose a potentially adverse environmental impact if not disposed of properly. A mature, million-barrel-per-day oil shale industry would produce over one-and-one quarter million tonnes of retorted shale during each day of operation.

Although the retorted, or processed, shale represents the largest by-product from oil shale retorting operations, results from detailed studies indicate that it can be managed in an environmentally acceptable manner. Laboratory and field tests have demonstrated the following properties: compaction to 1600 kg/m^3, using normal vehicular traffic; cementation strength to 1480 kPa, using only retorted shale and optimum water; permeabilities as low as 1×10^{-7} cm/s, using proper handling techniques. In addition, tests have shown that dusting, auto-ignition, and leaching pose no special problems. These research results indicate that properly managed retorted shale exhibits the properties of a low-grade cement.

Although the nature of retorted shale certainly depends upon the nature of the geological deposit from which the raw oil shale was mined, it depends, to a large extent, also upon the retorting technology used to process the raw oil shale. The information presented in this paper is obtained from the Paraho Oil Shale Demonstration carried out from 1973 to 1976 ([1]).

The Paraho semi-works retort is a cylindrical vessel, having a 2.5 m internal diameter and is capable of processing about 250-300 tonnes of raw oil shale per day. A schematic of the Paraho direct mode operations is shown in Figure 1. Raw shale, crushed and screened to +1.0 cm to -10.0 cm, enters the top of the retort, passes through the retort under the influence

0097–6156/81/0163–0183$05.00/0

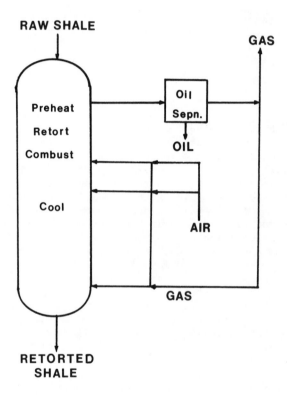

Figure 1.   Paraho direct mode operation

of gravity and controlled by the grate mechanism at the bottom.
The retorted shale still contains many of the larger, +5.0 cm to
-10.0 cm, pieces. This range in particle size found in the
retorted shale enhances its strength properties and minimizes
dusting while handling. The Paraho process uses counter-current
flows -- solids moving downward and gases moving upward. As the
shale moves downward through the retort, it passes through four
distinct zones as shown in Figure 1. The uppermost is the mist
formation zone where the shale is preheated by the rising gases
to retorting zone. In the next zone, the retorting zone, the
shale is heated so that its solid organic component, kerogen,
breaks down to form gas, oil and residual carbon, or coke. The
oil and gas are swept upward out of the retort to the oil-gas
separation equipment.

The shale enters the combustion zone where most of the coke
is burned to supply process heat. This reduces the organic
carbon in the retorted shale to approximately 2 wt%. Air,
diluted with recycle gas, assures even distribution of oxygen
across the shale bed and dilutes the oxygen to control the flame
temperature. One important feature of this combustion zone in
the Paraho process is the two-level distribution system. This
system assures sufficient heat for retorting while keeping the
combustion temperatures low enough to avoid excessive carbonate
decomposition. This carbonate decomposition wastes valuable
heat and energy through endothermic reactions and produces a
retorted shale higher in water-soluble oxides which would
increase leaching tendencies and cause a leachate higher in pH
and salt content. The shale finally enters the cooling zone
where it is cooled with recycle gas before it is discharged
from the retort. Within this zone the retorted shale reacts
with most of the hydrogen sulfide in the recycle gas. This
reduces sulfur emissions when a portion of this gas is utilized
and forms a variety of sulfur compounds in the retorted shale.
These sulfur compounds reduce the oxide content and promote
strength through cementation reactions. More thorough descriptions of the Paraho technology and the composition of the
retort products have been published previously (2,3).

Most of the material used in the retorted shale disposal
research was produced by the Paraho semi-works retort operating
in the direct mode operation. Another mode of operation, an
indirect mode, was also studied. In the indirect mode, air is
not introduced into the retort. Internal combustion does not
occur; none of the organic carbon remaining on the retorted
shale is utilized. Process heat for the indirect mode operation
is supplied by heating the recycle gas in an external heater.

During the recent Paraho operations, the potential problem
of retorted shale disposal was recognized. A seven-stage
retorted shale research program, jointly supported by the U. S.
Bureau of Mines, was carried out using both laboratory and field
studies (4). Highlights of this retorted shale research program

showed that retorted oil shale, produced by the Paraho process, can be effectively compacted and handled to produce strong and water impervious structures(5). These desirable properties of Paraho retorted shale are believed due to the formation of a low-grade cement by chemical reactions which occur during retorting.

In this paper the chemistry of Paraho retorted shale, the nature of the thermo-chemical reactions that can contribute to its cement-like properties, and the chemistry of the leachates obtained from permeability studies will be presented. Although civil engineering information now exists which permits the disposal of retorted shale in an environmentally acceptable manner, a better understanding of the thermal reactions of retorting and the chemical composition of retorted shale may suggest changes in retorting operations which would further lessen any possibly adverse environmental impact.

Experiment Design

Because the disposal of retorted shale is, ultimately, a field exercise, this paper will discuss the experimental design and data from field studies which have been carried out. Laboratory experimentation and data will be used to complement the results of field studies. Two field studies, compaction and permeability, were carried out during the Paraho research operations.

The field compaction studies were carried out in a relatively flat area, 2-3 km from the retorting operations (see Figure 2). The compaction site, measuring 55 m wide by 120 m long, was divided into two sections. In one section the retorted shale was placed dry; in the other, optimum water was added before placement. The material was hauled directly from the retorted shale disposal system and spread as soon as possible. No problems with dusting or auto-ignition were noted. The material was spread in 20-30 cm layers and subjected to various compactive efforts. Approximately 1200 m^3 (15000 tonnes) of retorted shale was used in these field compaction studies.

The field infiltration studies were carried out near the retorting operations. Two shallow ponds, 25 m diameter, were constructed using techniques developed during the earlier field compaction studies (see Figure 3). Both ponds were constructed out of Paraho retorted shale placed in layers to an overall thickness about 1 m. Both ponds had sloping sidewalls to obviate wall effects and to eliminate any wall-bottom interface. One pond was constructed with dry retorted shale using light compaction. The other pond was constructed of retorted shale, mixed with optimum water, and placed using heavy compaction. After construction, both ponds were filled with water and the infiltration rates were measured using staff gauges and flows through the drain lines.

U.S. Bureau of Mines

Figure 2.   Field compaction area

U.S. Bureau of Mines

Figure 3.   Field infiltration area

Results and Discussion

   Compaction. The field compaction studies confirmed earlier
laboratory studies regarding the effect of compactive effort,
moisture addition, and aging on density and strength. Shown in
Figure 4 is the relationship of compactive effort on the densities of retorted shale. At least three in-place density
measurements were made in each layer. Results show that densities averaging 1400 kg/m^3 (about 95 lb/cu. ft.) can be achieved.
   Optimum water is needed to achieve optimum strength. The
addition of water does not improve compactability. The strength
of the compacted retorted shale was measured using unconfined
compression(6). The relationship between this strength data and
added moisture at various seasoning times is shown in Figure 5.
The remarkable strength increase obtained with the addition of
optimum water indicates the occurrence of some sort of cementing
reaction. Further evidence of this cementing reaction is
apparent where the compressive strength gains with aging. Aging
60 days after the addition of optimum water produced compressive
strengths of nearly 1500 kPa (205 psi). The retorted shale
produced by indirect heat operations shows no strength.
   Infiltration. Infiltration data for the two ponds are
listed in Table I. Also listed are in-place and core densities,

TABLE I

FIELD INFILTRATION ANALYSIS

	Pond I		Pond II
	Initial	Cores	Initial
Moisture, wt%	22.1	18.5	0.0
Density, Bottom kg/m^3	1602	1697	1474
Sides kg/m^3	1602		1394
Strength, kPa		1482	
Permeability, cm/sec x 10^{-6}	0.3	0.6	2000

moisture contents, and compressive strengths. These data show
that Pond I (high compaction, optimum water) was well-
constructed. Densities matched those achieved in earlier laboratory and field compaction tests. The strength, measured in a
core sample (1480 kPa), exceeded those achieved during those
earlier tests. The field permeability, as measured by staff
gauge, when corrected for initial absorption and normal evaporation, approaches the value obtained from analysis of the core
(6 x 10^{-7} cm/s). Actual infiltration from the highly compacted
pond shows the permeation rate to be 3 x 10^{-7} cm/s.
   Pond II, receiving only light compaction and no added water,
shows a permeability rate of 2 x 10^{-4} cm/s. Although the

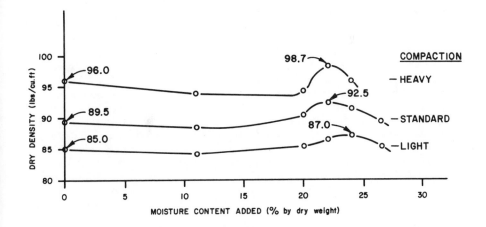

U.S. Bureau of Mines

*Figure 4.   Compaction test results. Paraho retorted shale, semiworks plant—
direct heat; 1.5-in. maximum size fraction.*

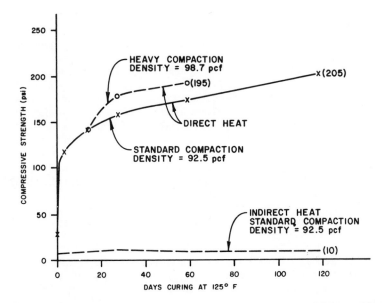

U.S. Bureau of Mines

*Figure 5.   Compression test results. Paraho retorted shale, semiworks plant;
.75-in. maximum size fraction.*

permeability of this material is quite high, effluents could be
contained in a disposal area using properly-placed, well-
constructed material such as used in Pond I. Even though the
loosely compacted Pond I exhibited a high permeability rate, an
additional field experiment indicated that permeability may not
pose a serious problem. After Pond II (light compaction) had
dried thoroughly for several months following the field infiltration test, a special test was conducted. The surface was
sprayed with 17,400 ℓ of water to represent a rainfall of 5 cm
in 30 minutes. No effluent occurred for nearly one full day. A
small seepage began the second day and continued for two days.
Only 7 ℓ were collected from the drain pipe. Essentially all of
the simulated rainfall was lost to absorption and subsequent
evaporation. This indicates that leaching and permeability may
not be a problem for Paraho retorted shale, even when lightly
compacted, because even heavy rainfall will not penetrate the
pile to significant depths.

   Chemical and Physical Properties. Paraho retorted shale is
described according to standard soils classification as a
silty-gravelly material(4). A size distribution diagram is
presented in Figure 6. Some of the favorable properties of the
retorted shale is attributed to this size distribution - like a
good aggregate mix, this material has the proper ratio of fines
to larger sized pieces so that voids between the larger
pieces are filled with fines. This relationship increases
density, promotes strength, and reduces dusting and erosion.
The chemical composition of retorted shale depends on the
composition of the raw shale and the retorting process. The
mineral composition of the Green River shale used in the Paraho
operations consists of a complex mixture of minerals. These
include: carbonates (50%), clays (40%), quartz (8%), and sulfides and others (2%). The principal carbonate mineral
undergoing thermal reactions during the normal retort conditions
is dolomite ($CaCO_3 \cdot MgCO_3$), or more properly ferroan ($CaCO_3 \cdot Fe_x$,
$Mg_{1-x}CO_3$) where a portion of the magnesium is replaced by iron.
It is believed that ferroan undergoes the following chemical
reaction during normal retorting conditions:

   (1) Ferroan + Heat $\rightarrow$ Calcite ($CaCO_3$) + Magnesia (MgO)
       + FeO + CO_2

   Many studies have been made concerning the mean chemical
analysis of Paraho retorted shale(7). Although it is important
to know this chemical composition, it is not helpful in assess-
ing the components responsible for the cement-like properties.
Much emphasis has been placed upon the formation of reactive
oxides, such as free lime and magnesia, from carbonate decomposition. Although free lime can be formed under laboratory
conditions(8), it has not been detected in the retorted shale
used in the field studies. Although free lime was not detected,

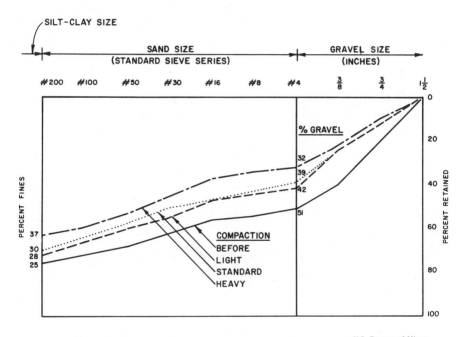

U.S. Bureau of Mines

Figure 6.   Gradation data. Paraho retorted shale, semiworks plant—direct heat;
1.5-in. maximum size fraction.

magnesia has been found in Paraho retorted shale. Sulfur
minerals, known to exhibit cement-like properties, have been
found in Paraho retorted shale(4). These include: anhydrite
($CaSO_4$), bassanite ($CaSO_4 \cdot 0.5H_2O$), gypsum ($CaSO_4 \cdot 2H_2O$). These
sulfur minerals present in the retorted shale may be there as a
result of the raw shale composition or as a result of absorption
of hydrogen sulfide by the retorted shale. It is believed that
the magnesia and sulfur minerals are responsible for the cement-
like properties of the Paraho retorted shale.

Many studies have been carried out concerning the analysis
of leachates from retorted shale. Results from these studies
are highly dependent upon the procedure that is employed. Listed
in Table II are some of the leachate data obtained during the

TABLE II

INITIAL LEACHATE COMPOSITION

	Loose Fill	Compacted
Permeation Rate, cm/sec	3.0×10^{-5}	3.2×10^{-6}
pH, pH Units	7.5	7.8
TDS, ppt	6.9	9.2
Calcium	407	157
Magnesium	47	37
Iron	0.05	0.07
Aluminum	< 0.05	< 0.05
Silicon	5	10
Sodium	1300	3200
Potassium	325	500
Chloride	580	790
Sulfate	3330	4320
Carbonate	19	66

All data in mg/ℓ except as noted.

retorted shale studies(4). As the compaction is increased, the
column experiments show that the leachate concentration is
increased, but the total amount leached is decreased. Another
experiment showed that leaching diminishes as the leachate is
recirculated. This indicates that leaching should not proceed
to great depths in a retorted shale disposal area. Batch experiments indicate that about 1 wt% of material is extracted from
the retorted shale. This meets established engineering
standards(4).

Data shown in Table II consists of materials which can contribute to salinity, toxic elements had not been considered. More recently, the U. S. Environmental Protection Agency has proposed an extraction procedure to determine hazardous wastes. Results obtained using the proposed EPA extraction procedure are shown in Table III for Paraho retorted shale. The low

TABLE III

LEACHATE DATA
EPA EXTRACTION

Arsenic	<	0.1	ppm
Barium	<	10	ppm
Cadmium	<	0.05	ppm
Chromium	<	1	ppm
Mercury		14	ppb
Lead		220	ppb
Selenium		23	ppb
Silver		30	ppb

concentrations shown in Table III indicate that this material is not a hazardous waste as indicated by the U. S. EPA. These low concentrations of toxic materials found in leachates from Paraho retorted shale using the proposed U. S. EPA extraction procedure would not be increased to hazardous levels if all of these materials normally present in the retorted shale were solubilized.

Conclusions

Detailed laboratory and field studies have shown that Paraho retorted shale can be compacted easily; is not subject to dusting, erosion, or auto-ignition; and can be handled to create structures of very low permeability. A basis for these beneficial properties can be found, in part, by an examination of the chemical and physical properties of the retorted shale. For example, it is believed that the strengths achieved are caused by the hydration of magnesia, reactions of the gypsum minerals, and the compaction of the silty-gravel mix.

However, more studies are needed to further define these chemical and physical properties. Results from these additional studies can further reduce the possibility of any potentially adverse impact from retorted shale disposal.

Acknowledgement

The retorted shale research studies discussed in this paper were carried out at the U. S. Department of Energy Anvil Points Research Facility located on the Naval Oil Shale Reserves Nos. 1 and 3 near Rifle, Colorado.

Literature Cited

1. Pforzheimer, H., Jr., "The Paraho Oil Shale Demonstration - A 1975 Progress Report," Oil Shale - Tar Sand Symposium, American Institute of Chemical Engineers, National Meeting, Los Angeles, CA, November 1976.
2. Jones, J. B., Jr., "The Paraho Oil Shale Retort," 9th Oil Shale Symposium, Colorado School of Mines, Golden, CO, 1976.
3. Jones, J. B., Jr. and Heistand, R. N., "Recent Paraho Operations," 12th Oil Shale Symposium, Colorado School of Mines, Golden, CO, 1979.
4. Holtz, W. G., "Disposal of Retorted Shale from the Paraho Oil Shale Project," U.S. Department of Interior, Bureau of Mines, J0255004, 1976.
5. Heistand, R. N. and Holtz, W. G., "Retorted Shale Research," 13th Oil Shale Symposium, Colorado School of Mines, Golden, CO, 1980.
6. American Society for Testing and Materials, "ASTM Standards," Parts 10 and 19, ASTM, Philadelphia, PA, 1974.
7. Heistand, R. N., Atwood, R. A., and Richardson, K. L., "Paraho Environmental Data; Part I, Process Characterization; Part II, Air Quality; Part III, Water Quality," U. S. Department of Energy, DOE/EV 0086, UC-66e & 91, 1980.
8. Heistand, R. N., Jones, D. B. and Morriss, L. M., "Free Lime in Retorted Shale," Energy Sources, 4, 195-202, 1978.
9. U.S. Environmental Protection Agency, "Hazardous Waste Management System," Federal Register, 45, (98), 33063-33285, May 19, 1980.

RECEIVED January 14, 1981.

An Investigation into the Potential Economics of Large-Scale Shale Oil Production (1)

BEN C. BALL, JR.

Adjunct Professor of Management and Engineering, Massachusetts Institute of Technology, Cambridge, MA 02139

If there is any aspect of energy upon which most informed people agree, it is that our nation's increasing reliance on foreign petroleum is not good for the United States. The unfavorable nature of that dependence may be seen as arising from national security, foreign policy considerations, and as stemming from strictly economic effects.

There is less agreement about which alternatives are less objectionable for the United States than importing so much oil. One broad alternative is to increase supplies of domestic substitute liquids like coal liquids or/and shale oil.

The debate over the alternatives has been exhaustive and public. Unhappily, all the alternatives seem to have significant difficulties associated with them.

Interest in shale oil is motivated largely by the enormous size of oil shale deposits in the United States. A further reason for interest in oil shale processing is that processes for the production of liquid fuels from oil shale appear cheaper than those that start from coal (2). This is primarily because oil shale contains a very much higher ratio of hydrogen to carbon, and process costs tend to correlate directly with the increase in the net H/C ratio required. This cost advantage is somewhat offset by increased materials handling required by shale. But, on balance, it is expected that most <u>liquid</u> synfuels will be produced from shale (3).

Industry seemingly does not regard shale oil ventures as attractive now. Dissatisfaction is most frequently expressed in terms of "non-economic" barriers - innumerable permits, changing environmental regulations, tax and pricing uncertainties, lease limitations, water rights conflicts, and legal challenges. The crucial barrier is the fact that shale oil simply costs more than imported oil. If shale oil cost less, we would probably see more determined and more successful efforts by both industry and government to surmount the non-economic barriers. ("Non-economic" is shorthand, of course; there are costs, often large ones, resulting from those barriers.)

0097–6156/81/0163–0195$06.75/0

Industry's continued interest in shale oil, despite its current unattractiveness, is sustained primarily by the belief that the real cost of imported oil will continue to rise and ultimately surpass shale oil at some unpredictable future date. Government assistance is sought by industry before that date on the grounds that: a) there is a public value, which cannot be directly captured by a company undertaking a shale oil venture now, in reducing imported oil and b) there is need for an immediate start in order to have significant shale oil production in place when the cost curves do intersect.

A secondary reason for industry's continued interest is the belief that the real cost of producing shale oil may be reduced through technological improvement. (There are quite different views on the prospects for reducing cost through improvement of current technologies. For example, Merrow ("Constraints on the Commercialization of Oil Shale", Rand/R-2293-DOE, September, 1978) is pessimistic, but Hutchins ("Oil Shale 1979", presented at the Twelfth Annual Oil Shale Symposium, April, 1979) is optimistic.) That belief raises the issue of how the process of technological change occurs, and what the consequences might be for two different paths of the shale oil industry. One set of consequences would result from the industry following the usual evolutionary path; a different set of consequences would result from an "industry-in-place" path.

Shale oil studies in both the private and public sectors have emphasized what we call here an "evolutionary" approach. Costs are estimated for a single plant by looking at one installation as a totality within itself, not as part of a complex, such as an industrial park, or as a shale oil industry. It is not clear whether the "evolutionary" approach is an oversimplification that tends to result in costs that are too high or too low, on the average, for a whole industry. In some ways, this approach is the cheapest. For example, the highest quality shale would be mined first, and the lowest-cost water would be used first; local environmental pollution would be lowest with the first plants; demand for labor and steel would be limited and would not drive up price levels.

However, other economies would result from the existence of a cluster of plants. For example, a separate grass-roots community need not be built for each plant - one larger (lower unit cost) community could serve several plants; product transportation costs would be lower for an industry pipeline than for any mode scaled for a single plant; unit equipment manufacturing costs would be lower if many units were replicated.

This latter set of possibilities encourages us to raise the question of the economics of an industry, once in place. Might not a shale oil industry be the beneficiary of economies that simply would not be applicable to a single plant. Might these economies by significant? Might an industry be viable whereas a plant or a few plants might not be? Investigating the fruitfulness of this line of thinking is the purpose of this study. The questions we are raising are of the kind one might ask when reflecting on U.S. shipbuilding dynamics early in World War II: the decision to build several Liberty ships a week resulted in structural and technical changes that permitted economies that simply were not possible when shipbuilding was considered a one-at-a-time process.

The present study attempts to contribute to the consideration of oil shale as a serious option by identifying technological opportunities to reduce substantially the costs of producing shale oil on a large scale, such as 2-5 million barrels/day as opposed to a small scale of an individual shale oil project of 50-100 MB/D. These opportunities involve the application of existing technology which has not been seriously considered on a small scale and the development of new technology which looks reasonably susceptible to successful development and which would have important impact on a large scale.   To focus on the questions suggested above, we note but do not consider a number of other important issues, though we recognize that they may well be controlling factors in the development of a shale oil industry in the United States.

- We do not consider how the industry will be built, but rather consider it already in place at steady state; in chemical terms, we are concerned with equilibrium rather than kinetics.
- We consider only the economic consequences of technological alternatives; we do not evaluate other alternatives, such as financial or tax devices for example, to reduce cost.
- We do not attempt to reevaluate process economics or make fine comparisons among various competing processes; we have made an effort to obtain the latest data available from the most active promoters, accepting their data at face value.
- We assume that the environmental specifications which must be met are those presently established.
- We do not take account of unique project features inapplicable on a large scale, for example, the recovery for sale of alkaline minerals along with the shale.
- We do not compare shale oil to other alternatives for reducing oil imports.
- We do not evaluate current or potential government policies affecting shale.

In other words, in this study we deliberately take a narrow technologist's view of the potential for reducing costs through technology in a large, distant-future shale oil industry.

Background

Oil shale processing has been practiced on an industrial scale since the 1860's. Much "coal oil" produced in the United States before the discovery of petroleum was in fact shale oil. Production of 2,500 B/D was maintained by the Scottish oil shale industry for long periods of time over its 100-year history. A Manchurian oil shale industry, begun in 1929, reached outputs of 35,000 B/D while under Japanese control during World War II. The Chinese expanded the Manchurian operation, and output during the Korean War is believed to have been as high as 40,000 B/D (4).

During the 1960's, shale oil R&D was being carried on by several of the major oil companies, and by The Oil Shale Company (TOSCO), newly formed expressly to become a major factor in a new shale oil industry. With the announcement of the sale of U.S. Government shale leases in Utah and Colorado in early 1974, the level of R&D was temporarily increased somewhat.

This lease sale, taking place at the height of the 1973-74 Arab oil embargo, elicited over 1/2 billion dollars in bids from several major oil companies plus TOSCO. These companies appear to have been acting largely on the belief that some combination of the following conditions would obtain: (1) world oil prices would continue to rise, and the cost of shale oil production would then be at a level that would make the industry viable at world oil prices, and/or (2) shale oil would be "needed", and therefore prices would be paid that would make its production profitable, regardless of the market prices and costs, and/or (3) the government would take whatever steps might be necessary to ensure that the necessary technology and regulatory environment would be available, and that Federal subsidies in some form would be available if needed for construction of early plants (5), and/or (4) improvements in technology or reduction of "non-economic" costs would reduce the real costs of shale oil.

Since the lease sale, each of the lessees has been conducting engineering and feasibility studies, studying environmental impact, etc., but only modest progress has been made in either the technology or the conceptual development of the shale oil industry with the possible exception of Occidental's modified in-situ process.

Technology

Oil shale processing technology is simple in principle. Oil shale contains a carbonaceous material called "kerogen". When oil shale is retorted, i.e., heated to about 900°F, the kerogen decomposes (pyrolyzes) to yield an oil (raw shale oil), gas, and residual carbon which remains in the shale. The total solid residue from retorting is known as spent shale. Typical, "rich" U.S. shales under consideration yield about 20 to 40 gallons of raw shale oil per ton of rock heated.

Research has been done on other ways of recovering shale oil from its rock, for example by extraction with solvents or by the action of microorganisms. No method other than heating has shown any real potential for commercial application.

The retorting of oil shale may be done in two general ways: above-ground or in-situ. For above-ground retorting, the shale rock is mined, crushed to appropriate sizes, and heated in steel vessels of various configurations located on the surface. For in-situ retorting, the shale rock is heated while it remains underground. (Occidental Petroleum's Modified In-Situ process, however, requires at least 20% of the shale resource to be mined and brought to the surface where it can be retorted conventionally.) Many variations of both above-ground and in-situ retorting have been investigated. Each variation has its advantages and disadvantages. No variation has been tested on a commercial scale in the United States although both above-ground and in-situ processes have been operated commercially in Scotland. No domestic shale oil project has ever exceeded 700-800 B/D - a number which can be compared with our current oil imports of 7-8,000,000 B/D.

Regardless of the retorting method used, the resulting raw shale oil is ordinarily "upgraded" to reduce contaminants - nitrogen, sulfur, and metals - so that it may then be processed further by the same techniques used to process crude petroleum.

The relatively small amount of oil recovered - roughly 10-15% by weight of the shale rock heated - means that there are substantial technical problems resulting from the sheer volume of rock that must be mined and transported to a commercial-scale processing plant which uses above-ground retorting. Furthermore, since the shale expands by as much as 50% during crushing, the volume of spent shale to be disposed of is greater than the volume of shale that was mined. Spent shale also often has a high content of alkaline minerals, a factor that must be considered in the disposal process. Interest in in-situ retorting stems largely from the fact that it can avoid handling much or all of the shale rock and spent shale handled in above-ground processes.

Oil shale processing currently requires about one to four barrels of water per barrel of shale oil produced. This water is used in the shale processing itself as well as for dust control, but the largest single amount, up to half or more of the total, is usually for environmentally acceptable disposal and revegetation of the spent shale. Water availability is a problem in the arid shale regions of the West, and opinions about its importance as a constraint on production are often expressed with intense emotion. As a result, one typical conclusion is that "...water is estimated to be the single most limiting restraint (on shale production)." (6) However, the same source points outs that Colorado water can be desalinated for about 5¢/barrel (7); at the extreme limit, fresh water can be brought to the area from 1000 miles away for well under $1/barrel (8). Also, there are other trade-offs between cost and level of water consumption. Thus, the cost of water is significant but need not be an absolute economic barrier if institutional regulations are overcome.

Technological Change

It is convenient to think of technological change occurring in five stages termed: (1) Invention, (2) Development, (3) Introduction, (4) Diffusion, and (5) Maturity. These stages are described in detail in the Appendix. The normal evolution of technology - shale oil technology as well as other technologies - would progress through each of these stages. Thus, a shale oil industry in a Maturity phase would make use of those mining, retorting, and upgrading technologies which had proved superior to competing technologies during extended commercial-scale operation in the Introduction and early Diffusion phases.

If an industry were put in place in some unspecified way, the Introduction and early Diffusion phases would be skipped. As the Appendix points out, the primary purpose of those phases is to narrow the range of cost uncertainty rather than to reduce the probable cost, although technical changes which result in reduced (or increased) cost certainly occur in those phases. Thus, the later Diffusion and Maturity phases would be entered, although with less certainty that the best technologies were being used.

A crucial question to be faced is the probability of these economies of an industry in place being greater than the diseconomies of skipping some intermediate stages. In general, the economies that might result from the industry-in-place approach fall into two categories. One is the economy of scale. An industry can solve problems more economically than individual plants and can justify the development of technology not otherwise supportable. Examples of economy-of-scale savings would include (as illustrations, not proposals):

- Mining. All or much of the Piceance Creek Basin in Colorado might be open-pit mined, with the resulting oil shale distributed to individual retorting sites.
- Combinations. An industry basis might better accommodate an optimum balance between surface and in-situ retorting.
- Infrastructure. An industry might support larger, more economical cities.
- Transportation. Pipelining the product out, for example, to existing refineries, might offer cost savings.
- Spent shale disposal may be more economical on an industry basis.
- Environmental Impact Statement. A simple EIS for the entire industry may well be more cost-effective than separate studies and statements for each plant.
- Environmental control (e.g., particulates, NO_x, SO_2) may be economical for an industry.

• Water supply and disposal could be much more practical for an industry, through such means as bringing in water from remote sources.

The other possible source of cost reduction lies in the dimension of mass production economies for the suppliers to the shale oil industry. If suppliers were to know and could count on the construction of an industry of, say, 5,000,000 B/D over a relatively short time frame, say 8 to 15 years, then perhaps economies could be realized through the planned mass production of retorts, mining machinery, pipe and valves, etc.

Mining Opportunities

Significant cost savings should be achievable in the mining operations necessary for producing shale oil on the scale considered here. However, the enormity of a mining operation moving 3 to 8 million tons per day of rock calls for innovative materials handling approaches by either identifying old technologies applicable to this new situation or developing new technologies for it. As an example, if labor productivity were not increased over the maximum current level of about 150 tons/man-shift in underground mines, the industry would need 20,000 to 50,000 underground miners - and supplying just that part of the total labor force would be an enormous problem.

The most obvious way to increase mining productivity is to mine on the surface rather than underground. Therefore, proposals to surface mine all or major portions of the Piceance Creek Basin should be reevaluated since that may be the most practical way to produce enough oil, especially considering the difficulty of attracting mining labor to the region.

A related proposal would examine the possibility of developing "surface" mines underground, i.e., large underground mines with perhaps 100-foot ceilings excavated as though they were on the surface.

There appear to be no technological barriers to the development or use, or both, of mining equipment on a much larger scale than now planned. Very large equipment - conspicuously, large-scale excavators and high-speed conveyors - has been built and operated economically, for example in surface lignite mining in Germany. Surface mining there involves stripping 900 feet (soon to be 1,600 feet) of overburden; that compares with a maximum Piceance Creek Basin overburden of about 1,800 feet overlying a maximum shale strata thickness of about 1,300 feet. Although there are no obvious technical limitations on increasing the size of mining equipment, there are two caveats: (1) size increases have to be coordinated among all elements of the mining system, and (2) continued increases in size do not invariably result in decreases in cost, i.e., some mining systems have shown that total costs (including maintenance, service factor, etc.) may be a minimum at some size less than the largest sizes tested.

Retorting in-situ is, in principle, the oil recovery strategy with potential for reducing the environmental problems and solids-handling costs of surface retorting. The key to in-situ retorting is "mining" in the sense of making the rock in place permeable so that heat can be introduced (or created) pervasively and oil (and gas) withdrawn efficiently. In practice, of the various in-situ methods hypothesized or tested, only modified in-situ (in which some rock is removed to provide void volume so that the remaining rock can be fragmented and made permeable) has commercial promise on a wide scale.

Continuous processes for in-situ or conventional mining to replace cyclic drilling/blasting/mucking would improve labor productivity and safety. Tunneling or honeycombing machines capable of handling the hard (relative to coal) shale rock are needed. Improved mining and controlled rubbling both depend on a better understanding of rock mechanics including the special case of rubbling to a controlled void in a confined volume.

A combination of in-situ and surface retorting may make best use of the shale resource in place. One can think of surface retorting the mined-out rock from a primary in-situ operation, or of in-situ retorting the rock left behind after underground mining for a primary surface operation.

Difficult environmental problems are associated with large-scale mining operations and will require solution. Coping with large aquifers above, between, and below shale strata is a major problem which may be easier to cope with on an industry scale (e.g., by grouting or dewatering on a large scale) than on a project-by-project basis. Fugitive dust is another problem, especially with surface mines. The crucial problem of spent shale disposal may be eased by high-temperature retorting which seems to reduce both the volume of and the soluble alkalis in the spent shale.

Several more speculative suggestions can be made for technologies capable of reducing mining cost significantly. A whole new in-situ system is possible. Rubbling by new methods - hydraulic cone fracture, chemical or nuclear techniques, mechanical leverage - can be hypothesized. Underwater mining could be a way of coping with major aquifer problems.

Retorting Opportunities

In-situ retorting is regarded as primarily a mining problem (see previous section) rather than a retorting problem in the usual sense. Most, though not all, improvements in in-situ retorting are expected from improved methods of preparing the retorts (tunneling, rubbling, etc.) rather than from improved methods of operating those retorts.

So far, only heating has been demonstrated to have potential for recovering oil from shale on a commercial scale. Exploratory R&D on other recovery techniques such as action of microorganisms, solvent extraction, and RF heating is not regarded as promising. Beneficiation or enrichment of retort feed by some mechanical or other means may be worth investigating.

Opportunities for improved technology in heated retorts, both specific suggestions and identified needs, can be classified in four groups shown below.

1. Economies of scale in retorting seem most likely if a major increase in production can be obtained in each retort train (or module) rather than by replication of small modules. The retort technology that appears capable of very large single-train throughputs (based on demonstrated solids-handling capacity in refining processes) is fluidized bed technology. Fluidized bed technology for shale retorting was investigated briefly and then abandoned many years ago and we are not aware of any current major projects. Nevertheless, advances in that technology, especially for operations with higher gas velocities and larger particles, justify another evaluation.

Operating under pressure is another general technique for increasing throughput in both conventional and fluidized bed retorts; it deserves evaluation.

2. Good utilization of resources in place means that retorting processes should be able to handle shales of different richness, crushed to different sizes, and located at different places and depths. Retorting of local coal along with shale rock may be advantageous in special circumstances. Thinking about retorting in this broader context means that different types of both surface and in-situ retorts will be employed in an optimum large industry and that there is value in developing retorting systems which have inherent feed flexibility.

3. In addition to having flexibility to accommodate different feeds, a retorting system could profitably have flexibility to make different mixes of products including oil, gas, and steam (or electric power). The optimum product mix would differ for different technologies, locations, and degrees of integration into the surrounding industry. Different retorting atmosphere gases (H_2, O_2/steam, etc.) offer one means by which product slate can be varied. Accessory equipment like fluid bed combustors may make it possible to convert energy in an economical and environmentally acceptable manner from one form to another more useful one, say coal or lean shale to low-Btu gas or carbon on spent shale to steam or electric power.

4. Costs for controlling or disposing of waste streams in an environmentally acceptable way are significant in shale oil production. Improved retorting technologies can help reduce those costs. Retorting at higher temperatures reduces soluble alkali in spent shale and thus reduces long-term leaching problems after spent shale disposal. Investigation of this effect in surface retorting should be undertaken. Cheaper treatment of contaminated water streams, from mining or retorting, with the objective of reuse or discharge, should be possible.

High-temperature retorting can also reduce the volume of spent shale to about (or perhaps even less than) the volume of the original rock, thus making it easier to dispose of all the spent shale by returning it to the mine.   However, high-temperature retorting does incur costs because of losses in thermal efficiency and increased gaseous emissions.

The alkalinity of the spent shale suggests possible use in gas scrubbers to remove acidic sulfur compounds.

Clean-up and use of low Btu gas from in-situ retorting is a particularly expensive operation. Cheaper "one-step" technologies are needed. Improved technology of this type would have a large impact.

In addition to the specific suggestions and needs identified above, there are obvious opportunities for cost-saving during equipment manufacturing by: (a) mass production methods for replicated pieces of equipment, and (b) shop fabrication replacing field fabrication wherever practical.

Upgrading Opportunities

There is little need to spend much time discussing the technology of upgrading raw retort shale oil to refinery feedstock. This opinion is based on several assumptions:

- End products of shale oil will be similar to the current end products of petroleum in quality characteristics, even if not necessarily in volume distribution.

- Conversion of raw shale oil to end products will occur at existing petroleum refinery sites, or at new refineries generally similar (in technology) to existing ones, but tailored to shale oil feed.

- Conversion will be carried out primarily by existing petroleum refining companies or combinations of existing companies who already have expertise.

- Large-scale production of shale oil involves very long lead times and, therefore, refiners will have ample notice of the need to design for large amounts of raw shale oil.

- Petroleum refining technology has shown its ability in the past to cope rapidly and efficiently with new feedstocks and changing product slates and qualities.

On the basis of these assumptions, one may conclude that upgrading technology would occur naturally and effectively in the petroleum refining industry when it becomes evident that large volumes of shale oil would be produced and would have to be refined. The most important economies of application in a large-scale industry could result from:

- Pipeline transportation of raw shale oil to existing refining centers. Movement of raw shale oil (in heated pipelines or with additives or other pretreatment) to existing centers would: (a) make use of existing refining capacity presumably idled by reduced supplies of imported petroleum, and (b) shift some demand for human, mechanical, and natural resources to locations better able to supply them than Colorado/Utah/Wyoming, which have some infrastructure limitations.

● Development or modification of refining catalysts and processes to make them less sensitive to contamination by the nitrogen present in raw shale oil.

● Rebalancing of new and existing refinery process capacity to regard shale oil as a primary feed rather than a contaminant - analogous to shifting from a sweet crude refinery to a sour crude refinery - with a corresponding shift of product slate (consistent with overall market demand) to best exploit the different optimum product mixes from shale oil and petroleum.

The "Systems" Approach

It would be unwise to consider cost reductions by looking only at the individual functional steps by which oil has traditionally been recovered from shale. The result could be sub-optimization, and the possibility of a whole new approach or system might be completely missed. Therefore, one should consider the systems approach, and from two aspects. The first concerns technology, including combinations of some individual functions. The second concerns implementation of industry development in such a way as to encourage systemic technological cost reductions.

Obvious examples of "systems" thinking about technology are referred to in the preceding sections as combinations of various approaches. Combinations of both in-situ and surface retorts should be able to best exploit the resource in place in some locations. The shale mined for modified in-situ, which creates the void needed for rubbling, would be charged to surface retorts and the exact balance between modified in-situ and surface retorting could be optimized depending on shale quality and depth, etc. Combinations of different types of retorts should make best use of mined shale and should make a product mix of maximum value. Integration of shale oil refining into the total refinery process should reduce refining costs. Other examples of combinations which serve multiple purposes could also be cited. A more basic approach is described below.

Imagine an extraction device which travels through the shale, breaking rock, heating the rubble, separating the oil and gas, cooling the solid residue and replacing the rock in the mined-out volume. The products would be shipped to the surface through pipes which follow the extractor. Air or other gases and/or liquids are fed to the device through pipes. Possibly, the extractor could be operated by remote control so that men would not ordinarily be required underground. A key issue in such a concept is the ability of the process to reduce the volume of the waste rock to the original volume. It appears that this may be achievable by high processing temperatures and compaction.

In order to reduce unit costs through mass production, perhaps 1000 units should be manufactured. In order to produce 5 million B/D, each unit might have a frontal area of about 10 square meters and would advance about 60 centimeters per minute.

The design of such a device would clearly call for a major technical effort. A number of important mining, mechanical, electrical, and chemical engineering problems must be faced. The entire unit would likely be more than 30 meters in length, weigh 500 to 1000 metric tons, and cost in production perhaps $30 million each. On the other hand, the revenue from such a unit even at 50% utilization could amount to $30 million per year, if the oil were sold at $20 per barrel.

No such device is now under development or has even been thought about seriously to our knowledge. And, of course, there may be little probability that such a system can be developed at acceptable cost, if at all. The example, however, illustrates that there are other ways of thinking about shale oil recovery that should at least be studied.

History suggests that the sheer existence of a significant industry provides the environment necessary for the kinds of systemic technological innovations that produce significant cost reductions. Therefore, we present an example of a form which might make such a significant industry possible. Such a form would also serve to:

- Stimulate inputs and contributions (of technology, skill, experience, perspective, and funds) from all relevant industries.
- Provide for Federal support at start-up without Federal control or a continuing Federal role.
- Provide for authentic participation at state, local, and public levels.
- Provide a mechanism appropriate to the enormous size of the task.

The example developed to permit these advantages would be the creation of a publicly held firm along the lines of COMSAT. Its purpose would be to produce shale oil and its by-products. The process firms presently active in the development of shale oil would be invited to provide process expertise and lease holdings. Mining companies, equipment manufacturers, engineers, and construction firms would be invited to provide expertise, accepting as payment a limited early profit plus an equity position. The Federal government would provide leases (land) and research funds which would be repaid out of earnings. State governments would provide assistance in meeting the social and economic impacts of construction and operation. Shale oil would compete in the marketplace, without price control, with a negotiated royalty to the Federal government. Principal funding would be through sale of equity to the public, with debt financing as appropriate. The creation of a strategic planning function capable of managing the effect of changing technology would be important.

Through such a vehicle, the rudiments of an "industry in place" would be created, so that new systemic ideas and concepts can emerge and so that economies of scale can be identified. R&D would be centralized at least in part, with the attendant increase in efficiency and synergy (as well as some accompanying loss of diversity). The focus would be on optimum exploitation of the shale oil resource from a total perspective.

Conclusions and Suggestions for Further Work

Production of shale oil on a large scale could provide opportunities for significant technological economies not otherwise realizable. Prompt accelerated development of small-scale shale oil production should be encouraged in the national interest. Production would facilitate, and may be essential to, the technology development that should occur both to reduce current uncertainties and to make informed decisions about any future large-scale industry. Further work is justified on more detailed evaluation of the technological opportunities, of their potential economic consequences, and of various structural options that would encourage accelerated development.

The greatest potential for savings in mining for surface retorts is treatment of part or all of the Piceance Creek Basin as a single surface mine - even though major aquifer disturbances and other environmental problems would be encountered and would have to be solved. Opportunities in mining for in-situ retorting are less well defined, but they seem to focus on continuous tunneling and controlled fragmentation, replacing cyclic methods of drilling/blasting/mucking.

The largest potential for surface retorting appears to lie in large fluidized bed retorts. Operations under pressure, or with retorting atmospheres other than air, look interesting for both fluid and non-fluid retorts.

Refiners faced by large quantities of raw shale oil feed are apt (in their traditional ways) to develop new refining technologies to handle that feed at significantly lower cost than now foreseen for brute force hydrogenation, followed by conventional petroleum refining.

The primary contributions from "systems" technology emphasizes the advantages in large-scale production of combinations of technology to exploit all resources most effectively, e.g., combinations of in-situ and surface retorting to make best total use of the shale resource in place, combined shale and coal retorting, and multi-product (oil, gas, electric power) retorts.

It is urgent to increase the rate of development of the shale oil industry in order to accelerate the rate of development of its technology. This increase would lead to a reduction of technical, economic, and environmental uncertainties and would put the nation in a position to exploit oil shale on a large scale rapidly, if it became necessary or desirable to do so. New large-scale structures involving both the private and public sectors would help and may be essential to accelerate development and to produce shale oil on the huge scale potentially desired. COMSAT is a possible model as a mechanism for the development and implementation of these suggested technologies. An R&D operation could be linked to such an organization through a wide range of funding, programming, and administrative devices.

Two types of further study would be useful for future consideration of new shale oil projects:

- Possible technological alternatives for a large-scale industry should be hypothesized and the economics for those alternatives should be estimated. Studies of that type would not yield costs of absolute accuracy, but the relative costs could help identify the most promising technologies for further R&D and the potential gain relative to current technology.

- Various structural options for a shale oil industry should be examined. Options should be described in detail with the advantages and disadvantages of each. This would contribute to a well-informed choice of an implementation mechanism that best fits policy constraints.

Literature Cited

1. Initial research on oil shale was conducted at the MIT Energy Laboratory by the author, Malcolm A. Weiss and Rober J. Barbara and was first reported in MIT Energy Laboratory Working Papers No. 79-012WP and 79-013WP. This original work was sponsored by grants from the Edna McConnell Clark, Ford, and Alfred P. Sloan Foundations. This paper draws on the initial research and summarizes aspects of a workshop on shale oil that was sponsored by MIT on June 4-5, 1979. Art Tybor of Gulf Science and Technology Company provided the editorial work to produce this paper in its present form.

2. Standford Research Institute, "A Western Regional Energy Development Study: Economics, Volume 1," SRI Project 4000, November, 1976, p. 7; Department of Energy, Policy and Evaluation Division, "Inside D.O.E.," May 18, 1979, p. 6.

3. "Recommendations for a Synthetic Fuels Commercialization Program," Synfuels Interagency Task Force Report to the President's Energy Resources Council, November, 1975, Vol. II, p. 18, p. H-27.

4. Hammond, Ogden H. and Boron, Robert E., "Synthetic Fuels: Price, Prospects, and Prior Art," American Scientist, July-August, 1976, pp. 407-417.

5. Whitcombe, J. A., "Shale Oil Production Costs and the Need for Incentives for Pioneer Plant Construction," TOSCO, February 1-3, 1976.

6. Ramsey, W. J., "Institutional Constraints and the Potential for Shale Oil Development," Lawrence Livermore Laboratory, UCRL-52468, July 6, 1978, p. 24.

7. Ibid., p. 16.

8. Probstein, R. F. and Gold, H., "Water in Synthetic Fuel Production," M.I.T. Press, Cambridge, MA, 1978, p. 59.

9. Jacoby, H. D. and Lawrence, H. Linden, "Government Support for the Commercialization of New Energy Technologies -- An Analysis and Exploration of the Issues," Policy Study Group, MIT Energy Laboratory Report MIT-EL 76-009, Cambridge, MA, November, 1976. (Prepared for ERDA under Contract No. E49-18 2295).

10. Allan, Gerald B., "Note on the Use of Experience Curves in Competitive Decision Making," Intercollegiate Case Clearing House, #9-175-174, Boston, MA, 1975.

11. Allan, Gerald B., "A Note on the Boston Consulting Group Concept of Competitive Analysis and Corporate Strategy," Intercollegiate Case Clearing House #9-175-175, Boston, MA, 1975.

12. Ibid., p. 108.

13. Ball, B. C., Jr., "Energy: Policymaking in a New Reality," Technology Review, October/November, 1977.

Appendix - The Process of Technological Change

The Nature of the Process. In order to evaluate properly the trade-offs in the "evolutionary" versus the "industry in place" alternatives, it is helpful to establish a clear view of how new technologies are, in fact, commercialized.

Commercialization of a new technology occurs, if it is available at a cost allowing the private sector an acceptable return on the total capital required, given the market prices of inputs, capital, and labor, given the regulatory restrictions, and given the marketplace.

A way in which this real-world process can be perceived is through the existence of four rather discrete stages which precede the establishment of a mature industry:

- Research or invention
- Development or demonstration
- Commercial introduction
- Commercial diffusion

Research or invention is the generation of an idea. A functioning process or product is established. Economic issues are not dealt with in depth at this stage; technical, market, and regulatory uncertainties are very high. Costs, prices, and markets are usually poorly known.

In the Development stage, design is optimized until the process or product is embodied in an actual model within a working environment. The principal function of this stage is to eliminate technological uncertainty and thus determine the expected cost of mature production (e.g., production following the Diffusion stage). However, the variance of this expected future cost may be rather high. This stage does not deal at all with market or regulatory uncertainties.

The Development stage need not, and in fact usually does not, require the construction of a full-scale production facility. Pilot plant is the usual approach here. The product may be real-life (e.g., a barrel of real shale oil), so that the product may be tested, but the production facilities are expected to be smaller than full size by virtue of the ability to scale. If they are readily scalable, then there are no significant technical uncertainties which require commercial-scale construction for their resolution. If a crucial sub-unit is not readily scalable, an alternative to a full-scale demonstration plant is to build a facility only of the crucial sub-unit, no larger than necessary to resolve the relevant technical uncertainties.

The purpose of the Development stage is, thus, twofold:

- To reduce technological uncertainty
- To determine expected mature costs

At the end of this stage, variance of the mature costs will be rather high. However, the expected value of this cost has been determined. If this cost is too high to offer adequate hope of profit (i.e., to offer hope that the technology will be commercialized) or if the cost necessary to commercialize lies within the variance but at an inadequately low probability, then the technology is not commercial. The project is dropped or perhaps the Invention stage is reentered.

The Development stage is not primarily intended to reduce costs. Rather, it determines them within a broad range, given the output of the Invention stage. It deals not at all with market or regulatory uncertainties.

It is the Commercial Introduction stage that deals primarily with these issues, while further narrowing the range of cost variance. It is here that full-scale production facilities are put into operation in order to reduce market uncertainties (e.g., marketing programs, distribution channels, maintenance organizations, market segmentation and differentiation, character of the technology and of the industry, and the value of mystique) and regulatory and legislative uncertainties (e.g., environmental, tax, delays).

It is only after these cost, market, and regulatory uncertainties have been reduced during the Commercial Introduction stage that the diffusion stage is considered. The Commercial Diffusion stage is marked by widespread production in a growing number of full-scale production facilities, widespread usage, and (normally) the entry of competitors. Actual costs begin to decrease as experience is gained.

What is the driving force for this process? Clearly, it is pursuit of economic gain by the individual actors in the private sector. This scheme might be viewed as a series of investment decisions, each preceding one of the four stages.

1. The decision to conduct research is a decision to invest in the possibility of an option to "develop" a new idea, should one be forthcoming.
2. The decision to "develop" a new idea is a decision to invest in an option to "introduce" a new product or process, should the Development stage indicate it technically feasible at attractive probable cost.
3. The decision to "introduce" is a decision to invest in an option to "diffuse", should the market, regulatory, and cost issues addressed in the Commercial Introduction stage result in a favorable resolution.

At no point in the process has a "profit" been made or have cash flows been positive, even undiscounted. Even the Commercial Introduction stage is not normally expected to be profitable in its own right, though some revenues may obtain. Rather, it is another in a series of investments.

4. The decision to diffuse is the decision to invest in multiple full-scale facilities and in market share, with the expectation of "profit", that is, within the planning horizon, the discounted cash flows will be positive, including the investment in the three earlier stages. (A complicating factor is the fact that, at the point of the diffusion decision, investments in prior stages are sunk costs.) At the point of the Commercial Diffusion stage, technical uncertainties are nil, market and regulatory uncertainties have been reduced to manageable levels, and costs are known with a relatively high degree of certainty. The significant uncertainty is competitive action, which would affect individual actors in the process more than the progress of the process itself.

Should the reduction of market, regulatory, and cost uncertainty, achieved during the Commercial Introduction stage, indicate a low probability of profitable diffusion, then obviously the process would be stopped or delayed until a significant change occurred in one of the key elements. In the latter case, the type of the change would indicate the stage in which it occurred, and therefore, the succeeding stage in which the process would pick up, for example:

- New idea (new technology) or introduction. Redevelop.
- Lower cost-introduction/development. Reintroduce.
- New market or regulatory climate.   Reintroduce or diffuse.

One would correctly expect the magnitude of the investment to increase significantly from invention through diffusion to maturity.   The successful invention (i.e., one that is eventually 'commercialized') normally has miniscule costs relative to the investment in the mature, diffused industry. Even the investment in "introduction" is very small relative to diffusion investment. In most cases, the cost of each stage (including Commercial Introduction) is not recovered during that stage.   If when examined at the end of its development, a technology appears to be commercial in the long run, it usually will be introduced and 'commercialized' by the private sector (9).

The cost of successful invention, development, and introduction are therefore small relative to that of diffusion.   One might say that it is the unsuccessful ones that are expensive. Viewed as a whole, the successful ones must more than pay for the unsuccessful.   This is usually viewed in the private sector as "risk", and is thought of, not as an added cost, but rather as the expected return necessary to justify "taking the risk", i.e., making the investments in invention, development, and introduction.

An additional word needs to be said about the declining costs in the mature phase following diffusion, as experience is accumulated.   It has been found (10) for a wide variety of products and a wide variety of industries that costs (in constant dollars) decline through experience as the product matures.   This is a well-known phenomenon for the manufacturing process ("the learning curve"); the principle applies similarly to the total infrastructure, i.e., manufacturing, management, distribution, marketing, etc. (the "experience curve").   This cost reduction is a function of the number of comparable units produced, and is expected to amount to a 20-30% reduction for each doubling of accumulated experience.   On a log-log plot, the curve is a straight line, with a slope of 70-80% (see Figure 1).

Several characteristics of this phenomenon are important to note here:

- The early points on the plot are scattered, and do not begin to take form until the system as a whole becomes organized and routine, well into the Commercial Diffusion stage.
- Largely, each firm follows its own experience curve. For

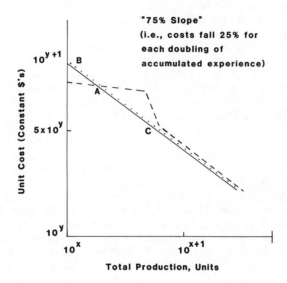

Figure 1.   Experience curve

example, if firm X led the Diffusion phase and had progressed down the experience curve in Figure 1 to point C at the point in time when firm Y decided to become a competitor, the latter would enter at, say, point B.

The implications of these characteristics are significant:

1. In a fragmented industry (i.e., many equal competitors) all competitors would follow the experience curve more or less together. Prices would be expected to follow the dotted line, with the ordinal difference between the solid and dotted lines representing "profit" or return on total investment. Under these conditions, a firm is not likely to diffuse unless this ordinal difference is positive at or very near the beginning of the Diffusion stage.

2. If one firm were to adopt an aggressive pricing strategy, it might become the initiator of diffusion at point B, but set its price along the dashed line in order to dominate the market. Only at point A in experience would it begin to break even on current production, but at point C in experience it could begin reducing prices more sharply and remain profitable. Of course, the incentive for such a strategy would be increased profit (e.g., higher present value of net cash flows, properly discounted for the time value of money and for risk), due to "investment in market share".

One of the principal strategic reasons for a firm investing in invention, development, and introduction is to give it "a head start down the learning curve", i.e., more accumulated experience would result in lower unit costs than competitors during diffusion. Strategically, this would lead to a dominant market share as maturity is reached (11). Other strategies are open to competition. Either market failure or inadequate expected profit would prevent a firm from adopting this particular marketing strategy.

A Summary View. Figure 2 presents a summary view of the process of technological change as outlined above.

- Invention is the generation of a new idea, with little knowledge of costs or of technical, market, or regulatory uncertainties. An investment represents an option to develop.

- Development is the design optimization of the idea until it is embodied in an actual model that will perform in the working environment.
  - Purpose: essentially eliminate technological uncertainty, and get an idea of the cost. In the language of the "Commercialization" paper (12), mature cost $C(X)$ is estimated, but with high variance $G^1(C(X))$.
  - Market and regulatory uncertainties are not dealt with.

	Invention	Development	Introduction	Diffusion	Maturity
Nature	Generation of a new idea.	Design optimization until embodied in actual model in working environment.	Establish initial production facilities, marketing program, distribution channels, maintenance organization, etc.	Widespread usage, with entry of competitors.	Equilibrium
Function	New idea.	1. Eliminate Technological uncertainty. 2. Estimate diffusion cost $C(X)$ with high variance $G^i\, C(X)$.	1. Reduce market and regulatory uncertainties. 2. Determine introduction cost $C^*(X^*)$ and thereby reduce cost variance from G^i to $G^d(C(X))$.	Market, expand, and compete profitably.	Expand profitably, but more slowly. Market and compete profitably.
Criteria of Success	A new idea with practical potential.	A product which management can expect to sell at a profit.	Not profit, but an expectation to diffuse successfully.	Positive net present value (including prior investments).	Net cash flow.
Investment in	Option to develop.	Option to introduce	Option to Diffuse	Profit	Net cash flow.
Cost	Unknown — Possibility of $C(X)$	Estimate of $C(X)$ — $C(X)$	$C^*(X^{**})$ determined — $C(X)$	$C(X)$ determined	$C(X)\cdot f(X)$ determined
Uncertainties — Cost	—	$G^i(C(X))$ — high	$G^d(C(X))$ — reduced	low	nil
Uncertainties — Technology	high	nearly eliminated	nil	nil	nil
Uncertainties — Market & Regulatory	—	not dealt with	reduced	low	low

Figure 2. Commercialization and the process of technological change

- Criteria of success: a product which management can expect to sell at a profit.
- Investment: option to introduce.

● <u>Introduction</u> is the establishment of initial full-scale production facilities, marketing programs, distribution channels, maintenance organizations, etc.
  - Purpose: reduce market and regulatory uncertainty.
  - Cost: determined as $C'(X^*)$, reducing the variance of $C(X)$ from $G^1(C(X))$ to $G^d(C(X))$.
  - Criteria of success: not profit, but option to diffuse profitably.

● <u>Diffusion</u> is widespread production and use, usually accompanied by the entry of competitors.
  - Purpose: profit, sometimes accompanied by a strategy to dominate the market.
  - Cost: $C(X)$ is determined, and the slope of the experience curve $C(X) = f(X)$, is established.
  - As maturity is approached, each competitor progresses down his own learning curve.

Thus, each stage performs its own function. For example, if the cost of a particular technology emerging from the Commercial Development stage is expected to be noncompetitive, the indication is to invent a new technology, not introduce the noncompetitive one. Similarly, if technology emerging from introduction does not appear profitable, the indication is to invent a new one, not diffuse the unprofitable one.

At the present time, even those enthusiastic about proceeding with the construction and operation of full-scale shale oil plants expect the cost to exceed competitive prices (i.e., the world oil price). Their argument for proceeding is based on the need to reduce uncertainties (whether technological or regulatory), and to have the plants ready when competitive prices rise to the level of their costs. Most of those who make these arguments believe that a government subsidy of some form (e.g., special tax treatment) is appropriate in order to provide private incentive for the construction of these plants.

The description of the process of technological change is useful in interpreting these arguments. We are now at the "development" stage; the cost uncertainty is high, but is expected to exceed break-even prices. As displayed in Figure 3, at the Development stage, probable cost is greater than break-even cost, $C(X) > C(BE)$.

This analysis indicates the technology is simply not viable. Effort is indicated at the Invention stage to develop a lower-cost technology. If technological risk is too high, effort is indicated at the Development (pilot plant) stage, not at the Introduction ("demonstration") stage. Effort at the Introduction stage is possibly appropriate to reduce regulatory uncertainty. (However, it needs to be emphasized that there are alternate methods for reducing regulatory risk which may well be much more cost-effective.) However, the purpose of doing so is not clear as long as the expected cost exceeds break-even, even after reducing the uncertainty. The argument for government subsidies or incentives would hinge on a demonstration that the private discount rate exceeds the public value, or that the social value of shale oil exceeds the market value (or, perhaps, the existence of some other form of market failure). In other words, if the break-even price is to rise from C(BE) to C(BE') over some time frame, then investment in Introduction/Diffusion may well be economically attractive now, even at C(X), depending on the discount rate. The question raised by this analysis is, if the investment is not attractive to the private sector now, how is it attractive to the public?

The process of technological change is normally driven by the expectation that C(X) < C(BE), the difference representing the possibility of a profit. This is represented in Figure 3 as C(X) < C(BE'). This relation must hold for each phase in the process for investment in the next phase to be attractive. If this relation does not hold at any phase, then the process properly ceases.

The Shakedown Period. Introduction and Diffusion reduce uncertainty, not expected cost. One of the ways in which this occurs is that, by simple trial and error, marginally equivalent methods, technologies, processes, combinations, and permutations are tried against each other, and the marginally best is thereby identified. This begins to occur during the Introduction stage and continues through the early Diffusion stage. Thus in shale oil, the various approaches to retorting would compete against each other in the real world, as would in-situ and modified in-situ; by the closing of the Diffusion stage, industry would have learned the optimum process, the key situational parameters, and how to obtain maximum profit, given any particular set of circumstances.

An example here may be helpful. During World War II, catalytic cracking of gas oil was discovered as a practical means of increasing the yield of high-octane gasoline (i.e., avgas) from crude. At the end of the Development stage, three competing processes were identified: FCC, TCC, and HCC. (Fluid catalytic cracking, Thermofor catalytic cracking, and Houdry catalytic cracking, respectively.) Any of the three was far superior to none, but it was not clear which one was best of the three. Therefore, all three competed in the real world, and by the middle of the Diffusion stage, the FCC was found to be superior to the two competing approaches in all applications. That is to say, against a refinery without catalytic cracking, any of the three processes was highly attractive. However, against a refinery with FCC, the other two were very unattractive.

The point here is that the cost advantage of FCC over TCC or HCC is an order of magnitude less than the cost advantage of any of the three processes over no catalytic cracking at all. Ap-

plying this point to shale oil, we can see that, as far as the
process of technological change is concerned, the important issue
is the range of expected costs of any of the competing processes,
relative to expected break-even cost.   This is illustrated in
Figure 4, which compares the expected costs of Processes A, B, and
C with the break-even cost C(BE').   The process of technological
change depends on $C_A(X)$, $C_B(X)$, and $C_C(X)$ relative to C(BE'), not
relative to each other.   However, during the shakedown period of
the process of technological change, the uncertainties of $C_A(X)$,
$C_B(X)$, and $C_C(X)$ relative to each other are reduced significantly,
and the appropriate processes are sorted out from the competing
ones.

"Experience" Cost Reduction.   It is important to distinguish
this "sorting out" during the shakedown period from the cost
reductions which occur during maturity.   The former is the determination of which process, technique, etc., is most cost-
effective.   Once this has been determined, then this knowledge
becomes the basis for the rest of the Diffusion stage and for the
Maturity stage.   It is only after the established process, technique, etc., has become repetitive that the continuing cost
reduction of the "experience curve" (as defined and discussed on
page 17-18) becomes applicable.   Thus, the shakedown period is one
of cost determination, by selecting the marginally optimum
process, while the experience curve effects continuing cost
reduction, resulting from the accumulation of experience in
repeating the same functions.

These two dynamics are not only different in both nature and
in consequences, they are also separated in time.   In fact, at any
single point in time, they are by definition mutually exclusive.

Applicability to This Study.   Having proposed a model for
understanding the process of technological change, and having
analyzed the present shale oil industry through the framework of
this model, hopefully now we should be able to articulate the
question this study intends to raise in more precise and succinct
terms.

If an industry were to be put in place, as compared with
evolving through the process of technological change, then we
would, in effect, be jumping from the end of the Development stage
to the end of the Diffusion stage.   Since we are focusing here on
technological costs, the major phase bypassed would be the shakedown period.   Thus, a non-optimum process or technique may be the
one selected for the industry in place.   To use again our
World War II analogy from the refining industry, we might have
built a refining industry on the basis of the HCC process.   The
question of this study is, then, what is the probability of the
economies of an industry in place being greater than the diseconomies of skipping the shakedown period?

This question can be seen graphically in Figure 4, if
Processes A, B, and C represent presently competing shale oil
techniques, and C(BE) represents the break-even cost of shale

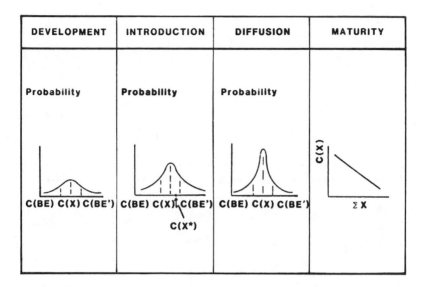

Figure 3. Cost uncertainties and break-even costs

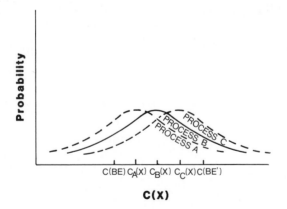

Figure 4. The shakedown

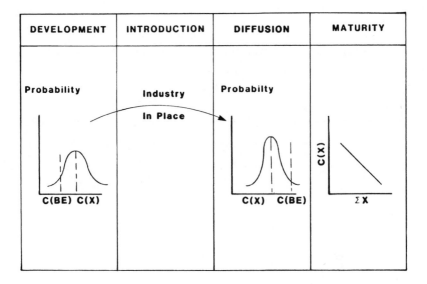

Figure 5.   An industry in place

oil.   What is the probability of the cost of shale oil from an industry in place being less than C(BE), <u>even if Process C is chosen as the basis for the industry?</u>

Our analytic framework permits asking this same question in an additional way.   Note that in the process of technological change, cost reductions occur at only the stages at each extreme of the process: Introduction on the one side and Maturity on the other.   Thus, normally, if a technology at the end of the Development stage has an expected cost greater than C(BE), then the technology is abandoned.   The question here is, could the economies of an industry in place reduce the expected cost from greater than break-even to less than break-even?   This is displayed graphically in Figure 5.

This picture raises quite naturally the question about the possible role of experience cost reduction (as this term is rather narrowly defined in this paper).   After all, this kind of cost reduction has played a rather spectacular role in other industries, IC's being the classic example.   However, in the shale oil industry, such reductions are not expected by anyone to be significant, principally for two reasons.   In the first place, the dynamics of limited resources is expected to be overwhelming from the very beginning.   In the second place, none of the components of the shale oil industry is new (i.e., mining, retorting, materials handling); we are already so far down the learning curve on each of them that additional accumulated experience within the shale oil industry is expected to result in negligible cost reductions.

Thus, the picture of shale oil is basically one of continually increasing, rather than decreasing, costs.   Any viability at all depends not on increasing economies but on increasing break-even costs (i.e., increasing world oil price).   This is a poorly understood notion and is contrary to most experience.   There are no analytical tools capable of dealing adequately with issues of marginal costs exceeding average costs (13).

Over against this, the question raised by this study is a rather fundamental one: When viewed from the perspective of any industry-in-place, are there possible economies not yet perceived, which might permit costs to decline (in real terms) rather than to rise over the long term?

RECEIVED June 19, 1981.

Commercial-Scale Refining of Paraho Crude Shale Oil into Military Specification Fuels

N. J. WASILK

The Standard Oil Company, P.O. Box 696, Toledo, OH 43694

E. T. ROBINSON

The Standard Oil Company, 4440 Warrensville Center Road,
Warrensville Heights, OH 44146

In September, 1977 the Standard Oil Company (Ohio) was con-
tracted by the U.S. Navy to refine up to 100,000 barrels of
crude Paraho Shale Oil into Military Transportation Fuels. The
objective of the program was to demonstrate that shale oil
could be converted into stable, specification military fuels
utilizing conventional refining technology and in sufficient
volumes to support an extensive engine testing program. Yields
of JP-5 (jet fuel) and DFM (diesel fuel marine) were to be
maximized while minimizing the yield of residual fuel.

The crude shale was produced by Paraho Development Corp.
over the three year period from 1976 to 1978. Paraho's Anvil
Point, Colorado works utilizes a vertical direct heat retort to
recover the oil from crushed shale (1).

For contractual reasons the program was divided into three
phases. During Phase I, the proposed shale oil processing
scheme was tested and developed in appropriate pilot plants.
Phase II constituted engineering preparation and the actual refinery run. Post run analysis and report writing were completed in Phase III.

Paraho Shale Oil

The unique nature of crude shale oil requires special consideration in handling and processing. Table I summarizes some
typical inspections of raw shale oil and a West Texas crude.
In comparison to conventional petroleum, shale oil has several
deleterious characteristics:

  (1) High nitrogen and oxygen content.
  (2) Low hydrogen/carbon ratio.
  (3) Low yield of 650°F minus material (< 30 vol. %).
  (4) Moderate arsenic and iron content.
  (5) Suspended ash and water.

0097–6156/81/0163–0223$05.00/0

Table I
Properties of Paraho Shale Oil and West Texas Sour Crude

	Paraho Shale Oil	West Texas Sour
Gravity, °API	20.4	34.1
Specific Gr. @ 60°F	0.9315	0.8545
Pour Point, °F	+85	Fluid @ -30
Viscosity, SSU		
@ 60°F	Too heavy	57.1
@ 100°F	213	43.1
@ 210°F	44.9	-
Viscosity-Gr. Constant	0.8899	0.722
Reid Vapor Pressure, PSI	-	5.1
Total Acid No., mg KOH/gm	1.988	0.265
Asphaltenes, wt.%	0.889	1.028
Ramsbottom Carbon, wt.%	2.977	2.65
B.S. & W., Vol. %	0.05*	0.30
Salt, lb/M Bbls.	4.9**	3.3
Elemental Analysis		
C, wt.%	83.68	-
H, wt.%	11.17	-
O, wt.%	1.38	-
N, wt.%	2.02	0.10
S, wt.%	0.70	1.40
Metals		
As, ppm	7.5	-
Na, ppm	0.3	-
K, ppm	0.17	-
V, ppm	0.17	4.4
Ni, ppm	2.4	2.6
Fe, ppm	53	2.0
TBP 650°F Point, vol. %	28.24	58.64
(True Boiling Point)		

*   (0.06 unsettled)
** (8.20 unsettled)

The high nitrogen content is probably the largest area of concern, as it is an order of magnitude higher than that found in petroleum. The technology for processing high nitrogen crudes is not nearly as advanced as comparable technologies for desulfurization or cracking (increasing yield of lower boiling hydrocarbons).

Nitrogen compounds are known poisons for many petroleum processing catalysts such as fluid bed catalytic cracking, naphtha reforming and hydrocracking catalysts. In addition, nitrogen compounds have been found to create stability problems in gasoline, jet and diesel fuels. Fuel bound nitrogen will also increase the NO_x emissions from practically any type of combustor. Finally, nitrogen compounds quite often have a peculiar and offensive odor which is uncommonly difficult to remove (2).

Shale Oil Refining Process

A schematic of the process developed for this program is shown in Figure 1. The crude shale oil is initially allowed to settle batchwise at above ambient temperature. This has been found to be effective in breaking the water/oil emulsion, thereby precipitating suspended water and ash to the bottom of the tank. The shale oil is also pumped through a 20 micron filter enroute to the hydrotreater to remove any entrained debris left in the tank.

After settling, the shale oil is mixed with hydrogen, preheated and passed through a guard bed. The purpose of the guard bed is to remove the organic iron and arsenic as well as any ash and solids which survived the settling and filtering procedure.

Following the shale oil pretreatment steps (settling and guard bed demetallization) the whole shale oil is catalytically hydrotreated at elevated temperature and hydrogen partial pressure. Hydrotreating, the most important processing step, is the catalytic reaction of hydrogen with sulfur, oxygen and nitrogen compounds to form H_2S, H_2O and NH_3, respectively, plus heteroatom-free hydrocarbons. In addition, aromatic saturation and cracking occur to some extent -- thereby increasing the hydrocarbon/carbon ratio and increasing the yield of military fuel feedstock (650°F minus material).

The hydrotreated shale oil is fractionated by distillation methods into gasoline, jet, diesel, and 650°F bottoms (residua). The jet and diesel fuel boiling ranges were determined experimentally to meet flash point and freeze or pour point requirements. Some of the residua was recycled back to the hydrotreater to increase jet and diesel fuel yields.

A final finishing step, acid and clay treating, was included to meet military specification gum and stability requirements.

Refinery Modifications

Prior to the shale oil operation, facilities modifications at the Toledo refinery were required to be able to receive, store and process the shale oil and its products without contamination from normal refinery stocks.

Raw shale oil was shipped from the Paraho facilities to Toledo by railroad tank car. An underutilized railcar rack was revamped to provide a new unloading as well as a product loading system. A new steam heated tank was built in which to store the shale oil as it was received over a 3 month period.

A hydrocracker which normally processes distillate fuels into gasoline products was modified to process the shale oil. New catalyst (Shell 324) was charged to the first stage reactor. A guard bed packed with alumina extrudate was placed in the feed preheat train. A 20 micron filter was installed on the inlet line from the shale oil storage tank. A new stripper tower was installed on the distillation tower to strip the DFM product. Numerous piping and instrumentation modifications were made to allow for a single stage hydrotreater operation.

For acid treating of the diesel fuel and jet fuel products a "new" acid treater was designed and built, the major vessel of which were refinery surplus equipment. These vessels included a settler, clay contactor and sludge storage tank.

To provide product storage for JP-5 and DFM, two tanks were removed from refinery service and cleaned prior to processing.

All lines used for shale oil material which interconnected with lines containing normal refinery stocks were either blanked or had the isolating valves chained and locked.

Refinery Logistics and Process Flow

When all the shale oil had been received, the storage tank was heated to 185°F, and an attempt was made to drawoff any free water. No free water was found. The shale oil received at Toledo measured only 0.07 vol.% sediment and water, (B.S.&W.), whereas earlier pilot plant samples contained 0.8 vol.% B.S.&W. The shale oil was pumped continuously from the tank through the 20 micron feed filter into the hydrotreater surge drum. From here it was pumped through the feed preheat section and guard bed together with hydrogen gas and into the reactor. Reactor effluent was cooled, water washed and recycle hydrogen and light ends removed, prior to entering a muiltidraw distillation column. Here four products were recovered from

the effluent: an overhead gasoline stock, a jet fuel cut (JP-5
or JP-8), a marine diesel fraction (DFM) and a bottoms residual
fuel fraction.   The gasoline stock was sampled, but not
recovered in bulk, instead it was used as feed to another
hydrocracker.   The JP-8 was acid treated on rundown to a
railcar, while JP-5 and DFM were run down to storage for later
acid treating.   Any off spec JP-5, JP-8 or DFM were returned to
the shale oil storage tank.   Part of the bottoms residua were
recycled through the hydrotreater to increase conversion, while
the remainder was used as cat cracker feed with a small amount
rundown directly to railcars for recovery as heavy fuel oil.

Refinery Run

The hydrotreating run began on November 4, 1978 and ended
on December 4, 1978.   In that time 73,100 barrels of the 88,225
barrels of shale oil received were hydrotreated.   However, some
of the products fom this volume were returned to the shale oil
storage tank as off specification product.   An excessively high
pressure drop across the Guard Bed caused the run to be
terminated before all the shale oil was processed.   The
hydrocracker was first shutdown on day 25 of the run because of
a high guard bed pressure drop.   The top 25% opf the Guard Bed
packing was removed because a black viscous sludge was present
on the top of the bed.   When returned to operation, the Guard
Bed soon redeveloped a high pressure drop and the run was
terminated due to contractural time limitations.

Original plans called for the JP products to be acid
treated on rundown to tankage or railcar.   This plan was
modified after acid treating startup problems resulted in poor
denitrification.   The JP-5 was rundown to tankage without acid
treating, as was the DFM, and both were treated after the
hydrotreating run was complete.   Fortunately, the acid treating
problems were resolved in time to treat the JP-8 on rundown to
a railcar.

The residual hydrotreated shale oil was mixed with regular
refinery cat cracker feed at a rate of 3%, with no detectable
shifts in yields or other adverse consequences.   Similarly, the
gasoline range cut had no detectable effects on hydrocracker
operations at 1.5% of feed.

The shale oil which remained after the processing run was
burned as boiler fuel.   No problems developed over the 1 month
combustion period.

Following conclusion of the run, an examination of the
Guard Bed contents revealed two separate problems, the sludge
at the top of the bed and FeS_x fines throughout the bed.   The
sludge was theorized to have been formed by a reaction between
shale oil, iron, and sulfuric acid.   The acid had been

unwittingly introduced into the shale oil feed tank by recycling off-spec JP-5 from the acid treater during startup. A large quantity of fines containing a high concentration of FeS_x was found throughout the bed. Apparently FeS_x had been depositing throughout the run and filled the interstitial spaces among the extrudate, thus causing a high pressure drop.

Material Balances

Essentially all of the conversion of 650°F plus bottom material to transportation fuel occurs in the hydrotreating step. Table II compares the overall material balance and yield and nitrogen levels obtained at Toledo with original pilot plant results. These data indicate that the denitrification activity of the catalyst was consistent with prior results, however the apparent yield structure was different. The differences in yields are attributed to two factors: (1) poorer distillation efficiency in the refinery operation and (2) lower DFM pour point and flash point targets during the refinery run. The actual conversion of 650°F plus bottoms material attained in the refinery run is very similar to the pilot plant results. The distillation curve of whole hydrotreated products (minus recycle) shown in Figure 2, illustrates this observation.

Net hydrogen consumption metered in the refinery run was significantly less than pilot plant results ($\sim$ 1500 versus 1050 SCFB). Chemical analysis of the various hydrotreated products indicate that the level of aromatic saturation, cracking and heteroatom removal for both refinery and pilot plant were nearly the same. The difference in measured hydrogen consumption is most probably a result of scaleup and pilot plant error. Needless to say, hydrogen consumption is a very important parameter in determining overall shale oil economics.

The total amount of each finished fuel produced is shown in Table III. In acid treating the yield losses were found to be porportional to nitrogen content and molecular weight of the fuel. For a 3300 ppm nitrogen JP-5 stock, yield loss was 4 wt.% and on a 3300 ppm nitrogen DFM the loss was 5.4 wt.%. Other losses incurred in the system were startup and line-out slop, heel left in feed tanks and treating vessels and losses during the clay column changes.

Product Analyses

Gasoline Stock. Analyses of the refinery and pilot plant gasoline stocks are shown in Table IV. Both materials are very similar in aromatic content, nitrogen level and octane number.

Table II
Shale Oil Hydrotreating Yields

| | Toledo Refinery | | | Pilot Plant | |
	Bbls.	Vol.%	Wt.%N	Vol.%	Wt.%N
Gasoline Stock (including Butanes)	8743	11.96	0.067	11.00	0.050
JP-5	9546	13.73	0.220	25.30	0.250
JP-8	490				
DFM	18939	25.90	0.340	34.50	0.430
Residual Fuel	37220	50.91	0.380	35.20	0.220
TOTAL	74939	102.50		106.00	
H_2 Cons. SCFB		1050		1500	

Table III
Net Fuels Produced After Acid/Clay Treating

	Bbls.
Gasoline Stock	7,718
JP-5	6,615
JP-8	462
DFM	16,357
Residual Fuel	37,220

Table IV
Gasoline Stocks Analyses

	Pilot Plant	Toledo
API Gravity	57.8	54.7
Reid Vapor Pressure, psi	1.3	5.6
Distillation	D-86	D-86
Initial Boiling Point, °F	190	100
10 Vol % Off, °F	226	249
50 Vol % Off, °F	258	283
90 Vol T Off, °F	288	317
End Point	332	370
% Recovered	99.0	98.0
% Residue	1.0	1.0
Paraffins	58.87	49.95
Monocyclo. Paraffins	29.61	31.62
Dicyclo Paraffins	9.97	2.40
Alkylbenzenes	9.97	15.20
Indans + Tetralins	0.11	0.51
Naphthalenes	0.33	0.32
Carbon No. Paraffins	8.01	9.36
Carbon No. Alkybenzenes	7.81	7.85
Nitrogen, Wt.%	0.040	0.078
Research Octane Number, clear	47	Not run

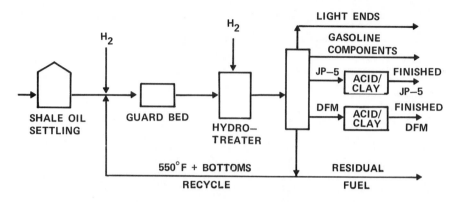

Figure 1.   Shale oil processing block-flow diagram

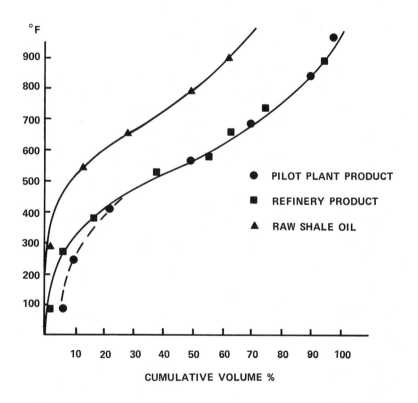

Figure 2.   T.B.P. distillation comparison of pilot plant and refinery whole hydro-treated product

Neither is suitable as a direct gasoline blending stock or as reformer feed. Additional hydrotreating is required to reduce the nitrogen content to levels acceptable to catalytic reforming, which is required to boost the octane number of this material.

Jet Fuels. Product JP-5, before and after acid treating is compared to pilot plant prepared material in Table V. Again both stocks have similar nitrogen, hydrogen and aromatic content. Note that the thermal stability of the untreated fuel is poor. However, once the nitrogen compounds are selectively removed by acid treating, the fuels' stability as determined by gum and JFTOT (ASTM D-3241) measurements is very good. In addition, storage stability characteristics of the fuels were tested by aging the material for 1 month at 140°F and then repeating the JFTOT and gum tests. The aging tests results, shown in Table VI for a composite sample of all treated JP-5 produced at the refinery, indicate that this fuel has very good storage stability properties.

Diesel Fuel Marine. Physical inspections of pilot plant and refinery DFM are compared in Table VII. As previously mentioned, the distillation (hence nearly everything else) are different due to refinery fractionation practices and altered target specs. Again, acid treating is required to meet fuel stability specifications, i.e. ASTM 2274 - (accelerated oxidation gum test). These fuels have good combustion properties, as shown by the cetane number ($\sim$50) and hydrogen contents (13 wt.% hydrogen).

Residual Fuel. The residual fuel produced by both the pilot and refinery meets all government specifications for low sulfur, high pour point #6 fuel oil. The residual fuels are in fact very "clean" as shown in Table VIII by the high hydrogen and low sulfur, metals, carbon and asphaltenes content. This stock is better utilized as cat cracker feed than residual fuel, since higher value gasoline and kerosene fuel can be easily produced via catalytic processing.

Product Fuels Distribution

All 6165 bbls. of the treated JP-5 produced at the Toledo refinery was shipped to Rickenbacher Air Force Base in Lockbourne, OH. The treated DFM was shipped to four destinations: 3021 bbls. were sent to General Motors Detroit Diesel, Allison Plant #5 in Indianapolis, IN, 8334 bbls. were shipped to Philadelphia Naval Base in Philadelphia, PA, 235 bbls. were sent to Wright Patterson Air Force Base, Fairborn, OH and 4785 bbls. went to the Defense Fuel Support Point in Cincinnati, OH. Of the 4670 bbls. of residual fuel reserved

Table V
JP-5 Analyses

A - Untreated JP-5

	Pilot Plant	Toledo	T-5624 K Mill Spec.
API Gravity	41.8	42.7	36<API<48 GR
Flash Point °F	157	158	140 Min.
Freeze Point, °F	-52	-57	-51 Max.
Existent gum (D-381) Mg/100 cc	12.2	Not Run	7.0 Max.
Distillation	D-86	D-86	D-86
IBP, °F	356	370	Report
10 Vol %, °F	380	384	401 Max.
50 Vol %, °F	415	400	Report
90 Vol %, °F	456	436	Report
End Point, °F	477	480	554 Max.
Nitrogen, Wt. %	0.32	0.29	-
Paraffins, Vol. %	43.9	42.5	-
Naphthenes, Vol. %	33.1	36.0	-
Aromatics, Vol. %	23.0	21.5	25% Max.
JFTOT, Visual (D-3241)	4 (Fail)	-	3

B - Treated JP-5

	Pilot Plant	Toledo	Mill Spec.
API Gravity	43.0	43.6	36<API<48 GR
Nitrogen, PPM	8	0.5	-
Total Acid Number, mg KOH/gm	Nil	0.005	0.0015 Max.
Water Separation Index, Modified	86	95	85 Min.
Existent gum (D-381) Mg/100 cc	0.6	1.4	
JFTOT @ 500°F (D-3241)			
Visual	2	1	3
Max. Spun Rate	10	0	17
Max. ΔP mm Hg	1.0	0.5	25
Paraffins Vol.%	46.0	43.7	
Naphthenes Vol.%	33.1	34.5	
Aromatics Vol.%	20.9	21.8	25% Max.

Table VI
Refinery JP-5 Stability Properties

	Unaged Fuel	Aged @ 140°F for 1 month
JFTOT Break Point, °F	625	500
Color	+ 30	+ 30
D-381 Existent gum Mg/100 cc	1.4	1.6
JFTOT @ 500°F, visual (D-3241)	2	2
JFTOT @ 500°F, Max. Spun Tube	1.0	3.0
JFTOT @ 500°F, Max. Spot Tube	2.0	2.0
JFTOT @ 500°F, Σ TDR	1.5	6.5
JFTOT @ 500°F, ΔP MM Hg	0.0	0.0

Table VII
Diesel Fuel Marine Analyses

A - Untreated DFM

	Pilot Plant	Toledo	F-16884G Mil Spec.
API Gravity	33.4	36.8	Report
Pour Point, °F	15	0	20 Max.
Flash Point, °F	290	162	140 Min.
Distillation	D-86	D-86	D-86
Initial Boiling Point, °F	507	396	-
10 Vol.% Off	529	456	-
50 Vol.% Off	553	512	R
90 Vol.% Off	595	562	675 Max.
Endpoint, °F	1.0	1.0	3 Max.
Nitrogen, Wt.%	0.40	0.33	
Cetane Index	50.1	52.5	45 Min.

B - Treated DFM

	Pilot Plant	Toledo	F-16884G Mil Spec.
API Gravity	34.8	38.1	Report
Carbon, Wt.%	86.75	86.27	-
Hydrogen, Wt.%	13.02	13.28	-
Nitrogen, ppm	90	3.9	-
Paraffins Vol.%	42.2	45.5	-
Naphthenes, Vol.%	25.8	25.5	-
Aromatics, Vol.%	32.0	29.0	-
Total Acid Number, Mg KOH/gm	0.029	0.010	-
Cetane Number	55.3	50.1	0.30 Max.
ASTM 2274 Mg/100 cc (accelerated to oxid. test)	0.37	0.51	2.5 Max

Table VIII
Residual Fuel Analyses

	Pilot Plant	Toledo
API Gravity	30.3	29.6
Pour Pt., °F	105	80
Rams Bottom Carbon, Wt.%	Not Run	0.096
Asphaltenes, Wt.%	0.244	0.059
Vis. @ 210°F, CST	6.45	2.00
Distillation	D-2887	D-2887
Initial Boiling Point, °F	689	331
10 Vol. % Off, °F	739	582
50 Vol. % Off, °F	830	732
90 Vol. % Off, °F	958	900
Endpoint, °F	1000	1032
Carbon Wt.%	87.32	86.71
Hydrogen, Wt.%	12.59	12.75
Nitrogen, Wt.%	0.33	0.44
Oxygen, ppm	102	182
Sulfur, ppm	20	20
Saturates, Vol.%	57.1	Not run
Aromatics, Vol.%	42.9	Not run
Iron, ppm	0.93	0.10
Arsenic, ppm	0.13	0.4
Vanadium, ppm	0.36	0.02
Sodium, ppm	0.79	0.6
Potassium, ppm	0.10	0.6

for shipment, 4345 bbls. were sent to the U.S. Navy at Mechanicsburg, PA, and the remaining 325 bbls. were shipped to the E.P.A. at the Naval Ship Yard in Long Beach, CA. These fuels are undergoing extensive engine testing and evaluation by the parties involved. In addition to the fuels produced, numerous samples of feed, intermediate and product streams were taken for health effect studies by the D.O.D. and D.O.E.

Conclusions

1. Fuels meeting military specifications and possessing good storage stability characteristics can be produced from shale oil, utilizing conventional refinery equipment.
2. The processing scheme utilized in this study requires:
    a. Settling and a guard bed to protect the hydrotreating catalyst.
    b. Hydrotreating to remove heteratoms, increase the hydrogen/carbon ratio and improve the 650°F minus liquid yield of shale oil.
    c. Acid and clay treating to meet thermal and storage stability requirements of the jet and diesel fuel.

Acklowledgement

This program was administered by the U.S. Navy Energy and Natural Resources R & D offices under the direction of Lt. Commander Lawrence Lukens.

In addition, we wish to acknowledge the long hours and skillful assistance and operation provided by the Toledo Refinery Operations Staff and the Central Engineering Division.

References

1. Jones, J.B., Heistand, R.N., "Recent Paraho Operations", 12th Oil Shale symposium Proceedings, Colo. School of Mines, april 18-20, 1979 pg. 184-194.
2. Robinson, E.T., "Refining of Paraho Shale Oil Into Military specification Fuels", IBID, pg. 195-212.

RECEIVED April 30, 1981.

Relation Between Fuel Properties and Chemical Composition. Chemical Characterization of U.S. Navy Shale-II Fuels

JEFFREY SOLASH[1], ROBERT N. HAZLETT, JACK C. BURNETT,
ERNA BEAL, and JAMES M. HALL

Naval Research Laboratory, Washington, D.C. 20375

As domestic and imported petroleum supplies dwindle and
petroleum increases dramatically in cost, it is imperative for
the Navy to consider future liquid fuel options. The Navy has
two thrusts in transportation fuels: (a) explore the relaxation
of fuel specifications and (b) examine alternate sources of fuels.
This paper deals with one of the alternate sources, shale oil.
    The bulk of the Navy's vehicles utilize middle distillate
fuels; a kerosene type jet fuel, JP-5, for aircraft and diesel fuel
marine, DFM, for ships and boats. Reasonable yields of these
fuels can be obtained from shale oil. Further, shale crude oil
has a good hydrogen content which allows upgrading to finished
fuel with modest additions of expensive hydrogen. Thus the
interest in Navy fuels from shale oil.
    The Navy has completed two crude production/refining exer-
cises with shale. The first of these, a 10,000 barrel operation
(Shale-I), is described in two reports (1,2). The second, a
73,000 barrel operation (Shale-II), was completed in 1979 at the
Toledo refinery of The Standard Oil Company (Ohio) (3). This
paper describes the chemical characterization of the JP-5 and
DFM from the Shale-II project.

Experimental

    Samples. One gallon samples of the various refinery streams
were obtained from Sohio throughout the approximately one month
of production. Periodic samples of finished JP-5 and DFM were
also obtained during the acid treatment process which was completed subsequent to the hydrocracking and fractionation steps.
Drum samples of the finished homogeneous JP-5 and DFM products
were also examined.

---

[1] Current address: Department of Energy, Germantown, MD, 20767.

Total Nitrogen. The fuel samples were pyrolyzed/combusted at 1000°C in a flow of argon/oxygen and the chemiluminescence for the reaction of NO with ozone measured (4). Types of specific nitrogen compounds found are discussed elsewhere in this book (5).

GC Analyses. The n-alkanes in the fuel samples were determined with a 100 meter OV-101 wall coated glass capillary column. The inlet split ratio was 50:1, the column oven was temperature programmed from 80 to 240°C, and the inlet temperature was 310°C. The internal standard procedure was used for quantitation.

LC Separation. Preparative scale liquid chromatography was performed with Waters PrepPak radially compressed silica columns. Fuel charges of 6 to 10 ml were carried through the column with n-pentane at a flow of 200 ml/minute. Refractive index, 254 nm ultraviolet, and 313 nm ultraviolet detectors monitored the LC effluent and keyed the collection of fractions.

Mass Spectrometry. Electron impact (EI) mass spectrometry was done at NRL on the effluent from a 6 ft. OV-101 packed GC column programmed from 70 to 210°C. Field ionization mass spectrometry (FIMS) was performed by SRI International on contract to NRL. In this latter analysis, the fuel sample was frozen on a solids inlet probe prior to insertion into the mass spectrometer. The spectra accumulated for each mass during a temperature program were normally totaled for data presentation (6). Molecules boiling below 140°C are lost or depleted with this technique but such compounds comprise a very small fraction of JP-5 or DFM. Since the ionization efficiency for hydrocarbon classes is currently under study, the FIMS data are utilized primarily in a qualitative sense.

NMR Examination. Fuel samples and fractions were analyzed by proton and ^{13}C NMR at the Naval Biosciences Laboratory. The spectra were taken on a Varian FT-80A.

Results

Nitrogen Content. The bulk of the shale oil nitrogen was removed in the hydrocracking step. All four products from fractionation of the hydrocrackate--naphtha, jet, diesel and heavy oil-- contained substantial amounts of nitrogen, however. The data in Table I indicate that the lighter products had less total nitrogen.

All products increased in nitrogen content as the refining run progressed. For instance, the 25 day hydrocrackate contained 2 ½ times the nitrogen found in the 12 day product. The jet and diesel fractions almost doubled in nitrogen over the same time span. The hydrocracking catalyst lost activity throughout the run.

The nitrogen content of the JP-5 and DFM fractions, the products important to the Navy, was too high to afford satisfactory stability. Extensive acid treatment with sulfuric acid reduced the nitrogen content in the finished fuels, however, to one ppm(w/v) for the JP-5 and 18 ppm (w/v) for DFM. As a consequence the finished fuels had excellent stability. Somewhat higher nitrogen contents would undoubtedly be acceptable with regard to stability but the Shale-II program demonstrates that stable fuels can be made from shale crude oil using standard refining processes.

n-Alkane Content. Shale fuels exhibit higher freeze and pour points than similar fuels made from most petroleum crudes. This is related to the symmetrical n-alkane molecules which are major components of shale derived fuels (7). The content of these molecules in the Shale-II middle distillate fuels is listed in Table II. The relationship between freezing point and composition is described in another chapter of this book (8).

FIMS Fingerprint. Field ionization mass spectrometry of a mixture affords a spectrum of the molecular ions since fragmentation is minimal. Thus a distribution of molecular sizes and hydrocarbon classes can be obtained from a single analysis. This is illustrated in Figure 1 which compares the FIMS fingerprints for JP-5 from Shale-I and Shale-II refining. Distinct differences can be noted. The preponderance of alkanes (C_nH_{2n+2}) is highlighted in Shale-I fuel which was produced by cracking the shale crude by delayed coking. Shale-II, using a hydrocracking process, produced a product much lower in alkanes. Analysis for total n-alkane content agrees with this finding, 37% in Shale-I JP-5 (7) and 22% for Shale-II. Other significant differences between the two jet fuels can be noted in the much higher peaks for substituted benzenes (C_nH_{2n-6}) and tetralins (C_nH_{2n-8}) in the Shale-II product.

Other differences can be noted in the FIMS data assembled in Table III. For instance, Shale-II also has higher peak sums for monocyclic alkanes (C_nH_{2n}) and dicyclic alkanes (C_nH_{2n-2}) than Shale-I. Data for a third JP-5 sample, a ten gallon quantity produced by fractionation of Paraho shale crude followed by 1200 psi catalytic hydrogenation of the jet fuel cut (9), is also shown in Table III. Again this fuel has a distinctly different FIMS fingerprint in response to the refining process used.

Preparative Scale LC. Separation of JP-5 and DFM on the Waters radially compressed silica column gave many fractions. This is illustrated in Figure 2 for six ml of DFM. Fraction one, beginning at 3.2 min, is the saturate fraction which was detected with a refractive index detector. Fraction 2, indicated by slight absorption on the 254 nm uv detector, corresponds to the olefin fraction. The subsequent fractions, as indicated by the strong absorption on one or both of the uv detectors, are comprised of

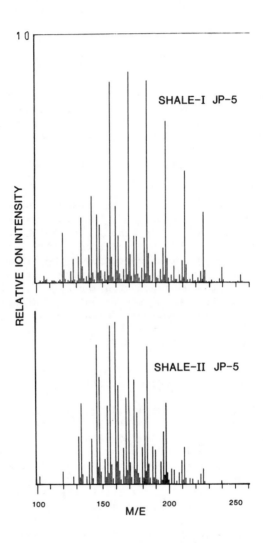

Figure 1.   Field ionization MS of Shale-I and Shale-II JP-5 jet fuels

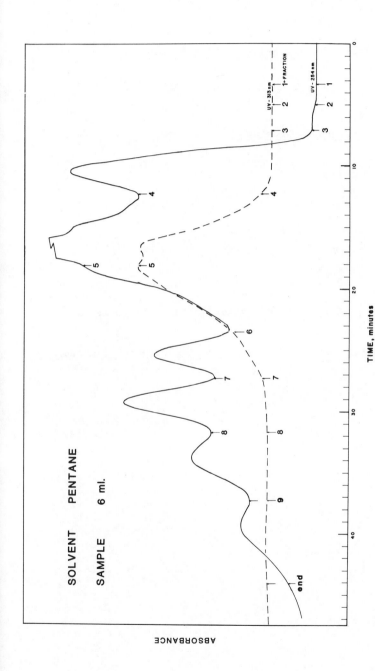

Figure 2. Preparative-scale LC separation of Shale-II DFM; 254-nm UV detector (——); 313-nm UV detector (– – –), RI detector trace not shown. Small numbers indicate times when fraction collection began; the large peak at 16–18 min on the 254-nm trace went off scale. Column, Prep PAK–500/silica; flow rate, 200 mL/min.

Table I.   Shale-II Refining Nitrogen Content*

Days of Operation	Hydro-crackate	Naphtha	Jet Pre-Acid	DFM Pre-Acid	Fractionation Residue
12	1400	---	1700	2500	1940
18	2000	---	2300	2900	2700
21	3000	640	2500	4000	----
25	3800	---	2900	4700	----

* PPM (wt/vol), repeatability ± 5%

Crude shale oil contained 2.1% nitrogen

Table II.   n-Alkanes in Shale-II Fuels

n-Alkane	Weight Percent JP-5	DFM
C_8	---	0.06
C_9	0.14	0.13
C_{10}	4.20	0.46
C_{11}	7.23	0.93
C_{12}	6.08	1.40
C_{13}	3.30	2.22
C_{14}	0.93	2.39
C_{15}	0.28	2.61
C_{16}	0.06	2.19
C_{17}	0.01	2.11
C_{18}	---	1.40
C_{19}	---	0.65
C_{20}	---	0.04
Total	22.23	16.59

Repeatability ± 4%

aromatic fractions. It is noteworthy that fractions 7,8 and 9 exhibit significant absorption at 254 nm but none at 313 nm. The JP-5 sample gave only five fractions in the same type of analysis.

Evaporation of the n-pentane solvent gave an estimate of the amount of the various fractions. The percentages normalized to total 100% are listed in Table IV. Recoveries of input sample amounted to 96 and 93% for the DFM and JP-5, respectively. The losses were due to evaporation of volatile components during the removal of the solvent. As expected, fractions 1 and 3 comprised the bulk of the fuel samples, 88.5% of the DFM and 95.3% of the JP-5. The Fluorescent Indicator Adsorption (FIA) method, ASTM D1319, gave data which generally agrees with the LC preparative scale separation. The JP-5 gave an aromatic content of 24.0% by FIA (versus 23.6% by LC, fractions 3,4 and 5) and an olefin content of 1.6% (2.9% by LC, fraction 2). The DFM had aromatics of 26.0% by FIA (versus 30.4 by LC, fractions 3 through 9) and olefins of 5% (versus 0.8 by LC, fraction 2) (10).

Mass Spectrometry of LC Fractions. The fractions from the preparative scale LC were subjected to GC/MS analysis with electron impact ionization. The total fractions were also analyzed by field ionization mass spectrometry with a direct insertion probe. The FIMS m/e plot for DFM fraction five is depicted in Figure 3. The two major hydrocarbon series observed in this fraction are C_nH_{2n-12} and C_nH_{2n-14}, naphthalenes and acenaphthenes. Trace amounts of the C_nH_{2n-10} and C_nH_{2n-8} series also appear in Figure 3.

The fraction seven FIMS plot (Figure 4) exhibits aromatic hydrocarbons with lower hydrogen contents. The two major series present in this fraction are acenaphthenes and fluorenes, but methyl phenanthrene or anthracene (m/e = 192) is also a significant component of fraction seven.

A summary of the hydrocarbon series in the nine DFM and five JP-5 LC fractions are listed in Tables V and VI. The data are qualitative in nature and based on both MS techniques, EI and FI. The trends with fraction number are as expected, hydrocarbons with less hydrogen appear in the later fractions. Further, the trend in aromatic ring size was 1 ring (fraction 3), 2 rings (fraction 4), and 3 rings (fractions 5-9). The JP-5 has very little three ring material but the DFM exhibits evidence for considerable amounts of acenaphthenes, fluorenes, and phenanthrenes/anthracenes.

The LC separation did not give sharp separation by ring size, however. For instance, tetralins appeared in fractions 3-5 and naphthalenes occurred in fractions 4-7. Larger molecules in a particular series eluted in later fractions. Significantly better separation has been observed with semi-prep LC columns.

Significant amounts of partially or fully saturated ring compounds were found in the jet and diesel products. Mono- and dicyclic alkanes were a major portion of the saturate fraction

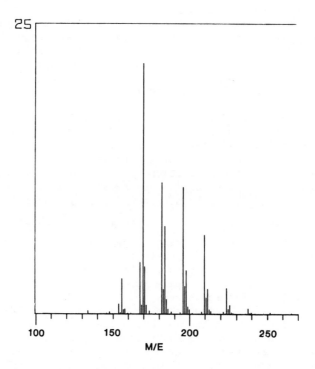

Figure 3.   FIMS of DFM, LC Fraction 5; major hydrocarbon series are C_nH_{2n-12} and C_nH_{2n-14}.

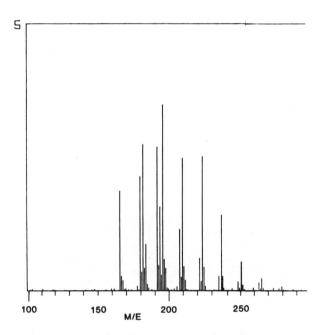

Figure 4.   FIMS of DFM, LC Fraction 7; major hydrocarbon series are C_nH_{2n-14}, C_nH_{2n-16}, and C_nH_{2n-18}.

Table III. Hydrocarbon Classes in JP-5 Samples
by FIMS*

Hydrocarbon Series	Shale-I (Coking)	Shale-II (Hydrocracking)	AF-Exxon (Fractionation & Hydrogenation)
C_nH_{2n+2}	50.8	30.4	40.6
C_nH_{2n}	12.2	16.9	20.8
C_nH_{2n-2}	4.1	7.1	11.2
C_nH_{2n-4}	1.9	0.8	3.2
C_nH_{2n-6}	16.6	19.6	14.4
C_nH_{2n-8}	12.2	23.8	7.3
C_nH_{2n-10}	1.7	1.0	2.2

* Ion intensities (total = 100)

Repeatability $\pm$ 5%

Table IV. Yields From LC Separation

Fraction	Percent Yield DFM	JP-5
1	68.9	73.6
2	0.8	2.9
3	19.6	21.7
4	7.1	1.6
5	1.2	0.3
6	0.6	---
7	0.7	---
8	0.5	---
9	0.7	---
% recovered	96	93

Repeatability $\pm$ 4%

Table V. Hydrocarbon Series in Shale-II DFM

Mass Series	LC Fraction								
	1	2	3	4	5	6	7	8	9
2n + 2	+++	++							
2n	+++	+++							
2n − 2	+++	+++							
2n − 4	++	+++							
2n − 6	+	++	++	+					
2n − 8		+	++	++	+				
2n − 10			++	++	+	+	+		
2n − 12			+	++	++	++	+	+	+
2n − 14				++	++	++	++	++	++
2n − 16					+	+	++	++	++
2n − 18						++	++	+	

+++ Major series in fraction

++ Significant series in fraction

+ Trace series in fraction

Table VI. Hydrocarbon Series in Shale-II JP-5

Mass Series	LC Fraction				
	1	2	3	4	5
2n + 2	++	+			
2n	+++	++			
2n − 2	+++	+++			
2n − 4	++	+++			
2n − 6	+	++	+++	++	+
2n − 8		+	+++	+++	+
2n − 10			+	++	++
2n − 12			+	++	++
2n − 14				+	++

+++ Major series in fraction

++ Significant series in fraction

+ Trace series in fraction

Table VII. Average Molecule in Fraction Three

Parameter	JP-5	DFM
Aromaticity	0.49	0.39
Aromatic Rings/Molecule	1.0	1.0
Average Mol. Wt.	164	206
Average Mol. Formula	$C_{12.2}H_{16.8}$	$C_{15.2}H_{23.3}$
Alkyl Substituents/Molecule	3.2	3.1
Carbons/Alkyl Substituent	2.0	3.0
Naphthene Rings/Molecule	0.5	0.7

and a fair amount of tricyclic alkanes were also found.
Tetralins/indanes were also found in abundance. Some partially
hydrogenated tricyclic aromatics -- C_nH_{2n-10} (tetrahydroacenaph-
thene, hexahydrofluorene, and octahydrophenanthrene) -- were also
observed. The presence of these types of compounds is evidence of
the high pressure hydrocracking step in the refining process.

NMR analyses. Fraction 3 from the LC separation was subjected
to proton nmr examination. The information from this examination
was treated by the method of Clutter and co-workers (11) to describe the average molecule. The calculated parameters are summarized in Table VII. The values obtained are consistent with the
other information in this paper and in the description of the
Shale-I JP-5 reported in an earlier article (7).

Discussion and Conclusions

The information presented in this paper shows that shale oil
has an excellent potential as a source for high quality middle
distillate fuels. The Shale-II program produced fuels with properties significantly improved compared to the properties of the
fuels produced in Shale-I. In particular, Shale-II fuels exhibit
vastly better stability, lower freezing points, and lower oxides of
nitrogen during combustion.

Testing of the Shale-II JP-5 jet fuel, which is currently
underway in four different gas turbine engines, shows good combustion performance. No problems have been encountered. Likewise,
testing of ship steam boilers, marine gas turbines, and diesel
engines on the Shale-II diesel fuel marine (DFM) is demonstrating
highly acceptable performance.

The composition of shale fuels may vary widely, however,
depending on the overall refining process. Much work is needed
to explore other refining options and to examine the effect of
refining on finished fuel composition and properties.

Acknowledgment

The authors thank Dr. S. E. Buttrill, Jr., of SRI International for performing the FIMS analyses and LCDR William Coleman
of the Naval Biosciences Laboratory for conducting the nmr
analyses.

Literature Cited

1. Bartick, H.; Kunchal, K.; Switzer, D.; Bowen, R.; Edwards, R.;
    "The Production and Refining of Crude Shale Oil into Military
    Fuels," Applied Systems Corp., Vienna, Va., ONR Contract
    N00014-75-C-0055, Aug. 1975..

2. Applied Systems Corp., Vienna, Va., "Compilation of Oil Shale Test Results," ONR Contract N00014-76-C-0427, Apr. 1976.

3. Robinson, E. T.; Wasilk, N. J.; "The Commercial Scale Refining of Paraho Crude Shale Oil into Military Specification Fuels," in this book.

4. Drushel, H. F.; <u>Anal. Chem.</u>, 1977, <u>49</u>, 932.

5. Nowack, C. J.; Del Fosse, R. J.; Speck, G.; Solash, J.; Hazlett, R. N.; "Relation Between Fuel Properties and Chemical Composition. IV. Stability of Oil Shale Derived Jet Fuel," in this book.

6. St. John, G. A.; Buttrill, S. E. Jr.; Anbar, M.; Ch. 17 "Field Ionization and Field Desorption Mass Spectrometry Applied to Coal Research," in <u>Organic Chemistry of Coal</u>, ACS Sym. Series No. 71, John Larson, Ed., 1978.

7. Solash, J.; Hazlett, R. N.; Hall, J. M.; Nowack, C. J.; <u>FUEL</u>, 1978, <u>57</u>, 521.

8. Affens, W. A.; Hall, J. M.; Beal, E.; Hazlett, R. N.; Nowack, C. J.; Speck, G.; "Relation Between Fuel Properties and Chemical Composition. III. Physical Properties of U. S. Navy Shale-II Fuels," in this book.

9. AFAPL-TR-75-10, USAF Tech. Rpt. "Evaluation of Methods to Produce Aviation Turbine Fuels from Synthetic Crude Oils, Phase 2," Exxon R&E Co., Linden, N. J., May 1976.

10. White, E. W.; private communication, Naval Ship R&D Center, Annapolis, MD, 1979.

11. Clutter, L.; Petrakis, L.; Stenger, R. L.; Jensen, R. K.; <u>Anal. Chem.</u>, 1972, <u>44</u>, 1395.

RECEIVED January 19, 1981.

Relation Between Fuel Properties and Chemical Composition. Physical Properties of U.S. Navy Shale-II Fuels

W. A. AFFENS, J. M. HALL, E. BEAL, R. N. HAZLETT,
and J. T. LEONARD

Naval Research Laboratory, Washington, D.C. 20375

C. J. NOWACK and G. SPECK

Naval Air Propulsion Center, Trenton, NJ 08628

The U.S. Navy has been involved for some time in the development of Navy fuels from alternative sources (shale oil, tar sands and coal). As a part of this effort, the Naval Research Laboratory and the Naval Air Propulsion Center have been studying the characteristics of these fuels (1,2). NRL and NAPC are currently participating in a program to characterize the products from the Shale-II refining process conducted by the Standard Oil Company of Ohio (SOHIO) at their refinery in Toledo, Ohio. This paper is concerned with a part of this program and is a summary of the work on the physical and related properties of three military type fuels derived from shale: JP-5 and JP-8 jet turbine fuels, and diesel fuel marine (DFM) (3,4,5). Another paper of this symposium (6) will discuss the chemical characterization of the fuels.

JP-5 (3) is a "high flash point" Navy fuel for carrier-based jet aircraft and helicopters and occasionally for shipboard power plants and propulsion. JP-8 (4), a U.S. Air Force jet fuel, is very similar to "Jet A" kerosene used by commercial jet aircraft in the United States and elsewhere. DFM (5) is a multipurpose distillate fuel used by the Navy for ship propulsion in steam generating, gas turbine, and diesel power plants.

The shale derived fuels used in these studies were derived from Paraho crude shale oil. The fuels were prepared by hydrocracking of the total crude, and then fractionation. Both the JP-5 and DFM Shale-II fuels were acid and clay treated in final finishing steps. The refining process which was used is described elsewhere (7).

A total of thirty-six Shale-II fuel samples have been examined including seventeen JP-5 samples, five JP-8 samples and fourteen DFM samples. Of the thirty-six samples, twenty-six were "finished" fuels in that they had been treated with sulfuric acid to remove organic bases, and ten were "pre-acid treatment" samples. Six of the finished samples did not contain additives but the remaining twenty samples did. The latter group included two pilot plant samples, a JP-5 ("J-PP") and a DFM ("D-PP").

GC Simulated Distillation

The boiling range of a representative sample of each of three types of fuels was determined by gas chromatography (GC Simulated Distillation) using ASTM method D 2887 (8). This was also done for representative petroleum derived JP-5 and DFM samples for comparison. Data are plotted for the jet fuels in Figure 1 and for DFM in Figure 2. JP-8 data have been omitted from Figure 1 since the Shale-II data for JP-5 and JP-8 are quite similar. The temperature for the JP-8 (Shale-II) averaged 4°C lower than for the JP-5 sample at the various percentages. The only exception was the 0.5% distilled point, for which JP-5 was 5° lower. It was concluded from the distillation data and other data which follow that the JP-8 Shale-II samples can be considered to be JP-5 for all practical purposes.

The Shale-II distillation temperature data, as seen in the figures, are somewhat low compared to that of the corresponding petroleum fuels. As a rule, data obtained by a GC simulated distillation do not agree with analogous data by actual distillation. Temperatures by the simulated distillation are lower than that of simple ASTM pot distillations (10) at the initial temperatures, higher near the end point temperatures, and in close agreement near the midpoint temperatures (3,4).

Miscellaneous Physical Properties

Specific gravity, freezing point and pour point data are shown in Table I. For each fuel four kinds of data are given (where available): the range of the data (minimum and maximum values obtained), the average value for all the samples examined, the military specification requirement for that property, and an average value for a representative petroleum derived fuel. Also shown in the table are the number of fuel samples which were examined in each case. This format is also used for Table II which will follow.

Specific Gravity. The specific gravities of the Shale-II jet fuels (one sample of each type) were very similar to each other, met specification requirements, and were about the same as that of an average petroleum derived fuel. The two Shale-II DFM specific gravities were very similar but slightly lower than that of an average petroleum derived fuel.

Freezing Point. With the exception of one JP-8 sample (J-11), all the samples of the jet fuels froze below the specification maximum. The single exception froze less than 0.5°C above the allowed value for JP-8, 50°C. The similar freezing points for the JP-5 and JP-8 samples reinforce the conclusion

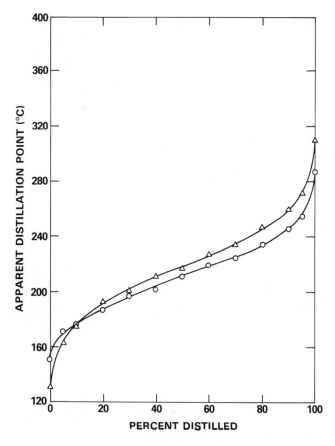

Figure 1.   *GC-simulated distillation of JP-5 fuels: petroleum (80–10) (△); Shale-II (J-18) (○).*

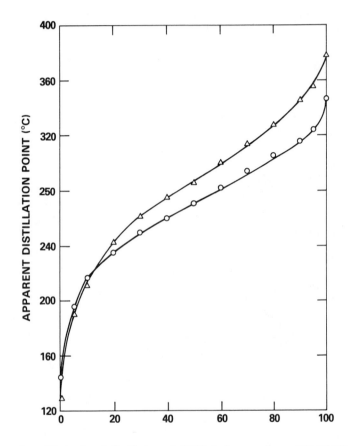

*Figure 2. GC-simulated distillation of DFM fuels: petroleum (PE-76-79) (△);
Shale-II (D-1) (○).*

TABLE I.   Miscellaneous Physical Properties

	Specif. Grav. (25/25°C)[a]	Freezing Point (°C)[b]	Pour Point (°C)[c]
JP-5 (10 samples)			
Range	–	-46.8 - -51.7	–
Average	0.8122[d]	-49.7	–
Specification	0.788 - 0.845	-46 (max.)	–
Petroleum[e]	0.818	-49	–
JP-8 (2 samples)			
Range	–	-49.6 - -50.4	–
Average	0.8098[d]	-50.0	–
Specification	0.775 - 0.830	-50 (max.)	–
Petroleum[e]	0.810	-54	–
DFM (2 samples)			
Range	0.8390 - 0.8393	–	-20.6[f]
Average	0.8392	–	-20.6
Specification	–	–	-6.7[g]
Petroleum[e]	0.850	–	-14

a – ASTM D 1217 (13)
b – ASTM D 2386 (14)
c – ASTM D 97 (15)
d – One sample tested.
e – Data for representative petroleum derived fuel (9,11,12)
f – Same result for both samples.
g – Maximum

TABLE II. Flammability and Ignition Properties

	Flash Point (°C)[a]	AIT (°C)[b]
JP-5 (6 samples)		
Range	55.1 61.2	–
Average	58.0	232[c]
Specification	60 (min.)[d]	–
Petroleum[e]	64	241
JP-8 (2 samples)		
Range	53.4 58.7	–
Average	56.1	238[c]
Specification	38 (min.)	–
Petroleum[e]	53	238
DFM (2 samples)		
Range	71–75	–
Average	73.4	238[c]
Specification	60 (min.)[d]	–
Petroleum[e]	79	240

a   ASTM D 56 (16)
b - ASTM D 2155 (17)
c - One sample tested
d - ASTM D 93 (20)
e - Data for representative petroleum derived fuel (9,11,12,21)

from the distillation data that the two types of jet fuels made in
the SOHIO process are very similar. The highest JP-5 freezing
point was that of the pre-acid treatment sample (J-7) which froze
at -46.8°C. The freezing point of jet fuel is greatly affected
by the concentration of the higher n-alkanes, such as n-hexadecane
(1). The relationship between freezing point and the concentration of n-hexadecane in the fuel appears to be consistent with
that of the Shale-I studies. The amount of the larger alkanes in
the Shale-II jet fuels is relatively low (6), a result of keeping
the distillation end point lower than normal (3,4). A comparison
of Shale-II and petroleum derived JP-5 distillation end points is
made in Figure 1, and was discussed previously. It was seen that
the Shale-II JP-5 end point is lower than that of the petroleum
fuel and this is in accord with the freezing point data.

Pour Point. The pour points of each of two samples of DFM
were 20.6°C. This value is well below the specification maximum of -6.7°C (4) and that of an average petroleum derived DFM
(11,12). As in the case of the jet fuel freezing points
discussed above, the lower pour point of the Shale-II DFM is
consistent with its lower distillation end point compared to
that of the petroleum DFM as seen in Figure 2.

Flammability and Ignition Properties

Flammability and ignition properties are shown in Table II.
As in the case of the miscellaneous physical properties (Table
I), the range of the data, averages, specification requirements,
and representative values for petroleum derived fuels are given
in the table.

Flash Point. Flash points were determined by the Tag
closed cup method (16) rather than by the Pensky-Martens method
(20) as called for in the specifications for JP-5 (3) and DFM
(5). The Tag closed cup, however, is specified for JP-8 (4).
The Tag method was chosen in order to have a basis of comparison
for all three fuels and because it gives values which are closer
to the lower flammability temperature limit which is important
from the standpoint of safety. For fuels in the JP-5/DFM flash
point range, the Tag method gives values which are 2-4°C lower
than that of the Pensky-Martens method (12). The JP-8 and the
DFM flash points are seen to be well above the specification
requirements of 38° and 60°C (4,5). In the case of the JP-5
samples, four of the six samples had Tag flash points which
were below the required 60°C (3). However, if we assume that
the Pensky-Martens flash points would average about 3°C higher,
four of the six samples would then meet the 60°C minimum and the
other two would be less than two degrees low. The Shale-II JP-8
flash point data are somewhat higher than that of an average

petroleum derived JP-8 and quite close to that of the Shale-II
JP-5.

Autoignition Temperatures. The autoignition data (AIT) shown
in Table II were determined by ASTM D 2155 (17). The Shale-II
JP-8 and DFM AIT values (238°C) were identical and similar to
that of their petroleum derived counterparts. The Shale-II JP-5
AIT (232°C), however, was slightly lower than that of the other
two fuels as well as that of a representative petroleum JP-5
(241°C), but was well within the 11°C reproducibility limit set
by the method (17). There are no AIT requirements in the military specifications for JP-5, JP-8 and DFM (3,4,5).

Electrostatic Properties

The electrical conductivity and charging tendency of jet
fuels are important for predicting electrostatic charge buildup
in fuel handling equipment, particularly filter separators.
Electrostatic charge buildup can result in a spark discharge
capable of igniting flammable vapors if they are present. This
is a frequent cause of accidental fires and explosions and is an
important factor in safety. Therefore, these properties were
measured on the Shale-II jet fuels to determine if these fuels
posed a lesser or greater hazard than their petroleum-derived
counterparts. The only electrostatic specification requirement
for current U.S. military fuels is that of an electrical conductivity range for JP-4 (3) and JP-8 (4). This requirement, however, is a recent one and did not apply to the JP-8 fuels of this
study.

Electrical conductivity was determined by the ASTM method
(18) and charging tendency with the EXXON Mini-Static Tester (19).
The latter method measures the amount of electrical charge
generated by flowing a fuel sample through a paper filter.
Electrostatic data are shown in Table III. Shale-I data (2)
are included in the table for comparison. The Shale-I fuels were
also derived from Paraho shale oil. However, the Shale-I fuels
were prepared by coking of the total crude, rather than by hydrocracking as in the case of the Shale-II fuels. After the coking,
the Shale-I fuels were then fractionated. For finishing steps,
the JP-5 was subjected to mild hydrotreatment, and the DFM was
treated by acid extraction. The Shale-I refinery process is
described in detail elsewhere (22). The petroleum data are
based on a fuel survey. The Shale-II values in the table are in
the normal ranges found for petroleum derived jet fuels. The
response to the addition of static dissipator additive, ASA-3,
is also normal. The sharp increase of charging tendency in the
fuel sample to which ASA-3 had been added at first glance appears
to be at cross purposes with the intent of an anti-static agent.
However, this is not the case, since most of the charge would

Table III. Electrostatic Properties of Shale Jet Fuels

Fuel	Source	Treatment	Conductivity (pS/m)[a]	Charging Tendency (pC/m^3)[b]
JP-5	Shale-I	–	246	c
"		Filtered[d]	215	7035
"	Shale-II	–	6.6	2100
"		1 ppm ASA-3 added	228	16600
"	Petroleum[e]	–	0.8 – 15	1500 – 4000
JP-8	Shale-II	–	5.3	890
"		1 ppm ASA-3 added	142	12300
"	(Specification)[f]		200 (min.) – 600 (max.)	–

a – ASTM D 3114 (18)
b – Exxon Minitester (Measured with Type 10 filter paper) (19)
c – Fuel contained a sediment which clogged the filter of the charging tendency apparatus
d – Filtered thru 0.45μ millipore
e – Data for representative petroleum derived fuels
f – MIL-T-83133A, 18 May 1979 (4)

relax very rapidly (less than one second) because of the
increased conductivity due to the ASA-3. However, it is seen in
Table III, that a concentration of more than 1 ppm ASA-3 would
be required for the Shale-II JP-8 sample to meet the new electrical conductivity specification requirement.

The Shale-I JP-5 exhibited abnormally high electrical
conductivity and charging tendency. This fuel was an off specification product containing sediment which clogged the filter
of the charging tendency apparatus making it impossible to
obtain a charge density measurement. The values shown in the
table were obtained after the sample was filtered through a
0.45µ Millipore filter.

Copper Corrosion

Tests for corrosion are of a qualitative type and are made
to determine whether the fuel is free of tendency to corrode copper bearing alloys in aircraft pumps. The results of the ASTM
copper strip corrosion tests (23) are shown in Table IV. The
samples in the table are grouped in accordance with their
refining treatment and by the additives the fuels were reported
to contain. In the table, the two pilot plant samples were
finished samples and contained both antioxidant (AO-29) and fuel
system icing inhibitor (FSII). The remaining twenty nine
samples were refinery prepared and are in three groups: the
first group of nine samples was taken before the acid treatment and contained no additives. The second group of six
samples was acid and clay treated but contained no additives.
The third group of fourteen samples was finished (acid and
clay treated) and was reported to contain AO-30 anti-oxidant.
The JP-5 samples in the third group were found to contain FSII
(24). The additives are identified in the table. The test
results are summarized on the right hand side of the table.

It is seen in Table IV that both pilot plant samples
(finished samples plus additives) passed the copper corrosion
test, as did most of the additive-free refinery samples. However, all fourteen of the additive-containing refinery samples
failed. These fourteen samples were all finished samples and
contained AO-30. Since the six DFM samples which failed the
test did not contain FSII, it is assumed that this additive did
not play a part. Since the two pilot plant samples (containing
AO-29) passed the test, and the fourteen refinery samples
(containing AO-30) failed, questions are raised concerning the
anti-oxidant additives which were used. These results need to
be related to the sequence of operations in the refinery process
and to the nature of the additives which were used. It seems
probable that either there was a problem with the acid treatment
process by which a corrosive species was produced which ended
up in the finished samples, or that the additives used may have
been contaminated. Both aspects may be involved.

TABLE IV. Copper Strip Corrosion Tests [a] - Shale II Fuels

Fuel	Treatment	Additives[b]	Number of Samples		
			Total	Passed	Failed
Pilot Plant Preparation:					
JP-5	Acid Treated	AO-29 & FSII	1	1	0
DFM	"	AO-29	1	1	0
		Total	2	2	0
Refinery Preparation:					
JP-5, JP-8	Pre-Acid	None	6	5	1
DFM	"	"	3	3	0
		Total	9	8	1
JP-5, JP-8	Acid Treated	"	5	5	0
DFM	"	"	1	0	1
		Total	6	5	1
JP-5	"	AO-30 & FSII	8	0	8
DFM	"	AO-30	6	0	6
		Total	14	0	14

a – ASTM D 130 (23).
b – Fuel System Icing Inhibitor (Ethylene glycol monomethyl ether) (3,4) – jet fuels only; Anti-oxidants "AO-29" (2,6-ditertiary-butyl-4-methyl-phenol) or "AO-30" (2,4-dimethyl-6-tertiary-butyl phenol).

Free sulfur (17 ppm) and mercaptans (10 ppm) have been detected in the Shale-II JP-5. Model studies found that the combined presence of these two species, each at about the 10 ppm level, can cause failure of the copper corrosion test. The anti-oxidant, AO-30, exhibited indications of reinforcing the effects of the sulfur species in the model studies.

An attempt was made to correct the copper corrosion problem by different types of fuel treatments (25). JP-5 samples were subjected to clay or silica gel filtration, or treatment with activated charcoal to remove the corrosive compounds. None of these treatments was successful. Samples were also treated with barium nitrate (to precipitate out sulfonates), sodium hydroxide (to extract mercaptans), and air bubbling to oxidize the corrosive compounds. These chemical treatments also were unsuccessful. However, JP-5 fuel (which failed the copper corrosion test) passed if benzotriazole, sometimes used to passivate copper surfaces, was added to the fuel in low concentrations (2 ppm) using FSII as a solvent. This technique is effective for reducing jet fuel attack on copper-nickel pipes used aboard aircraft carriers (26).

Conclusions

The physical properties of the Shale-II fuels were similar to that of equivalent fuels derived from petroleum. The differences observed could be minimized by modest changes in refining steps. Based on these results and other Navy R and D, shale oil can be considered a promising alternative source for the production of U.S. Navy distillate fuels.

Acknowledgment

The authors thank Mr. Charles Stansky of UOP, Inc. for determination of free sulfur in the JP-5 and for consultation on the copper corrosion problem.

The authors are also indebted to Mr. John De Guzman for assistance in obtaining the flash point and freezing point data.

Literature Cited

1. Solash, J.; Hazlett, R.N.; Hall, J.M.; Nowack, C.J.; Fuel, 1978, 57, 521.

2. Affens, W.A.; Leonard, J.T.; McLaren, G.W.; Hazlett, R.N., Preprints, Symposium on Oil Shale, Tar Sands, and Related Materials, Division of Fuel Chemistry, Amer. Chem. Soc., Sept. 1976, 21, (No. 6), 249.

3. Military Specification, Turbine Fuel, Aviation Grades, JP-4 and JP-5, MIL-T-5624L, 18 May 1979.

4. Military Specification, Turbine Fuel, Aviation, Kerosene Type, Grade JP-8, MIL-T-83133A, 18 May 1979.

5. Military Specification, Fuel Oil, Diesel Marine, MIL-F-16884G, 7 March 1973; Amend. 22 March 1978.

6. Solash, J; Hazlett, R.N.; Burnett, J.C.; Beal, E.; Hall, J.M., "Relation Between Fuel Properties and Chemical Composition. II. Chemical Characterization of U.S. Navy Shale-II Fuels", This Symposium.

7. Robinson, E.T.; Wasilk, N.J.; "The Commercial Scale Refining of Paraho Shale Oil into Military Specification Fuels", This Symposium.

8. "Boiling Range Distribution of Petroleum Fractions by Gas Chromatography", Amer. Soc. for Test. and Mater., ASTM D2887, 1973.

9. Shelton, E.M.; "Aviation Turbine Fuels, 1978," Bur. of Mines, Petrol. Survey 109, May 1979.

10. "Distillation of Petroleum Products," Amer. Soc. for Test. and Mater., ASTM D86 (1972).

11. "Distillate Fuel Economic Study," Nav. Ship Engr. Center, May 1974.

12. Affens, W.A.; "Shipboard Safety - A Meaningful Flash Point Requirement for Navy Fuels," Naval Research Laboratory Report 7999, Oct. 28, 1976.

13. "Density and Relative Density (Specific Gravity) of Liquids by Bingham Pycnometer," Amer. Soc. for Test. and Mater., ASTM D1217 (1976).

14. "Freezing Point of Aviation Fuels," Amer. Soc. for Test. and Mater., ASTM D2386 (1972).

15. "Pour Point of Petroleum Oils," Amer. Soc. for Test. and Mater., ASTM D97 (1971).

16. "Flash Point by Tag Closed Tester," Amer. Soc. for Test. and Mater., ASTM D56 (1975).

17. "Autoignition Temperature of Liquid Petroleum Products", Amer. Soc. for Tes. and Mater., ASTM D2155 (1976).

18. "D-C Electrical Conductivity of Hydrocarbon Fuels," Amer. Soc. for Test. and Mater., ASTM D3114 (1972).

19. Young, D.A.; "Mini-Static Test Procedure", Exxon Research and Engineering Co., Linden, N.J., June 1972.

20. "Flash Point by Pensky-Martens Closed Tester," Amer. Soc. for Test. and Mater., ASTM D93 (1974).

21. Coordinating Research Council, "A Survey of Electrical Conductivity and Charging Tendency Characteristics of Aircraft Turbine Fuels," CRC Report 478, April 1975.

22. Bartick, H.; Kunchal, K.; Switzer, D.; Bowen, R.; Edwards, R., "The Production and Refining of Crude Shale Oil into Military Fuels", Final Report of Applied Systems Corp., Vienna, Va. to the Office of Naval Research, under Navy Contract No. N-00014-75-C-0055, August 1975.

23. "Detection of Copper Corrosion from Petroleum Products by the Copper Strip Tarnish Test," Amer. Soc. for Test. and Mater., D130 (1976).

24. "Fuel System Icing Inhibitor in Hydrocarbon Fuels (Iodometric Method)," Fed. Test Method Std. 791B, Method 5327.3, Jan. 15, 1969.

25. Speck, G; "Correction of Shale-II Copper Corrosion Problem," Naval Air Propulsion Center, Final Report NAPC-LR-80-6, 22 April 1980.

26. Shertzer, R.; "Investigation of the Reduction of Thermal Stability of Fuel by Copper Contamination on Aircraft Carriers," Naval Air Propulsion Test Center, NAPTC-PE-14, January 1973.

RECEIVED January 19, 1981.

Relation Between Fuel Properties and Chemical Composition. Stability of Oil Shale-Derived Jet Fuel

C. J. NOWACK, R. J. DELFOSSE, and G. SPECK

Naval Air Propulsion Center, Trenton, NJ 08628

J. SOLASH[1] and R. N. HAZLETT

Naval Research Laboratory, Washington, D.C. 20375

The Navy has been interested in the use of alternate fossil fuels for sometime (1-4). Our interest is focused primarily in establishing the effects of chemical composition on fuel properties since such relations will lead to greater availability and better use of fuels. We recently reported some of our results on jet fuels derived from coal, tar sands and oil shale (1). Other papers in this series report on some aspects of oil shale derived fuels obtained from a large production experiment, Shale II, performed by Paraho, Inc. (5,6). In this paper, we report on some aspects of stability of a jet fuel prepared in an earlier Navy Program, Shale-I (3).

Previous work with shale oil derived middle distillates has noted the very high freezing point of these fuels (1,7). In addition, shale oil fuels which were high in nitrogen gave as much as 45% conversion of fuel bound nitrogen to NO_x emissions when burned under typical jet engine conditions (4). The high nitrogen content in shale oil jet fuels leads to particulates and gums upon standing at ambient temperatures in the absence of light (7).

Stability concerns the tendency of fuels to form particulates and/or coatings on engine surfaces under two different sets of conditions. One set of conditions is that of storage: weeks or months at temperatures of $\leqslant 40^{\circ}C$, quiescent exposure to air, and no light. The fuel encounters much different conditions in a jet aircraft: a few hours at temperatures up to $80^{\circ}C$ with agitation and exposure to air in the fuel tanks plus a minute or so at $150-250^{\circ}C$ in the fuel system components with only dissolved air present. Again, no light is present during the high temperature exposure. Shale oil derived fuels used in this work were much poorer than petroleum derived fuels under both stability regimes and a thorough study of the stability of these fuels was undertaken.

[1] Current address: Department of Energy, Germantown, MD, 20767.

Experimental

The shale oil derived jet fuel (designated Shale-I) used in this work was produced from a crude shale oil (supplied by Paraho, Inc.) by delayed coking, fractionation, and mild hydrotreatment at the Gary-Western refinery. The entire production operation has been fully described elsewhere (3). The physical properties of the jet fuel have been reported (1).

High temperature stability of the fuels was measured using an Alcor, Inc. Jet Fuel Thermal Oxidation Tester (JFTOT) (8). Low temperature (storage) stability was determined by measurement of gums, contamination and peroxide concentration (all by ASTM standard methods) before and after exposure to temperatures of $60^{o}C$ for four weeks. The fuels were stored in 1ℓ low actinic, dark pyrex glass bottles and were loosely covered to prevent exposure to airborne particulates. Air could still diffuse into the vessel. The vessels with fuel and various additives were thermostated at $60^{o}C$ for the specified length of time.

Isolation of shale oil jet fuel basic nitrogen compounds was accomplished by extraction with 1N aqueous HCl followed by neutralization of the HCl adducts (7). The basic nitrogen compounds thus obtained were analyzed by gas chromatography using a Perkin-Elmer model 3920B gas chromatograph equipped with a 100m OV-101 glass WCOT column and nitrogen-specific detector. This column separated the nitrogen compounds into at least 70 incompletely resolved components. Tentative identification of some of the components was made by combined gas chromatography-mass spectrometry (gc-ms) using a Hewlett-Packard model 5982 gc-mass spectrometer with a Hewlett-Packard model 5933A dedicated data system. The mass spectrometer was equipped with a 33m SE-30 SCOT column and was operated in the EI mode at 70 eV. In addition, the extracted basic nitrogen compounds were subjected to field ionization mass spectroscopy (FIMS). Ions produced by field ionization tend not to fragment and an accurate molecular weight profile of a mixture can be constructed (9).

Results and Discussion

Early work with refined shale oil clearly showed (7) that the jet fuel used (∿1000 ppm nitrogen) was unstable and rapidly plugged filters upon standing for several days. Removal of nitrogenous material by acid extraction or by passing the fuel over clay or silica gel gave improved storage properties. The chemical constitution of the nitrogen containing materials was sought in an effort to discover specific classes of compounds which could cause stability problems. It is well known that pyrroles and indoles are quite reactive toward air and light (10-14) and if present in large quantities in these fuels might account for the observed instability.

Basic Nitrogen Compounds. The Shale-I jet fuel contained 976 ppm nitrogen of which 860 ppm nitrogen was acid extractable. The neutralized extract was subjected to gas chromatography using an all glass system with a high efficiency capillary column. A chromatogram of the acid extract obtained using a nitrogen-specific detector is shown in Figure 1. As shown, retention time matching implies that the majority of compounds are pyridine-type bases. The mixture was also subjected to gc-mass spectroscopy. The total ion chromatogram is shown in Figure 2. The lower resolution SCOT column used on the mass spectrometer did not permit unequivocal assignment of each peak. Tentative assignments of the numbered peaks are noted in Table I. In many cases, the electron impact mass spectrum clearly showed the presence of more than one compound. However, the main compound type observed was alkyl substituted pyridine with lesser quantities of quinolines. We used another mass spectral technique to help confirm our gc-ms assignments. The FIMS results are tabulated in Table II. Since molecules tend not to fragment when field ionized, the FIM spectrum can be scanned for parent masses; compound classes and higher alkyl substituted homologs are readily recognized. The FIMS data confirm the presence of major amounts of pyridine compounds with lesser quantities of quinoline and tetrahydroquinoline types.

While ionization efficiencies for various classes of compounds under FI conditions are not known with certainty, we do not expect them to be very different for the aromatic nitrogen types observed here. We have observed that FIMS data on basic nitrogen compounds result in a higher than expected intensity for parent +1 peaks. This was observed for our basic nitrogen extracts but not for n-alkane or neutral fuel samples. We attribute this phenomenon to the presence of water in the basic nitrogen extracts; water rapidly loses a hydrogen atom to the radical cation generated by FI.

Extraction of the Shale-I jet fuel with HCl is approximately 90% efficient for removal of nitrogen containing material. Remaining in the fuel are 116 ppm of non-basic nitrogen compounds. Presumably, these compounds will be comprised primarily of pyrrole, indole and carbazole types. Only traces of substituted pyrroles and indoles were observed by FIMS in the basic nitrogen fraction (Table II). Shale oil nitrogen compounds have been characterized previously (15) and since carbazoles and pyrroles could not be titrated it is not surprising that they are also not efficiently extracted by 1N HCl.

High Temperature (Thermal) Stability. The high temperature stability of the Shale-I jet fuels was measured using the JFTOT technique (8). The thermal oxidative stability of the received fuel (976 ppm N) was measured. The fuel was then acid extracted, the isolated basic nitrogen compounds added back into the extracted shale fuel in varying quantity, and the thermal oxidative stability redetermined. A petroleum derived JP-5 was also subjected to JFTOT

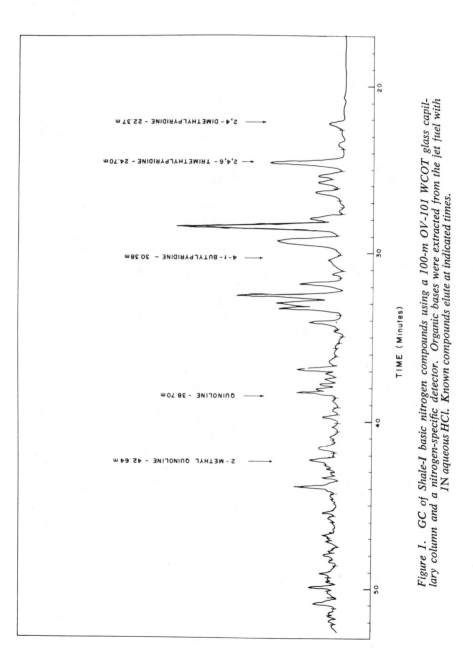

Figure 1. GC of Shale-I basic nitrogen compounds using a 100-m OV-101 WCOT glass capillary column and a nitrogen-specific detector. Organic bases were extracted from the jet fuel with IN aqueous HCl. Known compounds elute at indicated times.

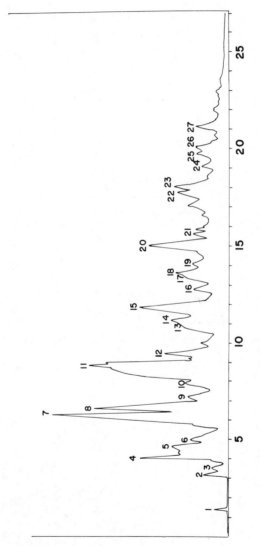

Figure 2. Total ion chromatogram of the basic nitrogen fraction from Shale-I jet fuel

Table I. Tentative Structural Assignments of GC-MS Peaks

Peak #[A]	Prominent Peaks m/e (Peak, Rel. Abundance)	Tentative Assignment
1	$78(M^+, Base), 77(M^+-1, 20\%), 52(15\%)$	benzene
2	$107(M^+, Base), 106(M^+-1, 50\%), 92(M^+-CH_3, 20\%), 79(M^+-HCN, 30\%)$	4-ethylpyridine
3	$121(M^+, 40\%), 120(M^+-1, Base), 107(M^+-CH_2, 25\%), 93(M^+-C_2H_4, 20\%)$	2-methyl-ethyl-pyridine
4	$121(M^+, Base), 120(M^+-1, 30\%), 106(M^+-CH_3, 21\%), 79(M^+-C_3H_6, 35\%)$	4-i-propyl pyridine
5	$121(M^+, 85\%), 120(M^+-1, Base), 107(M^+-CH_2, 25\%), 93(M^+-C_2H_4, 15\%), 79(M^+-C_3H_6, 35\%)$	2-propylpyridine
6	$121(M^+, Base), 120(M^+-1, 55\%), 106(M^+-CH_3, 50\%), 93(M^+-C_2H_4, 15\%)$	3-ethyl-4-methyl-pyridine
7	$135(M^+, 45\%), 134(M^+-1, Base), 121(M^+-CH_2, 45\%), 107(M^+-C_2H_4, 25\%), 106(M^+-C_2H_5, 30\%)$	2-propyl-methyl-pyridine
8	$135(M^+, Base), 134(M^+-1, 55\%), 121(M^+-CH_2, 20\%), 120(M^+-CH_3, 50\%)$	3,4-diethylpyridine
9	$135(M^+, 45\%), 134(M^+-1, Base), 121(M^+-CH_2, 30\%), 120(M^+-CH_3, 35\%), 107(M^+-C_2H_4, 65\%)$	2-propyl-methyl-pyridine
10	$135(M^+, Base), 134(M^+-1, 75\%), 121(M^+-CH_2, 15\%), 120(M^+-CH_3, 30\%), 107(M^+-C_2H_4, 28\%), 106(M^+-C_2H_5, 30\%)$	4-butylpyridine
11	$149(M^+, 15\%), 148(M^+-1, 33\%), 135(M^+-CH_2, 33\%), 134(M^+-CH_3, 56\%), 121(M^+-C_2H_4, Base)$	3-propyl-4-ethyl-pyridine

Table I - Continued

Peak #[A]	Prominent Peaks m/e (Peak, Rel. Abundance)	Tentative Assignment
12	$163(M^+,6\%),162(M^+-1,11\%),149(M^+-CH_2,53\%),148(M^+-CH_3,40\%),121(M^+-C_3H_6,\text{Base})$	3-propyl-4-ethyl-5-methylpyridine
13	$163(M^+,8\%),162(M^+-1,15\%),149(M^+-CH_2,60\%),148(M^+-CH_3,\text{Base}),134(M^+-C_2H_5,44\%),121(M^+-C_3H_6,30\%)$	3-ethyl-4-butylpyridine
14	$163(M^+,25\%),162(M^+-1,55\%),149(M^+-CH_2,34\%),148(M^+-CH_3,55\%),135(M^+-C_2H_4,\text{Base})$	2-propyl-3-methyl-4-ethylpyridine
15	$163(M^+,9\%),162(M^+-1,25\%),148(M^+-CH_3,18\%),134(M^+-C_2H_5,30\%),121(M^+-C_3H_6,\text{Base})$	2-butyl-4-ethylpyridine
16[B]	$163(M^+,27\%),162(M^+-1,20\%),147(45\%),121(M^+-C_3H_6,\text{Base})$	3,4-dipropylpyridine + tetrahydromethyl quinoline
17[B]	$176(M^+-1,11\%),163(M^+-CH_2,30\%),162(M^+-CH_3,37\%),147(M^+,80\%),146(70\%),143(M^+,\text{Base})$	C$_7$-pyridine + 3-methyl-quinoline + tetrahydro-methyl quinoline
18[B]	Complex spectrum	probable species include C$_6$-pyridine, C$_1$-quinoline, methyl-tetrahydroquinoline, ethyl tetrahydroquinoline
19[B]	$177(M^+,6\%),176(M^+-1,10\%),162(M^+-CH_2,18\%),161(M^+,18\%),135(M^+-C_3H_6,\text{Base})$	probable components: C$_7$-pyridine (one butyl group), ethyl-tetrahydroquinoline, methyl tetrahydroquinoline, methylquinoline

Table I - Continued

Peak #[A]	Prominent Peaks m/e (Peak, Rel. Abundance)	Tentative Assignment
20[B]	$177(M^+,8\%),176(M^+-1,15\%),160(M^+-1,15\%),134(M^+-C_3H_7,26\%),121(M^+-C_4H_8,Base)$	major: C_7-pyridine (with 2-pentyl gp)
21[B]	Complex spectrum	probable major components: C_2-quinoline, C_2-tetrahydroquinoline; minor: C_7-pyridine
22[B]	Complex spectrum	probable major components: C_2-quinoline; minor components: C_2-tetrahydroquinoline, C_7-pyridine; trace: C_4-tetrahydroquinoline
23[B]	Complex spectrum	probable major component: C_8-pyridine; very minor components; C_2-quinoline, C_2-tetrahydroquinoline 2
24[B]	$191(M^+,14\%),190(M^+-1,5\%),171(M^+,45\%),170(M^+-1,25\%),121(M^+-70,Base)$	major: C_8-pyridine, C_3-quinoline; minor: C_3-quinoline, C_2-tetrahydroquinoline
25[B]	$171(M^+,Base),170(M^+-1,30\%),156(M^+-CH_3,25\%),149(25\%)$	3-methyl-4-ethyl quinoline; minor: C_8-pyridine, other quinoline types

Table I – Continued

Peak #[A]	Prominent Peaks m/e (Peak, Rel. Abundance)	Tentative Assignment
26[B]	Complex spectrum	probable major components: C_9-pyridine, C_3-quinoline
27[B]	Complex spectrum	probable major components: C_9-pyridine + C_3-quinoline

[A], Refer to Figure 2 for numbered peak position in total ion chromatogram of gc-mass spectrum.

[B], EI spectra showed evidence of more than one compound.

Table II.   Field Ionization Mass Spectrum
Base Fraction from Shale-I JP-5

Series	Range of "n" Values*	Compounds	Relative Ion Count
$C_nH_{2n+1}N$	7 - $\underline{12}$ - 14	Piperidines	10
$C_nH_{2n-3}N$	7 - $\underline{9}$ - 15	Pyrroles	28
$C_nH_{2n-5}N$	7 - $\underline{9}$ - 16	Pyridines	1000
$C_nH_{2n-7}N$	9 - $\underline{11}$ - 16	Tetrahydro-quinolines	170
$C_nH_{2n-9}N$	8 - $\underline{13}$ - 15	Indoles	13
$C_nH_{2n-11}N$	9 - $\underline{11}$ - 14	Quinolines	157

* Underlined value of "n" indicates components in largest amount.

testing. The petroleum fuel had a breakpoint temperature of 275°C
and at 260°C did not produce significant tube deposit ratings (TDR)
or develop a significant pressure drop across the in-line JFTOT
filter. A number of nitrogen compounds, typical of those found in
this study, were then added to the petroleum derived JP-5 and the
high temperature stability redetermined. The results with shale
and petroleum fuels are displayed in Table III.

In previously reported stability work with shale oil derived
jet fuels (16) it was shown that the JFTOT thermal stability improved as the total nitrogen content decreased. In Table III, it
is observed that the thermal stability of the Shale-I fuel improves
as the concentration of basic nitrogen compounds decreases. In
previous work (16) the lower nitrogen contents of the shale oil
jet fuels were achieved by more severe hydrotreatment.

It can also be observed that there apparently are two major
modes of high temperature thermal instability and the effect of
basic nitrogen is different in each. If thermal stability is
measured only by tube deposits, a slight rise in breakpoint temperature is observed as the basic nitrogen content is reduced (breakpoint by TDR from 244°C to 254°C as basic N changes from 838 to 7
ppm). However, if the filter pressure drop is used for determining
breakpoint, then a much larger change, 227 to 279°C, is observed
as basic nitrogen content is reduced.

Pure compounds which are similar to those found in the Shale-I
basic nitrogen fractions (Tables I and II) were added to a petroleum based jet fuel of high stability (Table III). Most of the
basic nitrogen compounds used resulted in negligible deposit (TDR)
formation with the exception of 2-amino-3-methylpyridine. 4-t-
Butylpyridine showed evidence of filter plugging but only slight
deposits were formed. Pyrrole, however, was found to produce a
very high deposit rating (TDR) and also plugged the in-line filter.
Much more work with pure compounds in simple carrier vehicles is
necessary before definitive mechanistic inferences can be drawn
regarding the effects of the various classes of nitrogen compounds.

Storage Stability. The low temperature or storage stability
of the Shale-I fuel was followed by determining changes in peroxides, gums, contamination, and high temperature stability (JFTOT
behavior). The latter method was employed since deposit precursors,
which might form at low temperatures, could seriously degrade
engine operation if present in sufficient concentration. The test
fuel was placed in 1ℓ glass bottles which were loosely covered to
permit air diffusion to the fuel. Ten ml of distilled water and
1 g of iron filings were placed in each sample. These conditions
simulated actual storage tank conditions since water is always
present in fuel storage tanks and the fuel is frequently in contact
with uncoated metal surfaces of storage tanks. The samples were
maintained at 60°C for four weeks. The results of the storage
stability experiments are presented in Table IV.

Table III. High Temperature Stability of Jet Fuels[A]

Fuel Type	Organic Nitrogen, ppm		Breakpoint Temperature, B °C	
	Acid Extractable	Total	Heater Tube (TDR)	Filter
Shale Oil-Jet Fuel	860	976	–	232
	838[C]	954[C]	244	227
	97[C]	213[C]	243	232
	50[C]	166[C]	251	241
	7[C]	123[C]	254	279

	Additive Conc., ppm	260°C	
		Max TDR	ΔP, mm
Petroleum[D]	4-t-butylpyridine, 56	1	20
	2-t-butylpyridine, 49	10	1
	5-ethyl-2-methylpyridine, 107	11	3
	4-benzylpyridine, 56	7	2
	2-amino-3-methylpyridine, 134	45	14
	N,N-dimethylaniline, 82	6	5
	pyrrole, 100	32	Bypass[E]

A, Measured using Alcor, Inc. JFTOT according to ASTM Standard Method D-3241.

B, Breakpoint is defined as the temperature of test at which a maximum TDR of >17 is observed or a pressure drop of >25 mm Hg is attained across the in-line JFTOT filter.

C, Shale Oil JP-5 extracted with HCl, washed, and the isolated basic nitrogen compounds reintroduced to the shale oil fuel.

D, The petroleum derived jet fuel had a breakpoint temperature of 275°C and had negligible TDR or filter pressure drop at 260°C.

E, Pressure drop of >25mm developed after which the test continued for standard 2.5 hr. period with the hot fuel bypassing the filter.

Table IV. Results of Storage Stability Tests of Treated Shale-I JP-5 [A]

Experiment #	N-Additive, ppm [C]	Inhibitor [B], ppm	Storage Results				JFTOT 260°C Max TDR	
			Existent Gums, mg/100 ml		Peroxide, meq/kg			
			Before	After	Before	After	Before	After
1	0	0	0	0	0.14	60	1	10
2	8.4	0	0	1.4	1.4	64.3	9	13
3	25	0	0	5.4	1.0	96.8	4	27
4	125	0	0	1.6	0.2	42.5	5	48
5	0 [D]	25-DA	0	0	0	1.0	0	2
6	39 [D]	25-DA	0	0	0	0.6	0	2
7	123 [D]	25-DA	0	0	0.1	0.1	5	13
8	0	24-HP	0	0	0.7	0.7	4	9
9	5-ethyl-2-methylpyridine, 50	0	0	5	0.6	83	4	35
10	"	24-HP	0	0	0.6	0.6	0	0
11	2,5-dimethylpyrrole, 50	0	0	0.4	0.09	4.2	25	25
12	"	24-HP	0	0.6	0.07	0.5	26	25

A. Shale-I JP-5 containing 976 ppm nitrogen was first acid extracted then treated with silica gel to yield a nitrogen-free fuel. Conditions of storage: temp=60°C; time=4 weeks; no agitation; air allowed to freely diffuse into fuel.

B. Antioxidants used were commercial products qualified for Navy fuel use; DA=phenylene diamine (1,4-diamino benzene); HP=hindered phenol (2,6-di-tert-butyl-4-methylphenol).

C. Acid extracted nitrogen compounds added to nitrogen-free Shale-I JP-5 to bring nitrogen content to designated level.

D. Corrected for antioxidant nitrogen content.

Storage stability measurements have been performed on some shale derived fuel (17). In that study, a Paraho jet fuel (very similar to our Shale-I) was found to form some gums (increase in gums of about 2 mg/100 ml fuel after 32 weeks storage at 43°C) but there was only a small increase in acid number and no increase in viscosity. In our storage tests, we tried to determine the effects of basic nitrogen compounds on the storage stability of the Shale-I fuel. The combination of acid extraction followed by silica gel chromatography of the Shale-I fuel was found to be effective for removing all nitrogen containing compounds. The nitrogen-free Shale-I fuel showed some tendency to accumulate peroxides under our test conditions, but no appreciable gums were formed. In addition, the high temperature (JFTOT) stability of the aged nitrogen-free fuel was similarly acceptable (Table IV).

Increasing quantities of basic nitrogen compounds, which were acid extracted from the fuel, were then reintroduced into the fuel and the storage stability redetermined. As the concentration of basic nitrogen compounds increased from 8.4 to 125 ppm N, both the gum and peroxide concentration after storage rose to a maximum (25 ppm N) then fell back to lower levels (Table IV, expt. #2, 3, 4). However, the JFTOT deposit rating after storage was monotonically degraded by increasing nitrogen levels. The filter pressure drop was three mm or less for experiments #1-4 except for the 125 ppm N sample which exceeded 25 mm after storage.

The results imply a relationship between gum formation and peroxide concentration. It is possible that the relation between the gum and peroxide is of the form:

$$RH \xrightarrow[k_1]{O_2} [peroxide] \xrightarrow{k_2} gum$$

We propose that some fuel components, particularly those containing sulfur, nitrogen, oxygen, and olefinic functional groups, also react under storage conditions with peroxides. Condensation or dimerization of the free radical intermediates formed in these reactions can build the highly polar, medium molecular weight (400-500) gums observed in some studies (18). Antioxidants of either the phenylene diamine or hindered phenol type were effective for inhibiting both peroxide and gum formation in the current studies (Table IV, expts. #5, 6, 7, 8). The inhibitors also improved high temperature stability after storage.

The contamination level in experiments #1-#8 exhibited no patterns with nitrogen content. Further, the phenylene diamine antioxidant exerted little effect. In any case, the contamination did not exceed 2.4 mg/l in any of these tests.

A pyridine compound was found to storage degrade the Shale-I fuel faster than a pyrrole compound (Table IV, expt. #9, 11). After storage the Shale-I fuel doped with 50 ppm 5-ethyl-2-methyl-pyridine had an order of magnitude more gums and 20 times the peroxide level compared to the same fuel containing 50 ppm 2,5-dimethylpyrrole. Antioxidants were effective at inhibiting both gums and peroxides in the nitrogen doped fuels after storage (Table IV, expt. #10, 12), particularly for the pyridine compound.

5-Ethyl-2-methylpyridine caused a large change in JFTOT results after storage. The TDR increased from four prior to storage to 46 after storage. Correspondingly, the filter pressure drop changed from three mm to bypass condition (>25 mm in 120 minutes). In contrast, 2,5-dimethylpyrrole caused equally poor JFTOT performance before and after storage. Not only did the before and after tests give high TDR values, but the filter pressure drop exceeded 25 mm in six and ten minutes, respectively. The hindered phenol antioxidant was effective with the pyridine for maintaining good JFTOT behavior during the four week storage stability (no increase in TDR or filter pressure drop). This additive was not active in the presence of the pyrrole, however. The TDR values were about the same and the filter pressure drop exceeded 25 mm in seven and one-half and eight minutes, respectively, for the before and after storage tests.

Summary

High temperature thermal stability and storage stability experiments were conducted using Shale-I jet fuel. As basic nitrogen compounds are removed by acid extraction from the Shale-I fuel, JFTOT stability improves (especially filter pressure drop performance). After four weeks of accelerated storage, the Shale-I fuel containing basic nitrogen compounds formed more gums and peroxides, and exhibited degraded JFTOT performance. The basic nitrogen compounds extracted from the Shale-I fuel were characterized by way of various mass spectral methods. Compounds similar to those found in the basic nitrogen fraction were used as additives for JFTOT and storage tests on a petroleum fuel and nitrogen-free Shale-I fuels. Both pyridines and pyrroles contribute to fuel instability. Much more work must be performed in order to establish clear trends and to deduce a detailed mechanism of fuel degradation.

Acknowledgement

The authors thank Dr. S. E. Buttrill, Jr., of SRI International for conducting the field ionization mass spectral analysis on a Naval Research Laboratory contract.

Literature Cited

1. Solash, J.; Hazlett, R. N.; Hall, J. M. and Nowack, C. J.; *Fuel*, 1978, *57*, 521.

2. Eisen, F. S.; Sun Oil Company Final Report on U.S. Navy Con-
    tract No. N-00140-74-C00568, February 6, 1975.

3. Bartick, H.; Kunchal, K.; Switzer, D.; Bowen, R.; Edwards, R.;
    "The Production and Refining of Crude Shale Oil into Military
    Fuels," Applied Systems Corp. Final Report on Office of Naval
    Research Contract No. N-00014-75-C-0055, August 1975.

4. Klarman, A. F. and Rollo, A. J.; Naval Air Propulsion Center
    Report No. NAPC-PE-1, November 1977.

5. Solash, J.; Hazlett, R. N.; Burnett, J. C.; Beal, E. and Hall,
    J. M.; "Relation Between Fuel Properties and Chemical Composi-
    tion. II. Chemical Characterization of U.S. Navy Shale-II
    Fuels," in this book.

6. Affens, W. A.; Hall, J. M.; Beal, E.; Hazlett, R. N.; Nowack,
    C. J. and Speck, G.; "Relation Between Fuel Properties and
    Chemical Composition. III. Physical Properties of U.S. Navy
    Shale-II Fuels," in this book.

7. Solash, J.; Nowack, C. J. and Delfosse, R. J.; Naval Air Pro-
    pulsion Center Report No. NAPTC-PE-82, May 1976.

8. ASTM Method D-3241.

9. Buttrill, Jr., S. E.; "Analysis of Jet Fuels by Mass Spectrome-
    try," in Naval Research Laboratory Workshop on Basic Research
    Needs for Synthetic Hydrocarbon Jet Aircraft Fuels, Naval Air
    Systems Command, June 15-16, 1978, and references therein.

10. Frankenfeld, J. E. and Taylor, W. F.; Final Report under Naval
    Air Systems Command Contract No. N-0019-76-0675, February 1979,
    and references therein.

11. Witkop, B.; J. Amer. Chem. Soc., 1950, 72, 1428.

12. Witkop, B. and Patrick, J. B.; J. Amer. Chem. Soc., 1951, 73,
    713.

13. Saito, I.; Matsuura, T.; Nakagawa, M. and Hino, T.; Accts.
    Chem. Res., 1977, 10, 346.

14. Beer, R. J. S.; McGrath, L. and Robertson, A.; J. Chem. Soc.,
    1950, 3283.

15. Frost, C. M. and Poulson, R. E.; Amer. Chem. Soc., Div. Petro-
    leum Preprints, 1975, 20, 176.

16. Reynolds, T. W.; National Aeronautics and Space Administration, Technical Memorandum No. TM–X–3551, June 1977.

17. Brinkman, D. W.; Whisman, M. L. and Bowden, J. N.; Bartlesville Energy Technology Center, Report of Investigation No. 78/23, March 1979.

18. Ward, C. C.; Schwartz, F. G. and Whisman, M. L.; Technical Report #11 under Ordnance Project TB5–01–010, Bartlesville Energy Technology Center, July 1961.

RECEIVED January 19, 1981.

Pyrolysis of Shale Oil Residual Fractions

ROBERT N. HAZLETT, ERNA BEAL, THOMAS VETTER,
RICHARD SONNTAG, and WILLIAM MONIZ

Naval Research Laboratory, Washington, D.C. 20375

JP-5, the Navy jet fuel, must meet many stringent requirements if satisfactory performance in aircraft and fuel handling
and storage systems is to be attained (1). Among the critical
requirements are those for a low freezing point and a low viscosity. The freezing point is the property of concern in this
paper. Jet aircraft are exposed to low temperatures and the
fuels must not interfere with flying operations by freezing and
plugging filters. It has not been practical to make JP-5 from
some petroleum crudes because the specification freezing point
of -47°C (maximum) is difficult to meet along with the minimum
required flash point of 60°C. The freezing point situation
could be relieved by lowering the initial distillation point but
this would simultaneously decrease the flash point. Since mil-
lions of gallons of jet fuel are stored on most aircraft carriers,
the 60°C flash point is required to reduce the fire hazard due
to the fuel.

Thus we are emphasizing fuel freezing point phenomena in a
program to increase the availability of JP-5 from petroleum and
shale oil. Dimitroff et al (2) examined the influence of composition on freezing point of several types of fuels. They found
the saturate fraction of a fuel usually exerted the greatest
effect on freezing point but the aromatic fraction seemed to be
important in some cases.

The Naval Research Laboratory has related the freezing
point of JP-5 type fuels to the n-alkane content, specifically
n-hexadecane (1). This relationship applies to jet fuels derived from alternate fossil fuel resources, such as shale oil,
coal, and tar sands, as well as those derived from petroleum.
In general, jet fuels from shale oil have the highest and those
from coal the lowest n-alkane content. The origin of these
n-alkanes in the amounts observed, especially in shale
derived fuels, is not readily explained on the basis of literature information. Studies of the processes, particularly the

ones involving thermal stress, used to produce shale derived
fuels are needed to define how the n-alkanes form from larger
molecules. The information developed will significantly contribute to the selection of processes and refining techniques
for future fuel production from shale oil.

In this work, a shale crude oil residue was separated into
three chemical fractions. The fractions were then subjected to
nmr analysis to estimate the potential for n-alkane production
and to pyrolysis studies to determine an experimental n-alkane
yield.

Pyrolysis Mechanisms

A large n-alkane breaks apart by a free radical mechanism to
yield smaller hydrocarbons, both n-alkanes and 1-olefins. This
process, as originally diagnosed by Rice (3), ultimately yields
mostly small olefins with 2 to 4 carbon atoms. This behavior is
encouraged by high temperatures and low pressures. At the
moderate temperatures and higher pressures more typical of shale
retorting and delayed coking, however, Fabuss-Smith-Satterfield
(4) behavior occurs. In this situation, a single fragmentation
step occurs and equal amounts of n-alkanes and olefins form.
Further, the yield of hydrocarbons in the intermediate carbon
range is about the same. Unbranched olefins formed in the pyrolysis reactions readily convert to n-alkanes by hydrogenation.

Thus, formation of n-alkanes in the jet fuel distillation
range can be explained if large n-alkanes are present in the
crude oil source. Quantities of large n-alkanes are insufficient,
however, to explain the amounts found (up to 37%) in the jet fuel
made from shale (1). Other possible precursors to small straight
chain molecules are branched compounds or substituted cyclic compounds. Attack in a side chain obviously affords a path to an
n-alkane. Esters, acids, amines, and ethers also have the potential to form n-alkanes if an unbranched alkyl chain is present
in the molecule.

Carbon-13 nmr studies indicate that oil shale rock contains
many long unbranched straight chain hydrocarbon groups (5). The
shale oil derived from the rock also gives indication of considerable straight chain material with large peaks at 14, 23, 30, and
32 ppm in the C-13 nmr spectrum.

Experimental Studies

Separation. A residue from Paraho shale oil was obtained by
vacuum distillation at 40 torr to an end point of 300°C (equivalent to 420°C at one atmosphere pressure). The residue was then
separated on activated silicagel into a saturate fraction, an
aromatic fraction, and a polar fraction. The saturate fraction
was removed from the silica with n-pentane solvent, then the

aromatic fraction was removed with a 25:75 benzene: n-pentane
solvent. The polar fraction was desorbed with 25:75 benzene:
methanol solvent. Although the polar fraction required methanol
for desorption, it was only slightly soluble in methanol. It dissolved readily in benzene, however. The nitrogen content of
various eluates was determined by Drushel's method (6) as an indication of the separation efficiency. The pentane eluant contained
no nitrogen and the polar fraction (benzene:methanol) contained
97% of the recovered nitrogen. If 100% benzene was used to de-
sorb the aromatic fraction, up to 20% of the nitrogen was found
in the aromatic fraction. The nitrogen concentration in the
separated fractions was 2.5% in the polar, 0.13% in the aromatic
and less than 0.01 wt% in the saturate fraction. The input N
concentration in the residue was 2.2 wt%.

The distillation residue comprises 48% of the shale crude
oil. On a chemical basis, the polar compounds comprise 71%, the
saturates 13% and the aromatics 16% of the recovered residue.
Mass recovery from the separation was 85% but nitrogen recovery
was much less, 70%. The material retained on the silicagel, consequently, appears to be highly polar and high in nitrogen.

Carbon-13 nmr Analysis. Samples of the various fractions
were submitted to analysis by C-13 nmr. The C-13 spectrum affords
a distinct separation of the aromatic and aliphatic absorption
regions plus a good resolution of many peaks due to specific
molecular structure. Thus, a good amount of useful information
can be obtained even for a complex mixture such as a fuel fraction. With respect to the present study, the aliphatic region
of the spectrum is of particular importance.

Quantitative analysis of the aliphatic region was attained
by including a known amount of methanol in the sample as an
internal standard. A long unbranched fragment will exhibit peaks
at several positions in the aliphatic region of the spectrum.
The peak corresponding to the methyl end group (α-carbon) appears
at 14 ppm with reference to tetramethylsilane at zero ppm. The
CH_2 group adjacent to the methyl group (β-carbon) absorbs at
23 ppm and subsequent absorptions appear at 32 and 29.5 ppm for
the γ- and δ- carbons. Beyond this, all other CH_2 groups in a
long unbranched chain absorb at 30 ppm. Therefore, this latter
peak would be quite large for a long chain. In fact, the ratio
of the area of this peak to the α- β- or γ-peak can afford information on the average chain length of the unbranched fragment.

A spectrum for the aliphatic region of the polar fraction
from the shale residue is shown in Figure 1. The distinctive
peaks at 14, 23, 32, and 30 ppm demonstrate the presence of
significant amounts of long unbranched groups in this fuel fraction. The 29.5 peak appears as a shoulder on the 30 peak and
these two peaks were integrated together. Quantitation of the
spectral information using the methanol internal standard gives

the data listed in Table I. As expected, the content of long unbranched alkyl groups is greatest for the saturate fractions. Further, the straight chain alkyl groups in the saturate fraction are longer on the average than those in the aromatic and polar fractions. We conclude that there is a definite potential for making n-alkanes and 1-olefins in the jet fuel distillation range by cracking compounds found in the heavier shale oil cuts.

Pyrolysis. The residue fractions were stressed at temperature and pressure conditions typical of the petroleum refining process known as delayed coking (7). The conditions used were 450°C and about 90 psi pressure. Each thermal stress was conducted in a six inch long, 1/4 inch o.d. 316 s.s. tube closed at one end and fitted at the other end with a stainless steel valve via a Swagelok connection. The tube, with a weighed amount of sample (approximately 0.1 g), was attached to a vacuum system, cooled to -78°C, and pumped to remove air. The tube was then thawed and the cooling/pumping process repeated. The tubes were heated by inserting them into 9/32 inch holes in a six inch diameter aluminum block fitted with a temperature controller.

At the close of the heating period, the tubes were cooled to -78°C and the valve removed. A mixed solvent of n-pentane and benzene (50:50) was added to the tube which was then capped and warmed to room temperature. The solution and a subsequent rinse were transferred to a screw cap vial which was then stored in a freezer until analysis. The sample concentration in the solvent was typically 3 to 5%. A weighed amount of toluene was added as an internal standard prior to analysis.

The stressed samples were analyzed by two techniques, both based on gas chromatography. In the first, the solution with internal standard was injected into a 10 ft, 1/8 inch o.d., 5% OV-101 column which was programmed to 260°C at 12°/min after a 5.0 min initial hold at 60°C. The JP-5 cut was integrated as a single sum and compared to the internal standard to determine the yield of JP-5 from the pyrolysis experiment. The initial gc cut point for the JP-5 was set midway between n-octane and n-nonane and the final point midway between n-hexadecane and n-heptadecane. The gc baseline did not rise during this portion of the analysis, hence reliable integration was obtained.

The second gc technique determined the individual n-alkanes and 1-alkenes in the pyrolyzed sample. A 100 m wall-coated glass capillary gave the required resolution and the n-alkanes and 1-alkenes stood out as distinct, well resolved peaks. OV-101 or OV-17 wall coatings provide adequate separation. A carrier gas flow of one cc/min was combined with an inlet split ratio of 50:1 and a 310°C injector temperature. The column temperature was raised to 250°C at 4°/min after an 8.0 min initial hold at 80°C. Peak identification was based on retention time matching with n-alkane and 1-alkene standards.

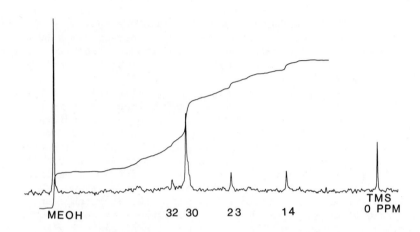

Figure 1. C-13 NMR spectrum of shale oil residual polar fraction; aliphatic region, TMS reference, methanol internal standard; integration trace (upper curve)

Table I. Carbon-13 nmr Examination
of Shale Oil Residual Fractions

Fraction	Wt. % Carbon in Aliphatic Region	Unbranched Alkyl-Groups*	Average Carbon Chain Length**
Saturate	100	40	43
Aromatic	60	21	14-22
Polar	56	30	20

* Sum of areas of absorption peaks at 14, 23, 30, and 32 ppm.

** For unbranched alkyl groups: based on ratio of 30 ppm peak area to average of 14, 23, and 32 peak areas.

Precision: ± 10%

Pyrolysis of the saturate fraction for 30 min at 450°C gave the n-alkane and 1-alkene yields shown in Figure 2. The n-alkanes predominated over the 1-alkenes at all carbon numbers for this sample. This was generally true for all fractions and all stress times. The 1-alkenes were less stable than the n-alkanes and the larger alkenes were very minor products for stress times 60 min and longer. Figure 2 indicates that the product exhibits a plateau in the 10-14 carbon number range, an integral part of the JP-5 distillation range.

The effect of stress time on yield is illustrated in Figure 3. The n-alkane + 1-alkene sum for each carbon number is plotted. For a 16 min stress the yields for carbon numbers 10 through 14 are almost identical. Consequently, one-step Fabuss-Smith-Satterfield pyrolysis (4) is controlling. The total yield increases at 30 min but the shift to a maxima at C-10 indicates product is forming and undergoing secondary decomposition. This trend is extended significantly at longer times such as shown by the 60 min data. Here the maximum is outside the JP-5 range and the yield of molecules with 16 or more carbons is quite low.

For the polar fraction, the combined n-alkane + 1-alkene yield increased up to 60 min stress time, then reversed (Figure 4). The yield of the larger molecules - 15 carbons and above - was drastically reduced at 180 min. Even at 16 min the products obtained in largest yield were on the low end of the JP-5 distillation range. This was consistent with the lower value found by nmr for the average unbranched alkyl chain length. The aromatic yield pattern fell between that for the saturate and polar fractions. The maximum yield for the aromatic fraction always fell at 10 or 11 carbons with a fairly sharp maximum.

A summary of the JP-5 yield data for all fractions stressed for various times at 450°C is presented in Table II. The saturate fraction affords the highest yield of JP-5 but the other fractions also give good yields at intermediate stress times. The polar fraction requires a longer stress time to attain its maximum yield of JP-5.

The potential n-alkane yields in the JP-5 cut are listed in Table III. These values were obtained by summing the capillary gc yields of n-alkanes and 1-alkenes for carbon numbers 9 through 16. This total was divided by the corresponding JP-5 yield in Table II to give the potential n-alkane yield.

All fractions attained similar maximum n-alkane yields, 20-25%. Surprisingly, the polar fraction gave the highest yields of potential n-alkanes. Further, the polar fraction gave a high conversion of the weight percent unbranched alkyl groups to n-alkanes, 24.9% (Table III) vs 30% (Table I). The maximum aromatic conversion ratio was even higher, 19.9 vs 21% whereas the saturate ratio was much lower, 22.7 vs 40%. The potential n-alkane yields for all fractions fell off at longer stress times.

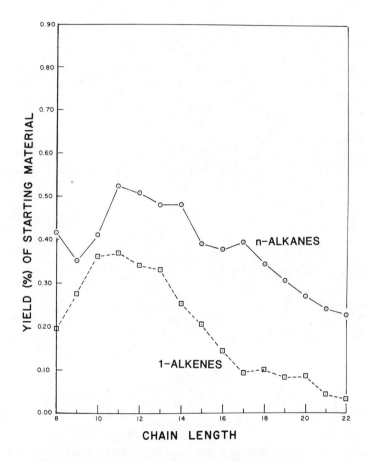

Figure 2. Pyrolysis of shale oil residual saturate fraction at 450°C for 30 min

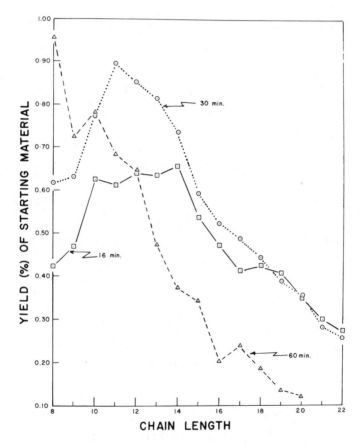

*Figure 3.   Pyrolysis of shale oil residual saturate fraction at 450°C.   The yield is
the sum of n-alkane plus 1-alkene for the indicated chain length.*

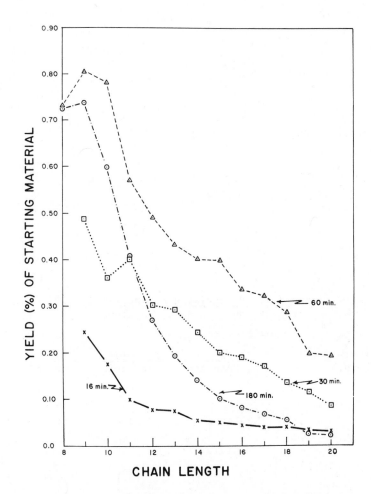

Figure 4. Pyrolysis of shale oil residual polar fraction at 450°C. The yield is the sum of n-alkane plus 1-alkene for the indicated chain length.

Table II. Product Yield*

Pyrolysis Time (min)	JP-5 Yield (Percent)		
	SAT.	AROM.	POLAR
16	20.4	18.8	5.7
30	28.0	23.6	14.1
60	27.3	23.9	19.6
120	–	12.0	16.3
180	–	–	16.8

* – Pyrolysis temperature – 450°C.

    Precision: $\pm$ 6%.

Table III. Potential n-Alkane Yield
from Various Residual Fractions

Pyrolysis Time (min.)	Yield		
	Saturate	Aromatic	Polar
16	22.7	14.4	14.7
30	20.8	19.6	24.9
60	15.5	19.9	21.7
120	–	15.1	24.9
180	–	–	20.1

* – Pyrolysis temperature – 450°C; yield in percent is sum
of n-alkanes + 1-alkenes for C_9 to C_{16} hydrocarbons
divided by JP-5 yield from Table II.

    Precision: $\pm$ 10%

Discussion and Conclusions

All three residual fractions afford good yields of JP-5 range material by pyrolysis at 450°C. This is particularly important for the polar fraction since it comprises 71% of the vacuum residue. The best yield of the JP-5 cut comes at different times for the various fractions, but a time in the 30 to 60 min range would appear to be the optimum time for good yield at 450°C for all three chemical fractions.

The polar fraction gave the highest potential n-alkane yield in the JP-5 cut. This indicates that the bulk of the polar molecules fragment close to the functional group, thus affording efficient production of n-alkanes and 1-alkenes. The data for the residual aromatic fraction also shows that fragmentation of the sidechain occurs close to the ring, probably between the β and γ carbons. The saturate fraction is less selective in the site of fragmentation since strongly activating groups are absent. Thus, a significant portion of unbranched alkyl moieties end up in branched chain and alicyclic hydrocarbons after pyrolysis.

The potential n-alkane yield for the saturate fraction decreases as pyrolysis time increases. On the other hand, the n-alkane yields go through a maximum with time for the aromatic and polar residual fractions. Pyrolysis times in excess of 60 minutes are preferred with respect to lower potential n-alkane yield but this would be at some loss in JP-5 yield.

Although all fractions gave potential n-alkane yields much higher than those found in JP-5 derived from petroleum, none of the shale residual fractions gave n-alkane yields approaching the 37% amount found in the Shale-I JP-5 (1). A temperature different from the 450°C used here might affect the conversion percentage. Further, the combined saturate, aromatic, and polar fractions may interact under pyrolysis conditions to give higher potential n-alkane yields than the fractions stressed independently. This thesis is being tested in current studies. In addition, the vacuum distillate from the shale crude, particularly the saturate fractions, can contribute markedly to n-alkane yield in a jet fuel (8).

Acknowledgement

The authors thank Dr. Hyman Rosenwasser of the Naval Air Systems Command for funding support.

Literature Cited

1. Solash, J.; Hazlett, R. N.; Hall, J. M.; Nowack, C. J.; "Relation between Fuel Properties and Chemical Composition, I. Jet Fuels from Coal, Oil Shale, and Tar Sands," *Fuel*, 1978, 57, 521.

2. Dimitroff, E.; Gray, J. T. Jr.; Meckel, N. T.; Quillian, R. D. Jr. Seventh World Petroleum Congress, Individual Paper No. 47, Mexico City, Mexico, Apr. 2 - 9, 1967.
3. Rice, F. O. J. Am. Chem. Soc., 1933, 55, 3035.
4. Fabuss, B. M.; Smith, J. O.; Satterfield, C. N. Adv. Pet. Chem. Refin. 1964, 9, 157.
5. Resing, H. A.; Garroway, A. N.; Hazlett, R. N. "Determination of Aromatic Hydrocarbon Fraction in Oil Shale by C-13 nmr with Magic-angle Spinning," Fuel, 1978, 57, 450.
6. Drushel, H. F. Anal. Chem., 1977, 49, 932.
7. Gary, J. H.; Hardwerk, G. E. Petroleum Refining, Ch. 5, Marcel Dekker, Inc., New York, N. Y., 1975.
8. Hazlett, R. N., "Free Radical Reactions Related to Fuel Research," Frontiers of Free Radical Chemistry, ed. W. A. Pryor, Academic Press, N. Y., N. Y., 1980.

RECEIVED February 18, 1981.

Synfuel Stability:
Degradation Mechanisms and Actual Findings

DENNIS W. BRINKMAN—U.S. Department of Energy, Bartlesville Energy
Technology Center, P.O. Box 1398, Bartlesville, OK 74003

JOHN N. BOWDEN—Southwest Research Institute, 8500 Culebra Road,
San Antonio, TX 78285

JOHN FRANKENFELD and BILL TAYLOR—Exxon Research and
Engineering, Box 8, Linden, NJ 07036

While substantial quantities of only a few experimental synfuels have been generated, those which are available have demonstrated the degradation problems that were predicted from work
with petroleum. The high heteroatom and unsaturate content of
syncrudes derived from shale and coal will necessitate closer
attention to processing parameters required to produce a commercially viable product. This paper presents basic and applied
data which should aid in the tradeoff decisions between further
costly processing and product stability. Because this is a
progress report on continuing work, many of the conclusions are
preliminary in nature.

Degradation Mechanisms

Considerable work has been published on degradation mechanisms for compounds found in petroleum[1-4]. Much of the previously reported research involved pure compounds in pure hydrocarbon solvents. The work reported here was performed with
additive-free #2 diesel fuel or JP-8, both of which are middle
distillate fuels in increasing demand. Much of this work is in
progress and only preliminary results can be presented here.

Structural Effects. The results of studies on structural
effects which have been carried out so far are summarized in
Figure 1. Here the nitrogen compounds are grouped as "strongly
deleterious", "moderately deleterious" and "relatively harmless"
with regard to their relative tendencies to form sludge in hydrocarbon fuels. The differences between groupings, especially
between strongly and moderately deleterious is quite large.
These limited data seem to indicate that, with few exceptions,
the deleterious compounds are those which contain heterocyclic
nitrogens with an alkyl group adjacent to nitrogen. Finally, as
observed previously[3,4] the 2,5-dimethyl pyrrole (DMP) configuration appears significantly more reactive than 2,4-dimethyl

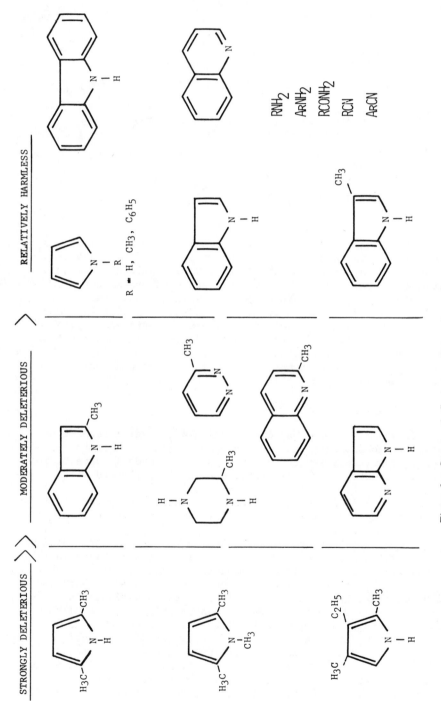

Figure 1.   Structural effects on sediment formation

pyrrole. These observations are based on limited data and must
be regarded as tentative. However, they do support previous
suggestions(3,4,5) that sediment from pyrrolic compounds arises
from oligomerization through the adjacent methyl groups (see
Figure 2). The partial structures shown in Figure 2 are supported by elemental, infrared and mass spectral analyses(3,4)
and provide a possible explanation for the need for alkyl groups
adjacent to nitrogen for large scale sediment formation. Additional work with other model compounds is being performed to
confirm these findings.

Compound Interactions. Interactions may be quite important
to storage stability of synthetic fuels, especially those derived
from shale and coal liquids. Previous work(3,4,6,7) has indicated that certain compounds, which do not produce sediment by
themselves, can contribute to or stimulate sediment formation in
others ("positive" interaction). In some instances, some materials interact to inhibit sediment formation ("negative" interaction). These interactions have been demonstrated for thermal
stability(8) and, to a very limited extent, for storage stabil-
ity(3,4). The results of preliminary interaction studies in the
present program are summarized in this section.

The results of a preliminary study to determine whether N-N
interactions can occur under conditions of dark storage are summarized and their significance analyzed in Table 1. In order to
determine whether an interaction actually occurred the data were
analyzed by means of 2 X 2 factorial experiments. A typical
design involving DMP and isoquinoline is shown in Figure 3. The
analysis shown in Figure 3 indicates a likely positive interaction
after 28 days and clear cut interaction after 56 days. Thus,
after 56 days the total sediment obtained with both nitrogen
compounds together (127.5 mg/100 cc) was more than double the sum
of the two which would be expected if they acted independently
(61.8 mg/100 cc). To determine the significance of the results,
the data were subjected to Students "t" test.(9) Results are
summarized in Table 1. These preliminary results suggest that
interactions can occur between DMP and various nitrogen containing
species. These have important implications for fuel stability.
Certain compounds, for example, trioctylamine and isoquinoline,
while relatively innocuous when present alone, can contribute
significantly to sediment formation in the presence of compounds
such as DMP. On the other hand, some materials, such as 2-methyl-
indole, may actually have a stabilizing effect. The results of
the four tests with 2-methylindole are especially interesting and
surprising. They all indicate a statistically significant
negative interaction. This needs to be confirmed in future experiments.

Previous work suggested that important interactions can occur
between nitrogen and sulfur or oxygen compounds(3,4,7,8).
Several of these interactions were "negative" (i.e., stabilizing).
Several experiments were performed in the present program to test

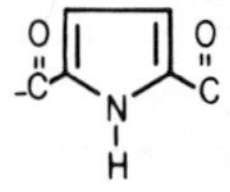

I

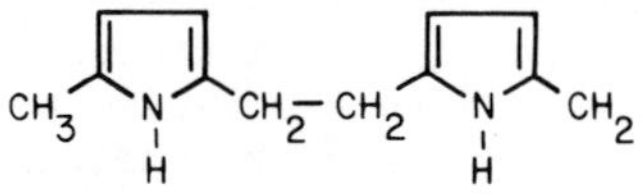

II

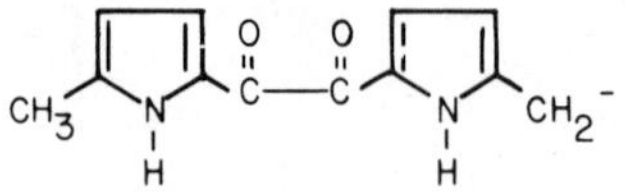

III

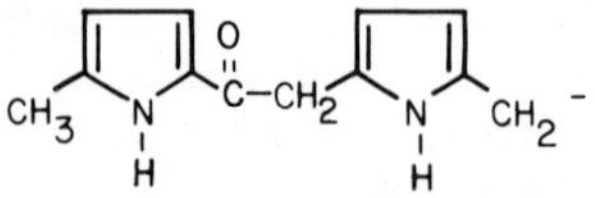

IV

Figure 2. Proposed partial structures for dimethylpyrrole sediment (5)

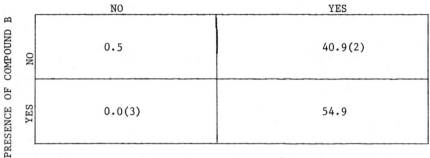

PRESENCE OF COMPOUND A

28-DAYS STORAGE AT 110°F

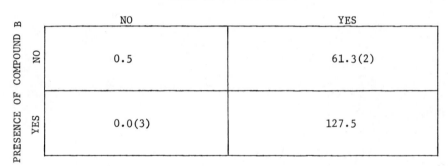

PRESENCE OF COMPOUND A

56 DAYS STORAGE AT 110°F

---

(1) Sediment shown as mg/100 cc.
(2) Amount expected from 150 ppm DMP alone.
(3) Amount from 1350 ppm Isoquinoline alone.

Figure 3. Sediment increase due to interaction between 2,5-dimethylpyrrole (A, 150 ppm) and isoquinoline (B, 1350 ppm) in No. 2 diesel (1)

Table I

Summary of N-N Interaction Runs

Compound A (ppm)	Compound B (ppm)	Storage Time (Days)	Type of Interaction[a]	Significance Test[b]
DMP (150)	3-Methylindole (1350)	28	Positive	Doubtful ($t = 1.9$, $p = 0.1$)
DMP (150)	3-Methylindole (1350)	56	Positive	Significant ($t = 5.2$, $.025 > p > .01$)
DMP (150)	Isoquinoline (1350)	28	Positive	Likely ($t = 3.5$, $.05 > p > .025$)
DMP (150)	Isoquinoline (1350)	56	Positive	Significant ($t = 6.3$, $.025 > p > .01$)
DMP (150	Trioctylamine (1350)	28	Positive	Doubtful ($t = 0.6$, $p = <0.1$)
DMP (150)	Trioctylamine (1350)	56	Positive	Significant ($t = 4.5$, $p = .01$)
DMP (150)	1,2,5-Trimethylpyrrole (150)	28	Positive	Highly Significant ($t = 73$, $p = <.005$)
2-Methylindole (750)	3-Methylindole (750)	28	Negative	Highly Significant ($t = >100$, $p = <.005$)
2-Methylindole (750)	3-Methylindole (750)	56	Negative	Highly Significant ($t = 86$, $p = <.005$)
DMP (150)	2-Methylindole (1350)	28	Negative	Highly Significant ($t = 52$, $p = <.005$)
DMP (150)	2-Methylindole (1350)	56	Negative	Significant ($t = 6.5$, $p = .05$)

(a) "Positive" interaction means combination gave more sediment than sum of two compounds tested alone.
(b) Student's test (see reference 9, section 4).

for these interactions in broad range fuels. The interactions discovered and their significance are summarized in Table 2. The thiols, especially the aromatic thiols, gave significant negative interactions with DMP at least up to 28 days storage (see also Figure 4). Such interactions were observed in earlier work, but the effect was reversed on long term storage[3,4]. It has been suggested that this was due to oxidation of the thiols to sulfonic acids; the former being inhibitors and the latter accelerators[4]. Longer term storage tests are being conducted to investigate this phenomena.

Surprisingly, no effects were observed with either decanoic acid or 2,6-di-t-butylphenol when tested with DMP in No. 2 diesel fuel. Work in purified decane has indicated a significant accelerating effect with most organic acids including decanoic while phenols are inhibitors[3,4]. It would appear that important N-S and, possibly, N-O interactions can occur in broad range fuels.

Effects of Base Fuel Hydrocarbon Content. The differences in sediment formation rates were observed with various diluents indicating the chemical characteristics of the base fuels can exert a significant influence on the amounts of nitrogenous sediment obtained. This may be due to differences in solubility characteristics of the base fuels or to the presence of trace impurities which accelerate or inhibit sediment formation. The effects of the hydrocarbon content of the base fuels is currently being studied with preliminary results reported here. These experiments are carried out by adding representatives of the most prevalent hydrocarbon types, n-paraffins, branched paraffins, naphthenes (cycloparaffins) and aromatics to the base fuels and determining their influence on sediment formation with various nitrogen compounds. The hydrocarbons are added at levels approximating their normal occurrence in most distillate fuels[10]. In addition, certain reactive olefins, known to contribute to gum formation in petroleum fuels, are being tested. The more highly refined JP-8 is being used for these experiments because adding small quantities of olefins to a complex fuel such as No. 2 diesel would likely lead to equivocal results.

Preliminary studies on hydrocarbon effects are summarized in Table 3. DMP at the 1500 ppm N level was employed as the nitrogen compound. The data obtained so far indicate only minor effects, if any, due to hydrocarbon type. However, additional work is required, expecially with more reactive species such as diolefins.

The effects of storage temperature on sediment formation were studied using 2,5-dimethylpyrrole as the model compound. Arrhenius plots for both #2 diesel and JP-8 are shown in Figures 5 and 6. The fairly linear plots permit estimation of apparent reaction activation energies of 10.7 kcal/mole in #2 diesel and 14.4 kcal/mole in JP-8. These are rather low and suggest some interactive or catalytic effects are involved.

Synfuel Test Results. A number of synfuels (meeting essentially all fuel specifications) and syncrude liquids produced from

TABLE II

Summary of Interactions Between 2,5-Dimethylpyrrole (DMP)
and S and O Compounds in No. 2 Diesel Fuel

Compound A (ppm)[a]	Compound B (ppm)[b]	Storage Time (days)	Type of Interaction[c]	Significance Test[d]
DMP (750)	Decanoic Acid (100)	14	None[e]	
DMP (750)	Decanoic Acid (100)	28	None[e]	
DMP (750)	Benzylphenyl Sulfide (3000)	14	None	
DMP (750)	Benzylphenyl Sulfide (3000)	28	None	
DMP (750)	p-Thiocresol (3000)	7	Negative	Significant ($t = 60$; $p = 05$)
DMP (750)	p-Thiocresol (3000)	14	Negative	Highly Significant ($t = 13.0$; $p < .005$)
DMP (750)	p-Thiocresol (3000)	28	Negative	Highly Significant ($t = 19.1$; $p < .005$)
DMP (750)	Thiophenol (3000)	7	Negative	Highly Significant ($t = 11.1$; $p < .005$)
DMP (750)	Thiophenol (3000)	14	Negative	Highly Significant ($t = 71.0$; $p < .005$)
DMP (750)	Thiophenol (3000)	28	Negative	Highly Significant ($t = 28.3$; $p < .005$)
DMP (750)	Dodecanethiol (3000)	14	None	
DMP (750)	Dodecanethiol (3000)	28	Positive	Not Significant
DMP (750)	2,6-Di-t-Butylphenol (100)	14	None	
DMP (750)	2,6-Di-t-Butylphenol (100)	28	None	

(a) N Basis.
(b) S or O basis.
(c) "Negative" means combination gave less sediment than sum of components alone.
(d) Reference 9.
(e) Positive interactions were observed in other fuel systems.

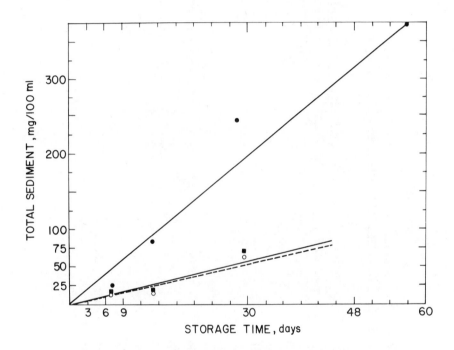

Figure 4. Interaction between 2,5-dimethylpyrrole and aromatic thiols in No. 2 diesel at 110°F: (○) DMP only, 750 ppm; (●) 750 ppm DMP + 3000 ppm p-thiocresol; — 750 ppm DMP + 3000 ppm thophenol.

TABLE III

Effects of Hydrocarbon Types on Sediment Formation
With 2,5-Dimethylpyrrole (DMP)[1]

Base Fuel	Hydrocarbon Added	Vol. % Added	Total Sediment (mg/100ml)[2]		
			14 Days	28 Days	56 Days
No. 2 Diesel	None	--	217.5	572.8	795.8
	s-Butylbenzene	15	176.1	833.3	-----
	Cyclohexane	20	152.0	888.0	-----
JP-8	None	--	108.5	313.7	586.3
	s-Butylbenzene	15	93.5	313.2	630.5
	1-Dodecene	5	112.0	311.2	685.5
	d-Methylstyrene	5	118.1	327.8	676.0

(1) DMP Level: 1500 ppm N; storage temp: 110°F.
(2) Average of 2 or more replicates; "total sediments" is
    sum of insoluble and adherent sediments.

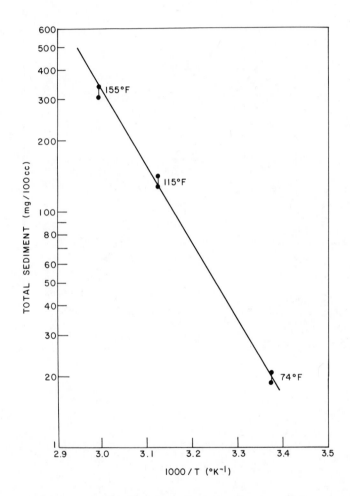

Figure 5.   Arrhenius plot of 2,5-dimethylpyrrole in No. 2 diesel fuel

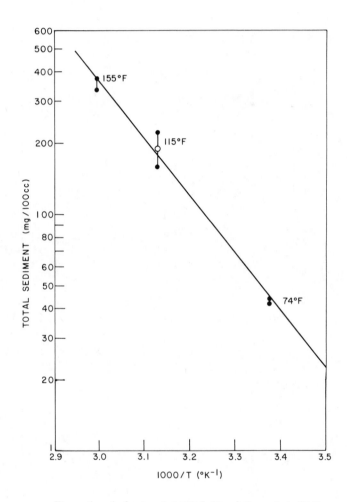

Figure 6.   Arrhenius plot of 2,5-dimethylpyrrole in JP-8

TABLE IV

Upgrading Effect on Composition and Stability
of Jet Fuel From Shale Oil

Properties	Original	Upgraded
Sulfur, total, wt-pct	0.015	0.005
Carbon, wt-pct	86.2	85.43
Hydrogen, wt-pct	13.32	14.42
Oxygen, wt-pct	0.28	0.05
Nitrogen, ppm	1500	3.2
Total gum after 32 weeks at 110° F, mg/100 ml	6.4	1.8

Table V

Elemental Analyses of Original Syncrude and
Gums After Prolonged Storage

	Element	Fuel	Gum	Gum, mg/100ml	Storage, Weeks
		Elemental Analysis			
Naphtha SRC-II (coal)				532	32
	C	84.94	65.99		
	H	12.78	6.55		
	N	0.32	8.59		
	O	1.92	12.91		
	S	0.72	2.00		
Middle Distillate SRC-II (coal)				1629	32
	C	86.28	75.60		
	H	9.05	6.65		
	N	0.98	5.46		
	O	3.36	10.99		
	S	0.32	0.67		
Heavy Distillate SRC-II (coal)				6434	4
	C	90.13	88.54		
	H	7.41	6.73		
	N	1.05	1.60		
	O	1.53	2.81		
	S	0.40	0.31		
Naphtha-EDS (#6 Illinois coal)				876	32
	C	85.25	70.01		
	H	12.45	6.65		
	N	0.223	6.26		
	O	1.92	10.27		
	S	0.61	6.82		
Naphtha-EDS (Wyodak coal)				1035	32
	C	85.14	66.28		
	H	12.56	6.19		
	N	0.21	7.21		
	O	1.84	17.36		
	S	0.21	2.86		
Gas Oil - Tar Sands				7438	16
	C	87.67	82.54		
	H	12.18	11.38		
	N	0.026	0.25		
	O	0.90	0.87		
	S	0.43	0.55		
Kerosene - Tar Sands				30.1	16
	C	87.05	83.52		
	H	12.42	8.41		
	N	Trace	Trace		
	O	0.30	7.34		
	S	0	0.01		
Naphtha - Tar Sands				20.7	32
	C	84.80	75.41		
	H	14.73	9.08		
	N	0.015	0.05		
	O	0.54	16.02		
	S	0.05	0.15		

TABLE VI

JFTOT Evaluations by ASTM Test Method D3241 Conducted
for 2.5 Hours at 260°C Control Temperature

Description (1)	Visual	Spun Tube	Spot Deposit	JFTOT Ratings ΔP, mm Hg/time, minutes		
Paraho shale oil JP-5(2)	4	24.5	34.5	1/30	1/90	1.5/150
Tar sands JP-5(3)	4	15	17	0/30	0.5/90	0.5/150
COED coal liquid JP-5(4)	4	12	24	2/30	76/90	197/150
Paraho shale oil Jet A(#4)(5)	3	15	18	1/30	1/90	1/150
Paraho shale oil Jet A(#23)(6)	4	17	19	0.5/30	0.5/90	0.5/150
Paraho shale oil Jet A(#10)(7)	4	30	35	1/30	1/90	1/150
Petroleum based JP-5	1	4	6	1/30	1/90	2/150

1) For detailed descriptions, see Ref.(11).
2) Paraho I, N = 1500 ppm.
3) Hydrotreated Athabasca kerosene.
4) Navy sample from W. Kentucky coal.
5) Refined from Paraho I material; N = 347 ppm.
6) Same as (5), N = 3.2 ppm.
7) Same as (5), N = 146 ppm.

shale, coal, and tar sands have been subjected to 110°F storage
for up to 32 weeks in sealed glass containers.[11,12,13] It is
normally accepted that one week of storage at 110°F is equivalent
to four weeks storage at ambient for middle distillates[14],
while equivalent to up to ten weeks at ambient for lighter fractions[15]. During this test samples were removed for analyses at
4, 8, 16, and 32 weeks and all stored samples were aerated every
4 weeks. While the experimental details have been published
elsewhere[11,12,13], in general the fuels refined to meet requirement of petroleum-based fuel specifications showed relatively
good stability. Table 4 shows an example of a jet fuel before
and after upgrading good stability. Table 4 shows an example of
a jet fuel before and after upgrading by additional hydrotreatment. As can be seen, the more severe the level of hydrotreating, the more stable the fuel. It is for this reason that the
stability specifications may dictate the ultimate processing
costs.

Elemental composition of several synfuels derived from coal
by two different processes and from tar sands are compared in
Table 5 to the composition of gum produced in each fuel during
prolonged storage. In some fuels considerable quantities of
sediment and gum were formed in a few weeks, therefore, the aging
was discontinued before 32 weeks were completed. Generally speak-
ing, the heavy distillates and gas oils (the more viscous products) produced the largest amount of deposits followed by the
middle distillates and then the naphthas. The elemental composition of the gums produced during storage show that the nitrogen,
oxygen and sulfur compounds tend to participate in the degradation
reactions. In the more viscous fuels the tendency toward higher
heteroatom concentration in the gum is much less, probably because
of considerable fuel entrainment.

In some applications, thermal degradation can be more of a
concern than storage stability. Table 6 presents data on several
middle distillate synfuels as compared to a petroleum-based fuel.
The tube deposits from the Jet Fuel Thermal Oxidation Test (ASTM
D3241) are significantly higher for the synfuels, but the pressure
buildup is normal except for one case. This indicates either
rapid reactions at the hot surface or slow agglomeration. In
either case, the deposit level is of concern and may dictate
further upgrading.

Conclusion

All information published to date implies that the production
of stable synfuels is possible but will require refining processes
altered from those now required for petroleum. Stability research
is currently focussing on both basic and applied considerations,
and the results are encouraging. By continuing these efforts, it
is hoped that stability will not be the limiting factor in providing adequate future fuel supplies.

Literature Cited

1. Whisman, M. L., Goetzinger, J. W., and Ward, C. C., "Storage
    Stability of Aviation Turbine Fuels," BOM RI 7325, 1969,
    23 pp.
2. Whisman, M. L., Cotton, F. O., Goetzinger, J. W., and Ward,
    C. C., "Radiotracer Study of Turbine Aircraft Fuel Stability,"
    BOM RI 7493, 1971, 30 pp.
3. Frankenfeld, J. W. and Taylor, W. F., "Alternate Fuels Ni-
    trogen Chemistry", Final Technical Report for Naval Air
    Systems Command AIR 310C Contract No. N0001976C0675,
    November, 1977.
4. Frankenfeld, J. W. and Taylor, W. F., "Continuation Study of
    Alternate Fuels Nitrogen Chemistry", Final Technical Report
    for Naval Air Systems Command AIR 310C, Contract No. N00019-
    78-C-0177.
5. Frankenfeld, J. W. and Taylor, W. F., "Continuation Study of
    Alternate Fuels Nitrogen Chemistry" Quarterly Progress Report
    No. 1, Naval Air Systems Command, AIR 310C, Contract No.
    N00019-78-C-0177, May, 1978
6. Taylor, W. F. and Frankenfeld, J. W., Ind. Eng. Chem. Product
    Research and Development, 17, 86 (1978).
7. Taylor, W. F. and Frankenfeld, J. W., "Development of High
    Stability Fuel", Final Report for Phase III, Contract No.
    N000140-74-C-0618, Naval Air Propulsion Test Center, December,
    1976.
8. Taylor, W. F. and Frankenfeld, J. W., "Development of High
    Stability Fuel", Final Report for Phase I, Contract No.
    N00140-74-C-0618, Naval Air Propulsion Test Center, Jan.
    1975.
9. Davies, O. L., Statistical Methods in Research and Production,
    Hafner Pub. Co., N.Y. (1958).
10. Frankenfeld, J. W. and Taylor, W. F., Ind. Eng. Chem. Prod.
    Res. Dev. 19 (1) 65 (1980).
11. Brinkman, D. W., Whisman, M. L., and Bowden, J. N., "Stabil-
    ity Characteristics of Hydrocarbon Fuels from Alternative
    Sources," BETC/RI-78/23, March 1979.
12. Bowden, J. N., "Stability Characteristics of Some Shale and
    Coal Liquids," BETC/4162-10, September 1980.
13. Bowden, J. N. and Brinkman, D. W., "Hydrocarbon Processing,
    July 1980, 77 pp.
14. Richie, J., J. Inst. Petrol., 1965, 51 (501).
15. Schwartz, F. G., Whisman, M. L., Allbright, C. S., and Ward,
    C. C., "Storage Stability of Gasoline," BOM Bulletin 660,
    1972, 60 pp.

RECEIVED February 18, 1981.

The Chemistry of Shale Oil and Its Refined Products

DONALD M. FENTON, HARVEY HENNIG, and RYDEN L. RICHARDSON

Union Oil Company of California, Science and Technology Division,
P.O. Box 76, Brea, CA 92621

"Oil Shale" is a term used to cover a wide range of
materials which are found in many parts of the United States.
The Green River oil shales are particularly high grade and are
the only U.S. deposits having adequate size and availability for
potential commercial value with present technology. The Green
River formation contains the equivalent of 1.8 trillion barrels
of shale oil. Assuming that only 600 billion barrels or one
third of this oil is ultimately recoverable, this would still be
20 times the U.S. proved crude oil reserves.

The Green River oil shale is a marlstone (calcareous mud-
stone) that was formed in shallow lakes about 45 million years
ago (1). The climate at this time probably varied from sub-
tropical to arid. During wet periods these lakes may have been
as large as 75 to 100 miles in diameter.

Sediment, mineral salts, minor plant debris and wind-
transported pollen were carried into the lakes by small local
streams, but the majority of the organic material that is in the
oil shale came from colonies of algae that thrived in the lakes.

The organic matter found in the Green River shales formed in
the deeper, central part of the lake. Rocks formed under these
conditions are characterized by thin, alternating layers of carbonate and organic matter. The layers vary in thickness from
0.01 to 10 millimeters.

The layers are believed to have been formed by the precipitation of calcium carbonate in early summer, when the surface
water temperature rises, followed by the seasonal high productivity of algae which occurs in late summer. The heavy carbonate
materials were deposited quickly; the organic matter settled more
slowly--which gave an alternation of light and dark laminations.

The typical composition of Green River oil shale is composed
of around 0-15% bitumen, extractable organics, and 85-100% kerogen, unextractable organics, see Table I. The kerogen is an
organic matrix of high molecular weight, containing on the average several saturated rings with hydrocarbon chains having an oc-
casional isolated carbon-carbon double bond and also containing,

0097–6156/81/0163–0315$05.00/0

in addition to small amounts of nitrogen and sulfur, approximately 6% oxygen. There is also the possibility that considerable amounts of non-crosslinked, long-chain compounds are trapped in the matrix.

If the nitrogen and sulfur are formally replaced by oxygen, for example by hydrolysis with each nitrogen and sulfur being replaced by the two oxygens and one hydrogen, then a simple formula weight is $C_{18}H_{28}O_2$ and the weight ratio of C/H is 7.7. This is about what would be expected for algae derived organics, since algae produce fatty acids in the C_{18} range as well as other hydrocarbons such as cartenoids at C_{40}. It has been shown that the extractable hydrocarbons from oil shale have a bimodal distribution at C_{17} and C_{29} supporting this contention ($\underline{2}$). Strong evidence for the biogenesis of kerogen was shown when it was found that the ratio of odd to even number of carbon atoms in the extracted hydrocarbons was as high as four to one. A ratio of one to one would be expected from a nonbiological source. The higher proportion of the odd number hydrocarbons would be anticipated if their source was the decarboxylation of algal fatty acids, since these acids are predominantly even number acids.

An interesting question is: how did these predominantly algal acids become crosslinked to form kerogen? It can be seen from the kerogen formula that there are on the average four units of unsaturation, while it is known that under some conditions algae form fatty acids that are 95% unsaturated, and with some acids, such as arachidonic, an essential fatty acid, there are four olefinic linkages. It has also been shown that these polyunsaturated algal acids, under mild heating, become crosslinked. It is clear that the unsaturated acids on diagenesis in the oil shale react to form naphthenes, the cyclic compounds found in kerogen. One reaction of this type is the Diels-Alder reaction which can occur at mild temperatures ($\underline{3}$).

While the Diels-Alder reaction is thought to be responsible for the organic crosslinking reaction, it is also proposed that there is a chemical attachment of the organic to the inorganic matrix. This attachment could arise from the interaction of the carboxyl group of the fatty acid with the calcium and magnesium ions on the inorganic surface, which could lead to the formation of insoluble calcium and/or magnesium soaps. In addition to the nitrogen found in porphyrins and related compounds, it is also proposed that the sulfur and nitrogen moieties found in kerogen result from attack of ammonia and polysulfides on the unsaturated fats leading to Willgerodt-type reaction products.

One big advantage of shale oil as compared to coal is the more favorable atomic composition of kerogen noted in Table II. The hydrogen content of kerogen is almost twice that of many coals, and the oxygen content is lower. The sulfur content of kerogen is similar to that of coal. The nitrogen is higher in kerogen. Consequently, less hydrogen is required to remove the

TABLE I

TYPICAL COMPOSITION OF
GREEN RIVER OIL SHALE

	(25 Gal/Ton Shale Oil) Wt%
Kerogen Content 15 wt%	
Kerogen Composition:	
Carbon	80.5
Hydrogen	10.3
Nitrogen	2.4
Sulfur	1.0
Oxygen (Varies with Depth)	5.8
	100.0
Simple Chemical Formula (Sulfur & Nitrogen Replaced by Oxygen)	$C_{20}H_{32}O_2$
Mineral Content 85 wt%	
Carbonates	48.0
Feldspars	21.0
Quartz	15.0
Clays	13.0
Analcite & Pyrite	3.0
	100.0

TABLE II

KEROGEN VS COAL

	Weight Percent			
	Kerogen	Coal		
		Bit	Subb	Lignite
Moisture and Ash Free				
Carbon	80.5	78.8	73.5	72.5
Hydrogen	10.3	5.7	5.3	4.9
Oxygen	5.8	8.9	19.7	20.8
Nitrogen	2.4	1.4	1.0	1.1
Sulfur	1.0	5.2	0.5	0.7
C/H Ratio	7.8	13.8	13.9	14.8

unwanted oxygen, nitrogen and sulfur, and less hydrogen is needed to bring the carbon/hydrogen ratio down to values required in liquid fuels such as gasoline, turbine and diesel fuels or heating oils.

Because of the impervious nature of the oil shale and the chemical nature of the kerogen, it is necessary to heat the shale to around 450°C (900°F) to thermally break up the kerogen. Under these conditions, kerogen decomposes to give oil (65-70%), gas (10-15%), coke (15-20%) and water (2-7%).

Also, during the retorting operation, there is significant loss of oxygen. About two-thirds is lost as carbon dioxide and about one-third as water. Because of the loss of carbon dioxide, the C/H ratio has beneficially decreased from 7.8 in kerogen to 7.3 in shale oil.

Some insight into the utility of shale oil can be gained by comparing its composition with coal-derived liquids and petroleum crude oil. See Table III. Two representative liquid products from coal are shown: COED product, produced by carbonization or coking, which, like retorting of shale, is a thermal step (4), and a liquid from the H-Coal process by coal hydrogenation (5). Arabian Light crude oil is also shown.

Of the two thermally produced liquids, shale oil has a better (lower) carbon-to-hydrogen ratio, and a lower specific gravity which indicates the absence of high boiling aromatics. Both have high pour points; shale oil because of long-chain paraffins, COED liquid because of heavy polyaromatics. The liquid yields per ton of raw material mined are in the same order of magnitude. The solid residue of shale retorting is largely mineral matter, while the solid residue from coal carbonization, called a char, is a usable fuel containing more energy than the oil fraction. Conversion of the COED liquid product to transportation fuels, however, is a more difficult task because of its high tar, lower hydrogen and higher hetero atom contents.

The hydrogenated product from coal, H-Coal liquid, is more aromatic than shale oil but somewhat comparable in hetero atom content even though a considerable amount of hydrogen has already been added to the product.

Arabian Light crude is a wider boiling material than crude shale oil and is lower in all hetero atoms except sulfur. It has a more favorable carbon/hydrogen ratio because it contains fewer aromatics and no olefins.

In the upgrading of crude shale oil, solids removal is first achieved by optimal centrifuging, settling and filtering. Next, arsenic removal is achieved with a catalyst-absorbent.

In the third step, the hydrotreating step, the sulfur, nitrogen, and oxygen containing compounds are hydrogenated over metallic sulfide catalysts to hydrogen sulfide, ammonia, water and hydrocarbons. Olefins present in the raw shale oil are also hydrogenated.

The hydrotreated shale oil (or syncrude) now, save for pour

TABLE III

CRUDE SHALE OIL,
COAL LIQUIDS, CRUDE OIL

	Crude Shale Oil	Coal Liquids		Arabian Light Crude
		COED*	H-Coal	
Gravity, Specific	0.92	1.13	0.92	0.85
°API	22.2	-4	23.0	34.7
Boiling Range, °C	60-540	-	30-525	5-575+
Composition, Wt%				
Nitrogen	1.8	1.1	0.1	0.8
Sulfur	0.9	2.8	0.2	1.7
Oxygen	0.8	8.5	0.6	-
C/H Ratio	7.3	11.2	8.1	6.2
Pour Point, °F	60	100	<5	-15
Viscosity, 100°F, SUS	98	133	-	44
Hydrogen Added				
Scf/Bbl Product	0	0	6000	0
Wt%	0	0	10	-
Yield, Gallons/Ton	25-35	30-48	60-90	-

*COED: Char Oil Energy Development

point, resembles crude oil more closely. The amount of hydrogen
consumed is listed in Table IV either as the volume of hydrogen
per barrel of product or the number of hydrogen atoms absorbed
per hetero atom, that is, nitrogen plus sulfur plus oxygen atoms.
The ratio of 10.8 exceeds the theoretical hydrogen consumption
because double bonds are saturated and hetero as well as other
compounds are hydrocracked.

The specific gravity and composition of hydrotreated shale
oil are compared to a syncrude from coal. Note that we have
converted crude shale oil to syncrude with much less hydrogen
than would be required for a similar product from coal: 1,350
SCF per barrel compared with 6,000 SCF per barrel or more, and
made a higher quality product, as indicated by the composition
and carbon/hydrogen ratio.

The high pour points, and also high viscosities of the raw
shale oil and of the hydrotreated shale oil, are a cause for
concern. It appears that both the raw shale oil with its high
nitrogen content, its high pour point and high viscosity and
the hydrotreated shale oil with its high pour point may not be
suitable for undedicated (to such oils) pipelines. In the absence of dedicated pipelines, conversion to pipelineable products
(gasoline, diesel fuel, jet fuel, etc.) at or near the retorting
site is one alternative. Another is to subject the raw shale
to a coking operation which lowers the pour point and, when
followed by hydrotreating, gives a low-sulfur, low-nitrogen oil
of about 45°F pour point. The hydrotreated shale oil can be
doped with a pour point depressant to give a 35 to 40°F pour
point oil acceptable in common carrier pipelines.

If the thermal coking has to be used to make a product
suitable for common carrier pipelining, an overall liquid yield
loss of 15% to 20% will be incurred.

Shale oil from the retort contains on the order of 10%
heavy naphtha, a precursor to gasoline. When hydrotreating the
shale oil to reduce the nitrogen content to 1,000 ppm, some additional naphtha is formed. The syncrude will have close to 14%
naphtha which is somewhat similar in quality to naphtha from
Light Arabian crude. See Table V. The octane number of the
naphtha is low and will have to be improved by catalytic reforming. Reforming primarily dehydrogenates naphthenic rings to form
high-octane aromatics, and also cyclizes or isomerizes low-
octane straight-chain paraffins and hydrocracks some of the high-
boiling paraffins. Reforming was developed to upgrade petroleum
naphthas and will also be required for comparable liquid stocks
from coal. The relatively high naphthene content of shale oil
naphtha permits reforming to high-octane gasoline with only
moderate yield loss, compared with Light Arabian naphtha.
Naphthas from coal generally contain aromatic rings as well
and so would give slightly better yields; but, because of the
higher number of hetero compounds, lose some advantage.

The Department of Defense is interested in alternative

TABLE IV

HYDROGEN REQUIREMENT TO
HYDROTREAT SHALE OIL

	Hydrotreated Shale Oil	H-Coal
Hydrogen Consumption		
Scf/Bbl Product	1350	6000
Atoms/Atom Hetero	10.8	----
Wt% Product	2.4	10
Gravity,		
°API	34	23
Specific	0.86	0.92
Pour Point, °F	+80	<5
Viscosity, 100°F, SUS	55	---
Composition, Wt%		
Nitrogen	0.08	0.01
Sulfur	0.002	0.2
Oxygen	–	0.6
C/H Ratio	6.5	8.1

TABLE V

SHALE OIL PRODUCTS VS PETROLEUM PRODUCTS

NAPHTHA (GASOLINE PRECURSOR)

Naphtha From:	Shale Oil*	Light Arabian Crude	Exxon Donor Solvent
Boiling Range, °C	70-205	25-190	70-205
50% Point, °C	154	123	177
Yield, Vol% Crude	13.6	26.7	10
Gravity, °API	51.6	63.0	30
Specific	0.77	0.73	0.88
Sulfur, ppm	9	320	4700
Nitrogen, ppm	34	---	2100
C/H Ratio	5.9	5.7	7.8
Octane Number			
Research, Clear	32.5	38.3	-
+ 3 ml TEL	61.9	63.6	-
Composition, wt%			
Paraffins	45	75	22
Naphthenes	44	14	42
Aromatics	11	11	36

*From shale oil which has been hydrotreated to reduce sulfur to 530 ppm. 1350 scf H_2 consumed per barrel of crude shale oil.

TABLE VI

SHALE OIL PRODUCTS VS PETROLEUM PRODUCTS

TURBINE FUEL

Source	JP-4 From Shale Oil	Typical JP-4
Boiling Range, °C	100–240	60–240
50% Point, °C	182	143
Gravity, °API	51.9	54
Specific	0.77	0.76
Sulfur, ppm	5	350
Freeze Point, °C	<-60	-62
Aromatics, Vol%	3.0	12.3
Smoke Point, mm	40	27.5
Thermal Stability, JFTOT at 260°C		
Pressure Drop, mm Hg	0	0.2
Preheater Deposit Code	0	1

TABLE VII

SHALE OIL PRODUCTS VS PETROLEUM PRODUCTS

DIESEL FUEL

Source	Diesel Fuel From Shale Oil	Typical
Boiling Range, °C	200–360	188–237
Yield, Vol%	42.3	--
Gravity, °API	37.2	36
Specific	0.84	0.84
Sulfur, ppm	19	2500
Nitrogen, Wt%	0.022	--
Pour Point, °F	−23	−4 to −48
Cetane Number	50	46
Viscosity, SUS @ 38°C	37.2	34.5

sources of turbine fuels for military aircraft. JP-4 is the large-volume fuel they require. See Table VI. Shale oil is well suited for yielding turbine fuels because of its relatively low aromaticity. All specifications for JP-4 are met by separating the JP-4 boiling range material from crude shale oil by distillation and hydrotreating that fraction.

Refining of jet fuels from coal syncrude poses more of a problem becuase of the high aromatic content.

The diesel fuel fraction from the raw shale oil is too high in sulfur and olefins and too low in cetane number and storage stability to meet specifications. Product which meets all specifications can be made, however, by hydrotreating crude shale oil followed by distillation, refer to Table VII. An increasing number of petroleum crudes also require hydrotreating of the diesel fraction to reduce sulfur content.

The portion of shale syncrude boiling above the diesel fuel fraction can be used as a premium low-sulfur fuel oil or cracked to produce more valuable lower-boiling transportation fuels such as gasoline, jet and diesel fuels. This fraction is a better material than the corresponding fraction from crude (such as Arabian Light), because the shale oil has been upgraded by prior processing: retorting, which thermally cracked the highest boiling fractions and reduced its carbon residue, and hydrotreating which reduced the sulfur and nitrogen contents. The corresponding crude oil fraction (from Light Arabian crude) still contains 32% (14% of crude) as a nondistillable asphalt. It is difficult to use as boiler fuel because of its 2.75% sulfur content. It is often utilized by blending it in bunker fuel or by converting it to acceptable distillate fuels by coking followed by hydrotreating.

LITERATURE CITED

1. Cane, R. F., "Developments in Petroleum Science 5," Chapter 3 (Teh Fu Yen and G. V. Chilingarian, ed.), Elsevier, N. Y. 1976, p. 27.

2. Ibid, p. 66.

3. Ibid, p. 51.

4. Synthetic Fuels Data Handbook, Cameron Engineers, Inc., 2nd Edition, 1978, p. 193.

5. Ibid, pp. 238-42; Shaw, H.; Kalfadellis, C. D.; Jahnig, C. E., "Evaluation of Methods to Produce Aviation Turbine Fuels from Synthetic Crude Oils-Phase One," Air Force Aero Propulsion Laboratory Technical Report AF-APL-TR-75-10, Final Report for Period 24 June 1974-24 January 1975, 12008 Exxon Pt 16 5-16-75MY, p. 168.

RECEIVED January 29, 1981.

The Reactivity of Cold Lake Asphaltenes

R. C. SCHUCKER[1] and C. F. KEWESHAN

Corporate Research Science Laboratories, Exxon Research and Engineering
Company, P.O. Box 45, Linden, NJ 07036

As known reserves of light crudes become depleted, the conversion of heavy crudes and residua to distillate fuels is becoming increasingly important. While reserves of Canadian and
Venezuelan bitumen and Arabian heavy oils represent vast, largely
untapped resources, their usefulness to a large extent depends on
our ability to chemically convert macromolecules such as asphaltenes and polar aromatics to smaller molecules boiling typically
in the mid-distillate/naphtha range. To optimize the utilization
of these feedstocks, we need a much better understanding of the
structure and reactivity of petroleum macromolecules, particularly asphaltenes.

While there has been a significant amount of research done
to date to elucidate structural characteristics of asphaltenes,
there appears to be no consensus of opinion even on major issues
such as the average size of asphaltene aromatic units. For example, proposed structures for Athabasca pentane asphaltenes vary
from the twelve-ring naphtho-ovalene structure of Speight (1) to
the two-ring sulfur polymer structure of Ignasiak et al (2).
With this kind of disagreement regarding crude asphaltene structures, it is easy to see why little progress has been made in the
area of asphaltene reactivity.

Recently it has been reported by Bearden and Aldridge (3)
that certain molybdenum catalysts can substantially reduce coke
formation in the hydroconversion of asphaltene - containing feeds
under thermal cracking conditions. We have now applied this
method to obtain asphaltene fragments in high yields for characterization of the structure of asphaltenes from Cold Lake crude.
The goal of our work has been to define the major building blocks
in Cold Lake asphaltenes in order to begin to bring together the
concepts of structure and reactivity. We have approached the
problem by carrying out mild, thermal hydroconversion reactions
on neat asphaltenes and characterizing both reactant and reaction

[1]Current address: Exxon Research and Development Laboratories,
P. O. Box 2226, Baton Rouge, Louisiana 70821.

products in detail. While previous research has concentrated on
crude asphaltenes, we have focused on reacted asphaltenes. By
combining structural and kinetic information obtained in this
study, we have been able to postulate a global asphaltene reaction mechanism which is consistent with all of our observations.

Experimental

     Cold Lake asphaltenes for this study were prepared by pre-
cipitation with n-heptane using a solvent to crude ratio of 20:1.
The precipitated asphaltenes were separated from the maltenes
(n-heptane solubles) by filtration, then washed with an equal
volume of n-heptane and dried at 100°C in vacuo. Total yield of
asphaltenes on crude was 12.6% (by weight). These asphaltenes
contained approximately 0.8% (by weight) toluene insoluble,
inorganic matter which was corrected for in subsequent yield
calculations. Elemental composition was measured by routine
analytical techniques. Oxygen was measured directly by neutron
activation analysis and not obtained by difference. Number average molecular weights were obtained by vapor pressure osmometry
(VPO) in toluene at 50°C. Nickel and vanadium concentrations
were measured by atomic absorption spectrophotometry. Mole fractions of aromatic carbon and hydrogen were determined directly by
pulsed Fourier transform nmr techniques. A summary of analytical
data for the reactant asphaltenes is given in Table I.

     All reactions were carried out as batch experiments in
tubing bomb reactors (30cc) using either Cold Lake asphaltenes as
precipitated or Cold Lake asphaltenes impregnated with a soluble
molybdenum catalyst which had been previously shown to reduce
coke formation in the hydroconversion of heavy hydrocarbons ($\underline{3}$).
In a typical experiment the reactor was charged with five grams
of asphaltenes and pressurized to 6 MPa with hydrogen. It was
then plunged into a preheated, fluidized sandbath, held for the
desired reaction time while agitating, removed from the bath and
quenched in cold water. The temperature of the reaction mixture
was monitored at all times using a thermocouple located in the
bomb. Typical heatup time from ambient temperatures to 95% of
reaction temperature was three minutes. At the end of a run
gases were vented through an H_2S scrubber into a gas bag. Hydrocarbon gases (C_1-C_4) were analyzed by gas chromatography using
flame ionization detection and 1,1-difluoroethane as an internal
standard. Toluene was used to remove the liquid and solid
products from the bomb and the toluene solution was filtered
to determine the coke (toluene insolubles) yield. After removing toluene from the filtrate by vacuum, n-heptane was added to
separate asphaltenes (toluene soluble, n-heptane insoluble) from
maltenes (n-heptane soluble). Coke and asphaltene fractions were
dried overnight at 100°C in vacuo. An overall material balance
was obtained by summing the coke, asphaltene, maltene and gas
fractions and for lower severity runs averaged between 97-101%.

TABLE I

ANALYSIS OF COLD LAKE CRUDE ASPHALTENES

C (WT.%)	80.64
H (WT.%)	7.64
O (WT.%)	1.84
N (WT.%)	1.60
S (WT.%)	7.95
Ni (PPM)	310
V (PPM)	815
Mn (VPO, TOLUENE, $50^{\circ}C$)	6640 ± 120
C_A (MOLE %)	47.3
H_A (MOLE %)	11.4
$(H/C)_{TOTAL}$	1.14
$(H/C)_A$	0.274
$(H/C)_S$	1.91
T_M ($^{\circ}C$)	209

Further separation of maltenes into resins (polar aromatics) and oils was achieved in selected cases by adsorption onto Attapulgus clay using a modification of ASTM D2007 (clay-gel separation).

Results And Discussion

The thermal hydroconversion of Cold Lake asphaltenes was studied initially to provide a basis for evaluation of catalytic effectiveness in subsequent work. Series of thermal runs were made at 335°C, 365°C and 400°C and the reaction products were separated as described previously. Several kinetic models were tried, but after examining the variability of our data, we decided on the simple first-order asphaltene decomposition model shown below:

$$A \quad \rightarrow \quad aA^* + bM \tag{1}$$

where A = weight fraction reactant asphaltenes

A^* = weight fraction reacted asphaltenes

M = weight fraction maltenes

a,b = stoichiometric coefficients (based on weight)

Rate expressions for total asphaltenes and maltenes were integrated to yield Equations (2) and (3).

$$A_t = a + (1-a)e^{-kt} \tag{2}$$

$$M = b(1-e^{-kt}) \tag{3}$$

Equations (2) and (3) were fit to experimental data using non-linear regression to obtain values of the first-order reaction rate constants and the stoichiometric coefficients at each temperature. The conversion data from the 400°C thermal run and the best fit of the kinetic model are shown in Figure 1. It is interesting to note that at the time of incipient coke formation (∼60 minutes) the asphaltene and maltene data deviate from predicted first-order behavior. From this we concluded that both asphaltenes and maltenes were participating in secondary coke-forming reactions. Further separation of the maltenes into resins (polar aromatics) and oils confirmed this to be true and showed that it was the resin fraction that was involved in coke formation.

The same experiments were run using asphaltenes impregnated with molybdenum. The conversions and best fit of the kinetic model at 400°C are shown in Figure 2. Previous work (4) had suggested that the molybdenum would sulfide and thus be able to activate hydrogen resulting in improved hydrogen transfer to radical fragmentation products. Increased hydrogen transfer

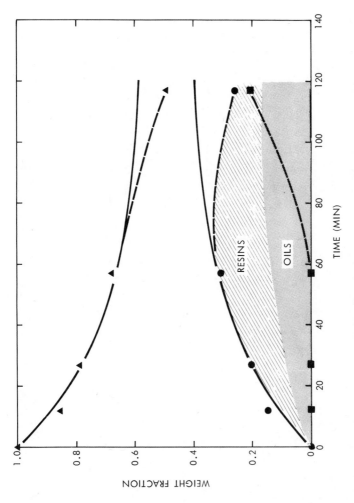

Figure 1.   Thermal hydroconversion of Cold Lake asphaltenes at 400°C and 6 MPa H_2: asphaltenes (▲); maltenes (●); coke (■); model (– – –).

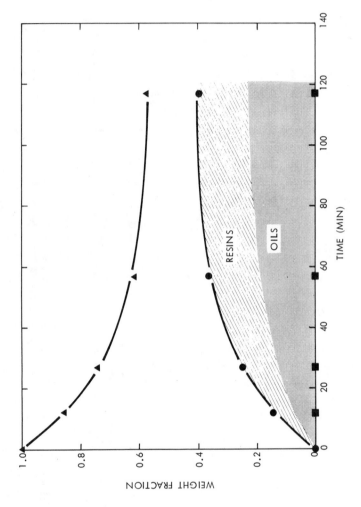

Figure 2.   Hydroconversion of Cold Lake crude asphaltenes with 200 ppm molybdenum at 400°C and 6 MPa H₂: asphaltenes (▲); maltenes (●); coke (■); model (– – –).

above the thermal base case would explain the stabilization of resin fragments shown in Figure 2 and the lower olefin/paraffin ratio in the gas illustrated in Table II for the C_3 gases.

The temperature dependence of the reaction rate constants obtained for the thermal and catalytic runs was assumed to follow the Arrhenius relationship and the resulting plot of these data is shown as Figure 3. As we can see, the catalyst had no real effect on the activation energy. It did, however, increase the rate of reaction at all temperatures. Interpretation of these data, though, is at best somewhat subjective. In complex reaction systems like these, the measured rate is generally considered to be that of the slowest or rate-limiting step in the reaction sequence. The low values of the activation energies obtained strongly suggest that primary bond breaking is not the rate-limiting step and that some other step such as hydrogen transfer might be. This is supported by the fact that the observed rate increased under improved hydrogen transfer conditions.

While the yield of asphaltenes and other products during the early stages of reaction are similar (as shown in Figures 1 and 2), the thermal asphaltenes exhibited lower H/C ratios and higher number average molecular weight ($\bar{M}_n$) and resulted in substantial coke formation. The unique behavior of the asphaltenes in the presence of molybdenum on the other hand provided us with an excellent opportunity to look closer at the structure of the reacted asphaltenes. Since these reactions were carried out neat, maltenes could be separated and analyzed directly. There were no maltenes initially so these molecules must at one time have been attached to the reactant asphaltene molecules. Furthermore, the reacted asphaltenes could also be analyzed to determine what chemical changes were taking place during reaction.

Elemental analysis showed some interesting results with regard to H/C, sulfur and nitrogen levels. Figure 4 shows a plot of the (H/C) values in the reacted asphaltenes and the product maltenes. As can be seen, the (H/C) ratio in the reacted asphaltenes drops continuously while that of the product maltenes rises continuously. The weighted average of the measured asphaltene and maltene fractions rises slightly indicating the addition of some hydrogen to the system. This is the kind of behavior that might be expected of an asphaltene structure containing a large, hydrogen deficient core to which are attached smaller, hydrogen-rich molecules. It is not consistent with the smaller asphaltene structure proposed by Ignasiak et al (2) for Athabasca asphaltenes.

Next the question of sulfur distribution was addressed. Sulfur in the asphaltene and maltene fractions was measured directly and that in the gas was obtained by difference. The result for this same series of runs is shown in Figure 5. What we found was that approximately 50% of the sulfur remained in

TABLE II

EFFECT OF HYDROGEN TRANSFER ON OLEFIN/PARAFFIN RATIO IN GAS PRODUCTS

TEMP. (^{O}C)	REACTION TIME (MIN.)	$C_3^=/C_3$	
		THERMAL	200 ppm MOLYBDENUM
365	42	0.18	0.08
	87	0.13	0.05
	177	0.07	0.03
	357	0.04	0.02
335	87	0.26	0.14
	177	0.15	0.06
	357	0.08	0.03
	747	0.04	0.02

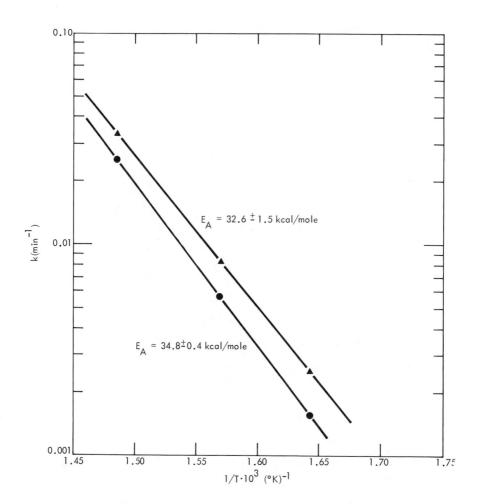

Figure 3. Arrhenius plot for hydroconversion of Cold Lake asphaltenes: 200 ppm molybdenum (▲); thermal (●).

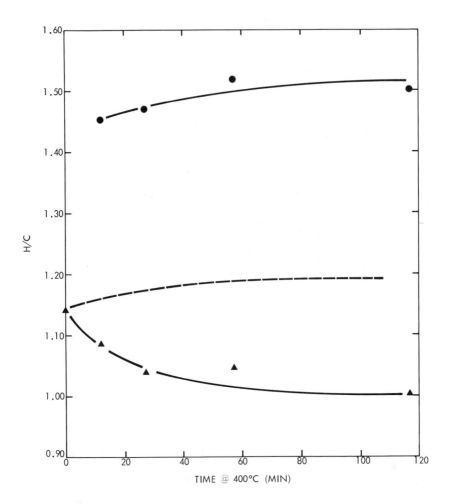

Figure 4.   Hydrogen-to-carbon ratios in reaction products: maltenes (●); total product (calculated) (– – –); asphaltenes (▲).

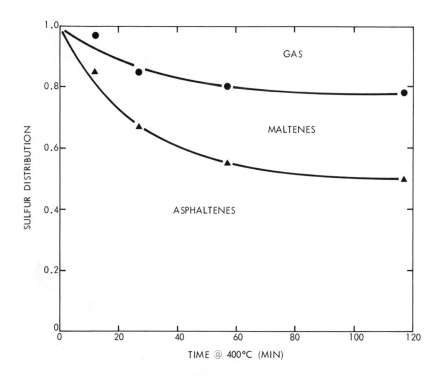

Figure 5.   Sulfur distribution in reaction products

the reacted asphaltene, 28% was found in the maltenes while 22% wound up in the gas (presumably as H_2S). Studies with model sulfur compounds (including dibenzothiophene, diphenyl sulfide, benzyl phenyl sulfide and dibenzyl disulfide) under the same reaction conditions led us to conclude that the majority of the sulfur in both the asphaltene and maltene products was either heterocyclic or an intermediate reaction product from the cleavage of diaryl or alkyl-aryl sulfide linkages. More easily cleaved bonds such as those in dialkyl sulfides or disulfides were found to be converted very quickly.

Nitrogen was also measured in the asphaltenes and maltenes and the results are shown in Table III. What we found was that, unlike sulfur which is distributed pretty evenly between the asphaltene core and the peripheral groups, nitrogen is primarily in the core structure. In addition, during reaction very little if any of the nitrogen is removed from the system. This suggests that nitrogen is in predominantly condensed heterocyclic structures in the core with only about 12-14% existing as smaller condensed nitrogen structures on the periphery.

Oxygen was measured only in the asphaltenes due to sample size limitations. Combined results indicated that over 50% of the oxygen was liberated during these reactions as gaseous species and this is in good agreement with recently published work of Moschopedis et al (5) suggesting the presence of carboxylic acid and aldehyde functionality.

In addition to elemental analyses, number average molecular weights ($\bar{M}_n$) were obtained on both asphaltene and maltene fractions from this series. The resulting curves are shown in Figure 6. The starting asphaltenes are observed to have a number average molecular weight of 6640 ± 120. This decreases monotonically to an apparent asymptote of 3400. At the same time, maltenes which are produced exhibit much lower molecular weights starting at 645 and decreasing to 415. It is not unreasonable at this point to postulate that the maltenes, once formed, continue to break down. Here again, the observed variation in average molecular weight is consistent with the concept that asphaltenes have a larger core structure to which are attached smaller (~1/10 the size of the core) groups. We are not saying that 3400 represents the molecular weight of the core structure. Experimental nmr and other VPO evidence points to the contrary. We are saying that at 400°C we have broken all bonds that can be thermally broken at a reasonable rate and are left with the core plus peripheral groups attached by much stronger bonds (i.e. biphenyl linkages, etc.) and some alkyl side chains.

One of the most powerful tools available to us for characterization of these fractions is nuclear magnetic resonance spectroscopy. Proton and ^{13}C Fourier transform nmr spectra were run in deuterochloroform on these same asphaltene and maltene samples and some of the spectra are shown in Figures 7 and 8. One of the first interesting points we find is that the asphal-

TABLE III

NITROGEN CONTENT OF REACTION PRODUCTS

REACTION TIME (MIN)	% ASPHALTENE CONVERSION	N/N_O ASPHALTENES	MALTENES
0	0	1.0	0
27	26.0	0.83	0.12
57	38.3	0.83	0.12
117	42.7	0.76	0.14

400°C, 200 ppm Mo

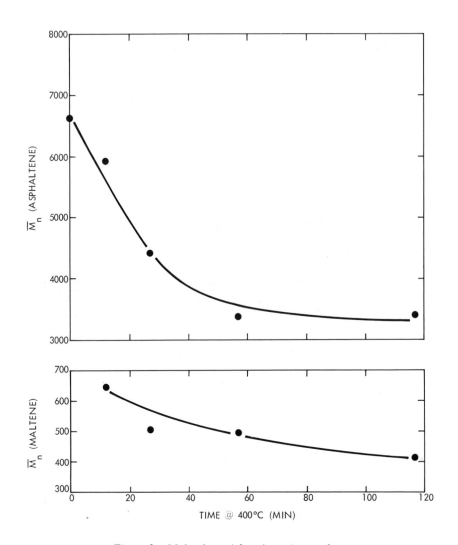

Figure 6. Molecular weights of reaction products

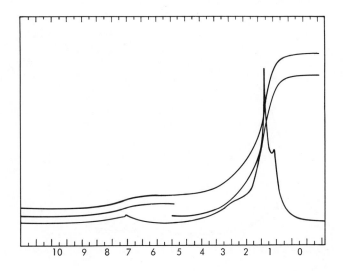

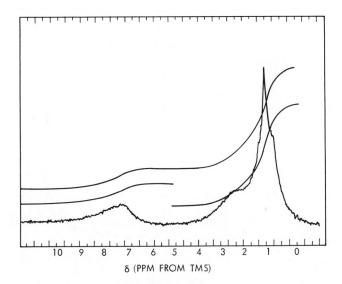

δ (PPM FROM TMS)

Figure 7.   H-1 NMR spectra of (top) crude and (bottom) reacted (400°C, 2 h) asphaltenes

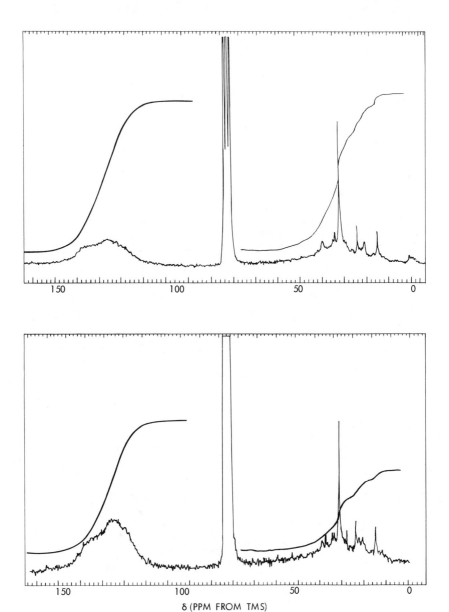

δ (PPM FROM TMS)

Figure 8.   C-13 NMR spectra of (top) *crude and* (bottom) *reacted (400°C, 2 h)*
asphaltenes

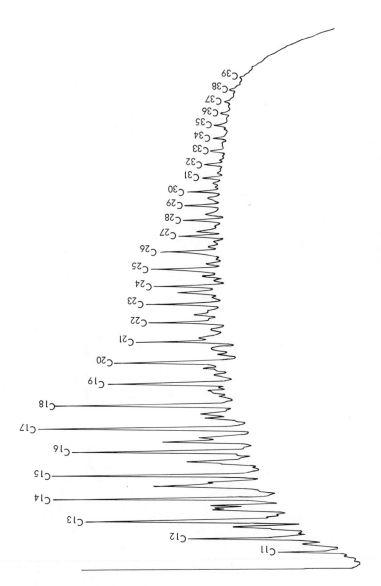

Figure 9.   GC of maltene fraction from run at 365°C, 6 MPa H₂, 3 h

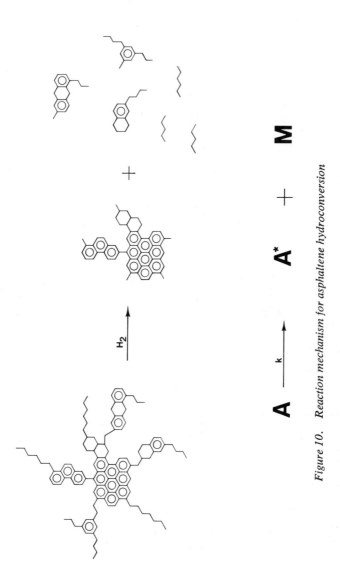

Figure 10.   Reaction mechanism for asphaltene hydroconversion

tenes with $\bar{M}_n$ = 3400 still have 40% aliphatic carbon. Both ^{13}C and ^{1}H spectra confirm these as predominantly paraffinic side chains although some naphthenic character still remains. These side chains need not be connected to the asphaltene core since the smaller peripheral groups are also known to be highly alkyl substituted. In general we can say that the increase in the fraction of aromatic carbon and hydrogen during reaction is consistent with (1) the loss of alkyl side chains, (2) loss of highly substituted aromatic and naphthenic groups, and (3) loss of naphthenic hydrogen. We believe that to a certain degree all of these are occurring but that (2) is the dominant reaction. We can also say based on subsequent experimental work using n-decyl benzene as a model alkyl aromatic that under these conditions (400°C, 120 min, 7 MPa H_2) β-scission of alkyl side chains is preferred 20:1 over α.

One maltene sample generated under somehwat milder conditions (3 hrs., 365°C, CoMo/γ-Al_2O_3) to minimize secondary cracking reactions was analyzed by gas chromatography and the resulting chromatogram is shown in Figure 9. It is clear that while the vast majority of the area is contained in the lower envelope, a definite pattern of regularly-spaced peaks is observ- -able above the base. These were identified by gas chromatography/mass spectrometry as n-paraffins ranging in length from C_{11} to C_{39}. The smaller peaks in between were identified as primarily iso-paraffins which may have been formed by isomerization during hydroconversion over the somewhat acidic CoMo/γ-Al_2O_3 or which may represent the natural distribution of isoparaffins in the alkyl side chains.

In summary, we have presented experimental evidence which supports the concept that Cold Lake asphaltenes have somewhat large, hydrogen-deficient core structures to which are attached alkyl side chains and highly substituted aromatic groups. We have shown that sulfur tends to be relatively evenly distributed between the core structures and the peripheral groups and that nitrogen is concentrated predominantly in the cores. The overall picture of asphaltene reactivity that has emerged from this is shown schematically in Figure 10. During mild hydroconversion, weaker linkages are thermally broken resulting in the formation of maltenes having a higher (H/C) and reacted asphaltenes having a lower (H/C). Some alkyl side chains are also lost predominantly by β-scission. In the absence of effective hydrogen transfer, some of these reaction fragments can recombine to form coke. With improved hydrogen transfer the coking reactions can be significantly delayed. Total conversion of these asphaltenes to maltenes would at this point seem to be an improbable goal; however, more research is needed in order to see how far the structural concepts developed here for Cold Lake asphaltenes can be generalized to others.

Literature Cited

1. Speight, J. G., "A Structural Investigation of the Constituents of Athasbaca Bitumen by Proton Magnetic Resonance
   Spectroscopy," Fuel, 1970, 49, 76-90.

2. Ignasiak, T., Kemp-Jones, A. V. and Strausz, O. P., "The
   Molecular Structure of Athabasca Asphaltenes. Cleavage of
   the Carbon-Sulfur Bonds by Radical Ion Electron Transfer
   Reactions," J. Org. Chem., 1977, 42(2), 312-320.

3. Bearden, R., Jr. and Aldridge, C. L., U.S. Patent
   4,134,825 (1979).

4. Bearden, R., Jr., private communication.

5. Moschopedis, S. E., Parkash, S. and Speight, J. G., "Thermal
   Decomposition of Asphaltenes," Fuel, 1978, 57, 431-434.

RECEIVED January 29, 1981.

Influence of Thermal Processing on the Properties of Cold Lake Asphaltenes: The Effect of Distillation

KENNETH A. GOULD and MARTIN L. GORBATY

Corporate Research Science Laboratories, Exxon Research and Engineering Company, P.O. Box 45, Linden, NJ 07036

A better understanding of the composition and properties of heavy feeds such as Cold Lake and Arabian Heavy oils is central to the development of improved upgrading technology. An important question which must be answered is to what extent these materials are thermally altered during refinery distillation. These heavy oils already contain large percentages of refractory materials such as asphaltenes, and it would be highly undesirable to increase the amount or degrade the quality of these components. We have, therefore, investigated the effect of heat treatment during distillation on the quantity and physical and chemical properties of asphaltenes. Cold Lake crude was chosen for this study since it is known to be a thermally sensitive material. Any changes caused by thermal treatment should, therefore, be more obvious than with a more stable feed. We report here the results of a variety of measurements made on the asphaltenes isolated from Cold Lake crude oil and from its vacuum distillation residue. It should be borne in mind that Cold Lake crude is subjected to the high temperatures of pressurized steam used in the production process and may conceivably have already undergone some thermal alteration. The present study, however, is designed primarily to learn if any further changes might occur during refining.

Background

The question of whether and to what extent asphaltenes are formed or altered during crude oil handling and processing has remained unresolved. In one investigation, samples of a Tartar mineral oil distillation residue were heated for five hours to 163°C and then for another five hours to 400°C to simulate conditions during distillation.(1) Both an increase in asphaltene content and a decrease in asphaltene H/C ratio were observed. In addition, distillation residues from various other crudes were heated to various temperatures for three hours and then pentane deasphalted. It was observed that asphaltene H/C ratios decreased rapidly above 300°C from 1.1 to 0.6.

0097–6156/81/0163–0347$05.00/0

These investigators also heated maltenes in sealed vials to various temperatures. The asphaltene yields obtained at 350°C, 400°C, and 450°C were 18, 32, and 36%, respectively. Although the conversions were approximately first order at the lower temperatures, they changed significantly at 450°C, the region of technical interest for many refining operations. Significant formation of new asphaltenes was seen to occur. Deasphaltened maltenes were also separated by alumina chromatography into a non-aromatic "gasoline" eluate, a strongly aromatic benzene eluate, and a resinous benzene-methanol eluate. Pentane insolubles were obtained from all three fractions upon heating at relatively low temperatures, although the rates were quite different. Resins gave the highest yields at the fastest rates while the aromatic oils showed about the same yield, but at a much slower rate. The yield and rate were lowest for the non-aromatic oils, and their pentane insolubles were mostly toluene insolubles and pyridine insolubles rather than asphaltenes. The report also claimed that asphaltenes were formed even at 20°C in the absence of air at relatively slow rates.

A study of the effect of heat on asphaltene decomposition at 350-380°C in a helium flow system (2) resulted in the following observations:

1. decomposition was found to be first order in asphaltenes
2. the percent coke make expressed as a percent of asphaltenes decomposed did not vary with the extent of cracking, implying that the mechanism is independent of the percent cracking.
3. a "20,000-fold increase in surface area" of the asphaltenes via introduction of carbon black (manner not specified) did not change the reaction rate
4. toluene insolubles were formed in amounts that decreased with increasing reaction time, implying that these products are intermediates in pyridine insoluble formation.

These observations led to the proposal of a free radical, chain reaction mechanism. Aspects of the mechanism include: (1) formation of small radical fragments which could abstract hydrogen and leave as light products, (2) reaction of stabilized free radicals (formed by hydrogen abstraction) which could interact with asphaltenes to form larger and larger condensation products, and (3) formation of toluene insolubles, i.e. linear condensation products, and pyridine insolubles, i.e. cross-linked products. These chain reactions could be terminated by formation of very stable radicals that could not react further.(2) This mechanism is in accord with the conclusions of Speight, who has stated that formation of paraffins during pyrolysis of Athabasca asphaltenes probably occurs via interaction of alkyl radicals with hydrogen produced during aromatization and condensation of polycyclic structures.(3) Carbon-carbon bond breaking in these asphaltenes was found to occur primarily β to aromatic rings.

In other work (4), x-ray analysis led to the conclusion
that not only did asphaltene melting point increase with increasing fractional aromaticity, f_a, but thermal sensitivity increased
in the same direction. Thus, asphaltenes with f_a 0.32 were more
sensitive and were transformed to a large extent to toluene
insolubles after one hour at 375°C. When f_a was 0.17 and 0.24,
only 18-32% conversion to toluene insolubles was observed.

Experimental

   Preparation of Asphaltenes. Asphaltenes were obtained by
n-heptane precipitation from either Cold Lake crude or vacuum
residuum using typical deasphaltening procedures. (i.e. One part
of residuum was refluxed for one hour with 10 parts of heptane.
The mixture was then filtered and the insoluble asphaltenes
washed several times with heptane and pentane and dried in vacuo
at 80°C.)

   Pyrolysis of Asphaltenes. Pyrolyses were performed using
the apparatus shown in Figure 1.(5) The appropriate material was
placed in a quartz tube with 24/40 ground joints and a dry ice
condenser was attached. After alternately evacuating and flush-
ing with nitrogen several times, the material was pyrolyzed at
the appropriate temperature for 10 min. Char and liquid yields
were calculated from the weights of the pyrolysis tubes and condensers before and after reaction.

   Analytical Data. Instrumental analyses and spectra were made
on the following equipment: infrared spectroscopy, Digilab FTS-
14 Fourier transform spectrophotometer; vapor pressure osmometry,
Hitachi-Perkin Elmer 115; gel permeation chromatography, Waters
Assoc. 200; nuclear magnetic resonance spectrometry, Varian
Assoc. A60 and XL100; thermogravimetric analysis, modified Stanton
thermobalance; differential scanning calorimetry, Perkin Elmer DSC
2; and electron spin resonance spectrometry, Varian Assoc. Century
spectrometer with E102 X band microwave bridge operating at 9.5
GHz.

Results and Discussion

   The findings discussed above (1-4) indicate that changes in
asphaltene quality and quantity during thermal treatment depend
strongly on both the origin of the oil and the severity of the
treatment. This means that specific questions concerning stability
can only be answered via studies on the particular oil at the
particular conditions of interest.

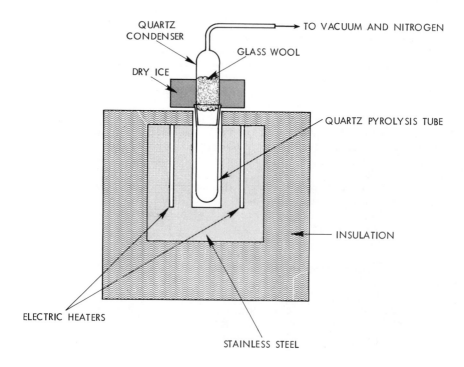

Figure 1.   Rapid heat-up pyrolysis unit

To provide raw material for this comparative study of untreated and heat-treated oils, asphaltenes from Cold Lake crude (crude asphaltenes) and from Cold Lake vacuum residuum (residuum asphaltenes) were prepared by n-heptane precipitation as described in the Experimental section. The Cold Lake residuum fraction was prepared by Imperial Oil Enterprises, Ltd. at Sarnia, Ontario, Canada. The distillation history of this bottoms fraction indicates that the pot material was subjected to temperatures as high as 314-318°C during atmospheric and vacuum distillation. The length of time at 300°C or higher was about two hours. This is well in excess of what would be experienced in a pipestill and should have provided ample time for any decomposition. It should be noted, however, that since it was possible to maintain the system vacuum at 0.35 mm, the maximum temperature experienced by the residuum was not quite as high as it might be during refinery distillation (e.g. ca 350°C).

Table I shows the yields of asphaltenes obtained from several deasphaltening operations on crude oil and bottoms. The yields on bottoms were normalized to yields on crude by correcting for the quantity of distillates in the crude.

Table I

Asphaltene Yields from Cold Lake Crude and Residuum

Source	% Asphaltenes (On Crude)
Residuum	10.6
Residuum	10.9
Crude	9.9
Crude	9.8
Crude	10.8

The average percentage of asphaltenes in the bottoms is 10.8% (based on crude) and is thus slightly higher than the average value of 10.2% for the crude oil. The 0.6% difference is, however, within the observed experimental variation of 1.0% and is therefore not considered significant.

The average elemental compositions for several preparations of crude and residuum asphaltenes are shown in Table II. As can be seen, the two asphaltenes are quite similar with the differences between them being less than the typical errors from analysis to analysis. The H/C ratios are almost identical.

Table II

Average Elemental Analyses for Crude and Residuum Asphaltenes

Asphaltene Source	% C	% H	% N	% S	Ni (ppm)	V (ppm)	H/C
Residuum	81.81	7.75	1.42	8.01	329	893	1.14
Crude	82.14	7.65	1.28	7.78	345	935	1.12

Both the number average molecular weights as determined by vapor pressure osmometry and extrapolated to zero concentration and the gel permeation chromatographic molecular weight distributions indicate that the crude and residuum asphaltenes do differ in molecular weight. The VPO results are summarized in Table III and comparative GPC traces are shown in Figure 2. As can be seen from these data, both techniques indicate that the crude asphaltenes have a significantly higher molecular weight than the residuum asphaltenes. This result is somewhat surprising since one would not a priori expect thermal cracking at such low temperatures, ∿320°C, even with a thermally sensitive crude such as Cold Lake. This explanation, however, cannot be ruled out. Another possibility which could account for lower molecular weights in the residuum asphaltenes, side chain dealkylation, can be eliminated on the basis of nuclear magnetic resonance results (vide infra). Another possible cause of the molecular weight reduction is thermally induced dissociation of $\pi\text{-}\pi$ complexes which may help to hold the asphaltene macrostructure together. Deasphaltening done at higher solvent-to-oil ratios, i.e. from 20:1 to 40:1, showed similar molecular weight differences between crude and residuum asphaltenes, implying that the ratio used here, 10:1, did not cause the observed differences.(6)

Table III

Number Average Molecular Weights
(M_N) for Crude and Residuum Asphaltenes

Asphaltene Source	M_N	Average M_N
Residuum	5120	
	4400	
	5850	5305
	5850	
Crude	8250	
	6120	6955
	6850	
	6600	

The two asphaltenes were also examined by infrared, nuclear magnetic resonance, and electron spin resonance techniques. Figures 3, 4, and 5 show the results of the IR analysis. It is immediately apparent that the two asphaltene spectra (Figures 3 and 4) are quite similar, showing no obvious qualitative differences. To learn if more subtle differences existed, a difference spectrum (Figure 5) was generated by computer using the data accumulated for Figures 3 and 4. This demonstrates that virtually complete cancellation can be obtained. The only residual absorption of any significance in this highly magnified spectrum is the small peak at 2950 cm⁻1. This may result from traces of residual solvent or it may represent a very minor difference between the two asphaltenes.

In the case of the magnetic resonance characterization, both ^{13}C NMR and proton NMR were employed to obtain the percentages of aromatic carbon and hydrogen. The results are shown in Table IV. Although the measured levels of aromatic hydrogen are within experimental uncertainty of each other, the difference in aromatic carbon is probably significant. Nevertheless, this difference is small and indicates that the aromatic carbon contents are quite similar. In addition, attempts to discern qualitative differences in the ^{13}C NMR were in vain. These results imply that very little, if any, dealkylation or aromatization has occurred during the crude distillation procedure.

Table IV

Aromatic Carbon and Hydrogen
Contents of Cold Lake Asphaltenes

Asphaltene Source	$\% \ C_A$	$\% \ H_A$
Crude	52.0 ± 1	13.7 ± 0.5
Residuum	50.4 ± 1	14.2 ± 0.5

Petroleum asphaltenes exhibit two general types of signals when examined by electron spin resonance techniques. One is the 16-line, anisotropic, vanadyl ($V=O^{+2}$) resonance of the solid state while the other arises from unpaired electrons which are present in the form of relatively stable free radicals. The crude and residuum asphaltenes were examined by ESR, and the relevant data are summarized in Table V.

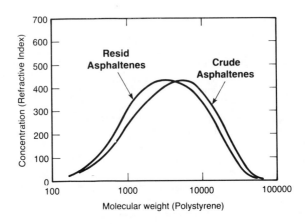

Figure 2.   Molecular-weight distributions of Cold Lake crude and residuum asphaltenes

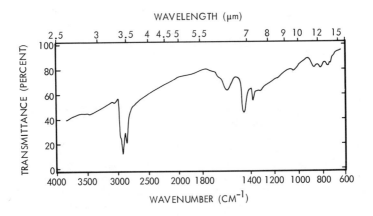

Figure 3.   IR spectrum of Cold Lake crude asphaltenes

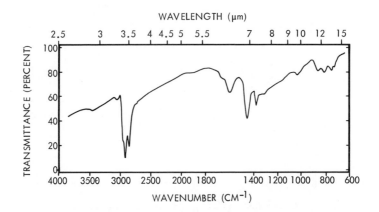

Figure 4.   IR spectrum of Cold Lake residuum asphaltenes

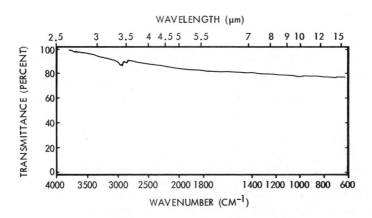

Figure 5.   Differential IR spectrum of crude and residuum asphaltenes

Table V

ESR Parameters for Cold Lake Asphaltenes

Parameter	Crude Asphaltenes	Residuum Asphaltenes
Vanadyl:		
$A_{||}$ (G)	174.0	174.4
$A_{\perp}$ (G)	56.3	56.7
$g_{||}$	1.9632	1.9629
$g_{\perp}$	1.9837	1.9813
Free Radical:		
g	2.00308	2.00307
linewidth (G)	6.4	6.6

It is apparent from the chemical shifts (g-values), the hyperfine coupling constants (A-values), and the linewidths that the free radicals and vanadyl species are in very similar environments in both samples. It was not possible to obtain meaningful values for the absolute numbers of spins per gram for either species, but estimates of the relative concentrations obtained by measuring peak heights indicate that the vanadyl and free-radical concentrations do not differ significantly between the two asphaltenes. It thus appears that heat treatment of Cold Lake asphaltenes to 320°C does not alter the nature or abundance of paramagnetic centers.

Since most of the physical properties of the asphaltenes did not show any major differences, thermal reactivity was investigated to discern any differences which might exist in chemical reactivity. Differential scanning calorimetry and thermogravimetric analysis as well as rapid pyrolysis were employed. The only notable features of the DSC analyses were what appeared to be glass transitions occurring at 175°C and 172°C for the crude and residuum asphaltenes, respectively. The TGA curves for the two materials were also virtually identical, differing by less than one percent volatile matter at any temperature. Both of these techniques thus indicate essentially no discernable differences in the two asphaltenes.

Similarly, when the pyrolysis behavior was studied in a rapid heating unit with a heatup time of one to two minutes, virtually identical residue yields were obtained.

Summary and Conclusions

The characteristics of Cold Lake crude and residuum asphaltenes have been compared by a number of instrumental and physical techniques. The asphaltenes were essentially identical in quality and quantity except that the crude asphaltenes exhibited higher average molecular weights as well as molecular weight distributions peaking at higher molecular weights than did the residuum asphaltenes.

The thermal history of these particular residuum asphaltenes is much more severe in terms of heating time than would ordinarily be the case for a refinery product from a pipestill since, in the present instance, a pot distillation was used. It therefore seems likely that refinery asphaltenes should be even less different from their respective crude asphaltenes than in this investigation, assuming that pipestill temperatures would be kept below the decomposition temperatures for the asphaltenes, i.e. less than about 350ºC. Furthermore, any differences should be further diminished in the event that a crude which is less thermally sensitive than Cold Lake is involved.

Since the Cold Lake crude used in this investigation has been exposed to the temperature of the pressuized steam used in the oil production, one cannot be certain that some thermal changes had not already occurred in the crude oil. To study this possibility the properties of cold bailed (i.e. recovered without steam injection) Cold Lake crude asphaltenes are being investigated by many of these same techniques and will be described in a future report.

Acknowledgments

We would like to thank R. B. Long for his assistance in the preparation of this manuscript, R. Rif for help with the experimental work, and the following individuals for their assistance in the various analytical measurements: L. Ebert, J. Elliott, B. Hager, B. Hudson, M. Melchior, E. Prestridge, W. Schulz, and B. Silbernagel.

Literature Cited

1. Hrapia, H. Meyer, D., and Prause, M., *Chem. Tech.*, 1964, 16, (12), 733.

2. Magaril, R. Z., and Aksenova, E. J., *Khim. Technol. Top. Masel*, 1970, 15, (7), 22.

3. Speight, J. G., *Am. Chem. Soc.*, *Div. Fuel Chem. Prepr.*, 1971, 15, (1), 57.

4. Bestougeff, M. A., and Genderel, P., *Am. Chem. Soc.*, *Div. Petrol. Chem. Prepr.*, 1964, 9, (2), B51.

5. Design supplied by R. J. Lang, Exxon Res. and Eng. Co., Baytown, Texas.

6. R. C. Schucker, private communication from these laboratories.

RECEIVED February 18, 1981.

Thermal Recovery of Oil from Tar Sands by an Energy-Efficient Process

K. M. JAYAKAR[1], J. D. SEADER, A. G. OBLAD, and K. C. HANKS[2]

Departments of Chemical and Fuels Engineering, University of Utah, Salt Lake City, UT 84112

Oil-impregnated rock deposits, more commonly referred to as tar sands, are found on every continent except Australia and Antarctica (1). The largest known deposits occur in northern Alberta, Canada, where two full-scale commercial plants for producing synthetic crude oil are in operation and two more plants have been approved for construction. Of the 24 states that contain tar sands in the United States, Ritzma (2) estimates that about 90-95 percent of these tar sands lie in Utah. Although the Utah deposits contain only about 25 billion barrels of in-place bitumen, compared to 900 billion barrels in Canada, as discussed by Oblad et al. (3), the Utah deposits represent an important potential domestic source of synthetic petroleum.

Operating plants in Canada employ a hot-water process for recovering bitumen from tar sands. Although Utah tar sands can be considerably different from Canadian tar sands with respect to physical and chemical properties (4), Sepulveda and Miller (5) have successfuly processed tar sands from high-grade Utah deposits with a modified hot-water process that uses high-shear conditions to overcome the higher viscosity of Utah tar-sand bitumens. More recent work by Misra and Miller (6) has been successful in processing medium-grade Utah deposits. Other methods for processing tar sands that have been studied extensively (1) include various in-situ techniques and mining followed by direct coking, solvent extraction, or cold-water separation. Of the other methods that use mined material as the feed stock, direct coking processes, generally referred to as thermal recovery methods, appear to exhibit the most promise as alternatives to hot-water processing because thermal recovery methods avoid handling of viscous bitumen, recovery of sediment from solutions, and recovery and recycle of water and/or solvents. In the work presented here, a new energy-efficient thermal process was developed and applied to tar sands from three Utah deposits.

[1] Current address: Eastman Kodak Company, Rochester, NY, 14605.

[2] Current address: Celanese Chemical Company, Pampa, TX, 78408.

0097–6156/81/0163–0359$05.00/0

Thermal Recovery Process

The concept of recovering liquid and/or gaseous hydrocarbons from solid hydrocarbon-bearing materials by thermal treatment has been known for several centuries (7). Thermal treatment essentially entails processing at high temperature. In most thermal processes, the feed material is heated in an inert or non-oxidizing atmosphere. The mode of heating and the operating temperature largely determine the type of changes occurring to the feed, which can include: 1) volatilization of any low-molecular-weight components in the feed, 2) generation of vapors by cracking reactions, and 3) conversion of part of the material into coke, by reactions such as polymerization. In the case of feed materials such as tar sand, which contain a significant amount of silica sand or other inorganic inert matter that remains substantially unchanged through the thermal treatment, coke is obtained as a deposit on the inorganic matter.

Thermal processing can require a substantial input of energy to provide the necessary sensible, latent, and reaction heats. However, as discussed by Oblad et al. (3), coke, when produced as above and subsequently combusted, can generally provide much or all of this energy requirement. Combustion, referred to some authors as decoking or burning, is therefore an important aspect of thermal-recovery methods.

Moore et al. (8) classify thermal processes into two general groups, direct heated and indirect heated, depending on whether pyrolysis and combustion steps are carried out in one or two reaction vessels. The processes further differ from each other with respect to fluidized-bed or moving-bed state of solids in each of the two steps. Table I shows a general process classification scheme that fits most known thermal processes. References are included in that table. Regardless of the thermal process used, as discussed in detail by Bunger (4), the synthetic crude oil product obtained cannot, in general, be used as a substitute for crude petroleum but must be upgraded to reduce sulfur and nitrogen contents, average molecular weight, and C/H ratio.

In all thermal recovery processes, tar sand is subjected to high processing temperatures, about 450-550°C for pyrolysis, and the residual coked sand is further heated to about 550-650°C during the combustion step. At these conditions, an acceptable thermal efficiency can only be obtained if a significant portion of the sensible heat in the spent sand is recovered and introduced back into the process. Almost all the processes in Table I provide for heat recovery from spent sand before it is discarded.

Perhaps the best-known fluidized-bed process is the one developed by Gishler and Peterson (17, 24, 25) in Canada. The process scheme resembles that of catalytic cracking as used in the petroleum industry. Tar sand is fed to the pyrolysis or coker bed, where the oil vapor produced is carried by the fluidizing gas to the product collection system. Coked sand is withdrawn from the coker and blown by preheated air into the burner where the coke is burned. A portion of the hot sand is recycled to the coker to supply heat for the pyrolysis step, with the remainder discarded through an overflow pipe in the burner bed. Two serious drawbacks of this process, as noted by Camp (1), are the large recycle of hot sand required and the high energy content of the net spent sand. Rammler (23) has described the application of the Lurgi-Ruhrgas process to tar sands. Like the Gishler and Peterson process, it uses sand as the heat carrier.

Development of an Energy-Efficient Thermal Process

The particulate nature of the mineral matter in most tar sands permits fluidized processing with several advantages: 1) disintegration of lumps of tar sand to individual particles upon the pyrolysis of the bitumen; hence such feeds do not have to be reduced to a small size prior to entry into the pyrolysis reactor; 2) relative ease of handling solids because fluidized solids flow through pipes like liquid; 3) high heat-transfer rates between fluidizing medium and solid particles; 4) nearly isothermal operation, which permits close control of the temperature of pyrolysis, a variable affecting product yields, quality and energy requirements; 5) high rates for mass transfer between particle surface and fluidizing medium, which is important for a high rate of feed per unit area without forming agglomerates; 6) accommodation of variations in bitumen content of feed by regulating the flow of fluidizing gas; and 7) ease of immersion of heat transfer tubes or heat exchangers in the fluidized beds with accompanying high heat-transfer coefficients. The last factor is particularly important for the type of process developed in this study and constitutes the primary reason for the choice here of fluidized pyrolysis. A fluidized bed recommends itself for burning coke for essentially the same reasons as for pyrolysis and was used, therefore, for the process developed here.

Previously developed processes employ various features to accomplish heat transfer for preheat and pyrolysis. These include 1) preheating the tar-sand feed, separately from the pyrolysis step, generally to recover heat from outgoing hot gaseous streams; 2) preheating the incoming process gas streams, generally to recover heat from spent sand or solids residue leaving the process; 3) transfer of heat from the burner to the pyrolysis reactor in the form of sensible heat of gases leaving the burner, generally by direct heat exchange with the contents of the pyrolysis zone; and 4) internal combustion of coke in the pyrolysis reactor itself with a controlled amount of oxidizing gas so that only a portion of the hydrocarbons in the pyrolysis zone, preferably coke, is combusted; 5) transfer from the burner to the pyrolysis step by recycle of hot, spent sand as a heat carrier.

Feature 1 has not been shown to be practical because, when preheated, tar sand becomes soft and sticky, making it impossible

to feed by common feeding devices such as a screw conveyor.
Feature 2 can be and generally is incorporated into most thermal
processes. However, a maximum of only about 25 percent of the
energy in the hot, spent sand can be recovered by preheating the
oxidizing gas for coke combustion. In Feature 3, the amount of
energy that can be carried by gases from the combustion zone to
the pyrolysis zone is relatively small. Feature 4 requires a
means for direct heat transfer between the two zones by conduc-
tion, convection, and/or radiation. Unless this can be accomplished on a large scale with little or no combustion of bitumen,
Feature 4 is not practical. Feature 5 is practical, but excessive
recycle of hot, spent sand is required, thus greatly increasing
the required sizes of pyrolysis and combustion reactors and
necessitating large devices to convey the sand.

Another possible means of transferring heat from the coke-
combustion stage to the pyrolysis stage is by the use of indirect
heat exchange not involving sand or gas. In the process developed
in this work, this means was implemented by incorporating heat
pipes to transfer the bulk of the energy required for solid preheat and pyrolysis from the coke-combustion stage. A heat pipe,
for the purpose here, may be defined simply as a completely
enclosed tubular device with very high effective thermal conduc-
tance, which transfers heat by two-phase circulation of a working
fluid (28).

In operation, heat is transferred to one end of the heat
pipe, causing the working fluid to vaporize. The vapor flows to
the other, cooler end due to the pressure gradient set up inside
the central vapor core of the heat pipe. There, the vapor con-
denses on the tube wall and inside a wick, transferring heat to
the surroundings. The condensate then returns to the warmer end,
thus completing the cyclic flow of the fluid. Because a large
amount of heat can be transferred by a heat pipe, its so-called
effective thermal conductivity can be extremely high. For application to thermal processing of tar sands, potassium was selected
as the working fluid.

The essential features of the reactor system for the new
thermal process developed in the work reported here are illustrated in the simplified process scheme of Figure 1. Freshly
mined and sized tar sand is dropped into the upper bed of a multi-
staged fluidized-bed column. The upper bed is a pyrolysis reactor, which is maintained at a temperature of generally between
400° and 550°C. Here, bitumen in the feed is cracked and/or
volatilized, leaving a coke deposit on the sand particles. The
oil vapors and light hydrocarbon gases produced are carried off
by the inert fluidizing gas to fines-separation and product-
recovery sections, while coked sand flows down by gravity through
a control valve to the burner section of the column where the
coke is burned to generate heat. The burner is maintained at a
temperature of generally between 550° and 650°C. Preheated air
is used to fluidize the solids in the combustion bed and to pro-

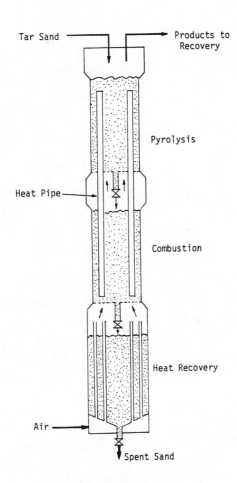

Figure 1. University of Utah process

vide oxygen for combustion. Gaseous products of combustion, mostly nitrogen and carbon dioxide, then flow upwards to fluidize solids in the upper bed as noted above.

A number of heat pipes, as required by the heat-transfer load, are placed vertically in the fluidized-bed column such that they extend into the pyrolysis and combustion beds as depicted in Figure 1. The heat pipes transfer excess heat generated in the burner to the pyrolysis reactor, thus maintaining the reactor and burner at proper temperatures.

Hot, spent sand leaving the burner flows down through a control valve to a heat-recovery section, where process air recovers heat from the spent sand. Additional energy can be recovered from the sand by heat exchange to produce steam. A more detailed description of the process is given by Seader and Jayakar (26).

The new process retains most of the simplicity of direct-heated processes. Solids move only downwards by gravity, the equipment is essentially a single vessel, and there is no recycle of solids. Most importantly, the heat-transfer features used-- heat pipes, heat recovery from spent sand to preheat process air, transfer of some heat by combustion gases, and some radiative heat transfer from coke-combustion stage to the pyrolysis reactor-- permit efficient management of the energy that is within tar sand itself to help achieve high energy efficiency. The heat pipes effectively link the pyrolysis reactor and the coke-combustion stage thermally without necessarily imposing any other constraints on the process such as flow patterns, reactor configuration, or dimensions of the column (except for the volume of heat pipes, which is a small fraction of bed volumes).

The basic process as outlined above is very flexible, and modifications and variations can be easily incorporated into it to further improve the overall efficiency and/or to make it more suitable for specific types of feeds. Thus, external fuel, recycle gas, or liquid fuels can be easily introduced into the burner in the case of lean tar sands. By providing for a purge gas stream off the top of the combustion bed, one can adjust the flow rate of fluidizing gas to the pyrolysis bed. If desired, after recovery, gas produced in the pyrolysis bed can be recycled back to that bed and used instead of combustion gases to fluidize it. This is very important for lean tar sands which would otherwise have very low product concentration in the combined exit gas stream, making product recovery difficult.

Laboratory Testing of New Process

A laboratory apparatus was used to demonstrate the new thermal process. It consisted of a 10-foot-high by nominal 2-inch diameter, two-staged, fluidized-bed column, a screw feeder for feeding tar sand, a hot cyclone and filter system for separation of fines from the products, and a product-recovery section consisting of condensers, phase separators, cyclones, and an electrostatic precipitator. A single 0.75-inch-diameter by 7-foot-long heat pipe extended into the pyrolysis and coke-combustion beds. The apparatus was completely insulated and instrumented with thermocouples, pressure taps, flow meters, and sampling taps. Electrical heaters and a propane burner were used to provide heat during startup conditions. The equipment was designed to handle a nominal feed rate of 5 lb/hr of tar sands containing up to 14 weight percent bitumen. Further details of the apparatus are given by Jayakar (27).

Several problems in solids handling were encountered in operating the laboratory apparatus. Originally solids were transferred from the pyrolysis bed to the combustion bed by means of a weir and dip leg. Because gas tended to flow up through the dip leg, this system was abandoned in favor of a simple solids downcomer with a specially designed solids flow-control valve. Although this valve permitted proper operation of the bed, it was a recurrent source of operating difficulty as it tended to stick after a few runs and had to be dismantled and cleaned every two to four runs. Flow of solids from the combustion bed was controlled by a similar valve, which presented no operating problems. Tar-sand feed materials were ground to particles or pieces no larger than about 1/4-inch in size. Materials tending to be sticky were dusted with fines or coal dust prior to feeding. The screw feeder did not plug as long as it was kept at a near-ambient temperature. Run durations were typically one hour after spending several hours to reach essentially steady-state conditions.
The experimental work was divided into three parts: fluidization studies at elevated temperatures, processing of tar sands in the pyrolysis section without use of the heat pipe, and operation of the complete heat-piped apparatus. Only typical results of some of the latter tests are reported here.
A total of 75 runs was made under thermal processing conditions at near-ambient pressure with tar sands from three different deposits: Tar Sand Triangle, Sunnyside, and Asphalt Ridge. Data from representative runs for feed materials from each of the three deposits are given in Table II. A complete accounting of all the bitumen in the feed material was generally not achieved mainly because of difficulties in removing oil product from the product recovery equipment. Thus, values reported for oil yield are believed to be low. Based on the best runs, it is estimated that for Sunnyside and Asphalt Ridge materials, a typical yield structure for near-optimal operating conditions would be: 70 wt% oil, 10 wt% gas, and 20 wt% coke.

Conclusions

1. The basic concept of a thermal process using pyrolysis and combustion stages coupled by heat pipes is workable and eliminates the need to recycle large amounts of sand.

Table I.   Classification of and References for Thermal Recovery
Processes

	Direct Heated	Indirect Heated
Moving-bed pyrolysis and combustion	Cheney et al. (9) Dannanberg and Matzick (10) Saunders (11)	Bennett (12) Berg (13) Fitch (14)
Fluidized-bed pyrolysis and combustion	Gifford (15) Peck et al. (16)	Gishler and Peterson (17) Nathan et al. (18) Roetheli (19) Murphree (20) Alleman (21)
Fluidized-bed pyrolysis and moving-bed combustion	Donnelly et al. (22)	No examples known
Moving-bed pyrolysis fluidized-bed combustion	No examples known	Rambler (23)

Table II.   Laboratory Results for Processing of Utah
Tar Sands

	Deposit		
	Tar Sand Triangle	Asphalt Ridge	Sunnyside
Run No.	58	67	74
Bitumen Content of Feed, wt%	4.70	11.67	10.56
Tar-Sand Feed Rate, lb/hr	3.85	3.90	4.41
Pyrolysis Bed Temperature, °C	475	482	449
Combustion Bed Temperature, °C	603	649	604
Oil Yield, wt%	49.5	52.7	45.4
Gas Yield, wt%	20.6	15.7	6.2
Coke Yield, wt%	22.0	7.8	17.2
Total Yield, wt%	92.1	76.2	68.8
API Gravity of Oil, 20°C	13.1	15.2	18.2
Viscosity of Oil, cps, 25°C	142	102	291

2. Tar sands containing as low as 8 percent bitumen can be thermally processed without external energy input to get satisfactory yields of oil. Tar sand with even lower bitumen content can be processed with good oil yield if a portion of the gas or oil products or some cheaper external fuel, such as coal, can be added to the combustion stage to provide energy.

3. Modifications of the process, such as introducing recycle of gas and oil, allowing for purge of some combustion gas, etc., can improve the energy efficiency of the process and the yields of oil and gas.

4. The process developed during the course of this work is simple, direct, and efficient. It is capable of wide application to processing of tar sands in Utah, Canada, and perhaps other deposits. Moreover, the concept of using heat pipes is of even broader applicability in the process industries in general and in energy-related industries in particular. For example, the basic processing concepts investigated here may have potential for application in the processing of oil shale and coal.

ABSTRACT

Tar sands from the Asphalt Ridge, Sunnyside, and Tar Sand Triangle deposits in Utah were processed in a small-scale, two-stage fluidized reactor system operating under continuous, steady-flow conditions. The oil products obtained were analyzed for viscosity, refractive index, density, sulfur content, distillation yield, and proton nmr spectra.

In the first stage of the reactor, mined and suitably sized tar sand is pyrolyzed at temperatures of 450 to 500°C in an inert atmosphere to crack and volatilize most of the contained bitumen, which is then condensed and collected to give a synthetic crude oil. In the second stage, coke formed as a by-product in the first stage is combined with air at temperatures of 550 to 650°C. The energy released during combustion in the second stage is transferred by a heat pipe to the first stage where the heat is utilized to provide for preheat and heat of pyrolysis of tar-sand feeds. Gaseous combustion products from the second stage, containing very little oxygen, are used to fluidize the pyrolysis bed. The process permits recovery of oil from tar sands with high energy efficiency in a once-through operation with respect to sand.

References

1. Camp, F. W., "Tar Sands" in *Kirk-Othmer Encyclopedia of Chemical Technology*, 2nd Edition, Vol. 19, John Wiley and Sons, New York, pp. 682-732 (1969).
2. Ritzma, H. R., *AIChE Symposium Series No. 155, 72,* 47 (1976).
3. Oblad, A. G., J. D. Seader, J. D. Miller, and J. W. Bunger, *AIChE Symposium Series No. 155, 72,* 69 (1976).

4. Bunger, J. W., K. P. Thomas, S. M. Dorrance, *Fuel 58*, 183 (1979).
5. Spulveda, J. E., and J. D. Miller, *Mining Engineering, 30*, 1311 (1978).
6. Misra, M., and J. D. Miller, *Mining Engineering, 32*, 302 (1980).
7. Gustafson, R. E., "Shale Oil" in *Kirk-Othmer Encyclopedia of Chemical Technology*, 2nd Edition, Vol. 18, John Wiley and Sons, New York, pp 1-20 (1969).
8. Moore, R. G., D. W. Bennion, J. K. Donnelly, "Anhydrous Extraction of Hydrocarbons from Tar Sands," Paper presented at local ISA Meeting, Calgary Section, April 1975.
9. Cheney, P. E., R. W. Ince, and C. M. Mason, U. S. Patent 3,487,002, December 30, 1969.
10. Dannanberg, R. O., and A. Matzick, "Bureau of Mines Gas-Combustion Retort for Oil Shale," U. S. Bureau of Mines Report of Investigation 5545 (1960).
11. Saunders, F. J., U. S. Patent 3,130,132, April 21, 1964.
12. Bennett, J. D., U. S. Patent 3,623,972, November 1971.
13. Berg, C. H. O., U. S. Patent 3,905,595, September 22, 1959.
14. Fitch, C. M., U. S. Patent 3,267,019, August 16, 1966.
15. Gifford, P. H., II. U. S. Patent 4,094,767, June 1978.
16. Peck, E. B., E. Tomkins, and D. G. Tomkins, U. S. Patent 2,471,119, May 1949.
17. Gishler, P. E., and W. S. Peterson, *Treatment of Bituminous Sand*. Canadian Patent 530,920, September 25, 1956.
18. Nathan, M. F., G. T. Skaperdas and G. C. Grubb, U. S. Patent 3,320,152, May 16, 1967.
19. Roetheli, B. E., U. S. Patent 2,579,398, December 18, 1951.
20. Murphree, E. V., U. S. Patent 2,980,617, October 13, 1959.
21. Alleman, C. E., U.S. Patent 2,647,077, July 28, 1953.
22. Donnelly, J. K., R. G. Moore, D. W. Bennion, and A. E. Trenkwalkder, "A Fluidized Bed Retort for Oil Sands," Paper presented at the AIChE Meeting, Florida, 1978.
23. Rammler, A. W., "The Production of Synthetic Crude Oil from Oil Sand by Application of the Lurgi-Ruhrgas Process," *Canadian Journal of Chemical Engineering, 48* (October 1970): 552-560.
24. Peterson, W. S., and P. E. Gishler, "A Small Fluidized Solids Pilot Plant for the Direct Distillation of Oil from Alberta Bituminous Sands," *Canadian Journal of Research, 28* (January 1950): 62-70.
25. Peterson, W. S., and P. E. Gishler, "Oil from Alberta Bituminous Sand," *Petroleum Engineer, 23* (April 1951): 553-561.
26. Seader, J. D., and K. M. Jayakar, *Process and Apparatus to Produce Synthetic Crude Oil from Tar Sands*, U. S. Patent 4,160,720, July 10, 1979.
27. Jayakar, K. M., "Thermal Recovery of Oil from Tar Sands," Ph.D. Thesis in Chemical Engineering, University of Utah (1979).
28. Dunn, P., and D. Reay, *Heat Pipes*, 2nd., Pergamon Press, 1978.

RECEIVED January 23, 1981.

Hydropyrolysis: The Potential for Primary Upgrading of Tar Sand Bitumen

J. W. BUNGER, D. E. COGSWELL, R. E. WOOD, and A. G. OBLAD

Department of Mining and Fuels Engineering, 320 WBB, University of Utah, Salt Lake City, UT 84112

Upgrading of high molecular weight, residual materials is becoming increasingly important as a result of decreasing availability of lighter feedstocks. Conversion processes for residual materials must contend with high heteroatom content, high molecular weight (low volatility), high aromaticity and high metals content not encountered to the same degree in lighter feedstocks. These characteristics result in higher process costs and typically lower conversion and yield of desired products. But as production recovery and processing costs rise, yield and conversion efficiency become increasingly important. As a result, conventional techniques for primary conversion of residual materials such as tar sand bitumen, e.g. coking, may prove economically unacceptable.

A possible alternative for the primary conversion of residual material is hydropyrolysis. Hydropyrolysis (HP) is a process for thermal cracking in the presence of hydrogen. This process has been shown to dramatically improve the yields of liquid and gaseous products compared to coking (1,2,3,4,5). Hydropyrolysis does not require the introduction of heterogeneous catalysts but requires elevated pressures. Through model compound work (5) and characterization (6) and processing (7) of high molecular weight tar sand bitumen, an understanding of the chemistry of this reaction is beginning to emerge. This paper reports our latest results and discusses the chemical changes effected by hydropyrolysis. The implication of the possible reactions to the suitability of various feedstocks for processing by hydropyrolysis is also discussed.

Experimental

Feedstock Source. Three feedstocks were used in this study. All were derived from Uinta Basin, Utah Tar Sand deposits. A Sunnyside bitumen was solvent extracted by procedures previously reported (6) from a freshly mined sample obtained from the old Asphalt Quarry northeast of Sunnyside, Utah. An Asphalt Ridge bitumen was extracted similarly from a sample freshly mined from

0097–6156/81/0163–0369$05.00/0
© 1981 American Chemical Society

the Uinta County Quarry southwest of Vernal, Utah. The TS-IIC
oil was used as received from the U.S. Department of Energy,
Laramie Energy Technology Center (LETC). The TS-IIC oil is
representative of the oil produced during an echoing in-situ
combustion oil recovery project conducted at Northwest Asphalt
Ridge by the LETC laboratories (8).

    Elemental Analysis and Physical Properties. Elemental
analysis was accomplished by conventional microanalytical techniques in a commercial testing laboratory. Densities were
measured on a Mettler/Paar digital density meter, model D.M. 40.
Number average molecular weights were determined by VPO in
benzene. Simulated distillation was accomplished using a 1/4" by
18" column of 3% dexsil 300 on chromosorb W, programmed from -30°
to 350°C at 10°/minute with a 4 minute hold at 350°C. The
detector was a flame ionization detector maintained at 400°C.
The percent nondistillable material was determined by using as an
internal standard, an equal volume mixture of C_9 to C_{16} n-alkyl-
benzenes (See also reference 9). ^{13}C-NMR spectra data were
obtained as reported in reference (3).

    Hydropyrolysis Process. Two hydropyrolysis reactors were
used in this study. The Sunnyside and Asphalt Ridge bitumen were
processed in a reactor consisting of a coiled stainless steel tube
3/16" i.d. x 236" long. This reactor has been previously
described by Ramakrishnan (1). The TS-IIC oil was processed in a
reactor originally developed for short residence time coal liquefaction. This reactor also consists of coiled stainless steel
tubes 3/16" i.d. The length of this tube system can be varied
from 20 to 120 feet, and has been previously described by Wood,
et al. (10). The length of the reactor for runs reported in this
paper was 100 feet. Average residence times were calculated from
the volumetric flow rates and the reactor volume at process conditions. The reaction mixture, which is predominantly H_2, was
assumed for purposes of this calculation to behave as an ideal
gas. The reactors were pre-sulfided with H_2S to inhibit catalytic
reactions from wall surfaces.

Results

    The elemental analysis and physical properties for the Uinta
Basin derived feedstocks are given in Table I. The elemental
analyses reveal compositions typical of Uinta Basin bitumens (11)
in that H/C ratios fall between 1.53 and 1.66, nitrogen contents
are appreciable (~1%) and sulfur content is low (<0.5%). The
physical property data reveal significant differences between the
three samples in that the Sunnyside bitumen exhibits the highest
molecular weight and, hence, the highest viscosity and lowest
volatility. The Asphalt Ridge TS-IIC oil exhibits the lowest
molecular weight with corresponding higher volatility and lower

TABLE I

Elemental Analysis and Physical Properties of Feedstocks

Property	Sunnyside (virgin bitumen)	Asphalt Ridge (virgin bitumen)	Asphalt Ridge (TS-IIC oil)
Carbon (wt.%)	86.3	86.2	86.7
Hydrogen	11.1	11.3	11.6
Nitrogen	0.8	1.1	0.7
Sulfur	0.35	0.4	0.5
Oxygen	1.4	0.9	<0.5
H/C atomic ratio	1.53	1.56	1.59
Specific gravity 20/20	1.003	0.981	0.959
API gravity	9.6	12.7	16
Average M.W. (VPO benzene)	778	713	410
Conradson Carbon Residue	14.1	9.1	6.8
% Distillable below 530°C	34	44	69
Viscosity kP 77°F, 200 sec^{-1}	1500*	69.3*	3.9

*Shear = .05 sec^{-1}

viscosity and density. An interesting property of the TS-IIC oil is the appreciable carbon residue exhibited considering this oil has been thermally produced in-situ. A greater portion of the heaviest and most carbonaceous material might have been expected to remain in the reservoir.

The three feedstocks were processed by hydropyrolysis at selected process conditions. Previous results (1,7) have shown that gas to liquid ratios increase sensitively with increasing temperature. This effect can be offset somewhat by decreasing the residence time. A variation in pressure does not have a major effect on product yields or gross properties, but pressures above about 1200 psig H_2 are required to inhibit coke formation.

Representative results for hydropyrolysis of the study feedstocks are given in Table II. The Sunnyside bitumen was processed at more moderate temperatures and longer residence times as a result of a significant propensity to coke at 525°C. The extraordinarily high velocities of gas used were required to prevent coking in the coiled tube reactor; however, more recent results with other reactor configurations indicate that a two-order of magnitude improvement on the recycle gas to feed ratios can be accomplished without significantly affecting the yields and without major coking problems. Run times for results shown in Table II were for one to two hours in length.

Results given in Table II show virtually 100% conversion of feedstocks to liquids and gases. Residual material shown for

TABLE II

Representative Results of Hydropyrolysis

Process Conditions

	Sunnyside (virgin bitumen)	Asphalt Ridge (virgin bitumen)	Asphalt Ridge (TS-IIC oil)
Temperature °C	500	525	525
Pressure (psig)	1800	1500	1800
Average residence time (sec)	30	18	5
Space velocity (LHSV)	1	1	1
Gas hourly space velocity			
(recycle and makeup)	1000	1000	1000
(approximate scf/bbl)	7×10^5	6×10^5	7×10^5

Yields

Weight % gases	27.3	27.3	12.8
liquid	73.9	73.7	85.6
residue	*	*	2.1
NH_3	0.38	0.61	0.1
H_2S	0.13	0.21	0.3
H_2O	1.15	0.79	negligible
Total yield	102.9	102.6	100.9
Hydrogen consumption			
(weight %)	2.9	2.6	0.9
(scf/bbl)	1800	1600	600

*Residual material for these runs were counted as liquids.

TS-IIC represents the material retained in a hot (350-400°C) catch tank and is believed to be indicative of the amount of material which is not volatilized during reaction. Extensive experimentation with hydropyrolysis has shown that actual coke production of much less than 1% is achieved. Details of minor coke buildup over extended runs have not yet been determined. The optimum conditions to obtain the desired yields and to prevent extraordinary coke formation will depend upon the feedstock properties and composition. Quantitative relationships between feedstock composition and optimum process conditions have not yet been conducted.

The amount of ammonia, hydrogen sulfide and water shown in Table II is inferred from the material balance on the respective heteroatoms; direct analysis of these compounds was not conducted. The values shown in Table II, along with the elemental analysis of condensable products and the gas analysis, were used to calculate the hydrogen consumption. Hydrogen consumption is not underestimated by the method of calculation (7) which first accounts for all of the carbon and heteroatoms fed and then sums the hydrogen content of the various components. The results of this study and those previously reported (7) indicate that hydrogen consumption varies in rough proportions to the non-condensable gas yield. Calculations of hydrogen requirements reveal that a hydropyrolysis plant could operate in hydrogen balance by steam-reforming the methane produced.

The C_1-C_5 gas analysis is given in Table III along with a coker gas from Asphalt Ridge bitumen (calculated from reference 7) for comparison. While the total amount of gas produced in hydropyrolysis is several times as high as with coking (~5 weight percent gas is produced in coking), it is apparent that hydropyrolysis reduces olefin formation relative to paraffin formation and that C_3's and C_4's are highly favored relative to methane. The rather erratic results of olefins to the paraffins ratio and C_5 production for the hydropyrolysis runs suggest the possibility of variable wall-effects (catalytic) or significant differences in molecular structure of one feed to another. Also, variations in reactor control (±6°C, ±100 psig, ±20% of residence time) may also influence these results.

Characteristics of hydropyrolysis liquid products are given in Table IV. Only modest improvement has been made in the H/C ratios and heteroatom removal, but notable improvements have been made in physical properties compared to the feed material. Average molecular weights of the virgin bitumens have been reduced in half and viscosities have been reduced by about 4 to 5 orders of magnitude. The reduction in molecular weight is significant in that the products will be much more amenable to catalytic hydroprocessing than the original materials. The low API gravity and high residue content of the Sunnyside products suggest a highly condensed material, probably unconverted from the original bitumen.

TABLE III

Gas Analysis

Compound	-------- Hydropyrolysis Gas -------			Coker Gas[7]
	Sunnyside (virgin bitumen)	Asphalt Ridge (virgin bitumen)	Asphalt Ridge (TS-IIC oil)	Asphalt Ridge (virgin bitumen)
	------- weight percent of C_1-C_5 gases -------			
Methane	29.7	25.9	27.8	45.4
Ethane	12.8	17.2	15.8	13.8
Ethylene	2.9	5.1	2.9	6.8
Propane	14.6	22.0	18.7	14.2
Propylene	13.8	5.1	6.7	13.5
Butanes	9.8	16.9	14.2	3.3
Butenes	5.9	5.0	1.6	2.4
C_5's	10.5	2.8	12.3	0.6
Total	100.0	100.0	100.0	100.0

TABLE IV

Characteristics of Hydropyrolysis Liquid Products

	Sunnyside (virgin bitumen)	Asphalt Ridge (virgin bitumen)	Asphalt Ridge (TS-IIC oil)
	---- Product Characteristics ----		
Carbon (weight percent)	86.9	86.8	86.2
Hydrogen	11.4	11.4	11.6
Nitrogen	0.7	0.8	0.7
Sulfur	0.3	0.3	0.2
Oxygen	0.5	0.3	1.2
H/C atomic	1.56	1.56	1.61
Specific gravity 20/20	0.967	0.903	0.920
API gravity	14.8	25.2	22.3
Average MW (VPO)	352	321	312
% distillable below 530°C	68	85	97
Viscosity 77°F cp, (shear sec^{-1})*	7000 (77)	8.1 (230)	246 (6)
Refractive index	too dark	1.52	1.503

*All products appear to exhibit Newtonian behavior in the shear ranges studied.

The original Sunnyside bitumen and the products were examined
by ^{13}C-NMR spectroscopy and found to possess a saturates to aromatic carbon ratio of 4.3 and 2.3, respectively. While these ratios
indicate a significantly more aromatic product has been formed,
the total aromatic carbon has increased only slightly, from 19%
in the original bitumen to 22% in the overall products, when gases
are taken into account. This result suggests that the molecular
weight reduction is occurring through cracking of saturates and
alkyl substituents, that the remaining liquids are relatively more
condensed, but that dehydrogenation to form aromatics has also
been inhibited.

      To further compare HP products with more conventional
materials, the smoothed boiling point distribution for the Asphalt
Ridge bitumen HP product was plotted against a similar curve for
the Asphalt Ridge coker distillate and a Wilmington, California
crude oil. Results given in Figure 1 show that HP products are
quite similar in boiling point distribution to a virgin heavy
crude oil. By comparison, the coker distillate possesses a
relatively high concentration of material in the heavy and vacuum
gas oil region. The Wilmington, California crude oil was chosen
for comparison because this crude is being conventionally refined
and has been shown to resemble Uinta Basin tar sand bitumen in
terms of the heteroatom and hydrocarbon compound types present (6).

      A further difference between HP products and coker distillate
is noted in the olefins content. Infrared spectral data taken
neat on these two products reveal olefin bonds at 1638, 988, 960,
904, and 880 cm^{-1} about 1.5 to 2.0 times as intense for coker
distillate compared to HP condensables. Based on analysis of
gases produced and on model compound work (5) which both show
hydropyrolysis inhibits olefin production, it is anticipated that
hydropyrolysis products will be more stable for storage, transportation, or distillation than coker distillates from the same
source.

Discussion

      The reactions taking place during hydropyrolysis are probably
dominated by free radical chemistry. Catalytic effects from
reactor components or trace minerals found in the feedstocks
cannot, however, be discounted. Cracking reactions are probably
initiated through thermally induced unimolecular bond scission.
The subsequent reactions involving the free radicals are those
which distinguish hydropyrolysis from thermal reactions in the
absence of high hydrogen pressure. Shabtai, et al. (5) have
postulated the reaction

$$R \cdot \; + H_2 \longrightarrow RH \; + H \cdot$$

as a significant reaction in the hydropyrolysis of n-decane. A
very modest activation energy of 14-15 K cal/mol is estimated for

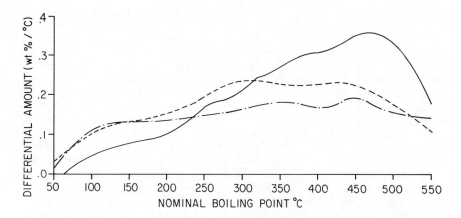

Figure 1. Distillation curves for selected tar sand products and Wilmington crude oil: Asphalt Ridge coker distillate (97% distillable, 27° API) (———); Asphalt Ridge hydropyrolysis condensables (85% distillable, 25° API) (– – –); Wilmington, CA crude oil (65% distillable, 20° API) (– · –).

this reaction on the basis of thermochemical data (5,12,13).
Considering the dominant partial pressure of hydrogen and
favorable activation energy, it is highly probable that many free
radicals present undergo the above reaction during hydropyrolysis.
This reaction has considerable significance. First, free radicals
present have an early opportunity to become saturated before other
bimolecular reactions can occur. Such processes as polymerization
or condensation which ultimately lead to high molecular weight
species or coke are inhibited. The results of both model compound
work (5) and those presented in this paper indicate that such
reactions are indeed inhibited. There is no evidence from the
model work and little in the work with tar sand bitumen to indicate that any products of a molecular weight higher than the
reactants are formed.

   Second, the production of a free hydrogen atom poses some
interesting implications. Should the hydrogen atom abstract a
hydrogen atom from a saturated carbon, the resultant free radical
may 1) undergo β-elimination to produce another hydrogen atom and
an olefin or 2) undergo β-scission to crack the molecule forming
an olefin plus a hydrocarbon free radical. Should the hydrogen
atom attack an unsaturated carbon such as our aromatic ring, a
dienyl radical is formed which 1) may rapidly undergo ring opening
with subsequent destruction of the aromatic ring or 2) become
saturated by a hydrogen from H_2, thus reducing the resonance
stabilization of the ring making it susceptible to further reaction. The possibility that this latter reaction is occurring is
supported, however weakly, by an increase in monoaromatics at the
apparent expense of polyaromatics. Previous work (7) has shown
that a monoaromatic/polyaromatic ratio of 0.3 is observed for
coker products (assuming coke as polyaromatics) but the ratio is
0.5 for hydropyrolysis products derived from the same feedstock.
There are, admittedly, molecular weight factors and dehydrogenation reactions in coking which could also influence this ratio.

   As a consequence of the reduced partial pressure of hydrocarbons, bimolecular reactions which result in hydrogen transfer
are inhibited. Such reactions which are highly significant in
liquid phase thermal reactions such as coking result in appreciable dehydrogenation of naphthenic rings with a corresponding
increase in aromatics content. Results from hydropyrolysis indicate that dehydrogenation of naphthenes occurs to some extent but
not nearly as much as with coking where the percentage of aromatic
carbon increases from less than 20% in the bitumen to over 30% in
the total products (assuming the coke contains principally aromatic carbon) (7). The inhibition of hydrogen transfer reactions
may be especially important for conversion of very high molecular
weight, naphthenic feedstocks such as tar sand bitumen.

   The effects of hydrogen on the thermal cracking of bitumen
are obvious in the results. Most dramatically, high carbon
residue material is converted in virtually 100% yields to liquid
and gaseous products. The effect is most pronounced for the

virgin bitumens; however, the effect for TS-IIC oil in which volatility is improved from 69% to 97% for a modest addition of 600 scf H_2/bbl is also appreciable. The liquid products formed from hydropyrolysis more closely resemble naturally occurring crude oils in terms of boiling point distribution than do coker distillates.

Uinta Basin bitumen exhibits a high nitrogen content which persists in the hydropyrolysis products. This is expected as the highest molecular weight species present in the original bitumen where the nitrogen is concentrated are converted to liquids. The high nitrogen content of HP products suggests that catalytic hydrotreating may be required prior to use of these liquids as a catalytic cracking feedstock. However, unlike the situation with shale oil which may contain 2% nitrogen and substantial quantities of pyrollic nitrogen (acidic) not commonly found in crude oils, the level of nitrogen in bitumen products is not above that which is handled by conventional refineries designed for high nitrogen crudes.

Hydropyrolysis processing is probably best suited for those feedstocks which can best utilize the inhibition effects of hydrogen on polymerization, condensation, and aromatization reactions. Such feedstocks are high molecular weight naphthenic materials which are susceptible to cracking but are easily converted to coke by liquid-phase bimolecular reactions.

Overall, process conditions for hydropyrolysis are no more severe than practiced now in catalytic hydrogenation processes. Considering the significantly increased yields of valuable liquid and gaseous products (compared to coking) and the rather simple process configuration, the economics of hydropyrolysis look promising.

<u>Summary</u>

Hydropyrolysis promises to be a process for reducing the molecular weight of residual materials without the formation of coke, without the introduction of heterogeneous catalysts and without an inordinately high consumption of hydrogen. Hydropyrolysis gains its attractiveness by trading off coke production for gas production. This is accomplished by the presence of hydrogen which is thought to inhibit undesirable bimolecular hydrocarbon-hydrocarbon reactions. Liquid products from hydropyrolysis more closely resemble virgin crude oils than do coker distillates in terms of boiling point distribution. Hydropyrolysis is expected to be most useful for the primary conversion of high molecular weight, moderate- to low-aromatic feedstocks, especially where high recovery costs place a premium value on improved yields in the conversion process.

Literature Cited

1. Ramakrishnan, R. "Hydropyrolysis of Coal Derived Liquids and Related Model Compounds," Ph.D. Dissertation, University of Utah, 1978.
2. Bunger, J.W.; Cogswell, D.E.; Oblad, A.G. Am. Chem. Soc., Div. Fuel Chem., Prepr. 1978, 23(4), 98–109.
3. Bunger, J.W.; Cogswell, D.E. In "Chemistry of Asphaltenes," Adv. Chem. Ser., accepted for publication, 1981.
4. Pruden, B.B.; Denis, J.M. Can. Chem. Proc. 1977, 61, 37–38.
5. Shabtai, J.; Ramakrishnan, R.; Oblad, A.G. "Hydropyrolysis of Model Compounds," Adv. Chem. Ser. 1979, 183, 297–328.
6. Bunger, J.W.; Thomas, K.P.; Dorrence, S.M. Fuel 1979, 58(3), 183.
7. Bunger, J.W. "Processing Utah Tar Sand Bitumen," Ph.D. Dissertation, University of Utah, 1979.
8. Johnson, L.A.; Fahy, L.J.; Romanowski, L.J.; Barbour, R.O.; Thomas, K.P. "An Echoing In-Situ Combustion Oil Recovery Project in a Utah Tar Sand," J. Petr. Tech. Feb. 1980, 295–304.
9. Poulson, R.E.; Jensen, H.B.; Duvall, J.J.; Harris, F.L.; Morandi, J.R. Analysis Instrumentation, Instrument Society of America, 1972, 10, 193–200.
10. Wood, R.E.; Wiser, W.H. "Coal Liquefaction in Coiled Tube Reactors," I & EC, Process Res. Dev. 1976, 15, 144.
11. Bunger, J.W. Amer. Chem. Soc., Div. Petr. Chem., Prepr. 1977, 22(2), 716.
12. Bensen, S.W. "Thermochemical Kinetics"; Wiley: New York, 1976.
13. Rosenstock, H.M.; Draxl, K.; Steiner, B.W.; Herron, J.T. J. Phys. Chem. Ref. Data, 1977, 6 (suppl. 1), I-774-I-783.

RECEIVED March 18, 1981.

INDEX

INDEX

Jacket design by Carol Conway.
Production by Candace A. Deren and V. J. Deveaux.

Elements typeset by Service Composition Co., Baltimore, MD.
The book was printed and bound by The Maple Press Co., York, PA.